# Corporate Behavior and Sustainability

'Anyone involved in the development of boardroom functioning will treasure this book because it provides another avenue to help academics and professionals become reflective, observant and introspective. This will be extremely helpful in gaining knowledge for improving business strategy and leading the business of sustainability. True experts on each topic have contributed in achieving this. Impeccable!'

Manoj K. Raut, CEO and Director, Institute of Directors

Companies can no longer expect to engage in dubious or unethical corporate behavior without risking their reputation and damaging, perhaps irrevocably, their market position. Irresponsible corporate behavior not only deprives shareholders of long-term returns but also ultimately imposes a cost on society as a whole. Sustainable business is about ensuring that entities contribute toward positive social, environmental, and economic outcomes. Bad business behavior is costly for stakeholders, for markets, for society, and the economy alike.

To ensure that a company behaves well, the buy-in of the leadership team is crucial. The full commitment of the board of directors, in conjunction with the senior managers of the organization, is required if an organization is to be socially responsible. In this sense, leadership does not reside with an individual (the CEO) within the organization but with all of those at the apex of corporate power and control. Effective change management requires enlightened and capable leadership to instigate and drive the process of embedding a sustainable and socially responsible corporate philosophy and culture that supports good business decision-making. A profound understanding of the requirements of such a leadership process will help corporate managers become highly effective change agents.

Governance will be the main driver of this change. For the economy and financial markets to become sustainable and resilient, radical changes in corporate leadership need to take place. Integrated reporting, government regulation, and international standards will all be important factors in bringing about this change.

As well as understanding the effects of corporate behavior on financial markets, such an understanding is also now imperative in relation to the social and environmental contexts.

**Güler Aras** is a professor of finance and accounting at Yildiz Technical University, Istanbul, Turkey, and the founding director of The Center for Finance, Governance and Sustainability (CFGS) at YTU. She is the former Dean of the business and economic faculty and Dean of the Graduate School. She has served as a visiting professor at Georgetown University, McDonough School of Business. Her research focus is on financial economy and financial markets with particular emphasis on the relationship between sustainability, corporate governance, corporate social responsibility, and corporate financial performance. She has published more than 20 books, has contributed over 250 articles in academic, business, and professional journals and edited several book collections. She also acts as an independent board member for many organizations.

**Coral Ingley** is Associate Professor of Management in the faculty of business and law at the Auckland University of Technology, Auckland, New Zealand. In 2006 she founded and is Director of the Centre for Corporate Governance at the university and is a member of the faculty's Work Research Institute. She has served as a visiting professor at Sorbonne University, Paris, ESC-Troyes, France, Maastricht University, the Netherlands, and Toulouse Business School, Barcelona, Spain. Her research focus is on corporate governance.

Finance, Governance and Sustainability:
Challenges to Theory and Practice Series
Series Editor:
*Professor Güler Aras, Yildiz Technical University, Turkey;
Georgetown University, Washington DC, USA*

Focusing on the studies of academicians, researchers, entrepreneurs, policy makers and government officers, this international series aims to contribute to the progress in matters of finance, good governance and sustainability. These multidisciplinary books combine strong conceptual analysis with a wide range of empirical data and a wealth of case materials. They will be of interest to those working in a multitude of fields, across finance, governance, corporate behavior, regulations, ethics and sustainability.

**Other titles in this series:**

**Sustainable Markets for Sustainable Business**
*Edited by Güler Aras*
ISBN 978-1-4724-3341-1

**Sustainable Governance in Hybrid Organizations**
*Linne Marie Lauesen*
ISBN: 978-1-4724-5130-9

**The Changing Paradigm of Corporate Governance**
*Edited by Maria Aluchna and Güler Aras*
ISBN: 978-1-4724-5201-6

**Cosmopolitan Business Ethics**
*Jacob Dahl Rendtorff*
ISBN: 978-1-4724-4708-1

**Strategy, Structure and Corporate Governance**
*Nabyla Daidj*
ISBN: 978-1-4724-5292-4

# Corporate Behavior and Sustainability

Doing well by being good

Edited by
Güler Aras and Coral Ingley

Routledge
Taylor & Francis Group

LONDON AND NEW YORK

First published 2017
by Routledge

2 Park Square, Milton Park, Abingdon, Oxfordshire OX14 4RN
52 Vanderbilt Avenue, New York, NY 10017

*Routledge is an imprint of the Taylor & Francis Group, an informa business*

First issued in paperback 2019

*British Library Cataloguing in Publication Data*
A catalogue record for this book is available from the British Library

*Library of Congress Cataloging-in-Publication Data*
A catalog record for this title has been requested

ISBN: 978-1-4724-5769-1 (hbk)
ISBN: 978-0-367-88066-8 (pbk)

Typeset in Sabon
by Apex CoVantage, LLC

# Contents

*List of figures*                                                    vii
*List of tables*                                                    viii
*About the authors*                                                   ix
*Series editor's preface*                                           xvii

Introduction: doing well by being good for sustainable business       1
GÜLER ARAS AND CORAL INGLEY


**PART I**
**Market behavior, stakeholders' approach and good governance**       7

1  Agency theory: explaining or creating problems? Good governance
   and ethical behaviour for sustainable business                     9
   GÜLER ARAS AND PAUL WILLIAMS

2  Using a stakeholder approach to understand success: empirical tests
   in Indian business                                                21
   SHALLINI S. TANEJA, JENNIFER J. GRIFFIN, PAWAN K. TANEJA,
   RADHA R. SHARMA, D. KIRK DAVIDSON AND RUPAMANJARI SINHA RAY

3  Behaviour in academe: an investigation into the sustainability of
   mainstream scholarship in management studies                      42
   MIRIAM GREEN


**PART II**
**Effective business behavior for corporate sustainability**         65

4  The walls between us: governance for sustainability               67
   PHILIPPA WELLS AND CORAL INGLEY

5  Governing corporate responsibility: the role of soft regulation          83
   ALICE KLETTNER

6  Corporate citizenship, ethics and accountability: the significance of
   the process of trust for corporate legitimacy in late modernity          103
   JACOB DAHL RENDTORFF

**PART III
Monitoring and reporting on sustainability                                  119**

7  Positioning of corporate social responsibility in media reporting: the
   role of media setting                                                    121
   JAMILAH AHMAD AND SURIATI SAAD

8  A pathway to corporate sustainability – social accounting                138
   DOUGLAS M. BRANSON

9  ESG matters in the boardroom                                             152
   ALISON L. DEMPSEY

**PART IV
The requirements for implementation of sustainability                       173**

10  The drivers of change                                                   175
    SUZANNE H. BENN

11  From ego to eco – theoretical challenges and practical implications of
    a "next generation" responsible leadership as a collaborative endeavor  199
    ELKE FEIN, JÜRGEN DEEG AND JONATHAN REAMS

12  Valuing corporate governance – a way out of the current impasse?:
    changing the leadership focus to behaviours and values rather than
    codes and compliance                                                    225
    BOB GARRATT

13  Defining and achieving good governance                                  234
    SHANN TURNBULL

    Conclusion                                                              252
    CORAL INGLEY AND GÜLER ARAS

    Index                                                                   254

# List of figures

2.1 Proposed Framework for Measuring Corporate Economic
    Social Performance by Stakeholder Approach     22
2.2 Scales for Community Expectations     28
2.3 Scales for Employees' Expectations     29
2.4 Scales for Customers' Expectations     30
2.5 Scales for Shareholders' Expectations     31
2.6 Framework for Measuring Corporate Economic and
    Social Performance     31
7.1 The Pillars of Corporate Social Responsibility     125
7.2 CSR News Coverage by Month (Jan–Dec 2013)     125
7.3 CSR News by Category (Jan–Dec 2013)     126
11.1 The "I-We-All-of-Us" Model     205
13.1 Generic Illustration of Network Governance     241

# List of tables

2.1   Analysis of Expert Opinions                                                                25
2.2   Sample Profile                                                                             26
2.3   Models Fit Indices                                                                         32
5.1   GRI Guidance on Governance of Sustainability                                               91
10.1  Total Direct Environmental Damage as a Percentage of Revenue
      for an Illustrative Selection of Primary, Manufacturing and
      Tertiary Sectors, Using Global Averages                                                   176
11.1  Levels of Self Development and Leadership                                                 207
11.2  Notions of Responsibility and Responsible Leadership
      on Different Levels of Self Development                                                   208
13.1  Mondragón Compound Board Compared with Unitary Board                                      244
13.2  Summarising Advantages of Network Governance for NEDs                                     247

# About the authors

## The Editors

### Güler Aras, PhD

Güler Aras is a professor of finance and accounting at Yildiz Technical University (YTU), Istanbul, Turkey, and a visiting professor at Georgetown University McDonough School of Business, Center for Financial Markets and Policy. She is the founding director of Center for Finance, Governance and Sustainability (CFGS) at YTU. She is the former dean of Faculty of Administrative and Economic Sciences and the former dean of the Graduate School. She served as a visiting professor at De Montfort University Leicester, UK and at University Sains Malaysia in Penang, Malaysia. Her research focus is on financial economy and financial markets with particular emphasis on the relationship between sustainability, corporate governance, corporate social responsibility, and corporate financial performance. Professor Aras has published more than 20 books and has contributed over 200 articles in academic, business and professional journals and magazines and edited several book collections. One of her most recent co-authored books is titled *The Durable Corporation: Strategies for Sustainable Development*, published by Gower, and addresses the topical issue of the sustainability of corporate activity. Her latest book, *Governance and Social Responsibility: International Perspectives*, was published by Palgrave Macmillan.

Professor Aras is the founding president of the International Financial Management Institute in Turkey (IMA, Turkish Chapter), and the Turkish Chapter of Transparency International. She has served as a board or a committee member of many national and international associations and research centers, including the Corporate Governance Association of Turkey (TKYD) and the Institute of Internal Auditing of Turkey. She is the editor of Gower book series, *Finance, Governance and Sustainability: Challenges to Theory and Practice* and the editor of Gower book series *Corporate Social Responsibility;* she has also served as an editor of *Social Responsibility Journal* and Emerald's *Development of Governance and Responsibility* book series until 2013. In addition, she is a member of a number of international editorial and advisory boards, and has spoken extensively at professional and academic conferences and has served as a consultant to a number of governmental and commercial organisations. She is a member of the Corporate Governance Committee of the Turkish Industry and Business Association (TUSIAD), an advisory board member of the Corporate Governance Association of Turkey (TKYD), and a member of Certified Public Accountant

(CPA-Turkey). Recently, she was elected as a member of the specialized committee of Minister of Development, Undersecretary of Treasury and Minister of Labour and Social Security Employment in Turkey.

### Coral Ingley, PhD

Coral Ingley is Associate Professor of Management in the faculty of business and law at the Auckland University of Technology, Auckland, New Zealand. In 2006 she founded and is director of the Centre for Corporate Governance at the university and is a member of the faculty's Work Research Institute. She has served as a visiting professor at Sorbonne University, Paris, ESC-Troyes, France, Maastricht University, the Netherlands, and Toulouse Business School, Barcelona, Spain. Her research focus is on corporate governance. She has published broadly on topics in governance including board competencies; board effectiveness; board roles and processes; sustainability and corporate social responsibility; risk management; director skills, independence, and human capital; environmental sustainability; urban governance, and stakeholder engagement. She has also published across fields of exporting; small, family, new, and entrepreneurial business; management and managerial competencies; marketing and service quality; strategic management; industrial networks; leadership and organizational culture; and business and regional economic growth.

Associate Professor Ingley's recent co-edited book is *Handbook on Emerging Issues in Corporate Governance* (World Scientific Press, 2010). She has also published recently on urban governance in the Asia-Pacific region, with chapters in *Environmental Sustainability in Urban Centers: Efficiency and new technologies in the provision of urban services* (2012) (A PECC Environmental Project 2009–2011). She has authored or contributed to more than 120 articles in academic, business and professional publications. She serves on editorial boards and as a regular reviewer for several academic journals.

Associate Professor Ingley is currently a member of a working group for the New Zealand shareholders association Beta Group designing the methodology and beta study among NZX top 50 companies for an index of corporate governance performance. She recently led a symposium on new challenges for directors at Auckland University of Technology and a workshop titled "Understanding Governance: A New Paradigm" at Toulouse Business School in Barcelona. She has also spoken at many professional and academic conferences and has served as a consultant to a number of governmental and commercial organizations. She is currently working with the New Zealand crown entity Accident Compensation Corporation as a team member delivering in-house teaching on leadership and as an individual expert responsible for researching and authoring a major research report commissioned by the corporation advising on delegated authorities.

## The Contributors

**Jamilah Hj Ahmad** is associate professor and currently the dean of the School of Communication, Universiti Sains Malaysia in Penang, Malaysia. Jamilah was invited as visiting professor at Universitas Gadjah Mada, Indonesia and Yildiz Technical University, Istanbul, Turkey. Jamilah is an accredited member and also fellow of the

Institute of Public Relations Malaysia (IPRM). Jamilah is also a panel member for Malaysian Qualifications Agency (MQA) for Communication and Media Studies since 2009. Jamilah also sits on the editorial board and is an issue reviewer for several international and local journals such as *Asia Pacific Public Relations Review (APPRJ)*, *Journal of Communication and Media Studies (JCMS)*, *International Journal of Business Management & Research (IJBMR)*, *Environmental Education Research Journal*, *Public Relations Inquiry Journal (PRI)*, *InSITE (Informing Science and IT Education)*, *Malaysian Journal of Education and Social Responsibility Journal (SRJ)* and since 2012 was appointed as chief editor for *GFTF Journal of Media and Communication (JMC)*.

**Suzanne H. Benn** is professor of sustainable enterprise in UTS Business School, University of Technology, Sydney. Suzanne has a background in the sciences and the social sciences. Her current research interests range across corporate sustainability and corporate social responsibility, business education for sustainability and leadership and organizational change for sustainability. Her interdisciplinary academic publications include four books and numerous refereed journal articles, book chapters and refereed conference papers. As well as conducting research funded through various Australian Research Council (ARC) projects, she has worked with many business and government organizations in order to progress understanding of change and leadership for sustainability. Her research currently is focussed on the circular economy and the implications for both social and environmental sustainability.

**Douglas M. Branson** holds the W. Edward Sell Chair in Business Law at the University of Pittsburgh, Pittsburgh, Pennsylvania, USA. He is a specialist in corporate law, corporate governance, finance, mergers and acquisitions and securities law. He previously taught for more than 20 years at Seattle University and has also been a distinguished visiting professor at a number of universities in the US, as well as Hong Kong, Australia, New Zealand, Europe, South Africa, and the UK. Professor Branson also holds a permanent faculty appointment in the master of law program at the University of Melbourne, Australia. He has published numerous articles and books on corporate law, corporate governance including publications on gender diversity and women on boards, and securities regulation, as well as business enterprise, the integration of the American League and a book based on visits to Vietnam. As an elected member since 1981, Professor Branson has been influential in framing the American Law Institute's recommendations for corporate governance and is a leading expert on the corporate law aspects of Alaska native corporations. Most recently, he has been a USAID consultant to the Ministries of Justice in Indonesia, Ukraine and Slovakia and to the Asian Development Bank advising on corporate law, capital markets law, corporate governance and securitisation issues. He is a life member of the American Law Institute.

**D. Kirk Davidson** is a Morrison Professor of International Studies at Mount St. Mary's University Maryland. He is an MBA from Harvard University and AB degree in economics from Princeton University, USA. He is PhD from Golden Gate University in San Francisco, California. He has worked with many companies in the US at various senior positions. He is a visiting professor at Georgetown University, the University of Maryland and an adjunct professor at George Washington University, Washington

DC, USA. His field of teaching, research and writing includes corporate social responsibility and sustainability. He is the author of two books which include *Selling Sin, the Marketing of Socially Unacceptable Products* and *The Moral Dimension of Marketing: Essays on Business Ethics*. He has written numerous book chapters, papers and journal articles, and he is currently engaged in a cross-cultural study of corporate social responsibility focusing especially on India and China. He is serving on the boards of various international journals as an editor and reviewer.

**Jürgen Deeg** is a long-term senior research fellow at the chair of business administration, leadership and organization; faculty of economics and business administration at the University of Hagen (Germany). He holds a degree in administrative sciences from the University of Konstanz and earned his doctorate in business administration at the University of Hagen. His work covers the fields of business administration, leadership, organization and human resource management. His main fields of interest are concepts and theories of human resource management, organization and leadership, change management, management in higher education and public administration.

**Alison L. Dempsey**, BA(Hon), JD, LLM, PhD, is an internationally experienced lawyer and business professional with over 20 years focusing in corporate governance, ethics, regulation and responsible business. She holds a doctorate in law (UBC Law 2012) and is the author of *Evolutions in Corporate Governance – Towards an Ethical Framework for Business Conduct* (Greenleaf Publishing, 2013). Her particular interest is in the role of mandatory and voluntary regulatory frameworks – in combination – enabling business and institutions in economically, environmentally and socially responsible practices, sustainable success and the mitigation of adverse impacts on society and the environment.

**Elke Fein** is a social scientist and lecturer at the University of Freiburg (Germany). She holds a Franco-German diploma in political science, a master's degree East European history and a PhD in political sociology. She has worked as a researcher in various academic contexts, among them in the fields of East European history (University of Freiburg) and in leadership and organization studies (University of Hagen, Germany) where she was the co-author of a master course in integral leadership. Elke Fein is also the CEO and managing director of the Institute for Integral Studies (IFIS) where she coordinates the EU-funded project Leadership for Transition (LiFT). She is currently working on a post-doc project on adult development and its implications on politics, societies and business and is serving as associated editor of a special issue of the *Behavioral Development Bulletin* focusing on uses of adult development theories in the social sciences.

**Miriam Green** has recently been awarded a doctorate from De Montfort University, UK. Her research focused on the representations of a major text about the management of innovation in mainstream management and management accounting scholarship. Her critique of such scholarship has centered on the need for complementing the dominance of objectivist, quantitative-based knowledge with subjectivist, qualitative approaches in order to produce inclusive, holistic and sustainable scholarship. This has implications for issues concerning organizational governance. She has published several articles mainly in *Social Responsibility Journal* and *Philosophy of Management*, and with David Crowther has co-authored a book, *Organisational Theory*. She is now interested in extending her work in mainstream management scholarship to researching its connections with neoliberal ideologies and practices. For many years, Dr Green taught various subjects including organization studies, work, employment and society and learning skills at London Metropolitan University. She is now teaching organization studies and research methods at Icon College of Technology and Management.

**Bob Garratt** is best known for his long-selling book *The Fish Rots from the Head: Developing Effective Board Directors*. Professor Garratt has an international consultancy practice in board review and development that has spanned from multinationals, the IMF in Washington and the Saudi Arabian Monetary Authority to small charities. He has long-term experience in developing business education in China, South-East Asia and Southern Africa. He is based in London and is Chairman of the Centre for Corporate Governance at the University of Stellenbosch, South Africa and visiting professor in corporate governance at Cass Business School, London.

**Jennifer J. Griffin**, professor, strategic management and public policy at the George Washington University School of Business (Washington, DC) and director, Global Strategies Program at GW's Institute for Corporate Responsibility. Jennifer examines corporate impacts and how managers innovate (or not) to engage stakeholders and manage responsibly as part of their corporate strategy. She has won the GW School of Business Teaching Excellence Award and has been nominated by students for the National Inspire Integrity Award as well as nominated seven times in the past nine years for the best professor in the school by the doctoral students. Author of a 2015 Cambridge University Press book, *Managing Corporate Impacts: Co-Creating Value*, she has won a Strategic Management Society research award and co-authored the best paper award in 20 years from the International Association for Business & Society (IABS). Jennifer has published case studies, chapters and articles in a range of management journals: *Public Administration Review, Group & Organization Management, Business & Society, Business & Politics, International Journal of Public Affairs, Corporate Reputation Review*, and *Public Relations Quarterly*, among others. Jenn is currently serving as the past division chair of the Academy of Management-Social Issues in Management (SIM) division.

**Alice Klettner** is a postdoctoral research fellow at the Centre for Corporate Governance at the University of Technology Sydney. Her research projects have included an Australian Research Council grant into the roles and responsibilities of company boards of directors as well as several collaborative projects with industry associations and government. These include work with the Australian Council for Superannuation Investors into board performance evaluation; research for Catalyst Australia regarding the governance of sustainability; and for the Australian Government's survey of women in leadership. Her background is as a lawyer, admitted as a solicitor in England and Wales and New South Wales, Australia. Prior to that, she obtained a first-class degree in natural sciences at Cambridge University. Her research interests include the role of regulation in promoting board effectiveness and the socio-legal factors driving corporate responsibility.

**Rupamanjari Sinha Ray** is an assistant professor of MDI Gurgaon. She has published research papers in the fields of international trade and environment, CSR and environmental responsibilities of firms and SEZs in reputed and refereed journals like *Indian Journal of Industrial Relations, Journal of Quantitative Economics, Economic and Political Weekly, Review of Market Integration,* etc. She has co-authored a book on CSR practices in India. She is constantly doing research in the fields of corporate social responsibility and environmental management system and also engaged in training and consultancy in this field of CSR.

**Jonathan Reams** is an associate professor at the Norwegian University of Science and Technology, where he teaches and does research on leadership development, coaching and counseling. He received his PhD in leadership studies from Gonzaga University. Jonathan Reams is also a co-founder of the Center for Transformative Leadership and serves as editor-in-chief of *Integral Review, A Transdisciplinary and Transcultural Journal for New Thought, Praxis and Research.* Jonathan Reams practices the cultivation of leadership through consulting and leadership development program design and delivery. He brings awareness-based technology to this work, focusing on how the inner workings of human nature can develop leadership capacities for today's complex challenges. He has done this for a diverse range of clients in the US, Canada and Europe.

**Jacob Dahl Rendtorff,** is professor of responsibility, ethics and legitimacy of corporations at Roskilde University, Denmark and he is also visiting professor in philosophy of management and ethical judgment at Copenhagen Business School. Rendtorff has a background in research in ethics, business ethics, bioethics, information ethics, political theory and philosophy of law. Rendtorff has written many articles and 12 books on issues of existentialism and hermeneutics, French philosophy, ethics, bioethics and business ethics as well as philosophy of law and he has been co-author and editor on more than 10 other books.

**Suriati Saad** is a PhD candidate in School of Management, Universiti Sains Malaysia (USM). Her research interest is in corporate social responsibility (CSR) and marketing communication. Suriati holds a master's degree from Universiti Sains Malaysia and bachelor's degree from Deakin University, Melbourne Australia. She is a fellow in School of Communication (USM) and has won Best Young Academician Award by Emerald Group Publishing Limited in 2012 presented at the 11th International Conference on Corporate Social Responsibility in Lahti, Finland.

**Radha R. Sharma** is raman munjal (Hero Motor Corp) chair professor of organizational behavior and HRD at Management Development Institute, India. She has been ICCR chair professor at HHL Graduate School of Management, Germany and visiting professor to various B-schools in Europe She has certifications in corporate social responsibility from the British Council; the New Academy of Business, UK; and the World Bank Institute. She has qualified GCPCL from Harvard Business School, USA; advanced professional certification in MBTI from Association of Personality Type, emotional intelligence certification from EI Learning Systems (USA). As a visiting professor she has taught courses on intercultural competencies, OB across cultures, psychometric testing, leadership, change management, case writing and case study in global MBA programs. Sharma has completed projects supported by World Health Organization, UNESCO, UNICEF, IDRC, Canada; McClelland Centre for Research and Innovation, Polish Academy of Sciences; Academy of Management, Humanistic Management Network, among others. Her publications include 12 books, research papers in *Frontiers in Psychology, Cross cultural Management: An International Journal, Journal of Management Development, Global Business Review,* among others. Her research interests are emotional intelligence, executive burnout, gender issues, change management and organisational transformation, socially responsible management, spirituality in management and humanistic management.

**Shallini Taneja** is an assistant professor in economics and business policy area at FORE School of Management, New Delhi. She is a fellow (PhD) from Management Development Institute (MDI), Gurgaon. She has around 11 years of experience in industry, teaching and research. She has attended and presented many research papers at national and international conferences. She has contributed chapters in edited books and published peer review articles in national and international journals. She is the reviewer and guest editor of various national and international journals. She has a published paper in *Journal of Business Ethics*. She has conducted the MDP's on Corporate Social Responsibility (CSR) for the middle level and senior managers as well as for the executive directors for the various companies (NHPC, GAIL, RITES, IRCTC, J.K. Cement, EXIM BANK, SBI etc.). Her areas of interests are corporate social responsibility, corporate social performance, stakeholder management, business ethics and environment sustainability.

**Pawan K. Taneja** is a faculty member at Indian Institute of Public Administration (IIPA), New Delhi. He has a rich and varied experience in teaching, research and industry for over 15 years. He has coordinated several operational research projects on various aspects of public health such as healthcare financing, health seeking behavior, monitoring and evaluation studies, modeling of impact of climate change on healthcare, and health systems research supported by UNICEF, WHO, BMGF, the UNION etc. He has published five books and 35 research papers in various peer-reviewed national and international journals (with impact factor) on various public administration, public health, finance and management issues. He has handled numerous training on various issues of management and administration, such as leadership development, qualitative and quantitative data analysis tools, impact assessment of interventions, monitoring and evaluation, project management, etc. His areas of research are operational research in public health, performance measurement and evaluation of public services, health economics and healthcare financing.

**Shann Turnbull** is a prolific author on reforming the theories and practices of capitalism. In Czechoslovakia and the People's Republic of China in 1991 he advised on reforms. A Harvard MBA based in Australia, Shann was a partner in a private equity group that purchased control and re-organized a dozen stock exchange traded firms. In this role and as a serial entrepreneur he became chair and/or CEO of listed firms, three of which he founded. His PhD established the science of governance by using bytes to ground social science in the natural sciences. In 1975 he wrote *Democratising the Wealth of Nations* and became co-author of the first course in the world to provide an educational qualification for company directors. In 2002 he authored *A New Way to Govern: Organisations and Society after Enron* and in 2011 became a co-founding member of the UK-based Sustainable Money Working Group.

**Philippa Wells** is an associate professor of law in the Federation Business School, Federation University of Australia. With considerable experience in the New Zealand and Australian tertiary sectors, her research and teaching interests lie in environmental policy and history and in corporate law and governance, particularly in relation to governance for sustainability.

**Paul F. Williams** is professor, Ernst & Young faculty research fellow, at NC State University. He is associate editor for critical perspectives on accounting (associate then editor for accounting and the public interest until 2010). He served as editorial board member for several journals such as *Advances in Public Interest Accounting, Accounting, Auditing and Accountability Journal, Accounting and Business Society, Accounting Forum, Alternative Perspectives on Accounting and Finance, Journal of Professional Responsibility and Ethics in Accounting, Accountancy, Business and the Public Interest, Issues in Accounting Education*. He published in renowned journals such as *Accounting, Organizations and Society, Business Ethics Quarterly, Critical Perspectives on Accounting, Accounting, Economics and Law, Accounting and the Public Interest, European Accounting Review, Accounting Education: An International Journal, The Accounting Historians Journal* and many others. He received Ernst & Young Outstanding Teacher Award in 1999 and the AAA Public Interest Section Accounting Exemplar Award, 2013.

# Series editor's preface

Businesses have substantial potential to contribute positively to sustainable markets and society. Their contribution can be two-fold: at the local level and at the global level. Because of their global reach and often their power over governments in countries where they are present, multinational companies are expected – and are well-placed – to play a major role in building and supporting sustainable markets. The contribution by organizations to sustainability is not only the province of for-profit entities: not-for-profit entities can also contribute in significantly different ways and they are also increasingly expected to work hand-in-hand as partners with business and government. The business models adopted by enterprises affect how they contribute to sustainable development. This contribution includes, but is not limited to, how they interact with each other in procurement, sub-contracting and other direct business decisions and arrangements.

In this book the corporate behavior and sustainability issue is argued in terms of theory, practice, regulation and principles. We hope that the reader will find the ideas presented here equally relevant and practical and, more importantly, helpful for improving business strategy for sound and sustainable business. The target groups for the book are broad and include academic researchers, teachers, postgraduate and doctoral students within study programmes, as well as policy-makers and regulators at the intersection of finance and sustainability. The book is also relevant to a variety of organizations including NGOs and those concerned with corporate social responsibility, business ethics, shareholder and stakeholder relationships, as well as corporate legitimacy and organizational public relations, where the ambition is to combine and/or transcend traditional financial, economic and social disciplines. The book also provides a valuable reader for further education and development of professional managers and consultants in the related areas of sound business strategy and sustainable development.

This book is the fourth book of the Gower book series *Finance, Governance and Sustainability: Challenges to Theory and Practice*. Today's developments within the field of sustainability and governance appeal to a growing audience in many aspects. The convergence between these three fields, finance, governance, and sustainability, has a high potential for effective solutions providing a wider perspective to the issues and barriers encountered about sustainability. The aim of the *Finance, Governance and Sustainability: Challenges to Theory and Practice* series is to fill this gap by bringing together the recent developments at the intersection of these three fields.

This series shares the studies of academicians, researchers, entrepreneurs, policy makers and government officers aiming to contribute to the progress and overcome the emerging barriers in corporate sustainability and sustainable development. In addition, by linking these studies to the research and development at the newly established Center for Finance, Corporate Governance and Sustainability, we will provide the most current coverage of these concepts with a global perspective. The series combines strong conceptual analyses with a wide-ranging empirical focus and a wealth of case materials. Also included are summary points, suggestions for further reading, web resources and an extensive bibliography. The level of presentation is for graduate students, academicians, business people as well as policy and decision-makers around the world.

Güler Aras

# Introduction

## Doing well by being good for sustainable business

*Güler Aras and Coral Ingley*

Corporate behavior is an important issue for business sustainability, not only for the entity itself, but also because organizations are corporate citizens and potentially their activities have an impact on other stakeholders. As corporate citizens their decisions and activities also impact ultimately on the wider community which, in effect, grants companies a social license to operate. Sustainable business is about ensuring that entities contribute toward positive social, environmental, and economic outcomes. Corporate sustainability is closely related to business behavior, corporate governance and sustainable market structures.

It is also important to create an understanding of where and how business can best contribute to sustainable markets, not only among the developed but also middle- and low-income countries where through globalization they are often key players. Irresponsible corporate behavior not only deprives shareholders of long-term returns but also ultimately imposes a cost on society as a whole. Recent waves of corporate misbehaviour have demonstrated the devastating consequences of excessive and ultimately destructive self-interest. Thus, as well as understanding the effects of corporate behaviour on markets, such an understanding is also now imperative in relation to the social and environmental contexts.

The power of various stakeholder groupings has changed radically in recent years. In particular, individuals have greater power to disenfranchise delinquent corporations and are more willing to use that power. Stakeholders are greatly empowered by electronic communications technology and the advent and efficacy of social media, with instantaneous global reach and potential for activism. It has taken corporations a long time to recognise and respond to the significance of the technological revolution that is resulting in an enormous advance in stakeholder democratisation.

Companies can no longer expect to engage in dubious or unethical corporate behavior without risking their reputation and damaging, perhaps irrevocably, their market position. At the very least, such damage from media scandals and potential legal action can be enormously costly, financially, as well as diminishing or destroying short- and long-term shareholder and stakeholder value. Conversely, sustained exemplary corporate behavior may potentially create greater social and economic value than markets, investors and corporations have hitherto fully appreciated.

Corporate concerns increasingly focus upon two main issues: good governance and social responsibility which are essential elements for a sustainable economic system. Much concern has been expressed as a result of revelations stemming from the economic and financial crisis. These revelations have exposed significant weaknesses and failures in governance at a corporate level and in markets and governments. Good governance and social responsibility operate at many levels from the global context to the corporate setting and are indisputably connected to sustainable behavior (Aras 2015a).

It is now becoming widely recognized that bad business behavior is more costly than good behavior for stakeholders, for markets, for society and all economies (Aras 2015b). Increasingly corporate social responsibility (CSR) and sustainability issues are regarded as strategic with a potential to generate important competitive advantages for companies that recognize the benefits of engaging in good business practices.

To approach the problems and considerations highlighted above, internationally recognized researchers and scholars in the fields of corporate governance, ethics, management, and sustainability studies have contributed chapters to this volume, each focusing on and providing balanced commentary as well as presenting findings from their analysis and research. This book is designed to address these debates in the context of business behavior and corporate sustainability. The topics covered are contained within four distinct parts. Part I considers corporate behavior from a stakeholder perspective; Part II focuses on effective business behavior for sustainable business; Part III discusses views and approaches to monitoring and reporting on sustainability performance; and Part IV considers the requirements for implementing good corporate practices for sustainability.

In the first chapter in Part I, Güler Aras and Paul Williams consider the agency problem in relation to stakeholders and corporate sustainability. The authors highlight the financial crisis in emphasizing the importance of corporate governance and corporate ethics for sound business. They argue that the weak internal controls, insufficient board oversight and lack of supervisory regulation of corporate governance revealed in the aftermath of the financial crisis were detrimental to both the performance of business and the financial markets. They assert that responsible corporate behavior exists in an environment of trust, ethical practices, moral values and the confidence of stakeholders in the corporate sector, including government, and the general public.

Chapter two by Shallini S. Taneja, Jennifer J. Griffin, Pawan K. Taneja, Radha R. Sharma, Kirk Davidson and Rupamanjari Sinha Ray adopts a multi-stakeholder approach to measuring success in Indian companies. The authors propose and test a framework that incorporates social and economic metrics in this context. They argue that combining effectively corporate social responsibility, financial performance and stakeholder management requires reconsidering what is meant by, and how to measure, success in a twenty-first-century firm. They posit that Western metrics of success that govern a firm's behavior often disregard or implicitly ignore social aspects of performance without accounting for the contributions from stakeholders involved in the value creation process.

In chapter three Miriam Green argues, on epistemological grounds, for the importance of having confidence in the validity of all scholarship and for its relevance to the understanding of the society or section of society for which the scholarship is relevant. She avers that scholarship affects people's understanding of the issues investigated and also has the potential to influence policy makers in government and other institutions. In the case of management studies, scholarship in sustainability has the capacity to influence the discourse about what organizations are, what they represent, how they function and, crucially, who has the power to effect sustainability policy. Because scholarship in this area also has – as it should – the capacity to instruct not only university and college students but also professional managers and consultants, it becomes vital that the knowledge imparted should meet pedagogic as well as epistemological standards.

Part II examines effective business behavior for sustainable business. In their chapter Philippa Wells and Coral Ingley explore issues relating to governance for sustainability and arguments that shape it. They debate the extent to which such a focus can be developed and pursued within the legal framework which provides as one of the directors' major fiduciary duties: the requirement to act in good faith and in the best interests of the company. The authors provide a brief overview of the major arguments and positions in relation to whether or not such values should form part of the strategic governance process. They reflect on whether and how the directors' duty to act in good faith can be applied so that directors can prioritize sustainability values and conclude with suggestions as to future avenues of research regarding governance for sustainability.

Alice Klettner considers in chapter five the governance structures and processes that can assist corporations to successfully integrate corporate responsibility into their business and improve the organization's long-term sustainability. She considers how instruments of soft regulation such as corporate governance codes and international reporting standards can guide this process and initiate change within corporations despite the seemingly weak voluntary status of these guidelines. The chapter introduces some emerging governance practices aimed at ensuring that corporate sustainability strategies are devised and implemented in conjunction with core operational strategies. These include the use of innovative methods of stakeholder engagement, board sub-committees and other leadership structures, and remuneration schemes that reward successful implementation of sustainability strategy.

Jacob Dahl Rendtorff outlines a theoretical framework for corporate citizenship, ethics and accountability in chapter six. In this chapter he shows that trust is essential for being good by doing good. The chapter first describes the significance of the process of emergent ethical trust and trusting in late modernity. The ethical idea of trust and trusting is then examined, where trust is based on the belief in the good moral intentions of the other. The role of trust and trusting in the process of leadership and organizing corporate culture is then discussed. With this analysis Rendtorff shows that the role and process of trust in the ethical culture of corporations is the foundation of good corporate citizenship.

Part III focuses on monitoring and reporting on sustainable business performance. This part begins with chapter seven by Jamilah Ahmed and Suraati Saad who highlight the role of media in encouraging responsible business behavior. The authors argue that the media has the capability to disseminate messages and influence audiences in developing perceptions, opinions or decision making, thereby playing an indispensable role in the dialogues around corporate social responsibility. In addition to its function as an independent monitor for corporations, the media often acts as a channel through which corporations communicate to the public. How media tell their stories about CSR has significant impacts on the public's and policy makers' expectations of companies and eventually influences the decision as to what extent companies will conduct their business in a socially responsible manner. The authors explore the

CSR and media scenario and how the media has framed and presented CSR. Their findings confirm that the media contributes to the construction of what CSR means in corporate practice by creating links between CSR and corporate activities, between CSR and media positioning, and between CSR and news value.

In chapter eight Douglas M. Branson traces a pathway to sustainability through social accounting over the last 40 years and highlights the importance to CSR of exemplary citizenship in communities, of which corporations are a part. Despite CSR having been at the fore since at least Earth Day in 1970, he notes that there is still no commonly accepted meaning of what social responsibility is or entails. Thus, he argues, has developed the first virtue accorded social accounting: by selecting the processes and fields of outreach the corporation wishes to monitor and report upon, the company defines for itself what corporate social responsibility means or should be. Being able to manage and continue to measure non-financial as well as financial performance is among a range of benefits of corporate social accounting discussed in the chapter. Branson highlights the wide spectrum of social audits, tracing their progression in sustainability reporting since 1990 showing an upward trend in universality in such reviews, at least among the larger corporations. Dominated by the major accounting firms, progress in such reporting has, he argues, resulted in anything from a 20-page sales pitch for the firm's social auditing services to denser reports of extraordinary length accessible only to individuals and organizations aware of the report's existence. He warns of a danger that form may triumph over substance and sight may be lost of the bigger picture on the accounting, reporting and sustainability landscape.

Alison L. Dempsey focuses in chapter nine on the role of the board of directors in her chapter on materiality with regard to environmental, social and governance issues in the corporate context. She highlights the higher expectations of board accountability in addition to their core oversight role, which are extending to non-financial dimensions of corporate activity. Not only are these changes in governance function a result of increased regulation and legal requirements aimed at reducing corporate misconduct: they also reflect normative and social expectations based on changes in attitudes toward the impacts of corporate activities. The chapter highlights the inadequacy of purely economic measures of corporate performance in capturing the full extent of factors required to ensure corporate success. While companies in the past have overlooked the non-financial aspects of their performance, there is now both a market-driven and a compliance imperative to their reporting obligations on a wider set of both non-financial and financial dimensions and risks affecting their business. She sets out ways in which boards can report proactively on the combination of financial and non-financial metrics to find a sustainable balance for efficient and effective current and future performance. The chapter concludes that adding non-financial reporting to the financial and governance matters on the board agenda recognizes the materiality of environmental and social issues to corporate performance, as well as how companies are held accountable and their ability to meet the increasing challenges presented by these issues.

Part IV considers the requirements for implementing good corporate practices for sustainability. In chapter ten Suzanne H. Benn examines the key issues that are driving organizational change for sustainability and the reasons that business and its networks need to come on board. Noting the importance of how relationships between business, civil society and government are harnessed for sustainable outcomes, Benn contends that we are, however, embedded in the conditions of a "world at risk" society, with increasing concern about the impacts of modernization that we ourselves have driven. She presents the concepts of "globalization from above" and "globalization from below" as two sets of actors which have emerged on the global stage in reaction to the potential adverse social and environmental effects of globalization and industrialization. This has given rise to the networked society, holding the private and public sectors accountable for their sustainability performance. The chapter notes also, evolving forms of regulation as a key driver of change for sustainability. New technologies and business models are a further driver of change, including innovations in energy efficiency, new forms of capitalism, an emphasis on cost avoidance and risk management and increasing expectations of better board and governance performance from large investors. Benn concludes that the reality for managers is that business success and sustainability are inextricably linked: social and environmental health are essential to corporate survival. The principles of community, interconnectedness and cooperation provide a model for corporations to move forward towards sustainability, generating new strategic directions, new levels of resource productivity and a way of understanding the corporation as a moral entity. She warns that, nevertheless, while there are increasing pressures toward a more sustainable world there are also powerful forces with an interest in maintaining the status quo and business as usual based on a wasteful economic growth paradigm. Benn maintains that to attain a truly sustainable global society, a working model is clearly needed, as well as the knowledge for creating the requisite transformative processes, and an understanding of the role of corporations in achieving this transformation.

Elke Fein, Jürgen Deeg and Jonathan Reams focus in chapter eleven on theoretical and practical implications of "next generation" responsible leadership. The authors note that the idea and concept of responsible leadership (RL) has gained increasing public and academic attention due to a general rise of awareness in business, research and politics concerning the challenges to sustainable development in an increasingly complex and globalized world. They also highlight the ongoing discussion about the meaning of responsibility and, thus, the requirements to be met by an evolving definition of responsible leadership. The chapter addresses these challenges by proposing a developmentally informed notion of responsible leadership, and then discusses collaborative forms of this approach. The overall argument in the chapter is summarized by Otto Scharmer's formula of a transformation "from ego to eco system perspectives" if leadership is to become more responsible towards a globalized world.

Bob Garratt argues in chapter twelve that in its current form, corporate governance as a bureaucratic compliance tool is increasingly seen as ineffective in ensuring the leadership efficiency and effectiveness of organizations. Yet effective governance is a powerful concept which, in Garratt's view, is a counter to the incompetence, ignorance and corruption that is undermining our organizations and societies. Thus, he argues, with widespread doubt about the effectiveness of corporate governance, it is time to reconsider its essence and create a new mindset to restore its relevance and our long-term survival. One of the main causes of this problem for corporate governance is, he believes, a public expectation that it is a silver bullet, based on structural interventions to solve all too human issues. Garratt regards the failure to meet this expectation is because the four main players – boards of directors, owners, regulators and legislators – do not act as an integrated system of learning. With little supervisory oversight of each player none see themselves as a key to developing effective leadership as an asset to stabilize and develop society. The chapter focuses on the requirements for a future corporate governance system that builds in learning systems, human behaviors and values rather than increasing compliance. With regard to codes and guidelines for effective corporate governance, Garratt advocates a broader and more diversity-embracing approach beyond the world of accountants, to restore public trust and to value organizational leadership which must involve human values and behaviors. He suggests that if a climate of self-enforcement of the moral values of accountability, probity and transparency – which are not only the foundations of effective leadership and corporate governance but are also both personal and measurable – combined with the basic duties of a director were ensured then increasingly dense codes that weigh against human nature and enterprise would not be needed. Garratt concludes the chapter with the hopeful suggestion that less time be spent on corporate governance codes and more time on understanding human nature and beliefs in relation to moral purpose and enterprise and their effects on the dynamics of markets.

In chapter thirteen Shann Turnbull contends that governance practices are not necessarily consistent with the objectives of good governance. One reason for the inconsistency is that there is little agreement as to the objectives of generic good governance, be it in the public, private or non-profit sectors. The objective of good governance suggested for all sectors in this chapter is the ability of an organization to further its purpose for its existence without imposing costs, harm and risks on society while acting equitably and ethically. Turnbull also indicates that in this way CSR is integrated into corporate governance while minimizing the extent, cost and need for government laws, regulations, regulators, legal actions and codes. He also argues that many laws, regulations and codes accepted and promoted by some regulators and governance-rating agencies include unethical counter-productive conflicts of interests. Turnbull concludes that the involvement of lay lawmakers is required to provide the leadership for achieving good governance.

Getting the right standards and tools in place to support, promote and benchmark responsible business practices is important for the future sustainability of the business world. Ethical management systems and various kinds of "social and environmental responsibility" standards for businesses are emerging and evolving. In this book we aim to contribute to, promote and support, "right" – that is, ethical and value creating – business behavior. Each chapter in the book addresses relevant and important aspects of corporate behavior and sustainability, not only from a theoretical perspective but also through practical analysis and implementation. The authors of this book have shared their views on the globally recognized and accepted understanding of our theme: doing well by doing good. We hope that the considered views presented in this volume are both informative and helpful in furthering debate, understanding and good practice for creating a sustainable but responsibly prosperous global environment.

## Bibliography

Aras, G. (2015a), 'Causality and Interaction: Sustainable Markets and Sustainable Business'. In *Sustainable Markets for Sustainable Business: Global Perspective for Business and Financial Markets*, Aldershot, Gower.

Aras, G. (2015b), 'The Future Perspectives: What Do We Need for Markets and Business Sustainability?', In *Sustainable Markets for Sustainable Business: Global Perspective for Business and Financial Markets*, Aldershot, Gower.

# Part I

# Market behavior, stakeholders' approach and good governance

# Agency theory

## Explaining or creating problems? Good governance and ethical behaviour for sustainable business

*Güler Aras and Paul Williams*

## Introduction

Corporate scandals (e.g., Enron, WorldCom) and the magnitude of the 2008 financial crisis has raised consciousness that Corporate Governance is an important issue for all institutions but particularly for corporate business. Weak internal controls, insufficient board oversight and lack of supervisory impact on corporate governance were detrimental to the trustworthiness of business and financial markets. Since the financial crisis, all countries are more aware of the importance of strong governance structures and good governance systems. Corporate governance can be considered as creating an organisational environment of trust, ethics, moral values and confidence among the organisation's stakeholders, including government and the general public. This is complicated by the fact that a corporation as a legal being has legal and ethical responsibilities, but without there being anyone explicitly charged with ensuring those responsibilities are fulfilled (Greenfield 2006). Many countries are now evaluating their legislation and regulatory policies pertaining to governance structures and taking steps to safeguard the sector and reduce the risk of severe financial distress in the future. Getting the right governance principles, standards and tools in place to support and promote responsible business practices is important for securing a sustainable business environment. However, businesses themselves need to be proactive and implement good governance principles and practices.

The latest financial crisis is a negative lesson in how good corporate governance is essential for a sound economy and fundamental to the operations of any good corporate citizen. In this chapter we will focus on how we can implement good governance principles for a sustainable and sound business environment. We will try to make the case that corporations conceived as merely a nexus of private contracts is inadequate as a perspective from which to consider how corporations should be governed. Corporations' role in the Great Recession, their role in the growing income inequality within even countries with advanced economies and their role in climate change all suggest that we need to rethink the way we approach their governance.

Many corporations are already adopting new perspectives motivated by their recognition that their long-term survivals depend on new modes of operations. Increasingly CSR, ethics and sustainability issues are regarded as strategic with potential to generate important competitive advantages for companies that recognise their success depends on engaging in good business practices – or business practices that are good.

## Managing managers via agency theory principles

A very simplistic characterisation of management describes managers as having the power to commit the organisation to whatever contracts and transactions they feel appropriate but as also having a fiduciary responsibility towards the owners of the business. For some four decades agency theory has provided the most prominent rationale upon which this dual, but conflicting, nature of management is allegedly rationally harmonised and corporate actions justified. Agency theory claims that the management of an organisation is undertaken on behalf of the shareholders of that organisation. It is a theory grounded in the ontology of neoclassical economics. It is not simply an economic theory but also a political ideology in that it presumes the superiority of free market solutions to social problems and the priority of protecting property rights as the legitimate priority of government. Consequently the management of value creation by the organisation is only pertinent insofar as that value accrues to the shareholders of the firm. Implicit within this view of the management of the firm, as espoused by Rappaport (1986) and Stewart (1991), amongst many others, is that society at large, and consequently all other stakeholders to the organisation, will also benefit as a result of managing the performance of the organisation in this manner. From this perspective therefore the concerns of management are focused upon how to manage the corporation performance for the exclusive benefit of shareholders. Corporate reports are, perforce, reports focused exclusively upon that kind of performance (Myners 1998). However, this view of an organisation has been extensively challenged by many writers,[1] who argue that the way to maximise performance for society at large is to both manage on behalf of all stakeholders and to ensure that the value thereby created is not appropriated by the shareholders but is distributed to all stakeholders. Others such as Kay (1998) argue that this debate is sterile and that organisations maximise value creation not by a concern with either shareholders or stakeholders but by focusing upon the operational objectives of the firm and assuming value creation and its equitable distribution are consequences of achieving proper corporate objectives (see, Aras and Crowther 2009).

Agency theory argues that managers merely act as custodians of the organisation and its operational activities and places upon them the responsibility of managing in the best interest of the owners of that business. According to agency theory all other stakeholders of the business are largely irrelevant and if they benefit from the business then this is coincidental to the activities of management in running the business to serve shareholders. This focus upon shareholders alone as the intended beneficiaries of a business has been questioned considerably from many perspectives, which argue that it is either not the way in which a business is actually run or that it is a view which does not meet the needs of society in general. For example, agency theory formed the primary rationale for stock-option compensation as a preferred method for rewarding managers since it allegedly aligned better their economic interests with the economic interests of shareholders. As Thomas Piketty's (2014) data have shown the biggest single factor contributing to the historically unprecedented gap in US income from labour between the top ten percent of earners and the bottom ninety percent is the tremendous growth in the compensation to corporate management precipitated by the advent of agency theory inspired compensation schemes.

An alternative theory of corporate management – stakeholder theory (Freeman 1984) – argues that there are a variety of stakeholders involved in the organisation and each deserves some return for their involvement. Management is the process of balancing these various interests. According to stakeholder theory therefore corporate value is maximised if the business is operated by its management on behalf of all stakeholders and returns are divided appropriately amongst those stakeholders in some way which is acceptable to all. However, a single mechanism for dividing returns amongst all stakeholders which has universal acceptance does not exist, and stakeholder theory is significantly lacking in suggestions in this respect. Nevertheless this theory has considerable traction and is based upon the premise that operating a business in this manner achieves as one of its outcomes the long-run optimisation of returns to shareholders. Stakeholder theory is premised on the recognition that corporations are "externality machines" (Greenfield 2006) and without due consideration of these externalities shareholder value maximisation may come at a very high cost to everyone else. The optimisation of returns to stakeholders is achieved in the long run through the optomisation of performance for the business in achieving a balanced consideration of all stakeholders' interests.[2] Consequently the role of management is to optimise the long-term performance of the business in order to achieve this end and thereby reward all stakeholders appropriately, including themselves as one stakeholder in a community of stakeholders. Agency and stakeholder theories can be regarded as competing normative theories of the operations of a firm; they lead to different operational foci and different conceptions of management's responsibilities and to different implications for the measurement and reporting of performance. It is significant however that both theories have one feature in common. This is that the management of the firm is believed to be acting on behalf of others, either shareholders or stakeholders more generally. They do so, not because they are the kind of people who behave altruistically but because they are rewarded appropriately and much effort is therefore devoted to the creation of reward schemes which motivate these managers to achieve the desired ends.

## From agency theory to corporate governance

The problem of managers' power to decide being exclusively harnessed for the benefit of others was remarked upon by Adam Smith (1776), the alleged father of "free markets". Smith (1776) noted this problem with management by remarking that it cannot be expected that the managers will watch other people's money and their own with the same anxiety. Therefore, negligence and profusion must always be, more or less, present in the management of a company. Almost 150 years later, when the business corporation had become dominant in the economic world, Berle and Means (1932) emphasised this problem of the separation of firm owners (the principals) and firm managers (the agents). They point out some of the key problems inherent in the separation of ownership and control.

An implication of Berle and Means study is that market forces could not be solely relied upon to countervail management power, suggesting that large corporations need more regulation by government of their affairs. A contrary argument to this conclusion about corporate governance was provided by Jensen and Meckling's (1976,

1994) study. It is the classic work on the application of agency theory in finance, and developed the concerns and ideas about owner-management separation into explicit, economic models on the behaviour of the agents. The principal-agent model provided a rational, economic decision theoretic solution to the conflict between managers and shareholders' interests. Jensen and Meckling provide important insights into the impact of agency relations within the firm and describe the nature of the agency relationship between the principal, owners of the firm, and the agents, managers of the firm. As both of the parties are rational economic actors, concerned only with maximising their own utilities, agency problems of equity will arise. Eisenhardt (1989, p. 58) states that "the origins of agency theory is directed at the ubiquitous agency relationship, in which one party (the principal) delegates work to another (the agent), who performs that work". However, this is done at the risk to the principals that the agents will not see their interests as consonant with those of the principals. Thus, the problem of corporate governance reduces itself to devising mechanisms to reduce the costs of agency, e.g., shirking, misdirection of resources, excessive risk aversion. Further, the theory claims that these mechanisms will emerge through the actions of economically rational principals and agents – mutual economic rationality leads to solutions to the agency problem. Persistent exploitation of principals by their agents would mean there is persistent economic irrationality, which agency theory assumes away. Thus, as a theory of corporate governance it could be accused of being tautologous. The classical papers by Fama (1980) Jensen and Meckling (1976), Ross (1973), Spence and Zeckhauser (1971), are examples of this economic formulation of the agency within the economics and finance disciplines.

Agency theory has profound implications about how to govern a modern corporation with a large number of shareholders whose collective capital is controlled and directed by separate shareholders. Miozzo and Dewick (2002) state that corporate governance is an important device as a means of reducing agency costs imposed by managers who are acting in their own interest. Jensen and Meckling (1976) model of agency costs and ownership structure holds a central role in the corporate governance literature. As the main problem is the conflict between the principal and the agent, the focus of this theory is on determining the proxies of agency costs and the most efficient mechanisms governing the principal-agent relationship. Some of the primary benefits of good governance are long-run viability, more efficient resource allocation, more or higher credibility, new market enhancement and the awareness of the needs of all stakeholders (Aras and Crowther 2008a). According to agency theory, corporate governance mechanisms serve to bring agents' behaviours into alignment with their principals' interests. The mechanisms of corporate governance define structures and rules forming the system and they will have significant effects on solving the agency conflict. A broad field of studies on agency theory concentrates on describing the different governance mechanisms to lessen the agency conflict (Aras 2015, Aras and Furtuna 2015).

The simplest model of agency theory assumes one principal and one agent and a modernist view of the world merely assumes that the addition of more principals and more agents makes for a more complex model without negating any of the assumptions. In the corporate world this is problematic as the theory depends upon a relationship between the parties and a shared understanding of the context in which agreements are made. With one principal and one agent this is not a problem as the two parties know each other. In the corporate world however the principals are equated to the shareholders of the company. For any large corporation however those shareholders are an amorphous mass of people who are unknown to the managers of the business. These shareholders also do not have harmonious interests; some shareholders take a long-term view while others a short-term one. Thus any corporate decisions will likely benefit some shareholders at the expense of other shareholders. Indeed there is no requirement, or even expectation, that anyone will remain a shareholder for an extended period of time. Thus there can be no relationship between shareholders – as principals – and managers – as agents – as the principals are merely those holding the shares – as property being invested in – at a particular point in time. So shareholders do not invest in a company and in the future of that company; rather they invest for capital growth and/or a future dividend stream and shares are just one way of doing this which can be moved into or out of at will. This problem is exacerbated, by the fact that a significant proportion of shares are actually bought and sold by fund managers of financial institutions acting on behalf of their investors. These fund managers are rewarded according to the growth (or otherwise) of the value of the fund. Thus shares are bought and sold as commodities rather than as part ownership of a business enterprise (Aras and Crowther 2009). This fact has led Lynn Stout (2012) to conclude that "shareholders" are a fiction – a convenient fiction to lend agency theory coherence. But as she concludes: "Recognizing these differences [among shareholders] reveals that the idea of a single objectively measureable 'shareholder value' is not only quixotic, but intellectually incoherent (Stout 2012, p. 60)."

## Mismanagement and corporate scandals

Such major scandals as the savings and loan failures in the late 1980s and 1990s; the Enron, Global Crossing, WorldCom and Tyco corporate scandals; Arthur Andersen's demise and the current crisis of the financial system have all been linked directly or indirectly to false, misleading or untruthful reporting. People presume that the information they receive about corporate activities, whether financial or otherwise, are "truthful." In a pragmatic sense corporate governance depends on the veracity of the information provided. This raises the important question of the veracity of the accounting provided by the corporation to others. Bayou et al. (2011) develop the implications of what it would mean for reporting for accounts about corporate performance to be "true." They argue that the role played by such information is not to enable economic prediction but to situate the corporation, i.e., to tell us about where it fits into the larger narrative society. The purpose of such situating is to provide information permitting reasoned action aimed at governing the corporation.

There is growing recognition of agency theory's failure as a foundation for understanding issues of corporate governance. Thus, the past thirty years have witnessed an ongoing research on corporate governance. After the corporate scandals such as Enron, Tyco, WorldCom and Parmalat, there have seen significant changes in the regulations and the relationships between management, boards and stakeholders globally. Through its evolution process, sets of laws and regulations have been established by developed countries. In UK, The Cadbury Report (1992), the Greenbury Report (1995) and the Combined Code (1998) have developed an adapted version of corporate governance codes in terms of corporate governance mechanisms.

In the USA, The Sarbanes-Oxley Act (2002) was enacted as a reaction to major corporate and accounting scandals and it aims to clarify the financial, board, CEO and stakeholder related applications. In 1999, the Organisation for Econnomic Co-Operation and Development (OECD) issued a set of corporate governance standards and guidelines to help countries to evaluate and improve the legal, institutional and regulatory framework for corporate governance in their homes. After these regulations, corporate governance mechanisms received a high priority on the agenda of policy makers, institutions, investors, companies and academicians. However the regulation was not enough to protect the economy from the 2008 financial crisis. The United States decided to re-regulate all markets with Dodd-Frank Wall Street and Consumer Protection Act (2010). This constituted a sweeping legislative reaction to the perceived regulator failures that had allowed the financial crisis to intensify uncontrollably into a global phenomenon (Clarke 2015). However, the Act has been criticised for not going far enough to diminish the power of Wall Street over the economy of the US.

## Stakeholders theory and investor protection

In the literature, there are many definitions of corporate governance and each emphasises different aspects of governance. OECD Principles of Corporate Governance (2004, p. 11) gives a broad definition of corporate governance, taking into account all parties involved into firm activities. In this report, "corporate governance" is defined as the system by which firms are directed and controlled. Also, corporate governance documents a set of relationships between a company's management, its board, its shareholders and other stakeholders.

Agency theory, or the shareholder theory of the firm, has been the paradigmatic theory of corporate governance. As already explained, the theory reduces the role of the management of a firm to acting as the agents of only the shareholders (the principals). The separation of ownership and control that is apparent in large modern-day (joint stock) companies, presently the most common way for a business to be organised, is another significant change since the days of Adam Smith. It is this separation that leads to what is known as the principal – agent relationship. It is also argued that within this role it is only appropriate for managers (the agents) to use the funds at their disposal for purposes authorised by shareholders (the principals) (Hasnas 1998, Smith and Hasnas 1999). Furthermore shareholders normally invest in shares in order to maximise their own returns. Consequently managers, as their agents, are obliged to target this end. In fact this is arguing that as an owner a shareholder has the right to expect his or her property to be used to his or her own benefit. Donaldson (1982, 1989) disagrees and suggests that it can be morally acceptable to use the shareholder's money in a different way if it is to further public interest. The ethical and moral acceptability of this suggestion has been questioned by Smith and Hasnas (1999), who point out that such an act would contravene Kant's (1804) principle that a person should be treated as an end in his or her own right rather than as a means to an end. By using shareholders' money for the benefit of others it is argued that the shareholders are being used as a means to further others' ends. This defence of shareholder theory is ironic given that the exact same principle is often cited to defend stakeholder theory (Aras and Crowther 2009). However, the argument is flawed because it is based on the false premise that the shareholders are actually the owners of the corporation, i.e., synonymous with it. The resources in law actually belong to the corporation, a separate legal being, and the managers are not agents of the shareholders, but agents of the corporation. In the early history of corporations they were governed by the ultra vires doctrine that stipulated that corporations were permitted to do only that which they were legally created to do, e.g., construct a canal or toll road. Corporations are creations of the state and it is the state that determines the limits of what corporations may or may not do, not shareholders. Over time, led by the U.S., corporate charters have virtually eliminated the requirement that corporations confine themselves to only limited activity so the ultra vires doctrine has faded in significance as a basis for corporate governance (Greenfield 2006). But simply because states have loosened substantially their reins over corporate behaviour does not negate the fact that corporations are creations of the state and shareholders merely one among many stakeholders with no superior status. Indeed, the reason there is a problem of corporate governance is that corporations are "persons" but without the ability to conduct themselves as actual humans can who are equipped with a conscience, a sense of shame and the capacity for compassion.

Accounting scandals in US, UK and crisis in the Asian countries have gained attention of investor protection issue in the last years. The task mainly related with protecting outsiders (minority shareholders, non-controlling shareholders) from insiders (controlling shareholders, large shareholders, managers and directors) expropriation or discretion with the help of the rights, regulations and laws. The literature on the importance of investor protection subject mainly begins with the pioneering study of La Porta, Lopez-de-Silanes, Shleifer and Vishny (LLSV) (1998–1999–2006) which mainly concentrate on investor protection, ownership concentration and CG in finance literature.

Corporate governance mechanisms serve to deal with the problems that arise from the separation of ownership and control. Furthermore, empirical evidence supports the effectiveness of these mechanisms in reducing the agency problem. Besides this, the corporate failures and scandals create an awareness of the importance of corporate governance mechanisms. The focus of corporate governance has turned to the evaluation of the efficiency and effectiveness of corporate governance mechanisms in terms of board size, board composition, the separation of CEO and Chairperson and audit quality (Aras and Furtuna 2015). However, the question is whether this focus on the minutiae of technical "corporate governance" will stifle more innovative thinking about what are more genuine problems effective corporate governance must address.

## Developing principles of good governance

### Good governance ethics and corporate performance

Good governance is essential for good corporate performance. Some of the primary benefits of good governance are long-run viability, more efficient resource allocation, more or higher credibility, reaching new markets and the awareness of the needs of all stakeholders,

An increasing number of country-level studies have provided empirical evidence of the positive effect of corporate governance on financial structure and the literature on corporate governance widely recognises debt as an important mechanism for solving agency problems in corporations characterised by separation of ownership and control. Corporate governance is an important mechanism for the debt holders to control the opportunistic behaviours of managers. By this way, corporate governance practices may reduce the cost of debt and the financial leverage (Aras 2015).

However, these efforts at governance reform are still largely predicated on an agency view of the corporation – creditors are merely another kind of "shareholder" whose interest in the corporation is purely financial. Even agency theorists acknowledge the importance of ethics; economic engineering has failed to prevent scandals, recessions, and any technical solution to the distribution problem (one that is looming as a more serious one for the social and political stability of even advanced societies). Agency theorists have acknowledged the indispensability of ethical behaviour to the functioning of a market economy (Noreen 1988). Much recent research in anthropology, psychology, evolutionary biology and even behavioural economics is causing fundamental reassessments of whether the idea of homo economicus, the assumption about human nature fundamental to neoclassical economic theory, is any longer sensible. What is emerging from all of the research is a view of humans as fundamentally ethical in their makeup. Rather than homo economicus humans are more aptly characterised as homo reciprocans, beings whose relationships are based on reciprocity rather than gaining advantage over one another. A persistent research finding is that humans possess an inherent "fairness sense" (Basu 2011; Corning 2011) and that humans are willing to incur considerable costs to themselves to affect a fair outcome. Human beings do possess, as Adam Smith (1976) claimed, a moral sense and it is this moral sense that provides the glue that enables humans to be the most social of all mammals.

The implications of this research for how we govern corporations are nothing short of revolutionary. Certainly a realistic understanding of human nature makes stakeholder theory a potentially more productive frame within which to consider corporate governance than one predicated on an empirically false belief about humans and human behaviour. An important implication for corporate governance is that whatever the mechanisms adopted they must satisfy the conditions of being "fair." Peter Corning (2011) has drawn the implication from our tribal evolution and the nature we evolved to live in such groups that societies are collective survival enterprises. The essential feature, as was essential to tribal survival, is that those societies are fair. Corporations are not ends in themselves but merely a human invention, a device for ensuring human survival. As such they are to be included in a system of governance designed to produce a fair society, one focused on assuring social justice and not necessarily maximum returns to shareholder.

One governance principle that devolves from a stakeholder view of corporate governance is for firms to develop a ". . . procedural justice-based model of authority. This model emphasised not the ultimate outcome of decisions but the fairness of the decision-making procedures" (Greenfield, ibid, p. 161). Many companies have already adopted this approach to their corporate social responsibilities by collaborating with various stakeholder groups in order to demonstrate the legitimacy of those activities. For such mechanisms to work it is essential that corporations be viewed not as a "nexus of contracts" but as system of "relationships". Of course firms by themselves cannot alone affect these governance changes. Reasonable changes in corporate law and laws redressing the imbalance of power between labor and capital will be necessary and some of these changes are already occurring. For example, many states in the U.S. now offer a Type B Corporation charter which charters the corporation to be a profit making enterprise for which profit is not the main objective, but profiting in socially responsible ways is more important.

## Do we need uniform standards and rules? Requirements for good business: standards, rules, principles

Standards, rules and principles for good business behaviour are extremely important and the question of standards for sustainable business is one which has been in existence for a long time. In doing so this emphasises the role of standards and principles in enabling the transferring of best practice. We would like to highlight the debates.

Good governance and its regulation provides important data concerning the benefits of developing global standards. However our argument is that standards and principles of business behaviour evolve through natural selection just as effectively as through imposed standards. Process is crucial to success. Therefore we consider that standards of good business behaviour should be organic and developed via a process of fair participation of affected stakeholders in the decision-making process. Standards of practice will evolve rather than be imposed as a one-size-fits-all set of rules. The rules that must exist are those that create and sustain the process of developing just practices.

Getting the right standards and tools in place to support, promote and benchmark responsible business practices is important for the future of business, communities and the planet. Codes of conduct, ethical management systems and various kinds of social and environmental responsibility standards for businesses are proliferating. But who wins and who loses as these tools and standards hit real-world markets and impact on producers in poorer countries?

- *What kinds of rules, principles and regulations are necessary to support and facilitate sustainability?*
- *Where is strong regulation needed for good business behaviour and where is it possible to rely upon market discipline to achieve balanced and sustainable social and corporate outcomes?*

Emerged economies demand uniform standards of corporate governance. This is the key driver for corporate governance convergence. The OECD Principles of Corporate Governance is the first conceptual framework for policy makers, companies and others around the world. However, all countries, emerging or emerged, have the problem of principal-agent costs and each has a distinctive set of rules to deal with this problem. In this point of view, corporate governance models differ in each country's business framework, as companies in different countries are operated under different business culture, legal and economic systems. Academic literature states that there cannot be a single governance model for every country because of the cultural differences (Aras and Crowther 2008b). They argue that culture is the most important determinant of the operation of governance models. According to the cultural differences, management styles, each country should establish its own governance model based on the four basic principles that are accepted globally: fairness, transparency, accountability and responsibility. Henry (2010) also argues that voluntary governance compliance can exist in each of country.

As a consequence of the major corporate scandals, accounting failures and ongoing concerns about corporate governance; board characteristics, independent directors, CEO-chairperson duality and audit quality have become the most discussed issue at the center of the policy debate concerning governance reform and the focus of considerable academic research.

## Conclusion

The social and economic problems facing humankind today will require considerable will on the part of everyone for their resolution. Climate change, growing income and wealth inequality, and widespread poverty (now even in rich countries of the world) will require responsible behaviour on the parts of everyone, most importantly corporations which are the entities that control a considerable amount of societies' wealth. Governing corporations so as to ensure they contribute to the well-being of society and the planet is a crucial issue. For the last forty years the dominant approach to corporate governance has been agency theory, which conceives of the corporation as a nexus of contracts among antagonistic economic actors, the most important of whom are shareholders and managers. Resolving the agency cost problem that emerges within any principal/agent relationship is viewed as the sole problem of corporate governance. Much recent historical evidence suggests this model is not a good model because it is based on utopian economics. As Corning explains it:

> But many so-called market failures really are not such thing. Rather, they represent basic structural deficiencies in the idealized model, and they cannot be fixed simply by tinkering with the machinery, like adding a few more regulations. They are designed to fail.
>
> (Corning 2011, p. 128)

Basing corporate governance on economic presumptions that are empirically invalid will not contribute to corporations being constructive participants in reducing the threats posed by environmental decline and growing relative poverty. We have provided an alternative, stakeholder-based approach based on the principles of fairness and shared decision making, which hold out greater promise for sustainable societies than those proffered by the market triumphalists that delivered corporate scandals and financial crisis.

## Notes

1  See for example Herremans et al. (1992), Tinker (1985).
2  See for example Rappaport (1986).

## Bibliography

Agrawal, A. and Knoeber, C.R. (1996), 'Firm Performance and Mechanisms to Control Agency Problems between Managers and Shareholders,' *Journal of Financial and Quantitative Analysis*, vol. 31, no. 3, pp. 377–398.

Aras, G. (2015), 'The Effect of Corporate Governance Practices on Financial Structure in Emerging Markets: Evidence from BRIC(K) Countries and Lesson for Turkey', *Emerging Markets Finance & Trade Journal (EMFT)*, vol. 51, no. 2.

Aras, G. and Crowther, D. (2008a), 'Governance and Sustainability: An Investigation into the Relationship between Corporate Governance and Corporate Sustainability', *Management Decision*, vol. 46, no. 3, pp. 443–448.

Aras, G. and Crowther, D. (2008b), Corporate Sustainability Reporting: A Study in Disingenuity?', *Journal of Business Ethics*, 87(Suppl. 1), pp. 279–288.

Aras, G. and Crowther, D. (2009), *The Durable Corporation: Strategies for Sustainable Development*, Gower, Aldershot.

Aras, G. and Kurt, D. (2013), 'The Effects of Stock Option Compensation on Managerial Risk Taking Behavior and Firm Financial Performance The Global Financial Crisis From a Different Perspective,' *International Journal of Economics and Finance Studies*, vol 4, no. 2, pp. 77–90.

Aras, G. and Kutlu Furtuna, O. (2015), 'Does Governance Efficiency Impact Equity Agency Costs? Evidence from Turkey,' *Emerging Markets Finance & Trade Journal (EMFT)*, vol.51, no. 2.

Basu, K. (2011), *Beyond the Invisible Hand*. Princeton University Press, Princeton, NJ.

Bayou, M., Reinstein, A. and Williams, P.F. (2011), 'To Tell the Truth: A Discussion of Issues Concerning Truth and Ethics in Accounting,' *Accounting, Organizations and Society*, vol. 36, pp. 109–124.

Berle, A. and Means, G. (1932), *The Modern Corporation and Private Property*. Macmillan, New York. (Electronic book.)

Berle, A. and Means, G. (1933), *The Modern Corporation and Private Property*, Commerce Clearing House, New York.

Clarke, T. (2015), 'Systemic Crises in Global Markets: In Search of Regulatory and Sustainable Solutions'. In Aras, G. (ed.). *Sustainable Markets for Sustainable Business: Global Perspective for Business and Financial Markets*, Aldershot, Gower, UK Finance, Governance and Sustainability: Challenges to Theory and Practice, Gower Book Series, UK.

Corning, P. (2011), *The Fair Society*. The University of Chicago Press, Chicago, IL.

Donaldson, T. (1982) *Corporations and Morality*, Prentice Hall, Englewood Cliffs, NJ.

Eisenhardt, K.M. (1989), 'Agency Theory: An Assessment and Review,' *Academy of Management Review*, vol. 14, pp. 57–74.

Fama, F. (1980), 'Agency Problems and the Theory of the Firm'. *The Journal of Political Economy*, vol. 88, no. 2, pp. 288–307.

Fama, F. and Jensen, M. (1983), 'Agency Problems and Residual Claims'. *The Journal of Law & Economics*, vol. 26, pp. 1–29.

Freeman, R.E. (1984), *Strategic Management: A Stakeholder Approach*. Pittman, Boston, MA.

Greenfield, K. (2006), *The Failure of Corporate Law*. The University of Chicago Press, Chicago, IL.

Hasnas J. (1998), 'The Normative Theories of Business Ethics: A Guide for the Perplexed,' *Business Ethics Quarterly*, January, pp. 19–42.

Henry, D. (2010), 'Agency Costs, Ownership Structure and Ownership Governance Compliance: A Private Contracting Perspective,' *Pacific-Basin Finance Journal*, vol. 18, pp. 24–46.

Herremans, I.M., Akathaparn, P. and McInnes, M. (1992), 'An Investigation of Corporate Social Responsibility, Reputation and Economic Performance,' *Accounting, Organizations & Society*, vol. 18, nos. 7/8, pp. 587–604.

Jensen, M. and Meckling, W. (1976), 'Theory of The Firm: Managerial Behavior, Agency Costs, and Ownership Structure', *Journal of Financial Economics*, vol. 3, pp. 305–360.

Jensen, M. and Meckling, W. (1994), 'The Nature of Man', *Journal of Applied Corporate Finance*, vol. 7 no. 2, pp. 4–19.

Kant, I. (1804), *Grounding for the Metaphysics of Morals*; many editions.

Kay, J. (1998), 'Good Business,' *Prospect*, 28 (March), pp. 25–29.

La Porta, R.F., Lopez-de-Silanes, F. and Shleifer, A. (1998), 'Law and Finance,' *Journal of Political Economy*, vol. 106, no. 6, pp. 1113–1154.

La Porta, R.F., Lopez-de-Silanes, F. and Shleifer, A. (1999), 'Corporate Ownership around the World', *Journal of Finance*, no. 2, pp. 471–517.

La Porta, R.F., Lopez-de-Silanes, F. and Shleifer, A. (2006), 'What Works in Securities Laws?' *Journal of Finance*, vol. 61, pp. 1–32.

Miozzo, M. and Dewick, P. (2002), 'Building Competitive Advantage: Innovation and Corporate Governance in European Construction', *Research Policy*, vol. 31, pp. 989–1008.

Myners, P. (1998), 'Improving Performance Reporting to the Market.' In Carey, A. and Sancto, J. (eds), *Performance Measurement in the Digital Age*, ICAEW, London, pp. 27–33.

Nooren, E. (1988) The Economics of Ethics: A New Perspective on Agency Theory, *Accounting, Organizations and Society*, 13(4), pp. 359–369.

OECD (2004), Principles of Corporate Governance, OECD Publication, France.

Piketty, T. (2014), *Capital in the Twenty-First Century*, Trans. Arthur Goldhammer, The Belknap Press of the Harvard University Press, Cambridge, MA.

Rappaport, A. (1986), *Creating Shareholder Value*. The Free Press, New York.

Rappaport, A. (1992), 'CFO's and Strategists: Forging a Common Framework,' *Harvard Business Review*, May/Jun, pp. 84–91.

Ross, S. (1973), 'The Economic Theory of Agency: The Principal's Problem,' *American Economic Review*, vol. 63, pp. 134–139.

Shleifer, A. and Vishny, R.W. (1997), 'A Survey of Corporate Governance', *Journal of Finance*, vol. 52, no. 2, pp. 737–783.

Smith, A. (1776), *The Wealth of Nations*, W. Strahan and T. Cadell, London.

Smith, A. (1976), *The Theory of Moral Sentiments*. Liberty Classics, Indianapolis, IN.

Smith, H.J. and Hasnas, J. (1999), 'Ethics and Information Systems: The Corporate Domain,' *MIS Quarterly*, March, vol. 23, no. 1, pp. 109–127.

Spence, A. Michael and Richard Zeckhauser. 1971. Insurance, information, and individual action. *American Economic Review* (May), 61(2): 380–387.

Stewart, G.B. III (1991), *The Quest for Value*, Harper Collins, New York.

Stout, L. (2012), *The Shareholder Value Myth*, Berrett-Koehler Publishers, San Francisco, CA.

Strahan, W. and Cadell, T., and Donaldson, T. (1989), *The Ethics of International Business*, Oxford University Press, New York.

Tinker, T. (1985), *Paper Prophets: A Social Critique of Accounting*, Holt, Rinehart & Winston, London.

# Chapter 2

# Using a stakeholder approach to understand success

## Empirical tests in Indian business

*Shallini S. Taneja,*Jennifer J. Griffin, Pawan K. Taneja, Radha R. Sharma, D. Kirk Davidson and Rupamanjari Sinha Ray*

## Introduction

For many organizations, performance measurements play an important role for translating strategy into desired behaviors and tracking success. By communicating expectations, monitoring progress, providing feedback, and motivating employees through performance-based rewards and sanctions certain behaviors are incentivized, reinforced, and sustained (Chow and Stede 2006). Yet, the success of business organizations is determined by internal business objectives, strategies, and efficient operations as well as by external, market and non-market factors such as macro-economic conditions, competition, customer satisfaction, suppliers, community, government, and other relevant stakeholders. Incentivizing, and improving, behavior that simultaneously enables an organization to survive in today's competitive markets while enabling it to thrive tomorrow is at the heart of sustainable development (Baron 2000, Brundtland 1987).

In part, what is measured is often the behavior that is incentivized. Researchers and practitioners across world are in accord that maximizing shareholder wealth is a necessity but by no means a sufficient condition for financial prosperity in the twenty-first century. Measuring success of a business organization is not simply a function of business's contribution to the welfare of its shareholder via solely economic outcomes. To survive and prosper, firms are required to bridge the economic and social systems by directing their efforts towards maximizing customer delight (Anantharaman 2007), employee's welfare (Waal 2003), social value, and environmental protection, among others (O'Rourke 2003, WBCSD 2002). The success of a business depends upon its contribution to stakeholder's wealth (Eells and Walton 1974 cited in Carroll 1999) requiring a more comprehensive measurement framework, that includes economic success (financial performance + operational performance) of the organization as well as the firm's stakeholder success (see Figure 2.1).

Economic performance measures have a century-long literature to support with return on investment cited by most studies for evaluating financial performance (Cooper 2004, Griffin and Mahon 1997, Waddock and Graves 1994, Waddock and Mahon 1991, Zhu 2004). Operational performance, on the other hand requires measures for raw material and labor inputs, as well as cost ratios (Mostafa 2007, Oh and Lööf 2009, Wang 2010, Zheng et al. 1998, Zhu 2000) and other operational expense ratios (Halkos and Tzeremes 2010, Le and Harvie 2010, Wang 2010).

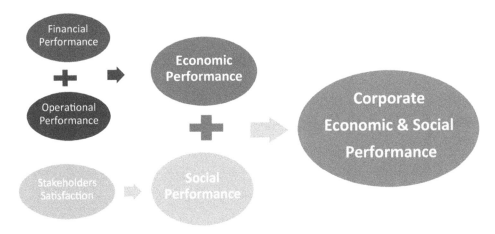

*Figure 2.1*  Proposed Framework for Measuring Corporate Economic Social Performance by Stakeholder Approach

A corporation's social performance (CSP), on the other hand, might be understood intuitively, yet remains a difficult task to express in concrete operational terms (Chow and Chen 2012, Labuschagne et al. 2005) due to differentiation in CSR practices in different socio-cultural settings (Taneja, Taneja and Gupta 2011).[1]

Given the inadequacies of a shareholder-only, financial view of a firm to incentivize corporate behavior, the main focus of this paper is to develop success metrics from a multi-stakeholder perspective (Freeman 1984) to measure success from the viewpoint of stakeholders (Griffin 2000). Specifically, the focus of this paper is to answer following two research questions:

- What relevant indicators should be considered to measure the success of a company to meet the expectations of stakeholders?
- What should be the framework to measure and control the individual and overall success to ensure meeting the expectations of all relevant stakeholders?

The article is organized as follows: the next section, briefly account for status of literature on measuring business success followed by a brief discussion on theoretical foundations and underpinnings used for the study. Section 2 includes the research methodology and explains the scale development process. Section 3 discusses the results of scale development process followed by a sub-section discussing the validation of the scales. The concluding section discusses the results with special reference to research questions and highlights the implications of the study, directions of future research, and contributions.

## 1  Literature review and theoretical underpinnings

In the twentieth century, many scholars suggested that a firm's primary loyalty is to its shareholders (Friedman 1970, Jensen 2002) which gave rise to a large volume of research directed at measuring shareholders' wealth (Avkiran and Morita 2010).

Accounting-based measures like Profit after Tax (PAT), Return on Investment (ROI), and Return on Equity (ROE) became popular metrics to evaluate organizational performance (Chow and Van der Stede 2006, Paulson et al. 2007, Yeniyurt 2003). However, a shift occurred in the late sixties and early seventies from accounting-based metrics to operational- or process-based metrics. Researchers were of the opinion to "forget the financial measures, [i]mprove operational measures like cycle time and defect rates, [and] the financial results will automatically follow" (Kaplan and Bruns 1987). Activity-based Management (ABM) systems, for example, focused on achieving customer value and company profit through the management of activities (Kaplan and Bruns 1987).[2] With painful or frustrating experiences due to cumbersome calculations and data-driven models, Kaplan and a new colleague devised the "Balanced Scorecard," a comprehensive model, merging operational measures with financial measures, giving both measures equal importance.[3]

In the 1980s and early 1990, issues such as democratization, good governance, accountability to society, transparency, green business, and sustainable development, etc. tied to a desire for a triple bottom line and fueled a debate for a socially responsible corporation. Corporate social performance (CSP) models integrated social and economic goals of organizations attracting worldwide attention (Post et al. 2002, Steckmest 1982, Waddock and Graves 1997). Wood (1991) elaborated upon the CSP concept to incorporate individual, organizational, and institutional levels of performance. Other scholars recast CSP as Corporate Social Responsiveness (Evans 2001, Frederick 2006, Gail and Nowak 2006) or focused on the firm's "social license to operate" (Gunningham et al. 2004, Sweeney 2006). The next decade of researchers explicitly connected corporate social actions with business strategy to align the multiple stakeholder-oriented actions with the company mission (Dyllick and Hockerts 2002, Griffin and Prakash 2014) and named it "corporate sustainable development" – business's attempts to meet the needs of organizational stakeholders without compromising the resources and interests of the local community, employees, and those same stakeholders (Dyllick and Hockerts 2002).

Griffin and Mahon (1997) and others criticized these individualized measures as too narrow when measuring a firm's social performance. Baumgartner and Ebner (2010) and López et al. (2007) argued that most studies considered CSP as a discreet element only. Researchers had ignored the multi-stakeholder nature of CSP and remained focused on a few social activities of business organizations such as: efforts for community welfare or community development (Chow and Chen 2012, Schreck 2011).

Several researchers (Baumgartner and Ebner 2010, Chow and Chen 2012, Erol et al. 2009, Schreck 2011) tried to assess corporate social performance through the lens of different stakeholders (Clarkson 1995, Donaldson and Preston 1995) in terms of their contribution to organizational wealth (Post et al. 2002). Scott (1992, p. 2) defined CSP as "social outcomes of firm behaviors" i.e. stakeholder satisfaction for organizational actions. Therefore, CSP, as a multidimensional construct, can be operationalized through a gap analysis to identify and analyze the expectations gap between stakeholder perceptions and the organization's actions (Griffin 2000, Mitnick 2000, Rowley and Berman 2000). To identify relevant metrics by using a gap analysis for various stakeholders, we look to stakeholder theory (Freeman 1984) as well as institutional theory (Buchholz and Rosenthal 1997, Covaleski et al. 1996, Scott 1983), and resource dependence theory (Lee et al. 2010, Pfeffer and Salancik 1978, Ulrich and Barney 1984) for guidance.

Stakeholder theory emphasizes "there are several different groups (stakeholders) within a society to whom an organization may have some sort of responsibility which it need to fulfill to survive and thrive and vice versa" (Bosse et al. 2009). Therefore, to ensure the alignment of managerial decision making, to meet the priorities and interests of different stakeholders – measurements of organizational success should be linked to specific stakeholders (Clarkson 1995).

In every business, stakeholders or stakeholder groups have a variety of resources and different expectations. Yet across nearly all businesses shareholders, employees, customers, and community are consistently four relevant stakeholders (Clarkson 1995, Cooper 2004, Wheeler and Sillanpaa 1997) and are the subject of this study. More specifically, shareholders include both institutional and individual owners; *employees* include permanent employees across three levels: top-, middle- and lower-level to include shop floor workers etc.; *customers* include both institutional and retail customers; and *local community* include representatives such as the beneficiaries and populations directly affected by the social initiatives of the companies.

Similar to stakeholder theory, institutional theory points out that organizations are affected by "common understandings of what is appropriate and, fundamentally, meaningful behavior" (Zucker 1983, p. 105). Business organizations are social institutions and cannot exist except in relation to the society within which they operate (Buchholz and Rosenthal 1997).

Resource dependence theory rests on fundamental assumption that every organization is comprised of internal and external coalitions which emerge from social exchanges formed to influence and control organizational behavior (Lee et al. 2010, Pfeffer and Salancik 1978, Ulrich and Barney 1984). The emphasis for managers is to secure a stable inflow of vital resources and reduce environmental uncertainty. To do so, organizations exercise power, control resources, and negotiate with other relevant constituencies (Carpenter and Feroz 2001, Michelli and Neely 2010, Modell 2001, Oliver 1991). Similarly, a performance framework is a tool, closely linked with the exercise of power, self-interest, and political advocacy in cut-throat competitive resource market (Michelli and Neely 2010, Pfeffer and Salancik 1978). Therefore, for survival and ensuring smooth access to critical resources, focal organization will always need to take into account and respond to these external demands (Pfeffer and Salancik 1978). These external demands in the form of stakeholders, expectations guides the business internal processes and end objectives (Carroll 2004, Huse and Rindova 2001, Kaplan and Norton 1992, Steurer et al. 2005).

## 2 Research methodology and scale development process

Since one main research objective of this paper is to develop and test a new standard instrument, which can be used for measuring the success of an organization, a sequential mixed method research design[4] (Creswell 2003) was used. The use of rigorous qualitative research facilitated the process of exploring the meaning and understanding of various constructs used for stakeholders' expectations. Use of a quantitative research approach provided scientific base to assess the magnitude and frequency of these constructs. Philosophical insights of qualitative research to identify stakeholders' expectations and scientific rigor of quantitative approach has helped to construct a standardized scale for measuring success of an organization, which can be used as a tool for strategic management.

To identify stakeholders' expectations, in the first phase, a qualitative research in the form of a comprehensive literature review was used. During this process more than 150 research publications showing corporate social performance in the form of expectations of shareholders, customers, employees, and local community were reviewed and identified. These identified expectations were converted into statements and semi-structured questionnaire form for each stakeholder separately.

To test the face[5] validity and content[6] validity a minimum of 20 experts (minimum 10 from industry[7] and 10 from academia)[8] on each stakeholder category were asked to rate the statements for their relevance and clarity using a 10-point (1 being least to 10 being highest) Likert scale. In addition to rating, experts were asked to validate and suggest changes in the form of addition/deletion/modification and group the items into factors.

On the basis of the experts' comments the instruments were refined and modified. Items having an average score less than 7.5 in relevance with standard deviation less than 1 and positively skewed were eliminated or merged with other items. A brief account of number items under each sub-construct after every stage is summarized in Table 2.1. The number of items was reduced by either merging the items or completely dropping them due to their low relevance. The shareholder expectations construct was greatly reduced since most of the corporate governance items had become mandatory guidelines as part of the corporate governance Clause 49A of the Listing Agreement to the Indian stock exchanges by SEBI.[9] In addition, experts suggested new items under a new factor, naming custodian of resources of the organization by not earning secret profits/insider trading, etc.

On the revised validated instruments, to collect data from stakeholders of listed manufacturing companies, a direct access to the stakeholders for filling these instruments without interference of the top management was discussed with concerned officials in the targeted sample companies. About 30 Indian manufacturing companies which qualify following six criteria in the top *Economic Times* 500 companies were contacted for this purpose.

1   Listed in national stock exchanges (BSE/NSE)
2   Minimum 20 year of existence
3   GRI/UN Global Compact/Sustainability Reporting/ CSR efforts reporting in annual reports
4   Involved in at least two CSR activities
5   Documented environmental policy
6   ISO or other quality and safety related standards

*Table 2.1* Analysis of Expert Opinions

| Stakeholder | No. of Indicators | | No. of Factors | |
|---|---|---|---|---|
| | Before Expert Rating | After Expert Rating | Before Expert Rating | After Expert Rating |
| Customers | 38 | 30 | 8 | 8 |
| Local Community | 41 | 27 | 8 | 8 |
| Employees | 40 | 33 | 8 | 7 |
| Shareholders | 50 | 24 | 6 | 7 |

Table 2.2 Sample Profile

| Name of the Company | Trident Ltd. | Godfrey Philips India Ltd. | Indian Oil Corporation Ltd. | JCT Ltd. | Maruti Suzuki India Ltd. | Nahar Spinning Mills Ltd. | Sona Koyo Steering Systems Ltd | Shreyans Industries Ltd. | Grand Total |
|---|---|---|---|---|---|---|---|---|---|
| **Nature of Ownership** | Private | Private | Public | Private | Public Foreign Joint Venture | Private | Private Foreign Joint Venture | Private | |
| **Nature of Business** | Paper & Terry Towels | Tobacco Manufacturer & Distributor | Oil Refinery & Distribution | Textile & Yarn | Cars | Textile | Steering and Car Spares | Paper | |
| **Sample Customers (N)** | 22 | 33 | 44 | 26 | 46 | 26 | 10 | 35 | 242 |
| Retail Customers | 50.0% | 45.5% | 47.7% | 30.8% | 89.1% | 46.2% | 0.0% | 51.4% | 52.1% |
| Institutional Customers | 50.0% | 54.5% | 52.3% | 69.2% | 10.9% | 53.8% | 100.0% | 48.6% | 47.9% |
| **Sample Employees (N)** | 33 | 31 | 38 | 43 | 25 | 18 | 53 | 61 | 302 |
| Top Level Management | 15.2% | 16.1% | 13.2% | 20.9% | 12.0% | 22.2% | 20.8% | 13.1% | 16.6% |
| Middle Level Employees | 15.2% | 41.9% | 18.4% | 44.2% | 40.0% | 38.9% | 35.8% | 27.9% | 32.1% |
| Lower Level & Workers | 69.7% | 41.9% | 68.4% | 34.9% | 48.0% | 38.9% | 43.4% | 59.0% | 51.3% |
| **Sample Shareholders (N)** | 33 | 30 | 35 | 32 | 31 | 34 | 31 | 30 | 256 |
| Retail | 78.8% | 80.0% | 85.7% | 71.9% | 80.6% | 85.3% | 80.6% | 66.7% | 78.9% |
| Institutional | 21.2% | 20.0% | 14.3% | 28.1% | 19.4% | 14.7% | 19.4% | 33.3% | 21.1% |
| **Sample Community (N)** | 21 | 30 | 46 | 32 | 36 | 30 | 33 | 30 | 258 |
| Company Supported NGOs/CSR Initiatives | 19.0% | 60.0% | 4.3% | 18.8% | 22.2% | 33.3% | 15.2% | 13.3% | 22.1% |
| Geographic Communities | 71.4% | 30.0% | 73.9% | 62.5% | 61.1% | 46.7% | 69.7% | 60.0% | 60.1% |
| Socio-Political Decision Making Structures | 9.5% | 10.0% | 21.7% | 18.8% | 16.7% | 20.0% | 15.2% | 26.7% | 17.8% |

After several rounds of discussions and presentations eight companies gave permission for further data collection from its stakeholders. These eight companies were a mix of public, private, foreign, joint venture, profit- and loss-making corporations representing manufacturing companies in India (see Table 2.2). The refined instrument with seven points Likert scales[10] was administrated on the stakeholders of the eight companies.

To test reliability of the instruments, these were pilot tested on all four stakeholder categories at Shreyans Industries Ltd, plant at Mandi Ahemadhgarh, Punjab, India with 61 employees, 35 customers, 30 shareholders, and 30 community members participating (see Table 2.2). To determine the initial plausibility of the factor structure[11] on the collected response, exploratory factor analysis (EFA) with Principal Components Analysis (PCA) by *Varimax with Kaiser Normalization* was carried out. Interpretation of the every factor was done through the variance accounted for by each individual factor. Further, to confirm the factor structure and internal consistency a parallel reliability analysis was conducted by estimating a reliability coefficient Cronbach's alpha (Cronbach 1951). In most of the factors the variance explained and Cronbach alpha values were higher than admissible limit. That is the total variance explained was equal to or greater than 60% and the value of Cronbach's alpha was above 0.60. In few cases where variance explained or Cronbach's alpha was less than permissible limits, factor were not ignored as sample size, i.e. number of respondents, were very less during pilot testing phase.

After the successful pilot test, the sample of stakeholders was selected by using quota sampling from representatives of local community (258), customers (242), shareholder (256), and employees (302) from the remaining seven companies. The final data was collected on a total sample of 1058 stakeholders (see Table 2.2). Since data sources for all four constructs were different, therefore, for further constructs scale refinement and validation four first order initial measurement models were constructed. Each construct was tested for uni-dimensionality[12] by using the Maximum Likelihood (ML) estimation method in Confirmatory Factor Analysis (CFA) approach[13] was adopted (Bentler 1995, Sureshchandar et al. 2002). The initial models of fitness were assessed and subjected to re-specification.

In the next stage, second order confirmatory factor analysis was performed based on the re-specified model and results were tested for satisfying criterion of uni-dimensionality, reliability, and validity (Byrne 1994). Re-specified nested models were reported by producing over-identified models (see Figures 2.2, 2.3, 2.4 and 2.5). To produce over-identified models regression path in each measurement component was fixed at 1. The criteria used to evaluate the items were: each item's error variance estimate; evidence of items needing to cross-load on more than one component factor as indicated by large modification indices; the extent to which items give rise to significant residual covariance; parsimony purpose; regression coefficient of each item; reliability of the item; and the reliability of the whole construct. In addition, the logic and consistency of data with the theoretical framework was considered when evaluating each item.

## 3  Results and discussion

### Scales for local community expectations

Scales for local community expectations (Figure 2.2) confirmed the CSR in action (Taneja, Taneja and Gupta 2011) and firm-level social actions (Mattingly and Berman

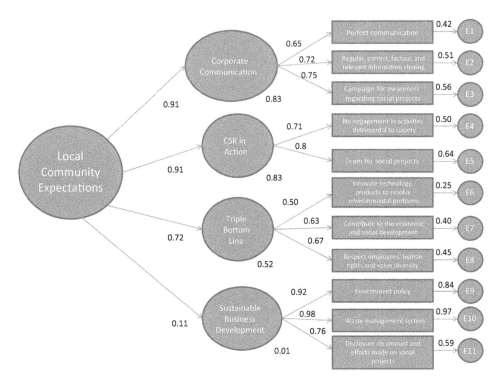

*Figure 2.2* Scales for Community Expectations

2006) frameworks asked to perform with social responsiveness (Carroll 1979), i.e. company should not engage activities which are detrimental to society and should have a dedicated team to for social projects (Hamann 2003, Porter and Kramer 2006, Rangan et al. 2012). Balmer and Gray (2000) pointed that companies' communications on social and ethical commitments seen as a component of the firm's corporate identity which ultimately enhance corporate performance (Berrone et al. 2007). Therefore, the local community of a company expects effective, factual, relevant, and regular communication of companies, action especially corporate social projects run for them (Berrone et al. 2007, Bruning 2002, Varey and White 2000). In the era of sustainable business development, local community also expects integration of triple bottom line (TBL) considerations in all business practices (i.e. policy, system, procedures, and reporting) (Jamali 2006). Local community expects companies to contribute to the economic and social development by innovating technology, products, and services to resolve environmental problems, respect employees' human rights (WBCSD 2001), and value diversity (Knoepfel 2001).

### Scales for employees' expectations

Employees of companies expect fulfillment of their social needs with a transparent recruitment selection system, clear job descriptions, and a healthy participative workplace environment supported by organizational systems for their development (see Figure 2.3). Fulfillment of expectations of the employees will lead higher job satisfaction;

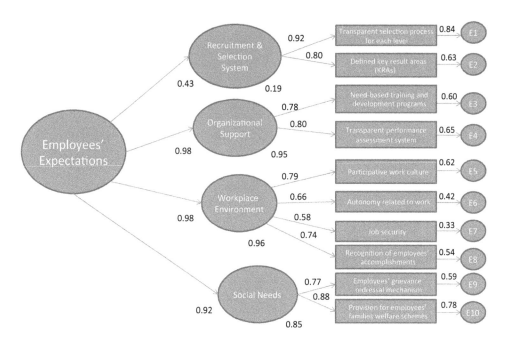

*Figure 2.3* Scales for Employees' Expectations

lower employees' turnover ratio, which has been directly linked to rising employee recruitment and training costs, low levels of employee morale, and customers' perceptions of service quality and lower profitability (Dermody et al. 2004). Allen et al. (2003) concluded that employees' perceptions of supportive HR practices such as participation in the decision-making process, growth and development opportunities, and fairness of rewards and recognition consistently positively related to increasing employees' productivity and efficiency.

### Scales for customer expectations

Meijer and Schuyt (2005) postulated for customer CSP acts as a double-edged sword. On one side, it motivates customers to buy a product but on the other hand, companies which don't perform a minimum acceptable level of CSP can face a boycott for the product from the customers. The developed scales in the customer expectations model found that in CSP, customers expect best CRM practices; quality products as specified by them, at fair price; and factual and informative promotional activities (see Figure 2.4). Fornel et al. (1996) reported similar findings and concluded that in the modem economy[14] customers expect customization and consistent reliability, as well as quality-driven products, rather than those driven by value or price. Therefore, to gain customer satisfaction which will only not enhance CFP (Kelsey and Bond 2001) but also CSP (Meijer and Schuyt 2005), efforts for price satisfaction (Matzler et al. 2007) are not sufficient; customize and quality product, customer relationship management, and socially responsible promotion practices are highly important (Matzler and Sauerwein 2002).

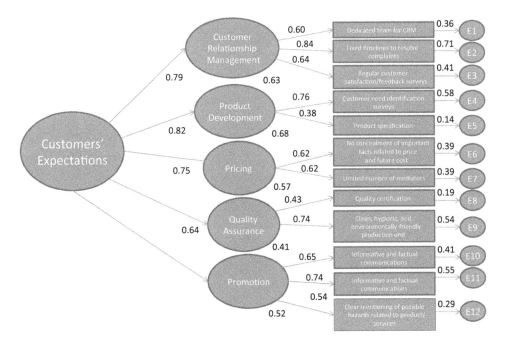

*Figure 2.4* Scales for Customers' Expectations

### Scales for shareholders expectations

Eccles et al. (2012) in a study on the impact of a corporate culture of sustainability on corporate behavior and performance concluded that companies that have voluntarily embraced a sustainable business culture over many years have significantly outperformed their counterparts over the long-term not only in terms of stock market but also accounting performance. The scale for shareholder expectations has also confirmed the same. Kaplan & Norton (1992) postulated that market value of a company is a function of the market's (existing and prospective shareholders) perception of a business's ability to generate returns today and in the future. In other words, shareholder value is the summation of firm's current financial performance and expectations for shareholders for future performance. Scales developed in the study emphasized that in future performance, shareholders expect that company should earn high return on assets for them by adopting ethical, socially responsible, and sustainable development practices. The company management should behave like a custodian of not just their resources but also of other stakeholders[15] as management creates value with its many stakeholders. Further, they should work for fulfilling their expectations but also of all other stakeholders for their sustainable development and growth in future (see Figure 2.5). Scales developed by the study are in line with characteristics[16] of future high-performance organizations listed in a global study on how to build a high-performance organization by the American Management Association (2007).

Figure 2.6 highlights the comprehensive performance measurement framework to assess the overall performance of firms.[17] Empirical studies on performance measurement had used simple linear aggregations, weighted or non-weighted approaches such

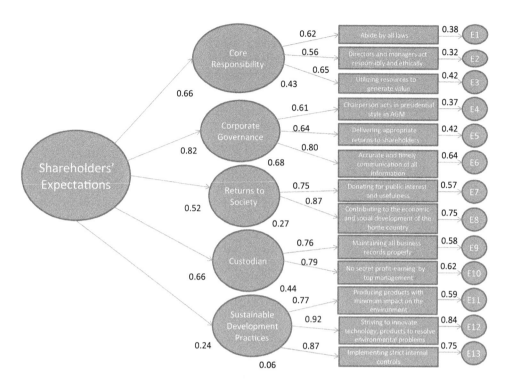

*Figure 2.5* Scales for Shareholders' Expectations

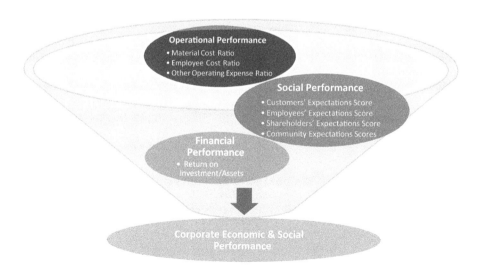

*Figure 2.6* Framework for Measuring Corporate Economic and Social Performance

as sustainability performance ranking, sustainability surveys, sustainability metrics, sustainability indexes, benchmarking, and accreditation processes (Chen and Delmas 2011, Freeman 2003, Kuosmanen and Kortelainen 2007, Székely and Knirsch 2005). The suggested performance measurement is comprehensive and balanced, as it values both negative and positive indicators to represent strengths and concerns regarding business practices for its sustainability.

### Scale validity assessment and testing of model

In absolute fit measures, the value of the chi-square divided by the degrees of freedom value (CMIN/DF) for each of the four models is less than the ideal value of 2.0 (Bollen 1989), indicates all models are well specified. Further, values of Root Mean Square Error of Approximation (RMRSEA), which accounts for the error of approximation in the population and tests the fit of unknown optimally chosen parameter values with the population covariance matrix (Brown and Cudeck 1993), ranged from 0.04 to 0.06 indicated models are either good or fair fit (see Table 2.3).

*Table 2.3* Models Fit Indices

| | Community Expectations Model | Employees' Expectations Model | Shareholders' Expectations Model | Customers' Expectations Model |
|---|---|---|---|---|
| Minimum Chi-square ($\chi^2$) Value (Minimum Discrepancy) (CMIN) | 57.935 | 57.281 | 89.618 | 81.114 |
| Degree of Freedom (DF) | 39 | 30 | 60 | 49 |
| Chi-square Value / Degree of Freedom (CMIN/DF) | 1.486 | 1.909 | 1.494 | 1.655 |
| Root Mean Square Error of Approximation (RMSEA) | 0.046 | 0.062 | 0.047 | 0.056 |
| **Absolute Fit Indices** | | | | |
| Root Mean Square Residual (RMR) | 0.092 | 0.049 | 0.147 | 0.053 |
| Goodness of Fit Index (GFI) | 0.958 | 0.954 | 0.947 | 0.936 |
| **Comparative Fit Indices** | | | | |
| Normed Fit Index (NFI) | 0.952 | 0.954 | 0.916 | 0.86 |
| Relative Fit Index (RFI) | 0.933 | 0.931 | 0.89 | 0.812 |
| Comparative Fit Index (CFI) | 0.984 | 0.977 | 0.97 | 0.938 |

Similarly, the incremental fit measures such as Goodness of Fit Index (GFI), Relative Fit Index (RFI), Normed Fit Index (NFI), and Comparative Fit Index (CFI), which are based on the comparison of the hypothesized model against some standard to highlight the complete co-variation in the data indicated strong evidence of uni-dimensionality the developed scales. The values of GFI, RFI, NFI, and CFI above 0.90 in all models imply that the models are good fit.

## 4 Conclusion

In many ways this research was inspired by a concern for all stakeholders. We were concerned that many stakeholders' expectations might have been lost or under represented due to an overriding concern for the shareholder. With the shareholder being paramount and regarded as the most important stakeholder in the management literature throughout the twentieth century we wanted to test for a stakeholder approach to businesses in the Indian context. A multi-dimensional approach to performance measurement is consistent with going beyond the traditional finance-only focus on shareholders, as a multi-stakeholder approach suggests the economic and social purpose of any organization is to distribute its wealth and increase the value of all of its stakeholders (Clarkson 1995). As a multi-stakeholder approach is evolving, managers are being held accountable for making their shareholders happy as well as being responsible for the sustainability of their business and business practices. With heightened expectations upon managers to keep stakeholders satisfied, this study is an initial attempt to understand what is meant by meeting stakeholders' expectations.

The instrument developed highlights four key stakeholder groups that are common to many businesses. The results of this study contribute to stakeholder theory by providing managerial insights into the multiple dimensions of what constitutes success from the viewpoint of four stakeholder groups. Findings from this research include: it is important for managers to identify, and respond to, the needs of key stakeholders, as different stakeholders have different expectations. This study identifies factors affecting corporate performance of an organization from the perspective of four key stakeholders. Business organizations, embedded within society, survive through strong, reciprocal stakeholder relations wherein they draw resources from society while creating value and returning value back to society in return. Knowing what is expected, and when expectations are not met, is an important aspect of the social contract between a business and their stakeholders that fuels the business cycle. This study provides Indian manufacturing companies with standardized scales to measure performance by identifying and testing key indicators of performance through a stakeholder approach. This study can help organizations design future strategies for business development by integrating social and economic goals for corporate performance.

This study contributes to a stakeholder approach to corporate performance, and suggests viable avenues for future research, in two different ways. First, this study identifies measurement factors from four key stakeholders using literature reviews and validated by expert opinion and extensive interviews. Due to the constraints of resources and time, the scope of the present research was confined to primary stakeholders: shareholders, employees, customers, and the local community. Future research can validate this study and extend its reach to additional relevant stakeholder groups.

Second, this research created four standardized instruments for measuring corporate performance based upon multiple manufacturing firms in India. Academics and practitioners can use these instruments to validate and test a multi-stakeholder approach to measuring organizational success that extends beyond the manufacturing sector within India. Comparing employee needs/expectations of the service sector to the employees of the manufacturing sector may create important insights into the differing skills, capabilities, retention, education, health and welfare needs of employees in tight (or easily substitutable) labor markets with specialized skills, for example. Alternatively, comparing the stakeholders' needs/expectations in the Indian context to other cultural contexts, including emerging or developed markets, is likely to uncover important socio-cultural expectations that are unique to India and others that are comparable across contexts. Scholars can also map these expectations with financial performance to develop a more comprehensive measure for examining a firm's likelihood of success.

## Notes

* Corresponding authors
1 Business organizations in India lag behind their Western counterparts on CSR practices (KPMG 2005). The main obstacles to CSR in India include ad hoc approaches by top management, lack of consensus on priorities within the firm, and problems related to measurement and evaluation of CSR activities (Krishna 1992), as well as external hindrances: unclear government policies, bureaucracy, poor monitoring, complicated tax systems, and poor infrastructure (CSM 2001). However, Indian businessmen have a well-established philanthropic orientation (Mishra and Suar 2010) with a religious-based foundation promoting giving, sharing, caring, donating goods/services, and sacrificing one's personal earnings for eternal gain of salvation (Kansal and Singh 2012). Most Indian companies focus their CSR activities on community development (PiC 2004). The advent of liberalization, globalization and entry of MNCs in Indian markets in 1991, and changed consumer and civil society expectations are pressuring business organizations to rethink and strategize its CSR activities. Chapple and Moon (2005) found that 72% of top 50 companies report CSR efforts on their website. In the most recent development, Indian Parliament has passed an historic The Companies Act of 2013 making it mandatory for companies to contribute 2% of profits for corporate social responsibility (CSR) activities.
2 Activity-based management (ABM) system draws on activity-based costing (ABC) as a major source of information. ABC is a methodology that measures the cost and performance of activities, resources, and cost objects. Resources are assigned to activities, then activities are assigned to cost objects based on their use. ABC recognizes the causal relationships of cost drivers to activities (Player and Keys 1999).
3 A balanced scorecard includes financial measures – the results of actions already taken. It further complements the financial measures with operational measures on customer satisfaction, internal processes, and the organization's innovation and improvement activities – operational measures that are drivers of future financial performance (Kaplan and Norton 1992).
4 A sequential mixed method research design is basically a multi-phase research using both qualitative and quantitative research methods. In this type of design objectives of research and findings of one phase guides the use of qualitative or quantitative approach in next phase.
5 In face validity one looks at the measure and sees whether "on its face" it seems a good reflection of the construct. Though face validity is probably the weakest way of demonstrating the construct validity, it does not in any way mean it is wrong, as the researcher on most occasions relies on subjective judgment throughout the research process.
6 Content validity is the degree to which the instrument provides an adequate representation of the conceptual domain that it is designed to cover. In content validity, the evidence

is subjective and logical rather than statistical (Kaplan and Sacuzzo 1993). The content validity of the instrument is generally ensured through a thorough review by experts (both academia and practitioners) in the field.

7  Criteria for selection of an experts from the industry was an executive who had carrying more than 15 years of experience in their relevant field.

8  Criteria for selection of expert from the academic was a full time associate or full professor working in a B- school (Kreber 2003).

9  The Securities and Exchange Board of India (SEBI) is the regulator for the securities market in India. More details http://www.sebi.gov.in.

10  Seven levels of agreement: 1 – Strongly disagree, 2 – Disagree, 3 – Somewhat disagree, 4 – Neither agree or disagree, 5 – Somewhat agree, 6 – Agree, 7 – Strongly agree on organizational social performance.

11  Testing the relationships between the observed and latent (factors) variables.

12  Uni-dimensionality refers to the existence of a single construct/trait underlying a set of measures. The usefulness of items within a measure depends on the extent to which they share a common core (Nunnally 1988). The concept of uni-dimensionality enables to represent the value of a scale by a solitary number (Venkatraman 1989). A comparative fit index (CFI) of 0.90 or above for the model implies that there is a strong evidence of uni-dimensionality (Byrne 1994).

13  A measurement model of structural equation modeling.

14  Which is based on production and consumption of increasingly differentiated goods and services.

15  "those groups without whose support the organization would cease to exist" (Freeman 1984, p. 23).

16  Proactive, Analytical, and Values-Driven; Clear, Consistent, and Customer-Focused; Well Led and Resilient; Involved with the Community; High Tech and High Touch; Transparent, Healthy, and Professionally Managed.

17  i.e. Corporate Economic Performance (CEP) and Corporate Social Performance (CSP).

## Bibliography

Ahire, S.L., Golhar, D.Y. and Waller, M.A. (1996), 'Development and Validation of TQM Implementation Constructs', *Decision Sciences*, vol. 27, pp. 23–56.

Ahire, S.L., Landeros, R. and Golhar, D.Y. (1995), 'Total Quality Management: A Literature Review and an Agenda for Future Research', *Journal of Production and Operations Management*, vol. 4, pp. 277–306.

Ali, M.A. and Malik, A. (2012), 'Corporate Social Responsibility: An Indian Perspective', *Paripex – Indian Journal of Research*, vol. 1, no. 9, pp. 26–28.

Allen, D.G., Shore, L.M. and Griffith, R.W. (2003), 'The Role of Perceived Organizational Support and Supportive Human Resource Practices in Turnover', *Journal of Management*, vol. 29, no. 1, pp. 99–118.

American Management Association (2007), How to Build a High-Performance Organization. *A Global Study of Current Trends and Future Possibilities 2007–2017*, Retrieved January, 1, 2010.

Anand, M., Sahay, B.S. and Saha, S. (2005), 'Balanced Scorecard in Indian Companies', *Vikalpa*, vol. 30, no. 2, pp. 11–25.

Anantharaman, S. (2007), 'Is Customer Delight a Viable Goal?', *The Hindu Business Line*, March 23, 2007. Available from http://www.thehindubusinessline.com (accessed October 19, 2013).

Anderson, J.C. and Gerbing, D.W. (1991), 'Predicting the Performance of Measures in a Confirmatory Factor Analysis with a Pretest Assessment of their Substantive Validities', *Journal of Applied Psychology*, vol. 76, no. 5, pp. 732–40.

Anderson, T.D. (1992), 'Another Model of Service Quality: A Model of Causes and Effects of Service Quality Tested on a Case Within the Restaurant Industry'. In Kunst, P. and Lemmink, J. (eds.). *Quality Management in Service*. van Gorcum, Amsterdam, pp. 41–58.

Avkiran, N.K., and Morita, H. (2010). 'Benchmarking firm performance from a multiple-stakeholder perspective with an application to Chinese banking', *Omega*, vol. 38, no. 6, pp. 501–508.

Balmer J.M.T. and E.R. Gray (2000) 'Corporate Identity and Corporate Communications: Creating a Competitive Advantage', *Industrial and Commercial Training*, vol. 32, no. 7, pp. 256.

Baron, D.P. (2000) *Business and its Environment*, 3rd Edition, Upper Saddle River, NJ: Prentice Hall.

Baumgartner, R.J. and Ebner, D. (2010), 'Corporate Sustainability Strategies: Sustainability Profiles and Maturity Levels', *Sustainable Development*, vol. 18, pp. 76–89.

Bentler, P.M. (1995), *EQS for Windows – User's Guide*, Multivariate Software, Encino, CA.

Berrone, P., Surroca, J., and Tribó, J.A. (2007), 'Corporate Ethical Identity as a Determinant of Firm Performance: A Test of the Mediating Role of Stakeholder Satisfaction', *Journal of Business Ethics*, vol. 76, no. 1, pp. 35–53.

Bollen, K.A. (1989), *Structural Equations with Latent Variables*, John Wiley, New York.

Boonstra, A. (2006), 'Interpreting an ERP-Implementation Project from a Stakeholder Perspective', *International Journal of Project Management*, vol. 24, pp. 38–52.

Bosse, D., Phillips, R.A. and Harrison, J.S. (2009), 'Stakeholders, Reciprocity, and Firm Performance', *Strategic Management Journal*, vol. 30, no. 4, pp. 447–56.

Brown, M.W. and Cudeck, R. (1993), 'Alternative ways of assessing model fit', in Bollen, K.A., Long, J.S. (eds.), *Testing Structural Equation Models*, Sage, Newbury Park, CA, pp. 136–62.

Brundtland, G.H., (1987), 'Our common future: Report of the 1987 World Commission on Environment and Development' United Nations, Oslo, pp. 1–59.

Bruning, S.D. (2002). 'Relationship building as a retention strategy: Linking relationship attitudes and satisfaction evaluations to behavioral outcome', *Public Relations Review*, vol. 28, no. 1, pp. 39–48.

Buchholz, R.A. and Rosenthal, S.B. (1997), 'Business and Society: What's in a Name', *The International Journal of Organizational Analysis*, vol. 5, pp. 180–201.

Buono, A.F. and Nichols, L. (1985), *Corporate Policy, Values, and Social Responsibility*, Praeger Scientific, New York.

Byrne, B.M. (1994), *Structural Equation Modelling with EQS and EQS/Windows – Basic Concepts, Applications and Programming*, Sage Publications, Thousand Oaks, CA.

Carpenter, V.L. and Feroz E.H. (2001), 'Institutional theory and accounting rule choice: An analysis of four US State governments' decisions to adopt generally accepted accounting principles', *Accounting, Organizations and Society*, vol. 26, pp. 565–596.

Carroll, A.B. (1979), 'A three-dimensional conceptual model of corporate performance', Academy of management review, vol. 4, no. 4, pp. 497–505

Carroll, A.B. (1999), 'Corporate Social Responsibility: Evolution of a Definitional Construct', *Business and Society*, vol. 38, no. 3, pp. 268–95.

Carroll, A.B. (2004), 'Managing Ethically with Global Stakeholders: A Present and Future Challenge', *The Academy of Management Executive*, vol. 18, no. 2, pp.114–120.

Chapple, W. and Moon, J. (2005), 'Corporate Social Responsibility (CSR) in Asia: A Seven-Country Study of CSR Web Site Reporting', *Business and Society*, vol. 44, no. 4, pp. 415–441.

Charnes, A., Cooper, W. and Rhodes, E. (1978), 'Measuring the Efficiency of Decision-making Units', *European Journal of Operational Research*, vol. 2, pp. 429–444.

Chen, C.M. and Delmas, M. (2011), 'Measuring Corporate Social Performance: An Efficiency Perspective', *Production and Operations Management*, vol. 20, no. 6, pp. 789–804.

Chow, C.W. and van der Stede, W.A. (2006), 'The Use and Usefulness of Non-financial Performance Measures', *Management Accounting Quarterly*, vol. 7 no. 3, pp. 1–8.

Chow, W.S. and Chen, Y. (2012), 'Corporate Sustainable Development: Testing a New Scale Based on the Mainland Chinese Context', *Journal of Business Ethics*, vol. 105, no. 4, pp. 519–533.

Clarkson, M.B. (1995), 'A Stakeholder Framework for Analyzing and Evaluating Corporate Social Performance', *Academy of Management Review*, vol. 20, pp. 39–48.

Clement, R.W. (2005), 'The Lessons from Stakeholder Theory for U.S. Business Leaders', *Business Horizons*, vol. 48, pp. 255–264.

Cooper, S. (2004), *Corporate Social Performance-A Stakeholder Approach*, Ashgate Publishing Company, London-Hants, UK.

Covaleski, M.A., Dirsmith, M.W. and Samuel, S. (1996), 'Managerial Accounting Research: The Contributions of Organisational and Sociological Theories', *Journal of Management Accounting Research*, vol. 8, pp. 1–35.

Creswell, J.W. (2003), *Research Design: Qualitative, Quantitative, and Mixed Methods Approaches*, Second Edition, Sage publications

Cronbach, L.J. (1951), 'Coefficient Alpha and the Internal Structure of Tests', *Psychometrika*, vol. 16, no. 3, pp.297–334.

CSM (Centre for Social Markets) (2001), 'Corporate Social Responsibility: Perceptions of Indian Business', CSM, Calcutta, India. Available from www.csmworld.org/public/pdf/social_respons.pdf (accessed January 18, 2009).

Dermody, M.B., Young, M. and Taylor, S.L. (2004), 'Identifying Job Motivation Factors of Restaurant Servers: Insight for the Development of Effective Recruitment and Retention Strategies', *International Journal of Hospitality and Tourism Administration*, vol. 5, no. 3, pp. 1–14.

Donaldson, T. and Preston, L.E. (1995), 'The Stakeholder Theory of the Corporation: Concepts, Evidence, and Implications', *Academy of Management Review*, vol. 20, no. 1, pp. 65–91.

Dyllick, T. and Hockerts, K. (2002), 'Beyond the Business Case for Corporate Sustainability', *Business Strategy and the Environment*, vol. 11, no. 2, pp. 130–141.

Eccles, R. G., Ioannou, I. and Serafeim, G. (2012). *The Impact of a Corporate Culture of Sustainability on Corporate Behavior and Performance* (No. w17950). National Bureau of Economic Research.

Erol, I., Caka, N., Erel, D. and Sari, R. (2009), 'Sustainability in the Turkish Retailing Industry', *Sustainable Development*, vol. 17, pp. 49–67.

Evans, K.G. (2001), 'Dewey and the Dialogical Process: Speaking, Listening, and Today's Media', *International Journal of Public Administration*, pp. 771–98.

Frederick, W.C. (2006), *Corporation, Be Good! The Story of Corporate Social Responsibility*, Dog Ear Publishing, Indianapolis, IN.

Freeman, A.M. (2003), The Measurement of Environmental and Resource Values: Theory and Methods. RFF Press, Washington, DC.

Freeman, R.E. (1984), *Strategic Management: A Stakeholder Approach*, Pitman, Boston.

Friedman, M. (1970), 'Social Responsibility of Business', *The New York Times Magazine*. September 13, pp. 32–33, 122–126.

Frooman, J. (1999), 'Stakeholder Influence Strategies', *Academy of Management Review*, vol. 24, no. 2, pp. 191–115.

Frooman, J. and Murrell, A.J. (2005), 'Stakeholder Influence Strategies: The Roles of Structural and Demographic Determinants', *Business & Society*, vol. 44, no. 1, pp. 3–31.

Gail, T. and Nowak, M. (2006). 'Corporate Social Responsibility: A Definition', Graduate School of Business, Curtin University of Technology, Working Paper No. 62.

Griffin, J.J. (2000), 'Corporate Social Performance: Research Directions for the 21st Century', *Business & Society*, vol. 39, no. 4, pp. 479–491.

Griffin, J.J. and Mahon, J.F. (1997), 'The Corporate Social Performance and Corporate Financial Performance Debate: Twenty-five Years of Incomparable Research', *Business & Society*, vol. 36, no. 1, pp. 5–31.

Griffin, J.J. and Prakash, A. (2014), 'Corporate Responsibility: Initiatives and Mechanisms', *Business & Society*, vol. 53, pp. 465–482.

Gunningham, N., Kagan, R.A. and Thornton, D. (2004), 'Social License and Environment Protection: Why Businesses Go Beyond Compliance', *Law & Social Inquiry*, vol. 29, no. 2, pp. 307–341.

Halkos, G. and Tzeremes, N. (2010), 'Performance Evaluation Using Bootstrapping DEA Techniques: Evidence from Industry Ratio Analysis', MPRA Paper 25072, University Library of Munich, Germany

Hamann, R. (2003), 'Mining Companies' Role in Sustainable Development: The 'Why' and 'How' of Corporate Social Responsibility from a Business Perspective', *Development Southern Africa*, Vol. 20, No. 2, pp. 237–254.

Handique, M. (2008), 'Companies Focus More on Social Responsibility Projects in Villages', livemint.com: *The Wall Street Journal*. Available from http://www.livemint.com/2008/03/11000146/Companies-focus-more-on-social.html (accessed February 29, 2012).

Huse, M. and Rindova, V.P. (2001), 'Stakeholders' Expectations of Board Roles: The Case of Subsidiary Boards', *Journal of Management and Governance*, vol. 5, no. 2, pp. 153–178.

Jamali, D. (2006), 'Insights into Triple Bottom Line Integration from a Learning Organization Perspective', *Business Process Management Journal*, vol. 12, no. 6, pp. 809–821.

Jensen, M.C. (2002), 'Value Maximization, Stakeholder Theory and the Corporate Objective Function', *Business Ethics Quarterly*, vol. 12 no. 2, pp. 235–256.

Kansal, M. and Singh, S. (2012), 'Measurement of Corporate Social Performance: An Indian Perspective', *Social Responsibility Journal*, vol. 8, no. 4, pp. 527–546.

Kaplan, R.M. and Saccuzzo, D.P. (1993), Psychological Testing: Principles. *Applications and Issues*, 3rd ed., Brooks Cole, Pacific Grove, CA.

Kaplan, R.S. and Bruns, W.J. (eds) (1987), *Accounting and Management: Field Study Perspectives*, Harvard Business School Press, Boston.

Kaplan, R.S. and Norton, D. (1992), 'The Balanced Scorecard – Measures that Drive Performance', *Harvard Business Review* (Jan–Feb), pp. 71–79.

Kelsey, K.D. and Bond, J.A. (2001), 'A Model for Measuring Customer Satisfaction Within an Academic Centre of Excellence', *Managing Service Quality*, vol. 11, no. 5, pp. 359–367.

Knoepfel, I. (2001), 'Dow Jones sustainability group index: a global benchmark for corporate sustainability', *Corporate Environmental Strategy*, vol. 8, no.1, pp. 6–15.

KPMG (2005), *KPMG International Survey of Corporate Responsibility Reporting 2005*, KPMG Global Sustainability Services, Amsterdam.

Kreber, C. (2003), 'The Scholarship of Teaching: A Comparison of Conceptions Held by Experts and Regular Academic Staff', *Higher Education*, vol. 46, no. 1, pp. 93–121.

Krishna, C.G. (1992), *Corporate Social Responsibility in India*, Mittal Publications, New Delhi.

Kuosmanen, T. and Kortelainen, M. (2007), 'Valuing Environmental Factors in Cost-Benefit Analysis Using Data Envelopment Analysis', *Ecological Economics*, vol. 62, no. 1, pp. 56–65.

Labuschagne, C., Brent, A.C. and van Erck, P.C.R. (2005), 'Assessing the Sustainability Performances of Industries', *Journal of Cleaner Production*, vol. 13, no. 4, pp. 373–385.

Le, V., and Harvie, C. (2010) 'Technical Efficiency of Manufacturing SMEs in a Transitional Economy: Evidence from Vietnam', *International Council for Small Business (ICSB)*. World Conference Proceedings.

Lee, J.W.C., Mohamad, O. and Ramayah, T. (2010), 'Outsourcing: Is the Social Exchange Theory Still Relevant in Developing Countries?', *Journal of Research in Interactive Marketing*, vol. 4, no. 4, pp. 316–345.

Lim, G., Ahn, H. and Lee, H. (2005), 'Formulating Strategies for Stakeholder Management: A Case-based Reasoning Approach', *Expert Systems with Applications*, vol. 28, pp. 831–840.

López, M.V., Garcia, A. and Rodriguez, L. (2007), 'Sustainable Development and Corporate Performance: A Study Based on the Dow Jones Sustainability Index', *Journal of Business Ethics*, vol. 75, pp. 285–300.

Lovell, C.A.K. (1994), 'Linear Programming Approaches to the Measurement and Analysis of Productive Efficiency', *TOP*, vol. 2, no. 2, pp. 175–224.

Mattingly, J.E., and Berman, S.L. (2006), 'Measurement of Corporate Social Action Discovering Taxonomy in the Kinder Lydenburg Domini Ratings Data', *Business and Society,* vol. 45 no. 1, pp. 20–46.

Matzler, K. and Sauerwein, E. (2002), 'The Factor Structure of Customer Satisfaction: An Empirical Test of the Importance Grid and the Penalty-reward-contrast Analysis', *International Journal of Service Industry Management,* vol. 13, no. 4, pp. 314–32.

Matzler, K., Renzl, B. Faullant, B. (2007) 'Dimensions of Price Satisfaction: A Replication and Extension', *International Journal of Bank Marketing,* vol. 25, no. 6, pp. 394–405.

Meijer, M.M. and Schuyt, T., (2005), 'Corporate Social Performance as a Bottom Line for Consumers', *Business & Society,* vol. 44, no. 4, pp. 442–461.

Michelli, P. and Neely, A.D. (2010), 'Performance Measurement in the Public Sector in England: Searching for the Golden Thread', *Public Administration Review,* vol. 70, no. 4, pp. 591–600.

Mishra, S. and Suar, D. (2010), 'Does Corporate Social Responsibility Influence Firm Performance of Indian Companies?', *Journal of Business Ethics,* vol. 95, no. 4, pp. 571–601.

Mitchell, R.K., Agle, B.R. and Wood, D.J. (1997), 'Toward a Theory of Stakeholder Identification and Salience: Defining the Principle of Who and What Really Counts', *Academy of Management Review,* vol. 22, no. 4, pp. 853–888.

Mitnick, B. (2000), 'Commitment, Revelation, and the Testaments of Belief: The Metrics of Measurement of Corporate Social Performance', *Business and Society,* vol. 39, no. 4, pp. 419–465.

Modell, S. (2001), 'Performance Measurement and Institutional Processes: A Study of Managerial Responses to Public Sector Reform', *Management Accounting Research,* Vol. 12, pp. 437–464.

Mostafa, M.M. (2007), 'Evaluating the competitive market efficiency of top listed companies in Egypt', *Journal of Economic Studies,* vol. 34, no. 5, pp. 430–452.

Nunnally, J.C. (1988), *Psychometric Theory,* McGraw-Hill Book Company, Englewood-Cliffs, NJ.

Oh, D.-H., and Lööf, H. (2009). '*Creating Innovations, Productivity and Growth: The Efficiency of Icelandic Firms'* (No. 162). Royal Institute of Technology, CESIS-Centre of Excellence for Science and Innovation Studies.

Oliver, C. (1991), 'Strategic responses to institutional processes', *Academy of Management Review,* vol. 16, pp. 145–179.

O'Rourke, A. (2003), 'A New Politics of Engagement: Shareholder Activism for Corporate Social Responsibility', *Business Strategy and the Environment,* vol. 12, pp. 227–39.

Paulson, K.A. and Hughes, S.B. (2007), 'Tracking Performance: When Less is More', *Management Accounting Quarterly,* vol. 9, no. 1, pp. 1–12.

Pfeffer, J. and Salancik, G.R. (1978), *The External Control of Organizations: A Resource Dependence Perspective,* Harper and Row, New York.

PiC (Partners in Change) (2004), *Third Report on Corporate Involvement in Social Development in India.* PiC, New Delhi.

Player, S., and Keys, D.E. (eds.). (1999), *Activity-Based Management: Arthur Andersen's Lessons from the ABM Battlefield* (Vol. 3). Wiley.

Porter, M.E., and Kramer, M.R. (2006), 'The Link between Competitive Advantage and Corporate Social Responsibility', *Harvard Business Review,* vol. 84, no. 12, pp. 78–92.

Post, J.E., Preston, L.E. and Sachs, S. (2002), *Redefining the Corporation: Stakeholder Management and Organizational Wealth,* Stanford University Press, Stanford, CA.

Rangan, K., Chase, L., and Karim, S. (2012). *Why Every Company Needs a CSR Strategy and How to Build It.* Harvard Business School, Cambridge, MA.

Rowley, T. and S. Berman (2000), 'New Brand of Corporate Social Performance', *Business and Society,* vol. 39, no. 4, pp. 397–412.

Schreck, P. (2011), 'Reviewing the Business Case for Corporate Social Responsibility: New Evidence and Analysis', *Journal of Business Ethics,* vol. 103, no. 2, pp. 167–188.

Scott, W.R. (1983), 'The Organization of Environments: Network, Cultural, and Historical Elements'. In Meyer, J.W. and Scott, W.R. (eds.). *Organizational Environments: Ritual and Rationality*, Sage, Beverly Hills, CA, pp. 155–175.

Scott, W.R. (1992). *Organizations, Rational, Natural and Open Systems* (3rd ed.). Englewood Cliffs, NJ: Prentice Hall.

Seiford, L.M. (1996), 'Data Envelopment Analysis: The Evolution of the State of the Art (1978–1995)', *Journal of Productivity Analysis*, vol. 7, pp. 99–138.

Seiford, L.M. and Thrall, R. (1990), 'Recent Developments in DEA: The Mathematical Programming Approach to Frontier Analysis', *Journal of Econometrics*, vol. 46, pp. 7–38.

Sergeant, J. (2005), Threats to Our Social License. Available from www.amro.com.au/index.cfm?p=1653 (accessed November 19, 2009).

Sethi, S. (1975), 'Dimensions of CSR', *California Management Review*, vol. 17, pp. 58–64.

Steckmest, F. (1982), *Corporate Performance: The Key to Public Trust*, McGraw-Hill, New York.

Steurer, R., Langer, M.E., Konrad, A. and Martinuzzi, A. (2005), 'Corporations, Stakeholders and Sustainable Development I: A Theoretical Exploration of Business–Society Relations', *Journal of Business Ethics*, vol. 61, no. 3, pp. 263–281.

Sureshchandar, G.S., Rajendran, C. and Anantharaman, R.N. (2002), 'Determinants of Customer-Perceived Service Quality: A Confirmatory Factor Analysis Approach', *Journal of Services Marketing*, vol. 16, pp. 9–34.

Susnienė, D. and Vanagas, P. (2005), 'Integration of Total Quality Management into Stakeholder Management Policy and Harmonization of their Interests', *Engineering Economics: Commerce of Engineering Decisions*, vol. 4, no. 44, pp. 71–77.

Sweeney, J. (2006), 'How to Measure Corporate Social Responsibility', *Eureka Street*, vol. 16 No. 6. Available from www.eurekastreet.com.au/article.aspx?aeid=875 (accessed December 15, 2011).

Szekely, F. and Knirsch, M. (2005), 'Responsible Leadership and Corporate Social Responsibility: Metrics for Sustainable Performance', *European Management Journal*, vol. 23, no. 6, pp. 628–647.

Taneja, S.S., Taneja, P.K. and Gupta, R.K. (2011), 'Research in Corporate Social Responsibility: A Review of Shifting Focus, Paradigms and Methodologies', *Journal of Business Ethics*, vol. 101, pp. 343–364.

Ulrich, D. and Barney, J. (1984), 'Perspectives in Organizations: Resource Dependence, Efficiency, and Population', *Academy of Management Review*, vol. 9 no. 3, pp. 471–481.

Varey, R.J., and White, J. (2000), 'The Corporate Communication System of Managing', *Corporate Communications: An International Journal*, vol. 5, no. 1, pp. 5–12.

Venkatraman, N. (1989), 'Strategic Orientation of Business Enterprises: The Construct, Dimensionality and Measurement', *Management Science*, vol. 35, no. 8, pp. 942–62.

Vos, J.F.J. and Achterkamp, M.C. (2006), 'Stakeholder Identification in Innovation Projects – Going Beyond Classification', *European Journal of Innovation Management*, vol. 9, no. 2, pp. 161–178.

Waal A. De (2003), "The future of Balanced Scorecard: An Interview with Professor Dr. Robert S. Kaplan", *Measuring Business Excellence*, vol. 7, no. 1, pp. 30–35

Waddock, S.A., and J.F. Mahon (1991), 'Corporate Social Performance Revisited: Dimensions of Efficacy, Effectiveness, and Efficiency', pp. 231–64 in J.E. Post (ed.), *Research in Corporate Social Performance and Policy*, vol. 12. Greenwich, CT: JAI.

Waddock, S.A. and Graves, S.B. (1994), 'Industry Performance and Investment in R&D and Capital Goods', *Journal of High Technology Management Research*, vol. 5, no. 1, pp. 1–17

Waddock, S.A. and Graves, S.B. (1997), 'The Corporate Social Performance Financial Performance Link', *Strategic Management Journal*, vol. 18, no. 4, pp. 303–319.

Wang, X. (2010), 'Data Envelopment Analysis: A Major Qualifying Project Report', Worcester Polytechnic Institutes.

Wang, C.L. and Ahmed, P.K. (2004), 'The Development and Validation of the Organisational Innovativeness Construct Using Confirmatory Factor Analysis', *European Journal of Innovation Management*, vol. 7, no. 4, pp. 303–313.

Wheeler, D. and Sillanpaa, M. (1997), *The Stakeholder Corporation*, Pitman Publishing, London, UK.

WBCSD (2001), *The Business Case for Sustainable Development: Making a Difference Toward the Johannesburg Summit 2002 and Beyond,* World Business Council for Sustainable Development, Geneva.

Wood, D.J. (1991), 'Corporate Social Performance Revisited', *Academy of Management Review*, vol. 16, pp. 691–718.

WBCSD (World Business Council for Sustainable Development) (2002), *The Business Case for Sustainable Development*, World Business Council for Sustainable Development, Geneva.

Zheng, J., Liu, X., and Bigsten, A. (1998). 'Ownership structure and determinants of technical efficiency: An application of data envelopment analysis to Chinese enterprises (1986–1990)', *Journal of Comparative Economics,* vol. 26, no. 3, 465–484.

Zhu, J. (2000), 'Multi-factor performance measure model with an application to Fortune 500 companies', *European Journal of Operational Research*, vol. 123, no. 1, pp. 105–124.

Zhu, J. (2004), *Quantitative Models for Performance Evaluation and Benchmarking: Data Envelopment with Spreadsheets and DEA Excel Solver.* Massachusetts: Kluwer.

Zucker, L.G. (1983), 'Organizations as Institutions' in *Research in the Sociology of Organizations, ed. S.B. Bacharach.* Greenwich, CT, JAI Press, Vol. 2 pp. 1–47.

Yeniyurt, S. (2003), 'A Literature Review and Integrative Performance Measurement Framework for Multinational Companies', *Marketing Intelligence & Planning*, vol. 21, no. 3, pp. 134–142.

# Chapter 3

# Behaviour in academe

## An investigation into the sustainability of mainstream scholarship in management studies

*Miriam Green*

## Introduction

It is important that one has confidence in the validity of all scholarship on episte-mological grounds, and also for its relevance to the understanding of the society or section of society for which the scholarship is relevant. The way scholarship is rep-resented has implications for the 'forming, framing and delimiting' of the concepts and discourse surrounding a topic and affects people's understanding of the issues (Chia 1996, p. 213). It also has the potential to influence policy makers in government and other institutions. In the case of management studies[1] it has the capacity to influence the discourse about what organisations are, what they represent, how they function and crucially who has the power to effect policy. Because scholarship in this area also has, as it should, the capacity to instruct not only university and college students, but also professional managers and consultants, it becomes vital that the knowledge imparted meets pedagogic as well as epistemological standards.

Pedagogy has been defined variously. Here Smith's (2012) ideas about pedagogy (and education) will be used as a framework:

> to educate is . . . to create and sustain informed, hopeful and respectful environ-ments where learning can flourish. It is concerned not just with knowing about things, but also with changing ourselves and the world we live in. As such educa-tion is a deeply practical activity . . . .
> (Smith 2012, http://infed.org/mobi/what-is-pedagogy/)

It seems crucial therefore for managers and consultants to understand the issues sur-rounding organisation and management practices, including knowledge of the struc-tures and processes in organisations, the influences on those by whatever factors are relevant, be they structural, environmental or the actions (including the non-actions) of human agents in organisations.

The content of this chapter is based on recent research into the representation of a text in the organisation, management and management accounting fields. The text is Burns and Stalker's (1961, 1966, 1994) *The Management of Innovation*. The book is about the management of change in organisations – a subject of huge relevance to pro-fessional managers and consultants. Mainstream representations of this book throw up important, widespread and lasting principles common to the dominant scholarship in these areas, and as will be shown, significant to matters of corporate behaviour and sustainable scholarship.

The structure of the chapter begins with definitions of theoretical frameworks and paradigms and an analysis of their different intentions regarding knowledge and their effects on the production of that knowledge. Burns and Stalker's text and its representations is used as an example. Decisions about meanings of texts have been regarded, particularly by post-structuralist writers such as Barthes and Derrida, to be problematic in that there are various 'interests' involved in such interpretations: the writer, the reader and the text itself. This analysis will follow Derrida's view that one should pay attention to the author's intentions, but ultimately the analysis should come from the text itself:

> Ultimately, it isn't my mark which will remain; as soon as it is launched onto the literary scene, it no longer comes from me. It doesn't relate to you; my trace slips away and falls into the world . . . At the risk of corruption, distortion and diversion, it is, nevertheless, my only chance of speaking to others.[2]

The analysis here therefore will look at the text in terms of the variables chosen, the arguments put forward, the weight of the topics discussed in terms of their length in relation to the book as a whole and finally the comments in the prefaces to the two later editions which comment on interpretations of the book.

A comparison is then made with interpretations of the book, mostly those appearing in mainstream scholarship but also including alternative views. The comparisons are largely about the presence or absence of topics concerned with organisational processes and the potential and actuality of human agents in organisations to support, distort or render dysfunctional policies and strategies implemented by managers in situations of change. Questions arise as to who has the power and prerogative to effect change in organisations. Is it solely senior managers, even only the chief executive, or do managers and more subordinate employees also have a part to play? The relevance of this to corporate behaviour and to the knowledge made available to students and by implication to professional managers and consultants is clear. It is argued here that broader, more holistic interpretations including analyses of influences by members of organisations at all levels on managerial policies and organisational processes are more sustainable in terms of the validity and legitimacy of the knowledge produced and of its practicality to practitioners in the field.

The second part of the chapter considers why mainstream scholarship has generally resisted this broader interpretation, continuing for over half a century to produce textbooks and research based on a narrower, structuralist approach, ignoring factors of human agency and organisational process. And this, despite serious and sustained critiques over the decades of the validity and practicality of this type of scholarship (see eg Merchant and Otley 2007, Otley 1980, 1995, Panozzo 1997).

Conventions and imperatives of the academy, including what is regarded as desirable material for publication by journal editors, supported by the all-important journal rankings and the influence of other disciplines, principally economics, are discussed. The desire for 'scientific' research has also been a strong argument for a focus on 'objective' scholarship such as studies of structure, and the rejection of more 'subjective' human factors constituting legitimate objects of inquiry (Bourdieu 1990, p. 27), despite contending views about subjectivities in science (see eg Kuhn 1970, Hanson 1972, Feyerabend 1993). Scholarship supporting managerialist agenda was encouraged by corporate sponsors of business schools, who were more interested in prescriptive problem-solving rather than on sociological understanding (Stern and Barley 1996). Broader political influences include having 'hard' management science, in the wake of the success of the USSR's Sputnik.

Questions then arise as to the future: will knowledge become more inclusive, encompassing more than the mainly structural factors present in mainstream scholarship and the knowledge produced? Although not all scholarship contains this narrower focus, can there be radical change in mainstream academic conventions given the influences and pressures for the continued legitimation of this type of knowledge. A strong imperative for its persistence, it is claimed here, is the power and influence, extending to education and academic institutions, of principles of neo-liberalism. If this argument is accepted, it has serious implications for the ability of the academy to be able to provide the knowledge and support required for more holistic scholarship which it is argued is important for 'good' corporate behaviour in organisations.

## Legitimacy of scholarship

There are different views as to what makes for legitimate scholarship. The most extreme approach or paradigm at one end of the sociological spectrum is positivism, which holds that all valid knowledge is neutral and value-free, and corresponds to an external reality that is not subject to human subjectivities and influence. According to this approach, to count as legitimate knowledge it must be able to be verified empirically, with research methods that are 'scientific', such as sampling, scaling and statistical analysis (Reiter and Williams 2002). In the social sciences this is often done through surveys such as questionnaires, where respondents are asked to plot their answers on a Likert-type scale with a range of preferred answers for each questions. These are then subjected to statistical analyses.

Along with these views and particularly relevant for management is the 'functionalist' approach or paradigm which advocates a study of formal structures and systems in organisations to the exclusion of informal groupings. This echoes the 'rationalist', non-subjective elements of positivism. It assumes that there is consensus within organisations and that they are ordered and regulatory. It is also managerialist in the sense that managers are viewed as having the power and prerogative to make decisions in their organisations and that other employees will follow their managers passively (Burrell and Morgan 1979). This type of scholarship, as indeed is the case with other approaches, has consequences for organisations and organisational governance, because it influences how people view organisations; what they see as the important and relevant issues to be researched and then to be acted upon; and who needs to be considered in terms of having the power and ability to make decisions and implement them. All this can affect the values, content and direction of governance in organisations, and determine what would be considered as 'being good' and therefore what would constitute 'doing well'.

The consequences following a particular approach might become clearer if one considers another paradigm in terms of where knowledge is thought to be located in the world, which issues should be studied, which are relevant and valid sources of information and which research methods would produce this view of legitimate knowledge. The interpretive paradigm is in some ways the opposite of the functionalist paradigm and its research methods are also very different from those advocated by positivism. According to Hatch and Yanow (2003), the interpretive paradigm advocates 'subjectivist' approaches. It claims that the social world is not like the natural world, and that knowledge of this world is acquired through understanding the human actors involved in this world (and within the confines of this chapter, in organisations). Therefore, rather than being concerned with 'objective' issues such as formal structure to the exclusion of the workings and influence of the informal groups that are often formed in organisations, subjectivist approaches require that human beings be studied. It is they who determine reality and therefore the knowledge about reality rather than knowledge being produced from a reality outside and independent of people (Bourdieu 1993). Therefore researchers need to know the understandings and interpretive frameworks that human actors are using for deriving meanings from their situations and, following on from that, for the actions they take.

In keeping with this approach, the research methods this approach advocates are also substantially different from those used by positivist researchers. Because in-depth knowledge is required about their respondents' interpretations, motivations and reasons for actions taken, surveys with questions predetermined by the researcher would be of little value. Instead what is advocated are in-depth investigations in order to acquire the necessary knowledge about the human actors being researched. Ideographic approaches such as participant observation or in-depth interviews are recommended (Hatch and Yanow 2003).

This affects what is considered important for researchers to investigate: rather than examining structures alone, researchers are likely to want to conduct research into organisational processes, including the influence on these processes of informal groups, often hidden from the eyes and knowledge of their managers (see eg Preston 1986). Researchers using an interpretive approach would probably want to find out the influence of organisational members on managerial strategies. They are unlikely to assume that decisions, including ones significant for their organisation's future, should be (and can be) made solely by senior managers.

The implications for organisational governance are significantly different from what they would be for researchers and practitioners following functionalist precepts. Here people are at the centre of the research, and organisational members at different levels and in different sections of their organisations would be likely to be the objects of research rather than only senior managers. The underlying assumption would be that because human actors and their perceptions are important in creating reality, this applies also to human interactions in organisations, whatever their level. Such an approach has very different implications for the ideology and values of preferred corporate behaviour. its view of organisations might be one where all the members, whatever their level of power and authority, might be contributing to what was happening in their organisation – its successes as well as its failures.

The analysis below will consider the paradigm in which most mainstream management scholarship is located, and what the messages would be for policies regarding corporate governance and sustainability – would enactments of these messages constitute 'doing well by being good'? However another issue has to be considered before looking in more detail at mainstream management scholarship. That is the question of epistemological and pedagogic standards which, one must assert, has to be the fundamental bedrock for any scholarship's claim to validity and legitimacy. This also should be the basis on which management practitioners accept or reject guidance from academics as to how organisations operate, what the problems might be and therefore how practitioners must frame their policies and strategies for implementation.

## Functionalist approaches in management scholarship

Epistemology, which can be defined briefly as what counts as knowledge or the relationship between the knower and what can be known, is closely linked with questions about ontology – the form and nature of reality, and therefore what can be known about it. Epistemology can be seen as the bridge between ontology on the one hand, and methodology on the other. Methodology constitutes the ways in which researchers can go about finding whatever they believe can be known (Guba and Lincoln 1998).

There are different approaches to and standards of what counts as knowledge. This question has been addressed in the natural and social sciences through examinations of the concept of paradigms and the knowledge constructed in different paradigms. Burrell and Morgan (1979) established a seminal framework for different sociological paradigms regarding the social sciences in general, but with an emphasis on approaches to organisations. They constructed four paradigms, which they defined in their introduction as follows:

> Each stands in its own right and generates its own distinctive analyses of life. With regard to the study of organisations, for example, each paradigm generates theories and perspectives which are in fundamental opposition to those generated in other paradigms.
>
> (Burrell and Morgan 1979, p. viii)

The theories and perspectives generated in mainstream scholarship have constituted what has been known as the 'functionalist' approach. This approach includes a wide range of perspectives, but the one used most frequently in mainstream management scholarship, and particularly in mainstream management accounting research is what Burrell and Morgan have called 'abstract empiricism' (Burrell and Morgan 1979, pp. 53–54). This is an 'objectivist' and determinist approach.[3] The organisation is treated as if it is in:

> the world of natural phenomena, characterised by a hard concrete reality which can be systematically investigated in a way which reveals its underlying regularities . . . . it is a world of cause and effect; the task of the management theorist is the identification of the fundamental laws which characterise its day to day operation . . . the individual is assigned an essentially passive . . . role . . . . [and where] objective factors in the work situation have a major influence upon behaviour.
>
> (Burrell and Morgan 1979, pp. 127–129)

This has had enormous implications for how organisations are viewed: what is considered to be the legitimate knowledge about organisations; what should be investigated and acted upon; and how the roles of members of organizations – i.e. employees- are to be understood.

The 'hard concrete reality' mentioned above has been interpreted by many mainstream scholars as the formal structures of organisations. Many management accounting scholars in particular used Burns and Stalker's (1961) conclusions from their research into 20 companies in England and Scotland. They found that whereas bureaucratic, hierarchical 'mechanistic' structures were appropriate in times of environmental stability, when the market and technology were rapidly changing organisations with decentralised, more flexible 'organic' structures fared better. These ideas were seized on, propagated and used as the basis for research by many management scholars over a period stretching for over 50 years into the twenty-first century.

Mainstream scholarship has thus focussed largely on organisation structures and systems. One example is Simons, a respected and influential management accounting scholar. Simons, as did many others, aimed to test Burns and Stalker's thesis through researching other companies. One of the researches he carried out was to test Burns and Stalker's ideas by carefully and painstakingly examining the stability/instability of the environment of a large number of organisations and then seeing whether the types of systems and structures present in their organisations corresponded to their environments in accordance with Burns and Stalker's research results. This has been a common interpretation in the mainstream literature of Burns and Stalker's ideas. Simons' research methodology was also commonly used in research applications of such work.

Simons' research methodology,[4] after his initial studies to select appropriate organisations for his study and questions for his research, was to send a questionnaire to senior managers of companies in both environments about their control systems. What is significant in terms of this chapter is firstly his object of inquiry. This was focussed solely on organisational systems of structures, excluding any issues surrounding or effects on the organisations studied of employee interventions in or resistance to managerial strategies regarding their organisations' structures. This supports Burrell and Morgan's analysis of one of the extreme approaches in functionalism being concerned with 'concrete' realities and not with issues involving the people in the organisations studied and their potential influence on this structural reality. Because only structure is considered, the assumption is that individuals lower down the organisations do not constitute an issue or problem that needs to be considered and would follow managerial strategies without question.

The fact that Simons, as was true of many other management scholars, such as Nouri and Parker (1998) and Chenhall and Langfield-Smith (1998), surveyed senior managers exclusively in their aim to test whether organisation systems and structures matched their environments, extends Burrell and Morgan's analysis that the functionalist approach regards individuals subordinate to senior management as essentially passive organisational members. This reliance for knowledge on senior managers does not take into account the organisational knowledge of employees subordinate to senior managers, negating the potential usefulness of their knowledge as well as their potential for action, which could either support managerial policies or work against them, rendering them dysfunctional. Much research has been done, often published in the same journals as the research described above, which has shown that senior management was often not in full possession of the facts about what was happening in their organisations lower down, and that formal structures did not always reflect what was really happening in organisations. Loft criticised the non-reckoning with humans as active agents in organisation processes:

> In Johnson and Kaplan's world view employees of the firm are 'merely' a factor of production with a cost to be minimised, they are not sentient beings but economic ciphers controlled by the wage contract.
>
> (Loft 1995, p. 41)

Not only that but an examination only of formal structures ignores informal group-ings, which by definition are the result of employee strategies and actions. In keeping with an essentially functionalist approach, concepts like formal structure and envi-ronment have been treated as ontological concrete realities and not subject to non-managerial influences such as informal structures or vulnerability to human agency (Willmott 1993). Preston, analysing the links between budgeting and organisational structure, pointed to the inadequacy of conventional emphases on formalised, hierar-chical structures. His topic of in-date budgeting information was difficult to get from formal information systems in high environmental uncertainty, and formal informa-tion was not able to encompass complex and unfamiliar environmental conditions adequately (Preston 1995). Based on earlier research (Preston 1986), he emphasised the fragility and fictional side to formal organisation communication systems and the different constructions that could be placed upon them by senior management in comparison with lower level managers (Preston 1995).

The ignoring of employees as latent active agents in organisational strategies and processes indicates another aspect of functional approaches: the promotion of the power and prerogative of managers. With attention paid to the assumptions behind such scholarship, the focus on managerial organisational knowledge and power; the absence and silence regarding the knowledge, attitudes and actions of other members in organisations; and the implications of these for power and control in organisations, and indeed for scholarship in these fields, all serve to bolster the idea that managers have the right and capability to effect change successfully. Possibilities of dysfunction or failure by management have not been incorporated in these analyses. Nor has their corollary – the potential of people in the organisation who are less powerful, but nev-ertheless might have sufficient influence through taking political action individually or in informal groups, to have the capacity seriously to upset or negate management policies.

## Burns and Stalker's approach

Burns and Stalker did not subscribe either to the idea that employees were passive or that they did not need to be taken into consideration with respect to managerial strategies and implementation of organisational policies. Although these authors had emphasised structure in suggesting a 'mechanistic'/'organic' dichotomy in stable and volatile environmental conditions, this constituted only one of the three variables they presented as significant for the success or otherwise of managerial change strategies. A large part of their book was concerned with organisational processes determined by human agency. After their linking organisational structure with the organisation's environment, they pointed to employee commitment as a crucial variable in deciding the direction and success of organisational change initiatives. Far from employees being seen as passive, Burns and Stalker spent a large part of their research time interviewing employees in different parts of the organisations they were studying at different levels in the hierarchy. Their findings included lengthy analyses of the substantial role employees paid in fostering or hindering the implementation of change strategies in their organisations. They discovered many failures in the change initiatives among the companies they studied, particularly in Scotland, attributable to various factors including human agency.

Employee commitment could be weakened or harnessed against managerial policies for many reasons: bureaucratic inertia as a preference to accepting a different, possibly more confusing structure; the effects of structural changes on employees' political and career interests; rivalry between people at different levels and between departments; and the privileges of the new scientific technocrats introduced to cope with the necessary new technological developments. These privileges could not only result in resentment by other employees, but could also constitute a threat to the authority of less technically knowledgeable managers (Burns and Stalker 1961). Burns and Stalker also had a keen respect for the power and influence of employees working in informal groupings on formal structures and managerial strategies. These and other authors regarded informal structures as not separate and dialectically distinct from formal structures, but as part of a single, holistic system, interleaved with and having effects on, these formal structures, as did formal structures on informal groupings (Willmott 1993).

And far from assuming that managerial strategies were infallible rather than being vulnerable to distortion, dysfunction or failure, Burns and Stalker's third variable was concerned with the capabilities of the chief executive having to deal with these organisations facing rapid technological and market change. Burns and Stalker dedicated three chapters to analysing the situations and difficulties confronting 'The Men at the Top'. These ranged from the perhaps obvious ones of the CEO (or MD, in those days) having enough knowledge about the changing environment, details about the issues, problems and processes in his[5] own organisation and how these would be impacted upon by a volatile market and technology. Burns and Stalker set out problems confronting the CEO regarding sufficient information about his organisation: the CEO was often isolated from members of the organisation further down, and thus did not know what they were thinking and feeling, nor about issues and problems being faced by them. The increased complexities of their expanding organisations in addition to new technologies and market demands demanded skills not always in the possession of chief executives. Lack of knowledge about what was happening in the organisation and sometimes lack of skill made a chief executive's task of dealing with the politics and rivalries of groups and individuals difficult, and just as more junior managers were being threatened by the technical knowledge of the newly recruited and privileged laboratory engineers, so too were chief executives, who had to handle people often acting largely outside the norms and rules of the organisation (Burns and Stalker 1961).

## Summary of principles of mainstream management scholarship

This comparison between Burns and Stalker's text and mainstream representations and research applications of this text is but an example of what has been prevalent in mainstream management scholarship – regarding interpretations of *The Management of Innovation* and also of other research in the areas of change. This has been true not only of research such as Simons' (1987) described above, but also what is taught and disseminated in educational institutions to students – some of whom will become managers in organisations. Examples of popular and widely used textbooks promoting such ideas including objectivist interpretations of Burns and Stalker's work are books by Daft (2001), Robbins (2003) and Mullins (2005).

To summarise: mainstream management scholarship when considering questions of organisational policy, strategy and change have regarded as ontologically 'real' and epistemologically valid issues to do with structures and systems of organisations. An underlying assumption is that the knowledge required for organisational change and policy-making in general rightly lies with management, which has the knowledge, capability and prerogative to plan and effect whatever changes are necessary for organisational success. Possibilities of managers' policies failing, or being subject to distortion or dysfunction are not considered. Actual failures, such as those not infrequently seen by Burns and Stalker in the companies they researched, are usually not mentioned. The difficulties faced by chief executives, such as those enumerated by Burns and Stalker in the companies they researched, have not been alluded to, let alone encompassed in mainstream research methodologies.

What else has been omitted or 'absented' from this discourse (Bhaskar 2008) are all aspects to do with human understandings and attitudes to such managerial initiatives. Thus the problems that Burns and Stalker found common to the organisations they studied regarding employee commitment or lack of it because of particular political and career interests; the rivalries between departments, particularly the newly recruited scientists and engineers, who also posed a threat to managers right up to their chief executive, were not mentioned in mainstream text books, nor generally made subjects for further research by later scholars.

The approaches that lie within this paradigm are deeply political, as indeed one can argue similarly about other, contrasting approaches. In this case the politics lies in the discourse, the assumptions and the practices about where power is concentrated, who has the prerogative to make decisions in organisations, and who has worthwhile knowledge relevant to researchers whose intentions are to further scholarship about organisations, in this instance, organisational change. As mentioned earlier, the assumptions are that managers have the power and prerogative to make such decisions, and there is no mention of the possibility (and from Burns and Stalker's and others' work[6] the actuality) of managerial failure. Absented is the potentiality (and the findings in Burns and Stalker's and others' research) for members of organisations lower down the hierarch to have the power and will to influence, distort and in severe cases render dysfunctional managerial strategies. The latent power of informal groupings working counter to managerial intentions and policies is not mentioned, again something emphasised by eminent organisation theorists such as Selznik (1948), cited in Burns and Stalker (1961).

## Alternative management scholarship

It must be noted that not all scholarship in the organisation, management and management accounting areas adhere to these principles. There has been alternative scholarship which has recognised the complexity of Burns and Stalker's analysis, its inclusion of political factors as explanations for organisational outcomes and the difficulties faced by some of the companies researched. One such early interpretation was the popular textbook by Pugh et al. who pointed out in 1964 that Burns and Stalker found that it was not at all easy to achieve organic systems, particularly if the organisation was being changed from a mechanistic one:

> The almost complete failure of the traditional Scottish firms to absorb electronics research and development engineers into their organizations leads Burns to doubt whether a mechanistic firm can consciously change to an organismic one.
>
> (Pugh et al. 1964, p.16)

This is a substantially different interpretation of Burns and Stalker's book. Although it remains within a discourse about structure, it highlights the fallibilities in structural change from a mechanistic to an organic system. That short paragraph also introduces the problem of human agency, in the shape of the new cadres of engineers. As elaborated above, these were difficulties acknowledged to be important by Burns and Stalker, and analysed by them at some length.

A reviewer in one of the most highly regarded US management journals, *The Administrative Science Quarterly*, recognised the sociological emphasis in *The Management of Innovation* and the importance of politics featured in it:

> Central to this is the analysis of the relationship between work-organization, political, and status structures of the concern. The dynamics of this relationship are the crucial relations emerging between the laboratory (development) and the workshop (production). How the necessary interpenetration between these two areas is avoided or stimulated is analyzed on several levels; as a threat to the existing code of conduct, as a disturbance of the existing status and political systems, and as an expression of contrasting occupational ideologies of scientists and managers.
>
> (Form 1963, pp. 271–272)

This constitutes a different representation of *The Management of Innovation*, in which status and political interests leading to potential rivalry and conflict are highlighted as a central issue. Form also acknowledged Burns and Stalker's inclusion of difficulties experienced by chief executives in trying to implement change strategies:

> The last section focuses on top management and the extent to which it can interpret the changing technical and commercial situations, adapt work organization to change, and elicit individual commitment to change. Obstacles and paths of action necessary for administration to induce innovation as a continuous process are suggested by the analysis.
>
> (Form 1963, pp. 271–272)

There are examples of alternative scholarship, more in keeping with Burns and Stalker's approach, in the same mainstream journals publishing objectivist, structure-focussed scholarship. One example used in Green (2013) is a paper published in *Accounting,*

*Organizations and Society*, the journal which contains much of the mainstream scholarship cited above. Chenhall and Euske (2007) carried out research into the adaptation in two military establishments of a change from a military, professional culture to one that was more managerially oriented. Chenhall and Euske's research was different from much mainstream management research in that it was broader in both content and method. This research was focussed on the processes involved in this cultural change. They found that different issues arose at different stages of the change process, which was influenced by the attitudes and reactions of organisational members at different levels in the organisations studied, and crucially at different stages of the change process. This provided a fairly detailed understanding of the interactions between management, members of the organisations and the processes involved in the change.

This type of knowledge was more easily acquired because of the research methods used. Rather than interviewing senior managers exclusively on structural features of their organisations, and then transposing this information into Likert-type questionnaires with pre-determined questions from pre-determined topics, Chenhall and Euske took their information from a variety of organisational members using a variety of research methods. Qualitative methods, included semi-structured interviews, giving important participants the opportunity to discuss the research findings, and observation at both formal and informal meetings. Other methods included archival research and a study of administrative processes (Chenhall and Euske 2007). (For a more detailed summary see Green 2013.)

Chenhall and Euske had wanted to do what they called 'richer' research, in which they looked at technical change in the social context in which it was taking place. They were interested in:

> integrating the technical approach to MCS [management control systems] with a behavioural approach that focuses on how individual users respond to MCS facilitated change.
>
> (Chenhall and Euske 2007, p. 608)

Despite the obvious advantages of this approach from the point of view of the knowledge acquired and its use for management scholarship, and from its practicalities about organisational processes and their interrelationship with organisational members' attitudes and actions, this type of research has remained a minority pursuit, dominated by the positivist, objectivist, functionalist approaches referred to earlier.

## Weaknesses in functionalist/objectivist scholarship

### Criticisms from within mainstream management scholarship

There were criticisms from within mainstream management scholarship about this type of objectivist scholarship, which was seen to be epistemologically invalid and also impractical. Some argued that it dealt in structural fantasy rather than the realities faced by organisations. Panozzo described this type of mainstream scholarship as being about highly idealised constructions rather than about what was happening on the ground. It was therefore irrelevant to organisational practice (Panozzo 1997).

Otley, a highly regarded management accounting scholar found fault with positivist management accounting research on many counts: the variables were ill thought out; there were other types of controls that needed to be taken into account along with management accounting information systems; managerial flair was another factor that needed examination; and research methodologies based on questionnaires were inadequate (Otley 1980). Such criticisms were repeated by Otley (1995) and by Merchant and Otley (2007).

What is interesting is that none of these critical interventions, despite the eminence of scholars like Otley, have made any impact on researchers, often publishing in the same journals in which the criticisms were made, particularly in *Accounting, Organizations and Society (AOS)*, one of the highest-ranking accounting journals which stood for broader, multi-disciplinary scholarship. Hopwood, the founder editor of *AOS*, claimed that the broader research traditions in his journal provided a good basis for accounting to go beyond abstract schemes for organisational change towards an exploration of actual organisational functioning (Hopwood, 2009). However much of management and management accounting research has continued to adhere to positivist, objectivist approaches. And if this type of scholarship is chosen as the basis for questions of 'good' corporate behaviour, the outcomes may be less than what is required to have sustainable corporate behaviour that does 'well by being good'.

### Scientific credentials of positivist scholarship

As mentioned, positivist, objectivist scholarship particularly in the social sciences, has claimed to be 'scientific' as a warrant for its legitimacy and for conforming with positivist principles. The most extreme version of positivism, logical positivism, regarded the nature of science to constitute knowledge acquired through a radical empiricism from only observable factors verifiable through sense data rather than through theory or the logic of deduction. The techniques had to be quantitative: sampling, scaling and statistical analysis. It had the advantage also over more subjectivist methods of being neutral and value-free (Turner 2001). Similarly, according to Neurath, a leading logical positivist, for sociology, and presumably other social sciences, to be accepted as sciences, they had to engage in the scientific methods of inquiry mentioned above in order to find regularities between observables eventually to connect all logically compatible laws into a unified science (Halfpenny 2001).

However this is only one, and an increasingly controversial, view of what is science. Positivism and particularly logical positivism have been contested from as early as the mid-twentieth century (Halfpenny 2001). A few decades later this view of science and scientific method was challenged by eminent historians and philosophers of science, and also by social theorists. Kuhn (1970), Hanson (1972), Feyerabend (1993) and Bourdieu (1990) have all expressed different, broader views about what constitutes science and its practices, challenging the above definitions and characterisations. No longer was it necessary to regard valid knowledge as being confined to observable factors. Kuhn, for example, in his book on scientific revolutions defined science as 'any field in which progress is marked' (Kuhn 1970, p. 162). Science definitely did include theory. A new paradigm, for example, produced new theoretical generalisations, new methods and applications. Theories already existed and if only the same ones were followed, this would impose a limitation on scientific progress – problems would be circumscribed in keeping with existing assumptions, as would acceptable solutions, thereby inhibiting scientific development (Kuhn 1970).

The use exclusively of quantitative methods was also invalidated by Kuhn. He saw no problem in carrying out qualitative as well as quantitative research. Kuhn mentioned Joule's experiments as an example of how the two were interdependent. Quantitative laws often emerged through paradigm articulation, which Kuhn regarded as qualitative. He asserted that

> ... so general and so close is the relation between qualitative paradigm and quantitative law that, since Galileo, such laws have often been correctly guessed with the aid of a paradigm years before apparatus could be designed for their experimental determination.
>
> (Kuhn 1970, p. 29)

Neither was science regarded as value-free – on two counts. First, human consciousness and community norms were important in decisions about deciding on what was regarded as valid scientific activity. Scientific practices, acceptable paradigms, what were considered to be valid scientific problems and solutions were all subject to consensus within particular scientific communities (Kuhn 1970). And finally science did not constitute a unified scientific method. Both Kuhn and Feyerabend argued that science was *not* about steadily increasing the sum total of knowledge[7] through 'experiment and observation kept in order by lasting rational standards' or by 'strict and unchangeable rules' (Feyerabend 1993, p. xi, 11). In fact, quite the opposite pertained. Kuhn described the scientific revolutions he was writing about as 'non-cumulative developmental episodes' (Kuhn 1970, p. 92).

Secondly, researchers in the natural sciences, as in the social sciences, were neither objective nor value-free. The 'situatedness' of the researcher, her social background, and her academic training and approach would serve to influence the type of knowledge produced (Sarbin and Kitsuse 1994, p. 11). This could determine the results and interpretations of any research undertaken. One example of researchers giving different explanations has been given by Hanson, who noted that the dawn would be interpreted differently by the astronomers Tycho Brahe and Kepler. Either the sun was moving above the horizon or the earth was rotating away to reveal the sun. Hanson, an eminent philosopher of science, explained this not because the data was in any way different, but because of '*ex post facto* interpretations of what is seen' (Hanson 1972, p. 8).

With regard to the social sciences, much nearer to the mainstream scholarship discussed in this chapter, Bourdieu was highly critical of claims to scientific legitimacy. He argued that what was being done in the social sciences was scientific form rather than scientific substance:

> The mania for methodology or the thirst for the latest refinements of componential analysis, graph theory, or matrix calculus assume the same ostentatious function as recourse to prestigious labels or fascinated attachment to the instruments – questionnaires or computers – most likely to symbolise the specificity of the craft and its scientific quality.
>
> (Bourdieu et al. 1991, pp. 70–71)

In fact scientific research involved painstaking work which had constantly to be re-evaluated in the interests of rigour and the allowing of new ideas to come to the fore. He evaluated much sociological positivist research as more to do with 'scientific-ity' than with empirical rigour and scientific legitimacy. Despite its scientific format it did not involve the careful and continuous consideration and reconsideration of the assumptions underlying the 'object of inquiry' crucial to proper scientific inquiry (Bourdieu et al. 1991).

Thus, if these scholars have legitimate arguments against a narrow interpretation of what constitutes science and scientific method, there is no reason to exclude the more 'subjectivist' approaches to scholarship. In terms of management scholarship this would involve a study of human understandings, interpretations and their expressions in action either in favour of or against managerial strategies, along with qualitative methods of inquiry the aims of which generally include finding out the reasons for and effects of human agency.

### Subjectivist aspects of objectivist scholarship

There is a further twist in this argument: as stated above, scholars pursuing objectivist, positivist methods have claimed scientific neutrality and researcher objectivity on the grounds of the quantitatively oriented research methodologies and the objects of inquiry chosen – non-human, non-subjectivist matters, as for example, organisation structures. However, as pointed out, there are subjectivist elements in management and management accounting scholarship despite any assertions to the contrary. The choice by the researcher of the respondents who provide information which crucially influences the direction, content, analysis and conclusions of the research becomes a subjective one. This is particularly so if other people with relevant information which potentially differs from that of the managers' are excluded (Green 2013). It matters that the results of the research frame are is presented by the researcher as legitimate knowledge. This then becomes accepted as legitimate knowledge by those informed by the research – for example professional managers, consultants and students. It consequently becomes common knowledge among the general public, including the boundaries of the analysis, without questioning what has been omitted.

Claims for subjectivities in objectivist scholarship do not stop there. Following on from the points made above, there is also the question of which questions are asked and the range of the information obtainable from them. Questionnaires arguably reflect the researcher's ideas about what is relevant and legitimate rather than necessarily presenting the concerns of the respondents. They also provide a very restricted picture of the issues significant to organisations, managerial strategies, organisational processes and the understandings and interests of members in various parts and at different levels of the organisation (Green 2013).

## Explanations for the persistence of objectivist approaches to management scholarship

These are powerful objections to the epistemology held to be legitimate in most mainstream scholarship: the research methods used to acquire knowledge about organisations; the claim that such approaches are in any case not 'scientific' knowledge;

the pointers to objectivist scholarship being driven in important aspects by subjective choices; and the examples of fuller, richer scholarship involving humans as active agents in organisational strategies and processes. Thus it would not be unreasonable to expect there to be more room for and validation of alternative, more subjectivist scholarship which would include qualitative methods of inquiry. Because of the 'absenting' (Bhaskar 2008) of what has been found to be important influences on the directions and successes of managerial policies and strategies for implementation, one could also expect there to be an expectation, if not insistence, on the inclusion of analyses of the actions and reactions of organisational members in different positions to managerial policies, and also more focus on organisational processes which have been found to be integral to the shaping of organisational systems and structures.

However, surprisingly, this has not been the case. Various reasons have been suggested (Green 2012, 2013). These have ranged from the insistence and legitimation in the academy of objectivist scholarship, through wider political pressures particularly in the US, to broader ideological positions which have driven epistemological values and standards in positivist directions. What is validated and to a large degree standardised in the academy is significant – this is the place where knowledge, including representations of others' scholarship, is produced, through published research, textbooks and pedagogy, and therefore becomes the reference point for the way knowledge is framed in terms of what are considered to be legitimate and important subject areas for study, and where relevant sources for this knowledge are to be found.

### The academy

The various pressures in the academy that have driven epistemological legitimacy to objectivism include journal editors' preferences for objectivist scholarship, bolstered by the all-important academic journal rankings, which confer prestige and significantly also resources on their institutions (Bhagat 1979). Journal editors of the most prestigious journals such as the *Administrative Science Quarterly* have preferred an 'objectivist' mould using 'hard quantitative measures of structures and attitudes' (Burrell and Morgan 1979, pp. 223–224, fn.37). It has been emphasised that there have also been papers published in this and other such journals which have had different scholarly approaches including more subjectivist ones (Green 2009). However, the majority of papers published in these high-ranking journals have been consistent with objectivist preferences.

Various theorists have argued that the ranking and consequent hierarchization of journals has led to a marketisation or commification of academic journals. The universities or departments of those ranked highest have been granted more resources. What is relevant there is that the scholarship in these journals has tended to be objectivist and structuralist as described above of mainstream management scholarship (Putnam 2009). This has reinforced this type of scholarship at the expense of more multi-paradigmatic and more qualitative knowledge and the development of different ideas.

This direction has been supported, particularly in US universities. Other pressures for conservative scholarship in the management fields came from university heads of department. According to Pfeffer and Moore (1980) it was easier for departmental heads to stay in post if in their departments there was paradigm consensus and conformity among the scholars. This was another boost for conventional mainstream orthodox approaches. A further pressure on universities to promote mainstream scholarship lay on those less able to take their student application numbers for granted, as it was thought such scholarship was more attractive to students (Manns and March 1978). This argument is extended in Green (2012).

The managerialist focus of traditional mainstream management scholarship was encouraged by corporative influences on business schools, particularly in the US. Practical problem-solving rather than sociological understanding and critical analysis were promoted. The focus or 'object of inquiry' (Bourdieu 1993) shifted to commercial companies from a previous interest in public service and government agencies, reinforced by corresponding career incentives for academics (Stern and Barley 1996).

### Wider political pressures

From the 1950s, there have been wider pressures in the US for 'harder', more rationalist and quantitative-based scholarship in the management area. Developments regarding the mainframe computer led to the language of cybernetics being adopted in managerial discourse, and Soviet technological progess with its launching of the Sputnik in 1957 increased technical competition and encouraged the adoption of curricula in business schools with an emphasis on more scientific approaches, using statistics and quantitative methods (Barley and Kunda 1992). Stern and Barley highlighted their effect on the content of what was taught, the sociological perspectives and methodologies used, and it legitimated certain ontological and epistemological positions as to what constituted the 'reality' out there and what then counted as knowledge. Willmott explains this as a:

> scholarly tradition fashioned in North America during the Cold War at a time when academic rigor was conflated with respectability gained from prostration before a Method ascribed to the natural sciences, irrespective of the ontology of the phenomena under discussion.
>
> (Willmott 2011, p. 436)

Later on the conservative Thatcher government in the UK was also not in favour of sociological inquiry, which might have given more attention to human agency and organisational processes (Fournier and Grey 2000). The influence of the New Right in the 1980s led to cutbacks in social science departments, particularly in sociology. The anti-sociological sentiments and actions against sociology departments under Mrs. Thatcher's government had the effect of closing many down altogether, and driving sociologists as well as organisation theorists into business schools. An unintended consequence of this, however, was that the entry of would-be social science scholars into business schools encouraged a cross-fertilisation of management studies with critical social science scholarship (Fournier and Grey 2000).

### Broader ideological positions: managerialism

As suggested earlier, objectivist scholarship can be seen, despite its claim to be value-free and neutral, to be deeply political. Marxist and later critical theorists have variously analysed the link between what has been legitimated as mainstream knowledge and dominant interests. Foucault is famous for the links he made between power and knowledge (Foucault 1980). Because of the pervasive acceptance of this type of knowledge, its discourse became part of everyday usage, further bolstering its assumptions of power and the legitimacy of current holders of such power (Clegg 2002).

In terms of management scholarship, claims of links between knowledge and power most notably are present regarding the powers and prerogative of managers, as argued earlier. Various critical theorists, such as those in the 'Frankfurt School' have pursued this issue (Alvesson and Deetz 2006). In terms of the discourses used, Lukacs analysed the ways the terms 'naturalisation' and 'universalisation' served to legitimate managerial power and prerogative as something to be seen as natural and universal (Alvesson and Deetz 2006). A different and hard-hitting analysis of the use of discourse, this time as a way of obfuscation, was made by Habermas. He coined the phrase 'systematically distorted communication', through which he showed how employees could be weakened in potential confrontations with management, through their being given access only to partial or misleading information about the organisations they were working in (Habermas 1972).

Habermas was also against the emphasis on objectivist aspects of organisations to the exclusion of human agency, and significantly, human participation in decision making. He contrasted objectivism or 'technical' reason, which focussed on control over objectified processes and which excluded employees from managerial policies, with human interests or 'practical' reason, which encouraged participation and the development of consensus among all the actors in a situation. Habermas's third category, 'emancipatory' knowledge constituted a situation where people had autonomy and responsibility and thus where knowledge and interest became one, rather than being reduced to 'technical control of objectified processes' (Habermas 1972, p. 316). If this precept were followed, this would have implications for organisational governance, in the first instance regarding the power and prerogative, not only of managers but of employees at all levels of their organisations.

As pointed out earlier, the dominance of objectivist scholarship in management studies has served to accord power and legitimacy to managers by assuming their prerogative and capability to effect change, and for regarding them as the only source of information necessary to understand organisational matters. They have also disempowered potential rival sources of power and information regarding organisations by absenting from the discourse organisational members outside the ranks of senior management. According to Bourdieu, objectivist scholarship has resulted in an analysis in which power and politics have been neutralised by omission (Bourdieu 1990).

### Broader ideological positions: neoliberalism

Neoliberalism is, arguably, an important and at present powerful influence on the direction of scholarly approaches in the management area. It is unlike classical liberalism. The latter is limited in the sphere of economics to the maximisation of free trade and competition with minimal state interference, and politically with individual liberty on an egalitarian basis (Brown 2005). Neoliberalism on the other hand is far more extensive in the political and social as well as economic spheres. It involves the extension and dissemination of market values into all aspects of society. Market values, according to neoliberal values should also pervade institutions and social, political, normative and educational values. Weber (1946) was prescient regarding its implications: all actions, discourses and policies would be evaluated according to profitability; moral responsibility would be equated with rational action.

In terms of education, scholarship, as already mentioned, is commodified through the ranking of the journals in which papers are published rather than through the quality of the work itself (Willmott 2011). This, regardless of quality, becomes the dominant narrative. Market values enter as 'appropriate' learning is produced for student consumers who 'purchase' a defined quantum of knowledge which becomes 'services' to enhance their own careers (Hogler and Gross 2009, p. 4). It follows that because objectivist scholarship is dominant in the academy, what becomes regarded as legitimate epistemologically is scholarship which concentrates on what is subject to rational calculation, in this case organisational systems and structures, excluding discourses and research into matters to do with power, politics, human understanding, intention and agency.

This may go some way to explaining the imperviousness to the highly critical comments made about inadquacies in management scholarship, as well as the ignoring of the arguments made above for a more eclectic and inclusive scholarship which would lead to a broadening of the 'object of inquiry' to include human interests and concerns, enriched through the addition of qualitative, deeper methods of research. The emphasis and sole value placed on rationalist, calculable approaches can overcome criticisms regarding questionable epistemological standards, and their limitations on knowledge of organisational processes through their exclusion of potentially significant factors which would increase understanding of how organisations actually work in practice.

## Conclusion

This has serious implications for matters of organisational governance. In fact neoliberal principles and the scholarship resulting from it, if allowed to continue its extension into all aspects of organisational life, could reduce issues of governance in organisations to rational, calculable topics to do with the promotion of market values. There would be no room for and no value placed on what have commonly been regarded as concerns of corporate governance – social obligations to non-shareholder stakeholders, including employees and local communities, for example (OECD Principles of Corporate Governance 2004, Article VI). Integrity and ethical behaviour is another instance of what has been required by board members (Cadbury 1992).

Dominant, mainstream management scholarship has supported neoliberal principles by ignoring those aspects eschewed by neoliberalism – human concerns, power and action which are potentially disruptive of managerial strategies to the point of rendering them dysfunctional. One might argue that ideology is one thing, but when scholarship is removed from the practicalities of organisational processes, successes and failures, its sustainability in the long term might be at risk. But rather than relying on the inadequacies of current mainstream scholarship being reversed, one could argue that if one wants to do 'well by being good', and if being good includes ensuring ethical practices and social values, one may have to fight for these.

Many authors have acknowledged the difficulties in countering neoliberalism as it has pervaded our lives so fully. Two such authors have claimed difficulties in withdrawing from its policies and practices 'without dismantling one's own existence' (Lilley and Papadopoulos 2014, p. 980). Suggested ways forward have been broader than looking specifically at scholarship. They have included challenging neoliberalism's calculativeness with an alternative vision of the good (Brown 2005); fighting on all fronts for democratic governance, economic, political, cultural equality and justice by making world-wide alliances (Harvey 2005) and working both within existing institutions and outside (Mouffe 2005). There is certainly a need to challenge current mainstream management scholarship for the sake of 'doing well by being good'.

## Notes

1 In this chapter 'management' includes management accounting and organisation studies.
2 "Au fond, ce n'est pas moi qui signe, dès que c'est lancé sur le marché littéraire, ça ne vient plus de moi, ça ne s'adresse pas à toi, la trace m'échappe, elle tombe dans le monde . . . le risque de perversion, de corruption, de dérive est en même temps la seule chance de m'adresser à l'autre" (Derrida 2005, p. 26).
3 The concept of objectivism will be discussed below.
4 Methodology has been defined as how researchers can go about finding whatever they believe can be known (Guba and Lincoln 1998, p. 201).
5 In the 1950s, when Burns and Stalker did their research, the CEO would almost certainly have been a man.
6 See e.g. Lawrence and Lorsch's (1967a,b) work on differentiation and integration in organisations and the likelihood of conflict because of the different interests working against integration.
7 Extreme functionalist, particularly positivist views held that knowledge was cumulative and acquired through scientific methods which would add to the total knowledge about the external world – an idea refuted strongly by Feyerabend (1993, p. 21).

## Bibliography

Alvesson, M. and Deetz, S. (2006), 'Critical Theory and Postmodernism Approaches to Organizational Studies'. In Clegg, S.R., Hardy, C., Lawrence, T.B. and Nord, W.R. (eds.). *Handbook of Organization Studies*. 2nd Ed. Sage, London, pp. 255–283.

Barley, S.R. and Kunda, G. (1992), 'Design and Devolution: Surges of Rational and Normative Ideologies of Control in Managerial Discourse', *Administrative Science Quarterly*, vol. 37, no. 3, pp. 363–399.

Bhagat, R.S. (1979), 'Book Review. Developing an Interdisciplinary Science of Organizations by Roberts, K.H., Hulin, C.L. and Rousseau, D.M.', *Administrative Science Quarterly*, vol. 24, no. 2, pp. 333–337.

Bhaskar, R. (2008), *Dialectic: The Pulse of Freedom*. Routledge, London.

Bourdieu, P. (1990), *The Logic of Practice*. Trans. Nice, R. Stanford University Press, Stanford.

Bourdieu, P. (1993), *Sociology in Question*. Trans. Nice, R. Sage, London.

Bourdieu, P., Chamboredon, J-C. and Passeron, J-C. (1991), *The Craft of Sociology: Epistemological Preliminaries*. Krais, B. (ed.). Trans. Nice, R. Walter de Gruyter, Berlin.

Brown, W. (2005), *Edgework: Critical Essays on Knowledge and Politics*. Princeton University Press, Princeton.

Burns, T. (1961), Preface to the Second Edition. In Burns, T. and Stalker, G.M. *The Management of Innovation*. 2nd Ed. Tavistock Publications, London.

Burns, T. (1994), Preface to the Third Edition. In Burns, T. and Stalker, G.M. *The Management of Innovation*. 3rd Ed. Oxford University Press, Oxford.

Burns, T. and Stalker, G.M. (1961), *The Management of Innovation*. Tavistock Publications, London.

Burns, T. and Stalker, G.M. (1966), *The Management of Innovation*. 2nd Ed. Tavistock Publications, London.

Burns, T. and Stalker, G.M. (1994), *The Management of Innovation*. 3rd Ed. Oxford University Press, Oxford.

Burrell, G. and Morgan, G. (1979), *Sociological Paradigms and Organisational Analysis: Elements of the Sociology of Corporate Life*. Ashgate, Aldershot.

Cadbury, A. (1992), *Report of the Committee on the Financial Aspects of Corporate Governance*. Gee, London. (December)

Chenhall, R.H. and Euske, K.J. (2007), 'The Role of Management Control Systems in Planned Organizational Change: An Analysis of Two Organizations', *Accounting, Organizations and Society*, vol. 32, pp. 601–637.

Chenhall, R.H. and Langfield-Smith, K. (1998), 'The Relationship Between Strategic Priorities, Management Techniques and Management Accounting: An Empirical Investigation, Using a Systems Approach', *Accounting, Organizations and Society*, vol. 23, no. 3, pp. 243–264.

Chia, R. (1996), *Organizational Analysis as Deconstructive Practice*. Walter de Gruyter, Berlin.

Clegg, S.R. (2002), 'Lives in the Balance: A Comment on Hinings and Greenwood's Disconnects and Consequences in Organization Theory?' *Administrative Science Quarterly*, vol. 47, no. 3, pp. 428–441.

Daft, R.L. (2001), *Organization Theory and Design*. South-Western College Publishing, Cincinnati, OH.

Derrida, J. (2005), *Sur Parole: Instantanés philosophiques*. La Tour d'Aigues, Editions de l'Aube.

Feyerabend, P. (1993), *Against Method*. 3rd Ed. Verso, London.

Form, W.H. (1963), 'Book Review: The Management of Innovation 1962 [sic]'. *Administrative Science Quarterly*, vol. 8, no. 2, pp. 271–272.

Foucault, M. (1980), *Power/Knowledge: Selected Interviews and Other Writings 1972–1977*. Harvester, Brighton.

Fournier, V. and Grey, C. (2000), 'At the Critical Moment: Conditions and Prospects for Critical Management Studies', *Human Relations*, vol. 53, no. 1, pp. 7–32.

Green, M. (2009), 'The Embedding of Knowledge in the Academy: "Tolerance", Irresponsibility or Other Imperatives?' *Social Responsibility Journal*, vol. 5, no. 2, pp. 165–177.

Green, M. (2012), 'Objectivism in Management Knowledge: An Example of Bourdieu's "mutilation"?' *Social Responsibility Journal*, vol. 8, no. 4, pp. 495–510.

Green, M. (2013), *What Counts as Knowledge? Parameters of Validity for the Meaning and Representation of a Contingency Theory in the Organisation, Management and Management Accounting Literature*. Ph.D. thesis. De Montfort University.

Guba, E.G. and Lincoln, Y.S. (1998), 'Competing Paradigms in Qualitative Research'. In Denzin, N.K. and Lincoln, Y.S. (eds.). *The Landscape of Qualitative Research: Theories and Issues*. Sage, Thousand Oaks.

Habermas, J. (1972), *Knowledge and Human Interests*. Trans. Shapiro, J. Heinemann, London.

Halfpenny, P. (2001), 'Positivism in the Twentieth Century'. In Ritzer, G. and Smart, B. (eds.). *Handbook of Social Theory*. Sage, London, pp. 371–385.

Hanson, N.R. (1972), *Patterns of Discovery: An Inquiry into the Conceptual Foundations of Science*. The University Press, Cambridge.

Harvey, D. (2005), *A Brief History of Neoliberalism*. Oxford University Press, Oxford.

Hatch, M.J. and Yanow, D. (2003), 'Organization Theory as Interpretive Science'. In Tsoukas, H. and Knudsen, C. (eds.). *The Oxford Handbook of Organization Theory*. Oxford University Press, Oxford, pp. 63–87.

Hogler, R. and Gross, M.A. (2009), 'Journal Rankings and Academic Research', *Management Communication Quarterly* [Online] vol. 20, no. 10: doi:10.1177/089335419, (accessed January 30, 2010).

Hopwood, A.G. (2009), 'Accounting and the Environment', *Accounting, Organizations and Society*, vol. 34, pp. 433–439.

Kuhn, T.S. (1970), *The Structure of Scientific Revolutions*. 2nd Ed. Chicago University Press, Chicago.

Lawrence, P.R. and Lorsch, J.W. (1967a), *Organization and Environment: Managing Differentiation and Integration*. Harvard Business School Press, Boston, MA.

Lawrence, P.R. and Lorsch, J.W. (1967b), 'Differentiation and Integration in Complex Organizations', *Administrative Science Quarterly*, vol. 12, no. 1, pp. 1–47.

Lilley, S. and Papadopoulos, D. (2014), 'Material Returns: Cultures of Valuation, Biofinancisalisation and the Autonomy of Politics,' *Sociology*, vol. 48, no. 5, pp. 972–988.

Loft, A. (1995), 'The History of Management Accounting: Relevance Found'. In Ashton, D., Hopper, T. and Scapens, R.W. (eds.). *Issues in Management Accounting*. 2nd Ed. Prentice Hall, London, pp. 21–44.

Manns, C.L. and March, J.G. (1978), 'Financial Adversity, Internal Competition and Curriculum Change in a University', *Administrative Science Quarterly*, vol. 23, no. 4, pp. 541–552.

Merchant, K.A. and Otley, D.T. (2007), 'A Review of the Literature on Control and Accountability'. In Chapman, C.S., Hopwood, A.G. and Shields, M.D. (eds.). *Handbook of Management Accounting Research*. vol 2. Elsevier, Amsterdam, pp. 785–802.

Mouffe, C. (2005), *The Democratic Paradox*. Verso, London.

Mullins, L.J. (2005), *Management and Organisational Behaviour*. 7th Ed. Prentice Hall, Harlow.

Nouri, H. and Parker, R. (1998), 'The Relationship Between Budget Participation and Job Performance: The Roles of Budget Adequacy and Organizational Commitment', *Accounting, Organizations and Society*, vol. 23, no. 5, pp. 467–483.

OECD (2004), Principles of Corporate Governance, Article VI. Available from http://www.oecd.org/dataoecd/32/18/31557724.pdf (accessed May 8, 2015).

Otley, D. (1980), 'The Contingency Theory of Management Accounting: Achievement and Prognosis', *Accounting, Organizations and Society*, vol. 5, no. 4, pp. 413–428.

Otley, D. (1995), 'Management Control, Organisational Design and Accounting Information Systems'. In Ashton, D., Hopper, T. and Scapens, R.W. (eds.). *Issues in Management Accounting*. 2nd Ed. Prentice Hall, London, pp. 45–64.

Panozzo, F. (1997), 'The Making of the Good Academic Accountant', *Accounting, Organizations and Society*, vol. 22, no. 5, pp. 447–480.

Pfeffer, J. and Moore, W.L. (1980), 'Average Tenure of Academic Department Heads: The Effects of Paradigm, Size and Departmental Demography,' *Administrative Science Quarterly*, vol. 25, no. 3, pp. 387–406.

Preston, A.M. (1986), 'Interactions and Arrangements in the Process of Informing', *Accounting, Organizations and Society*, vol. 11, no. 6, pp. 521–540.

Preston, A.M. (1995), 'Budgeting, Creativity and Culture'. In Ashton, D., Hopper, T. and Scapens, R.W. (eds.). *Issues in Management Accounting*. Prentice Hall, New York.

Pugh, D.S., Hickson, D.J. and Hinings, C.R. (1964), *Writers on Organizations: An Introduction*. Hutchinson, London.

Putnam, L.L. (2009), Symbolic Capital and Academic Fields. *Management Communication Quarterly*. [Online] vol. 20, no. 10, doi:10.1177/0893318909335420 (accessed January 30, 2010).

Reiter, S.A. and Williams, P.F. (2002), 'The Structure and Progressivity of Accounting Research: the Crisis in the Academy Revisited', *Accounting, Organizations and Society*, vol. 27, no. 6, pp. 575–607.

Robbins, S.P. (2003), *Organizational Behaviour*. 10th Ed. Pearson Education, New Jersey.

Sarbin, T.R. and Kitsuse, J.I. (1994), 'A Prologue to Constructing the Social'. In Sarbin, T.R. and Kitsuse, J.I. (eds.). *Constructing the Social*. Sage, London, pp. 1–18.

Simons, R. (1987), 'Accounting Control Systems and Business Strategy: an Empirical Analysis', *Accounting Organizations and Society*, vol. 12, no. 4, pp. 357–374.

Smith, M.K. (2012), 'What is Pedagogy?' *The Encyclopaedia of Informal Education*. Available from http://infed.org/mobi/what-is-pedagogy/ (accessed February 21, 2015).

Stern, R.N. and Barley, S.R. (1996), 'Organizations and Social Systems: Organization Theory's Neglected Mandate', *Administrative Science Quarterly*, vol. 41, no. 1, pp. 146–162.

Turner, J.H. (2001), 'The Origins of Positivism: The Contributions of Auguste Comte and Herbert Spencer'. In Ritzer, G. and Smart, B. (eds.). *Handbook of Social Theory*. Sage, London, pp. 30–42.

Weber, M. (1946), *From Max Weber: Essays in Sociology*. Trans. Gerth, H.H. and Wright Mills, C. (eds.). Oxford University Press, New York.

Willmott, H. (1993), 'Breaking the Paradigm Mentality,' *Organization Studies*, vol. 14, no. 5, pp. 681–719.

Willmott, H. (2011), 'Journal List Fetishism and the Perversion of Scholarship: Reactivity and the ABS List', *Organization*, vol. 18, no. 4, pp. 429–442.

# Part II

# Effective business behavior
# for corporate sustainability

# The walls between us

## Governance for sustainability

*Philippa Wells and Coral Ingley*

## Introduction

It is probably a truism to state that over the last couple of decades, companies (or corporations), particularly the large transnational corporations (TNCs), have attracted increasing levels of public attention in relation to the environmental impact of their activities. To some extent this could be due to the high profile of corporates in the modern economy and society (with the 44 companies included in Global Trend's 100 largest economic entities generating over 11 percent of global GDP [Global Trends 2013] and with some of the largest and most powerful having political allegiances and/or influence over policy makers), and with the high media profile afforded dominance more generally, especially when their activities and operations are identified as having negative impacts.

Examples of such negative publicity in the context of environmental pollution and damage alone include, but are by no means limited to, Union Carbide (gas and toxic chemical leak, Bhopal – India), Coca-Cola (extraction of water and its pollution – India), Royal Dutch Shell (water and land pollution – Nigeria), Chevron (toxic waste from oil drilling – Ecuador) and British Petroleum (water and land pollution – United States). These instances lead to weightier questions around the responsibility for, and liability of, such corporations for these impacts (Strine 2008).

It is also the case that the process of governance (particularly, although not only, when involving strategic planning) has been the subject of much public, political and academic debate and the expectations placed on those with legal responsibility for strategic and policy decisions (the board of directors) have grown almost exponentially over the last few decades. Legal compliance is one driver for such decisions but increasingly, boards are being called on to recognize, quantify and manage environmental issues as part of their long-term strategy (Klettner et al. 2013, Mansell and Prill 2003).

Most prominent as a focus for such debate and pressures is the question of sustainability, and how those involved in governance should embed a broader social responsibility to realize sustainability values (Aras and Crowther 2008, Mansell and Prill 2003, Ong 2001, Russell et al. 2007). This focus arguably stands as a challenge to a focus for governance which has long been formulated and vociferously defended – the shareholder value maximization model (SVMM) (similar in principle to the contractarian and shareholder primacy models) (Smith 1998) which effectively creates legal walls between the company and society. The SVMM sits uneasily alongside the model which demolishes those walls: the stakeholder or communitarian model, based on stakeholder theory. This theory holds that a company as a social player must consider the impact of its activities on those having an interest in the company (and vice versa) (Freeman 1984). Hence these two models center on quite different sized and defined groups whose interests must be prioritized in the governance process.

"Hybrid" frameworks also stand between and around these two polarities, including the Enlightened Shareholder Value Model based on the "idea that corporations should pursue shareholder wealth with a long-run orientation that seeks sustainable growth and profits" (Ho 2010, Millon 2010, p. 1), the Entity Maximization and Sustainability Model, which "proposes that the object of a company is to foster entity wealth, involving directors [in] endeavoring to increase the overall long-run market value of the company" (Keay 2010a, p. 35) and, more recently, the concept of Social License to Operate, defined as "the demands on and expectations for a business enterprise that emerge from neighborhoods, environmental groups, community members, and other elements of the surrounding civil society" (Gunningham and Sinclair 2002, p. 307).

However, a caution is indicated: all of these models to a greater or lesser extent acknowledge stakeholder concerns in sustainability (and otherwise) largely as the means of ensuring on-going profitability of the company rather than ensuring environmental sustainability as an end in itself. Further complicating the debate is the range of views as to how and why those responsible for governance of organizations will move to adopt and pursue such values. It could be argued (as has Coulson-Thomas 2014) that companies (or corporations) generally will only move to govern for (environmental) sustainability if forced or at least encouraged to do so by way of regulation and other legal instruments. Therefore, such suitable instruments should be implemented to permit, if not require, those responsible for the governance of companies to move towards articulating and applying such principles. This might in turn require a redefinition of the duties of directors. Other commentators just as stoutly maintain that the market is the most effective and efficient way of instilling such values as business will react to a market opportunity if it is there, including "going green" (Zhang et al. 2008). Market discipline is said to be of particular effectiveness in a context of comparative regulatory neutrality (meaning that it would not be considered worth relocating operations to regions or countries with weak environmental compliance requirements) (Heyvaert 2012).

Of relevance to this discussion, in 2005 the Australian Corporations and Markets Advisory Committee (CAMAC) was asked *inter alia*, to consider whether the law should be changed to encourage companies to adopt socially and environmentally responsible business practices and whether social and/or environmental reporting should be mandated. CAMAC concluded that existing law was sufficient to enable "responsible corporate conduct . . . in relation to . . . the environment . . . through the maintenance and strengthening of the legislative and regulatory framework" (CAMAC 2006, p. 167).

The logic driving CAMAC's conclusion appears to be that the existing law, including directors' duties, is sufficiently flexible to permit moves by companies to embrace sustainability while the competitive/market advantage implicit in the development of such practices will drive businesses, including corporates, down this path much sooner and more effectively than would any level of direct government or regulatory intervention.

Of further relevance is the extent to which, and how, those companies are moving down this path. Opinions are mixed. Perera, Putt de Pino and Oliviera (2013) report that 300 of the companies on the *S&P 500* Index report their greenhouse gas inventories each year to the Carbon Disclosure Project and some (including Alcoa, Citi, Johnson and Johnson and Siemens) are making genuine efforts to reduce their environmental impact, thereby promoting sustainability. Also, "a perusal of annual reports published by the Global Reporting Initiative (GRI) in 2002 provides evidence of the millions of dollars spent annually by companies . . . in the pursuit of corporate sustainability" (Russell et al. 2007, p. 36). However, there are also accusations levelled against companies for "greenwashing" and "greenspeaking" (Beder 2002, Kim and Lyon 2011, Strasser 2011): that is, going through the motions but not translating these to real action.

With the above in mind, three further preliminary points can be made. First, there remains much debate and discussion around what the shareholder and stakeholder models (and their variations) imply for a company addressing the question of whether to move to governing for sustainability. Second, there remains uncertainty over what is meant by "sustainability", what values it embraces, and how best it can be achieved. Finally, there is the problematic question of how to frame sustainability, as this can color attitudes, opinions and conclusions about it and its importance. To elaborate a little: corporate social responsibility (CSR) is one of the main frameworks within which sustainability has been considered (Aras and Crowther 2008, Dowse 2009, Caswell 2004a, 2004b, Greenberg 2007, Horrigan 2007, Legge 2008, Standen 2006a, 2006b, Waring 2008). There is also little doubt that for many corporates the principles of CSR have grown in importance. In 2005 the *Economist Intelligence Unit* reported a 1 percent increase from 2000 (54–55 percent) in the percentage of corporate executives indicating that corporate social responsibility (CSR) was central to, or an important consideration in, decisions. A *Conference Board* report a year later reported 66 percent of surveyed multinationals as indicating that CSR/sustainability issues were growing in importance (Farrar 2008).

However, CSR, while sometimes providing a context in which to consider governance for sustainability, also has drawbacks. Not all business leaders view CSR as positive, with "some companies see[ing] . . . CSR as the thin end of a very threatening wedge. They see themselves becoming at the mercy of NGOs and other activists who will . . . divert their attention from developing their company" (Davis 2006, p. 107).

Another objection which can be levelled against this framework lies in the nature and potential scope of CSR. A full discussion is beyond the scope of this chapter but suffice it here to say that CSR can embrace activities, such as charitable works, community projects and education, which do not necessarily form, or stem from, the core activities of the organization (American Law Institute 1994) and, furthermore, may have little or nothing to do with them. Embedding sustainability in this framework runs the danger of its being lost, confused and subject to criticism by association. We propose that governance for environmental sustainability should be treated separately to CSR, as resources are core and integral to the company's activities (and those of other economic entitles) and the misuse or mismanagement of those resources has contributed to broader environmental and social problems (Sethi 2005, Russell et al. 2007).

This chapter explores aspects of the governance for sustainability issue and arguments that shape it, with particular emphasis on the extent to which such a focus can be developed and pursued within the legal framework provided by one of the directors' major fiduciary duties: to act in good faith and in the best interests of the company. This duty has been codified, albeit with variance in wording, scope, consequences and emphasis, in s131, Companies Act 1993 (NZ); s181 Corporations Act 2001 (Cth, Australia) and s172 Companies Act 2006 (UK) and is recognized and applied in case law in all of the above jurisdictions as well as such countries as the United States and Canada. (Accordingly, this discussion refers only to countries where such a duty is imposed.) The chapter focuses on four areas in turn. The first two sections provide some background and context (specifically definition and scope), of the term "sustainability" and a brief overview of the major arguments and positions in relation to whether or not such values should form part of the strategic (governance) process. The third section reflects on whether and how the directors' duty specified above can be applied in such a way as to permit directors to prioritize sustainability values (as defined in the preceding section), while in the conclusion suggestions are made as to future avenues of research regarding governance for sustainability. "Corporation", "corporate" and "company" are used synonymously throughout.

## Sustainability – what does it mean?

"Sustainability" as a term is neither clearly understood nor consistently applied (Cowan et al. 2010, Dunphy et al. 2003, Keay 2008). Some proponents envisage a viable entity (financial sustainability) (Dyllick and Hockerts 2002, Keay 2008, 2010) thereby adopting an inward looking perspective, while others look outwards, defining an entity as sustainable if accounting appropriately for the broader social and/or environmental impact of its activities (Buchholz and Rosenthal 2005, Shrivastava 1995). Taking both of those aspects into account, Caldelli and Parmigiani (2004, p. 159) define sustainability as "the activities, demonstrating the inclusion of social and environmental aspects in the normal business operations of a company and its interaction with stakeholders." In addition, and more broadly, sustainability can be considered in economic terms (indicating success for an economic system [e.g. capitalism], industry or unit; it can refer to social concerns [determining the maintenance or continued success of a social group (e.g. democracy)]; or to environmental matters [e.g. allowing the continued well-being of an eco-system or part thereof]; or a combination of all three [Pesquex 2009].

Environmental sustainability is the main focus for this chapter. A broadly used definition in the context of sustainable development of the environment emerged from the *Brundtland Report* (Pesquex 2009, p. 234) which stated that development could be defined as sustainable only if "it meets the needs of the present without compromising the ability of future generations to meet their needs". However, such a definition is contested. Sustainability can be seen as requiring "the maintenance of the integrity of the ecology" (Idris 1990, p. 16), placing the environment squarely at the center and demanding adoption of baseline values representing at least the minima required to maintain that integrity.

At the other end of the spectrum, the environment is seen as a factor in a broader sustainability equation. From this perspective, economists argue that true sustainability emerges where the costs and benefits involved in the use of properly priced environmental resources are balanced against each other and against other social inputs such as labor and capital that contribute to the realization of socially desired objectives such as public health, adequate sustenance and material wealth – essentially a market model writ large. For such economic thinkers the failure to establish an appropriate price for environmental resources, and their resultant misuse or overuse leads to unacceptable environmental degradation (Beder 2002, Hardin 1968).

Given all the above, law makers and public and private policy bodies increasingly are looking to corporations (and business and/or other commercially oriented organizations more generally) to show leadership in the adoption of processes and strategies that incorporate principles of such sustainability, either specifically by reference to the environment or within a broader CSR framework. However, as stated above, this raises questions as to how and why corporations can and do recognize and adopt "sustainability" as a good (or vital) principle and whether expectations can or should be held of those responsible for governance who should and/or can advance such principles via the governance process. These questions are explored below, first, by addressing the question of whether environmental sustainability is considered an appropriate focus for governance decisions (by reference to the two contrasting models, shareholder value maximization model [Friedman 1970] and the stakeholder approach [Freeman 1984], as identified above). Second, a discussion of one of the main duties of directors: the fiduciary duty to act in good faith and in the interests of the company, considers whether this obligation might be a driver or a constraint on the furtherance of sustainability principles via the governance process.

### Shareholder versus stakeholder perspectives

The shareholder value maximization model (and similar conceptualizations of the relationship between the corporation and its shareholders) assumes that shareholders "own" the company (Friedman 1970), are potential beneficiaries of contracts negotiated by the board on behalf of the company (Bainbridge 2012, Stout 2012) or at least have a claim to the residual assets not subject to claims of creditors (Mygind 2009, Stout 2002). Therefore any attempt by its controllers, the board of directors, to divert shareholder money into outside endeavors with no perceived commensurate benefit to the company, and therefore to the shareholders, is tantamount to theft (Friedman 1970). If individuals other than shareholders suffer loss for breach of an express or implied contract with the company, the law provides the means for recovery (Sundaram and Inkpen 2004). Equally then, shareholders have legal protection against misuse or misdirection of their funds.

According to this view, pursuit of socially desired objectives is the domain of governments and other democratic institutions. If there is a perceived gap in the law that prevents the achievement of such objectives, it is up to society to press for change through democratic and legal processes. However, if resultant or potential changes to law could or would increase the costs to companies via higher compliance costs, then those companies have an obligation to shareholders to implement strategies to minimize their impact on the company – including relocation (an application of competitive advantage), or taking action (which might include lobbying lawmakers) against such change. Examples of such action include Doward 2013 (cigarette producers against plain packaging); Union of Concerned Scientists 2012 (corporations opposing climate change policies); News Corp for changes to anti-bribery laws).

Writers critiquing this view of the corporation and focus of corporate governance argue that such a model is anachronistic in the context of a global economy with transnational corporations (TNCs) and other huge companies having possibly millions of individual shareholders (Legge 2008), or millions of investors via institutional shareholders, which is not quite the same thing. It is highly unlikely, if not impossible, for highly dispersed shareholders to exert any influence over the decisions of the boards of such companies. Moreover, where funds are invested through institutional shareholders, individuals may not know where their capital has been placed. Hence the capital markets may not be sufficiently cohesive, powerful or informed to push corporates to change their strategic model to be more responsive to social change and expectations.

In addition, a shareholder-oriented perspective fails to address the stark modern reality that corporate operations and policy have impacts not only on the myriads of shareholding investors but also far beyond them, including interest groups and individuals across the community, country and globe (Greenberg 2007, Horrigan 2002, Kolk and van Tulder 2010, Stout 2012). Shareholder models also fail to acknowledge and account for the political influence and power that such corporations can and do bring to bear where the broader legal framework is weak (Hoovestal 2013) and/or where corporate governance expectations are low or obscure (reflective of the shift in power from weak to strong company constituencies) (Galanis 2011).

The stakeholder model, with its definition and acknowledgment of a range of interest groups, has appeal for critics of the shareholder models as a conduit through which the interests of those affected by corporations can and should be acknowledged and considered by those making decisions. However, problems have also been identified with the stakeholder model, these problems sitting apart from the question of whether stakeholders have any legitimacy as constituents which can be enforced against the company (Ho 2010). They include the following: identification and definition of interests to which decision-makers in corporations should and do pay attention (Mitchell et al. 1997); fuzziness and uncertainty implicit in measuring, addressing and managing those interests (Orts and Strudler 2009); and the potential for opportunism by stakeholders (Werder 2011) with negative impacts for both other stakeholders and the corporation.

The particular issues for governance for sustainability that are raised by these two opposing models will be addressed later in the chapter, but it is relevant first to explore the following question: if governance for environmental sustainability is to be expected of companies, are existing statutory and legal frameworks, specifically in this case the duty to act in good faith and in the best interests of the company, adequate to at least permit, if not ensure, that environmental sustainability principles are furthered via the governance process? This question is considered below.

## The duty to act in good faith and in the best interests of the company

Codified in a similar form under general and corporate law in a range of jurisdictions, the duty to act in good faith and in the best interests of the company has long been recognized in common law as one of the obligations fundamental to a director's position as a fiduciary. Historically speaking, the first corporations in America were envisaged as achieving a public purpose (out of 317 companies established between 1780–1801, nearly 66 percent were involved in transport, 20 percent in banking or insurance and 10 percent in the provision of local public services). Therefore, those original corporations have been seen as owing, at least by implication, duties not solely to shareholders but to a wider citizenry, with the best interests of the company likewise having a broad scope (Sommer 1995). In the UK (and countries inheriting its legal system such as Canada, Australia and New Zealand), this fiduciary duty was formulated at a time when directors were deemed equivalent to trustees having control over the assets of the unincorporated joint stock company and with equivalent responsibilities to the beneficiaries, in this case the contributors of capital. This formulation of the duty clearly foreshadows the shareholder value maximization model and resonates with Friedman's (1970) stance, persisting as a yardstick for appropriate behavior through to the modern corporation via the concept of agency (as originally articulated in *Aberdeen Rail Co v Blaikie Bros* [1854] 1 Macq. 461 @ 471 per Lord Cranford LC) (Langton and Trotman 1999). However, along with the shift in both concept and context for the governance of companies came a change in the focus of such a duty regarding the beneficiaries (or principal, to use agency parlance): rather than being a collective term for the investors as a group or as individuals, the company was recognized in law as a separate person. As such, it was now seen as having its own rights and responsibilities and, more specifically, as having its own interests recognized and furthered by the directors when making their decisions. This shift poses a problem for the directors in determining what is in the best interests of the company. Note that it is neither possible to expect, nor is it necessarily appropriate, to deem the interests of a majority or major voting bloc of investors as reflective of the company's interests. At the same time though, it is incumbent on the directors to identify something against which the company's best interests can be identified, measured and prioritized. The problem lies in determining that "something".

One possible solution is to rely on the courts. After all, determining the concept, shape, focus and size of this fiduciary duty are clearly legal questions. However, it is normally acknowledged by the courts that nothing in business is certain but, rather, decisions "are fraught with risk [and often made] on the basis of hunch and manifestly sparse data" (Manning 1984, p. 1482). The common law courts have historically been reluctant to hold a breach of duty without evidence of some significant problem with the decision or its process. Such a stance is indicated by such wide-ranging cases as *Saloman v Salomon and Co* [1893] A.C. 22 (no breach because no intention to prefer), *Bishopsgate Investment Management Ltd (in liquidation) v Maxwell (No 2)* [1994] 1 All ER 261 (breach for "mis-motivation"), *Coulter v E.L. Huckerby and Associates Inc* (1998) 41 B.L.R. (2d) 264 (breach where wrongful diversion of funds), *Regentcrest Ltd v Cohen* [2001] 1 B.C.L.C. 80 (no breach where directors honestly believed their decision was in the best interests of the company) and *Equiticorp Industries Group Ltd (in liquidation) v BNZ* (1993) 11 ACLC 952 (no breach where a subsidiary's funds were applied to the debts of the group). Even after the codification that has occurred in various jurisdictions, the position remains little changed – apart from a heightened expectation that directors are attuned to the needs and demands of their role, and knowledgeable about the business and the market context in which their company operates. The application of the business judgment rule means that the Court remains reluctant to second-guess board decisions. Provided that "an intelligent and reasonable person in the position of a director for the company . . . [could] have reasonably believed that the transactions were for the benefit of the company" (as stated in *Equiticorp Industries Group Ltd [in liquidation] v BNZ* [1993] 11 ACLC 952 at 983 by two judges, Clarke and Cripps JJA), directors generally are deemed to have adhered to the requirement.

Clearly, the proverbial ball is most often back in the directors' court. Provided directors make decisions that an intelligent and reasonable person would have made in comparable circumstances and in the interests of the company, and provided they do so with diligence and care, they would be deemed to have complied. However, this is not especially helpful when determining whether this duty permits or requires directors to take into account issues of environmental sustainability. Certainly, as previously asserted, views as to whether they can, or should, do so are inconsistent. Those arguing for the pricing mechanism would likely claim that as it is the responsibility of participants in the democratic process to determine whether and how different resources should be used, while users, including corporations, can only deal in accordance with the rules of the game; that is, regulations, policies and requirements which shape the markets for those resources. Those holding to the view that integrity of the environment must be maintained would more likely assert a broad obligation of corporations, again articulated via legal requirements, to maintain that integrity. Either way, directors must decide how to address the implications flowing from the use of resources while abiding by the rules and obligations. The merit or otherwise of such a decision would then be assessed in light of the directors' duty.

With the SVMM as a driver, decisions around whether or not the company should adopt sustainability principles would be shaped by whatever would maximize the benefits (including return to shareholders). However, justification for the use of this model presupposes that it is the shareholders' assets that are protected and increased. This premise in itself can be challenged in a variety of ways and contexts. *Trucost* (2013) in a detailed report (covering various industry sectors and regions) estimates *inter alia*, that the unpriced natural capital inputs (in order of cost, greenhouse gas emissions, water use, land use, air pollution, land and water pollution and waste) to the global primary production and processing sectors in 2009, alone, were US $7.3 trillion, or 13 percent of total overall global economic output (Trucost 2013). More disturbingly, *Trucost* reports that none of its top 20 corporations in this sector would be profitable if required to account adequately for the environmental costs they incur, a finding which implies that society (however defined) is subsidizing (via degradation, pollution and exploitation) private benefits enjoyed by investors (potentially an example of market failure: inappropriate pricing mechanisms leading to mis- or over-use of resources [Beder 2002]).

Those adopting a stakeholder perspective would likely assert that the broader social and environmental impact of corporate operations across the globe means that the best interests must embrace the values held by those who expressly or tacitly permit or support those operations. Thus, for example, should a TNC base its operations in an environmentally sensitive rain forest where local fauna and human populations are heavily reliant on the local ecology, then that TNC must ensure its operations are ecologically sound, even if the local law does not require it and even where this means lower returns for shareholders. However, those holding to such a stakeholder perspective might struggle to establish how some such ecological values could be either articulated or reconciled with those of specific stakeholder groups and how they then translate into identifiable and specific risks and opportunities for the corporation (Orts and Strudler 2009). Even if such human constituent groups can be identified, prioritized and considered, there remains a major problem, long recognized (Gravelle 1996–7, Ng 2011, Postglione 2010), for those arguing in favor of the environment and its sustainability. Essentially the problem concerns whether the environment (or each of its constituent parts) has a defined or definable interest which can be articulated, supported and enforced. Issues also emerge concerning what happens where there is conflict between the interests of a sector of society (such as prospective or actual employees or property owners) which can articulate the sector case, and the interests of the (mute) environment. Further debates relate to conflicts of interest between sectors of the community (on any level) enjoying different levels of power; and where there are conflicting environmental priorities (such as preservation of a wetland versus integrity of a forested land area), how those priorities can be ordered and whether it should be up to the corporation to make such determinations.

All of the above arguments seem to highlight an insurmountable problem. However, some precedent exists for asserting that this important directors' duty reasonably embraces environmental sustainability as being in the "best interests" of the company, an assertion for which several possible rationales can be offered. These rationales are linked to two main functions commonly associated with the board: compliance and performance.

The first board function discussed here is the compliance function. The duty requires that decisions are in the best interests of the company but by implication it also demands that first and foremost there is compliance with legal requirements (which are likely, in the context of environmental regulation, to include reporting against mandatory standards, paying taxes for use of scarce resources or on specified emissions such as carbon, or implementing required anti-pollution measures). Although shareholders are not legally responsible for compliance they are indirectly affected by failure to comply – such consequences being financial cost to the company (fines and other penalties), reputational damage (including criticism, boycotts and loss of trust) and possibly loss of viability for the company itself.

There is also a second aspect to the matter of compliance: because market confidence and legitimization are imperative (Keay 2010b) (and sometimes because the law says so), the interests of other stakeholders (most specifically, and normally, creditors) must be taken into account when and if relevant. The point can be made that the environment, or parts thereof, is not a "creditor" or other relevant discrete group or interest which can legitimately and reasonably be considered by directors – the concept being too general, too broadly defined and lacking any *locus standi* against the company. However, if the conclusions reached in the *Trucost* (2013) report, or any similar findings based on some objective measure of value, can be accepted as a reasonable representation of real costs presently unaccounted for by corporations, this seems to place the environment in a position analogous to that of creditors and therefore provides a ground on which the issue of environmental sustainability can and should be incorporated into company accounting practices and strategy.

The second board function to be discussed is that of performance. As identified earlier in this chapter, the corporation – and, by extension, every shareholder – can and increasingly does enjoy the advantages which flow from the exploitation of market opportunities connected to the adoption by the corporation of environmental sustainability strategies (and similarly, suffer if these strategies are not implemented) (Hult 2011, Lourenço et al. 2012, Willard 2012). So what are those advantages and how can they be pursued by directors while at the same time complying with the duty? With reference to the Canadian context, Mansell and Prill (2003) concluded that companies improve performance and reduce risks by adopting sustainability strategies. Directors will satisfy (the Canadian equivalent to) this duty provided they review and analyze the information on the costs/benefits of proposed strategies and conclude, on reasonable grounds, that their decisions are for the benefit of the company. Although such strategies might benefit other stakeholders such as employees and local communities, this does not preclude their being of benefit also and by extension to shareholders.

More specifically, Graci and Dodds (2008) argue that business organizations benefit financially and enduringly from stronger moves to "going green". This conclusion is shared by others such as *Jantzi Sustainalytics*, an organization which, in a report on the value of environmental (and social) considerations for companies in the natural resources sector (energy, mining and forestry), identified positive links between sustainability performance (principally operations, climate change policies and the supply of environmental products) and the drivers of strong financial performance (operational efficiency, a supportive political and regulatory environment, access to natural resources and access to labor) (Jantzi Sustainalytics 2011). Esty and Winston (2009), Murray and Ayoun (2010) and Rainey (2006) are among many others who consider that it is no longer an issue of whether sustainability should be central to governance: it is a matter of how and how quickly. Such a stance potentially raises a further question: if directors fail to address sustainability principles in the corporate's governance process, could they then breach this duty? This question is not explored here but raises some interesting possibilities for further consideration.

However, claims that companies will pursue sustainability because of a market advantage do not convince those who argue that corporations will only respond if forced to do so via regulation. To consider this argument further we examine, briefly, so-called "constituency" statutes and other similar moves through hard and soft law to at least authorize directors to take into account concerns other than those of shareholders. Some 30 American states including Iowa, Louisiana and Florida (as well as countries such as Japan, Germany and Canada (Standen 2006a)) now permit directors, when determining the best interests of the company, to consider the interests of non-shareholders (Bainbridge 1992). Although permission of this sort can be seen as offering a conduit for the recognition and incorporation of non-shareholder interests, including those of the environment, studies have concluded that directors have used this approach "more as a rationalization for deferring to their discretion than as a principled justification for consideration of constituent interests" (Springer 1999, p. 12); that is, as a mechanism for "opting out" rather than "opting in", and as a means of protection against accusations that might be levelled against them for failure to act in the company's best interests (Bainbridge 2012). It does not help that there is little guidance offered either in the statutes themselves, the courts or the literature as to how these provisions are to be applied or even whether they create legal rights for any who consider they are affected (Bainbridge 2012).

Also worth mentioning, more for what they do not say about environmental sustainability, are the Principles of Corporate Governance (OECD 2004) (now republished as G20/OECD Principles of Corporate Governance 2015), specifically Principle 4. "The corporate governance framework should recognize the rights of stakeholders established by law or through mutual agreements and encourage active co-operation between corporations and stakeholders in creating wealth, jobs, and the sustainability of financially sound enterprises" (OECD 2004, p. 21). The wording here clearly points to financial viability as the determination of sustainability (an inward oriented perspective or, more charitably, one that refers to pricing mechanisms for the environment rather than base-line standards). The Principles of Corporate Governance (American Law Institute 1994) are also noteworthy, particularly s2.01(1) in that while stating, as a priority, the "enhance[ment] of profit and shareholder interest", provide in s2.01(1)(b) (2) for boards to take into account ethical considerations and (3) devote a "reasonable" level of resources to public welfare, humanitarian, educational and philanthropic purposes. This wording is interesting: arguably environmental sustainability could fit into any of the words under (3) but more in the sense of charitable munificence (an aspect of CSR) than as a central aspect of corporate endeavor.

Connecticut is somewhat unusual in North America in mandating regard of non-shareholder concerns (which may include the environment) via the Conn. Gen. Stat 33–756(d). Similarly, the UK Companies Act 2006, s172 (articulating the directors' fiduciary duty to promote the success of the company) specifically requires that directors have regard, *inter alia*, to the "long-term consequences" and the "impact on the community and the environment". It is notable that this requirement was considered highly contentious at the time in seemingly shifting the focus of governance from the short-term benefit for shareholders to the broader long-term context (Standen 2006b) and for articulating "an obligation [on directors] to have regard to [competing] factors" (Farrar 2008, p. 496). However, both the Act and section are silent on the extent to which directors need to incorporate such considerations into decisions and the relative weight they should be accorded (Farrar 2008). Keay (2010b), in his lengthy discussion on this section, finally concludes that despite stated (reforming) intentions of government and policy-makers in introducing this new provision, the way in which it is interpreted and applied is little different to what was happening under previous common law. In the end, having "regard" is a long way from a requirement to "incorporate" or "pursue". Neither of these pieces of legislation requires those involved in governance to pursue environmental sustainability, a result that leaves it essentially in a vacuum, subject to the vagaries of the markets and investor sentiments (or what directors believe those sentiments to be).

What is it possible to conclude, therefore, about whether and how the duty of directors to act in good faith and in the best interests of the company works to encourage governance for sustainability? If directors are encouraged to incorporate sustainability as part of their fiduciary obligation, to what extent and how effective might such encouragement be? We draw some conclusions around these questions below.

## Conclusion

It is possible for directors to pursue governance for sustainability provided they are confident that there is (some) market benefit in so doing and, therefore, a strategy that recognizes and furthers the benefit to shareholders. The Court is unlikely to judge directors as being in breach of their fiduciary duty to act in good faith and in the interests of the company for decisions made on this basis, provided they can demonstrate a careful, considered process and conclusion which supported such an approach.

Debates surrounding the issue of how to advance legal theories and norms relating to directors' duties to advance a modest notion of corporate social responsibility within the framework of corporate governance are many and remain unresolved (Waitzer and Jaswal 2012). Recommendations being promoted are mostly based on the assumption that clarification of the role and accountability of directors manifestly involves a move towards greater scrutiny regarding the interests which directors should consider and the commitment of directors to long-term value maximization.

Statutory and "soft" law provisions do little to change the *status quo* where specific provisions focus more on compliance aspects than on corporate performance. Governance for sustainability thus remains driven by boards and CEOs of companies, shaped by groups and sectors which can exert influence (e.g. shareholders, depending on number and type; the media, via reports and articles; customers through purchase decisions; and governments via threatened or actual law reform). While historically consistent, the "soft" law approach could be considered too tentative in view of the impact of business on the environment and the serious environmental issues facing humanity (Mac Cormac and Haney 2012).

Civil society, within which corporations are citizens (Waitzer and Jaswal 2012), may be less advanced than we would like to believe in deconstructing the walls between the company and its external environment, even if stakeholder theorists see this as the most desirable outcome. Without a satisfactory anchoring mechanism for sustainability and a lack of standardized reporting requirements for critical (and arguably material) social and environmental elements, there remains a risk of director liability where such objectives are prioritized. It may also be that without fundamental change the gap is unbridgeable between what is expected from the corporate sector and what can realistically be achieved. On the assumption that the gap can be narrowed, one approach with regard to the environment might be to expand the fiduciary duty of directors to include an obligation to future generations to minimize the corporation's environmental impacts (Henderson 2011). While this option represents a direct challenge to the shareholder value maximization model, the lag between cause and effect from externalizing the costs of environmental harm may not be value maximizing after all but instead simply transfer such costs onto future generations.

An alternative is to develop a framework which encompasses an appropriate and generally agreed definition of sustainability, a generally agreed measure and valuation for environmental inputs and outputs, regulatory neutrality (thus removing non-sustainable competitive advantage) and an acknowledgement by both the private and public sectors as to the key social and economic roles played by business. Research which conceptualizes and tests such a framework and opens the debate as to how it could be developed into policy and statute would be useful as a vehicle for bringing sustainability more effectively within the purview of corporate purpose. The determination of proper corporate purpose, directors' duties and accountability depends ultimately on an understanding of the role of the corporation in our society and the core values which underpin that role.

## Bibliography

American Law Institute (1994), *Principles of Good Corporate Governance*, American Law Institute: Philadelphia, PA.

Aras, G. and Crowther, D. (2008), 'Governance and Sustainability: An Investigation into the Relationship Between Corporate Governance and Corporate Sustainability', *Management Decision*, vol. 46, no. 3, pp. 433–448.

Bainbridge, S. (1992), 'Interpreting Nonshareholder Constituency Statutes', *Pepperdine Law Review*, vol. 19, pp. 991–1025.

Bainbridge, S. (2012), *The Shareholder Wealth Maximization Principle Versus Non-Shareholder Constituency Statutes*. Available from http://www.professorbainbridge.com/professorbain bridgecom/2012/05/the-shareholder-wealth-maximization-principle-versus-non-shareholder-constituency-statutes.html.

Beder, S. (2002), 'Economy or Environment: Competitors or Partners?' *Pacific Ecologist*, vol. 3 (Spring), pp. 50–56.

Buchholz, R. and Rosenthal, S. (2005), 'Toward a Contemporary Conceptual Framework for Stakeholder Theory,' *Journal of Business Ethics*, vol. 58, pp. 137–48.

Caldelli, A. and Parmigiani, M. (2004), 'Management Information Systems – A Tool for Corporate Sustainability,' *Journal of Business Ethics*, vol. 55, pp. 159–171.

Caswell, T. (2004a), 'Sustainability: A Vital Agenda for 21st Century Good Governance: Part 1', *Keeping Good Companies*, vol. 56, no. 2, pp. 85–90.

Caswell, T. (2004b), 'Sustainability, a Vital Agenda for 21st Century Good Governance: Part 2', *Keeping Good Companies*, vol. 56, no. 3, pp. 149–153.

Cherapanukorn, V. and Focken, K. (2014), 'Corporate Social Responsibility (CSR) and Sustainability in Asian Luxury Hotels: Policies, Practices and Standards,' *Asian Social Science*, vol. 10, no. 8, pp. 198–209.

Corporations and Markets Advisory Committee. (2006), *The Social Responsibility of Corporations*. Australian Government, Canberra, Australia. Available from http://www.camac.gov.au/camac/camac.nsf/byheadline/whats+newmedia+release+csr+report.html.

Coulson-Thomas, C. (2014), *Governance, Sustainability and Regulation*. Available from https://www.academia.edu/9057970/Governance_Sustainability_and_Regulation.

Cowan, D., Dopart, P., Ferracini, T., Sahmel, J., Merryman, K., Gaffney, S. and Paustenbach, D. (2010), 'A Cross-sectional Analysis of Reported Corporate Environmental Sustainability Practices', *Regulatory Toxicology and Pharmacology*, vol. 58, no. 3, pp. 524–538.

Daily Mail Reporter. (2011), 'News Corp Gave $1million to Business Lobby that Campaigned Against U.S. Laws that Would Punish It for Bribery in Britain. July 15', *Mail Online*. Available from http://www.dailymail.co.uk/news/article-2015089/News-Corp-gave-1million-business-lobby-campaigned-U-S-laws-punish-Bribery-Britain.html.

Davis, A. (2006), *Best Practice in Corporate Governance. Building Reputation and Sustainable Success*. Gower, Aldershot.

Doward, J. (2013), 'Plain Packaging Lobbyists Under Fire Over Links to Tobacco Company', *The Guardian*. April 28. Available from http://www.theguardian.com/business/2013/apr/28/plain-packaging-lobbyists-links-tobacco-company.

Dowse, J. (2009), 'Citizens Within Corporates – Parts to be Played to Gain Value from Sustainability,' *Keeping Good Companies*, vol. 60, no. 1, pp. 10–15.

Dunphy, D., Griffiths, A., and Benn, S. (2003), *Organizational Change for Corporate Responsibility*, 2nd Ed. Routledge, London, England.

Dyllick, T., and Hockerts, K. (2002), 'Beyond the Business Case for Corporate Sustainability', *Business Strategy and the Environment*, vol. 11, no. 2, pp. 130–141.

Esty, D. and Winston, A. (2009), *Green to Gold: How Smart Companies Use Environmental Strategy to Innovate, Create Value, and Build Competitive Advantage*. Yale University Press, New Haven, MA.

Farrar, J. (2008), *Corporate Governance, Takeovers, Principles and Practice*, OUP, Melbourne, Australia.

Freeman, R. (1984), *Strategic Management: A Stakeholder Approach*. Pitman, Boston, MA.

Friedman, M. (1970), 'The Social Responsibility of Business is to Increase Its Profits', *New York Times Magazine*. September 13.

G20/OECD (2015) Principles of Corporate Governance, OECD, Available at: <http://www.oecd-ilibrary.org/docserver/download/2615021e.pdf?expires=1469936136&id=id&accname=guest&checksum=6FC9D1C90C33B1716F76042440162E04>.

Galanis, M. (2011), 'Vicious Spirals in Corporate Governance: Mandatory Rules for Systemic (Re).Balancing?' *Oxford Journal of Legal Studies*, vol. 31, no. 2, pp. 327–363.

Global Trends (2013), *Corporate Clout 2013: Time for Responsible Capitalism*. Available from http://www.globaltrends.com/knowledge-center/features/shapers-and-influencers/190-corporate-clout-2013-time-for-responsible-capitalism.

Graci, S., and Dodds, R. (2008), ' "Why Go Green?" The Business Case for Environmental Commitment in the Canadian Hotel Industry,' *Anatolia*, vol. 19, pp. 251–270.

Gravelle, R. (1996–7). 'Enforcing the Elusive: Environmental Rights in East European Countries', *Virginia Environmental Law Journal*, vol.16, pp. 633–694.

Greenberg, D. (2007), 'Making Corporate Social Responsibility an Everyday Part of the Business of Business: Offering Realistic Options for Regulatory Reform,' *Bond Law Review*, vol. 19, no. 2, pp. 41–57.

Gunningham, A. and Sinclair, D. (2002), *Leaders and Laggards: Next-Generation Environmental Regulation*, Greenleaf, Sheffield, UK.

Hardin, G. (1968), 'The Tragedy of the Commons,' *Science*, vol. 162, no. 3859, pp. 1242–1248.

Henderson, G. (2011), 'A Fiduciary Duty to Minimize the Corporation's Environmental Impacts,' *University of Oslo Faculty of Law Research Paper No. 2011–32*.

Heyvaert, V. (2012), 'Regulatory Competition – Accounting for the Transnational Dimension of Environmental Regulation,' *Journal of Environmental Law*, vol. 25, no. 1, pp. 1–31.

Ho, V. (2010), 'Enlightened Shareholder Value: Corporate Governance Beyond the Shareholder-Stakeholder Divide,' *Journal of Corporate Law*, vol. 36, no. 1, pp. 59–112.

Horrigan, B. (2002), 'Fault Lines in the Intersection Between Corporate Governance and Social Responsibility,' *University of New South Wales Law Journal*, vol. 25, no. 2, pp. 515–555.

Horrigan, B. (2007), '21st Century Corporate Social Responsibility Trends – An Emerging Comparative Body of Law and Regulation on Corporate Responsibility, Governance, and Sustainability,' *Macquarie Journal of Business Law*, vol. 4, pp. 85–122.

Hoovestal, L. (2013), *Globalization Contained: the Economic and Strategic Consequences of the Container*. Palgrave Macmillan, New York.

Hult, G.T. (2011), 'Market-Focused Sustainability: Market Orientation Plus!', *Journal of the Academy of Marketing Science*, vol. 39, no. 1, pp. 1–6.

Idris, S. (1990), 'Going Green – A Third World Perspective,' *Chain Reaction*, vol. 62, pp. 16–17.

Keay, A. (2007), 'Tackling the Issue of the Corporate Objective: An Analysis of the United Kingdom's "Enlightened Shareholder Value Approach"', *Sydney Law Review*, vol. 29, no. 4, pp. 577–612.

Keay, A. (2008), 'Ascertaining the Corporate Objective: An Entity Maximization and Sustainability Model', *Modern Law Review*, vol. 71, no. 5, pp. 663–698.

Keay, A. (2010a), 'The Ultimate Objective of the Company and the Enforcement of the Entity Maximization and Sustainability Model,' *Journal of Corporate Law Studies*, vol. 10, no. 1, pp. 35–71.

Keay, A. (2010b), *The Duty to Promote the Success of the Company: Is it Fit for Purpose?* University of Leeds School of Law, Centre for Business Law and Practice Working Paper, Leeds, England, doi: http://dx.doi.org/10.2139/ssrn.1662411.

Keys, T. and Malnight, T. (2010), *Corporate Clout Distributed: The Influence of the World's Largest 100 Economic Entities*. Strategy Dynamic Global Ltd. Available from https://www.globaltrends.com/reports/?doc_id=500537&task=view_details.

Kim, E., and Lyon, T. (2011), 'Strategic Environmental Disclosure: Evidence From the DOE's Voluntary Greenhouse Gas Registry,' *Journal of Environmental Economics and Management*, vol. 61, no. 3, pp. 311–26.

Klettner, A., Clarke, T. and Boersma, M. (2014),'The Governance of Corporate Sustainability: Empirical Insights into the Development, Leadership and Implementation of Responsible Business Strategy,' *Journal of Business Ethics*, vol. 122, no. 1, pp. 145–165.

Kolk, A. and van Tulder, R. (2010), 'International Business, Corporate Social Responsibility and Sustainable Development', *International Business Review*, vol. 19, no. 2, pp. 119–125.

Langton, R. and Trotman, L. (1999), 'Defining "the Best Interests of the Corporation": Some Australian Reform Proposals,' *Flinders Journal of Law Reform*, vol. 32, pp. 163–181.

Legge, J. (2008), 'Making Corporations Responsible', *Dissent*, no. 27, pp. 31–6.

Lourenço, I., Branco, M., Curto, J. and Eugénio, T. (2012), 'How Does the Market Value Corporate Sustainability Performance?' *Journal of Business Ethics*, vol. 108, no. 4, pp. 417–428.

MacCormac, S. and Haney, H. (2012), 'New Corporate Forms: One Viable Solution to Advancing Environmental Sustainability,' *Journal of Applied Corporate Finance*, vol. 24, no. 2, pp. 49–56.

Manning, B. (1984), 'The Business Judgment Rule and the Director's Duty of Attention: Time for Reality', *Business Law,* vol. 39, no. 4, pp. 1477–1501.

Mansell, R. and Prill, B. (2003), 'Beyond Environmental Compliance, with a View to the Best Interests of the Company'. In Sarra, J. (ed.). *Corporate Governance in Global Capital Markets*. UBC Press, Vancouver, BC, pp. 174–188.

Martinelli, A., and Midttun, A. (2010), 'Globalization and Governance for Sustainability,' *Corporate Governance*, vol. 10, no. 1, pp. 6–17.

Millon, D. (2010), *Enlightened Shareholder Value, Social Responsibility, and the Redefinition of Corporate Purpose Without Law.* Washington and Lee Legal Studies Paper No. 2010–11. doi: http://dx.doi.org/10.2139/ssrn.1625750.

Mitchell, R., Agle, N. and Wood, D. (1997), 'Towards a Theory of Stakeholder Identification and Salience: Defining the Principle of Who and What Really Counts,' *Academy of Management Review*, vol. 22, no. 4, pp. 853–886.

Murray, D. and Ayoun, B. (2010), 'Hospitality Student Perceptions on the Use of Sustainable Business Practices as a Means of Signaling Attractiveness and Attracting Future Employees,' *Journal of Human Resources in Hospitality and Tourism*, vol. 10, no. 1, pp. 60–79.

Mygind, N. (2009), 'Stakeholder Ownership and Maximization', *Corporate Governance*, vol. 9, no. 2, pp. 158–174.

Ng, T. (2011), 'Environmental Rights: Progressive Development or Obfuscation of International Human Rights Law?' *The Original Law Review*, vol. 7, no. 3, pp. 72–104.

OECD. (2004), *Principles of Corporate Governance.* OECD, Paris, France, http://www.oecd.org/dataoecd/32/18/31557724.pdf.

Ong, D. (2001), 'The Impact of Environmental Law on Corporate Governance: International and Comparative Perspectives,' *European Journal of International Law*, vol. 12, no. 4, pp. 685–726.

Orts, E.W. and Strudler, A. (2009), 'Putting a Stake in Stakeholder Theory', *Journal of Business Ethics*, vol. 88, no. 4, pp. 605–615.

Paramasivan, T. (2009), *Sustainability Reporting.* Available from http://www.experiencefestival.com/wp/article/sustainability-reporting.

Perera, A., Putt del Pino, S., and Oliveira, B. (2013), *Aligning Profit and Environmental Sustainability: Stories from Industry.* World Resources Institute, Washington, DC.

Pesquex, Y. (2009), 'Sustainable Development: A Vague and Ambiguous Theory,' *Society and Business Review*, vol. 4, no. 3, pp. 231–245.

Postglione, A. (2010), *Global Environmental Governance: The Need for an International Environmental Agency and an International Court of the Environment.* International Court of the Environment Foundation: Emile, Belgium: Bruylant.

Rainey, D. (2006), Sustainable Business Development: Inventing the Future Through Strategy, Innovation, and Leadership. In *E-books Corporation* (ed.), Cambridge University Press, Cambridge, England.

Russell, S., Haigh, N. and Griffiths, A. (2007), 'Understanding Corporate Sustainability: Recognizing the Impact of Different Governance Systems.' In Benn, S. and Dunphy, D. (eds.). *Corporate Governance and Sustainability*. Routledge, Abingdon, England, pp. 36–56.

Sethi, P. (2005), 'Investing in Socially Responsible Companies is a Must for Public Pension Funds: Because There is No Better Alternative,' *Journal of Business Ethics*, vol. 56, no. 2, pp. 99–129.

Shrivastava, P. (1995), 'The Role of Corporations in Achieving Ecological Sustainability,' *The Academy of Management Review*, vol. 20, no. 4, pp. 936–960.

Smith, D.G. (1997–8), 'The Shareholder Primacy Norm,' *Journal of Corporate Law*, vol. 23 (Winter), pp. 277–323.

Sommer, A. (1995), 'Whom Should the Corporation Serve? The Berle-Dodd Debate Revisited 60 Years Later', *Delaware Journal of Corporate Law*, vol. 16, pp. 33–56.

Springer, J. (1999), 'Corporate Constituency Statutes: Hollow Hopes and False Fears,' *Annual Survey of American Law*, vol. 85, no. 1, pp. 43–84.

Standen, M. (2006a), 'CAMAC's Discussion Paper on Corporate Social Responsibility: Is it Time for a Change?,' *Keeping Good Companies*, vol. 58, no. 2, pp. 98–103.

Standen, M. (2006b), 'The Corporation in Society: Time to Revise its Role?' *Australian Law Reform Commission Journal*, no. 87, pp. 12–16.

Stout, L. (2002), 'Bad and Not-so-bad Arguments for Shareholder Primacy,' *Southern Californian Law Review*, vol. 75, pp. 1189–1212.

Stout, L.A., (2012), *The Shareholder Value Myth: how Putting Shareholders First Harms Investors, Corporations, and the Public*, 1st Ed. Berrett-Koehler, San Francisco, CA.

Strasser, K. (2011), *Myths and Realities of Business Environmentalism Good Works, Good Business or Greenwash?* Edward Elgar Publishing Limited, Cheltenham, England.

Strine, L. (2008), 'Human Freedom and Two Friedmen: Musings on the Implications of Globalization for the Effective Regulation of Corporate Behavior,' *University of Toronto Law Journal*, vol. 58, no. 3, pp. 268–317.

Sundaram, A. and Inkpen, A. (2004), 'The Corporate Objective Revisited,' *Organization Science*, vol. 15, no. 3, pp. 350–363.

Sustainalytics (2011), *Sustainability and Materiality in the Natural Resources Sector*. Sustainalytics, Toronto, CA. Available from http://www.sustainalytics.com/sustainability-and-materiality-natural-resources-sector.

Trucost (2013), *Natural Capital at Risk: The Top 100 Externalities of Business*. Trucost Plc, London. Available from http://www.trucost.com/published-research/99/natural-capital-at-risk-the-top-100-externalities-of-business.

Union of Concerned Scientists (2012), *A Climate of Corporate Control, How Corporations Have Influenced the U.S. Dialogue on Climate Change and Policy*. UCSUSA, Cambridge, MA.

Von Geibler, J. (2012), 'Market-based Governance for Sustainability in Value Chains: Conditions for Successful Standard Setting in the Palm Oil Sector,' *Journal of Cleaner Production*, vol. 56, pp. 39–53.

Waitzer, E. and Jaswal, J. (2012), 'The Good Corporate Citizen,' *Advances in Business Ethics Research*, vol. 1, pp. 127–172.

Waring, P. (2008), 'Rethinking Directors' Duties in Changing Global Markets,' *Corporate Governance*, vol. 8, no. 2, pp. 153–164.

Werder, A.V. (2011), 'Corporate Governance and Stakeholder Opportunism,' *Organization Science*, vol. 22, no. 5, pp. 1345–1358.

Willard, B. (2012), *The New Sustainability Advantage: Seven Business Case Benefits of a Triple Bottom Line* (Completely Revised 10th Anniversary Edition.). New Society Publishers, Gabriola Island, BC.

Zhang, B., Bi, J., Yuan, Z., Ge, J., Liu, B. and Bu, M. (2008), 'Why Do Firms Engage in Environmental Management? An Empirical Study in China,' *Journal of Cleaner Production*, vol. 16, no. 1, pp. 1036–1045.

Chapter 5

# Governing corporate responsibility
## The role of soft regulation

*Alice Klettner*

## Corporate responsibility

Famously debated in 1932 by Berle and Dodd in the *Harvard Law Review* (Berle 1932, Dodd 1932, Wells 2002), there has been a resurgence of interest in corporate responsibility in the last two decades and a growing expectation that companies should take action and report on their efforts to be more responsible. Perhaps more importantly, there has been a huge change in corporate practice in the area of corporate reporting. Professional services firm KPMG has monitored the number of companies publishing information on corporate responsibility since 1993. Using a sample made up of the 100 largest companies in each of 34 countries, reporting on corporate social responsibility went from 12% in 1993 to 71% in 2013 (KPMG 2011, p. 21). In the 250 largest global companies there has been an increase in corporate social responsibility reporting from 35% in 1999 to 93% in 2013 (KPMG 2011, p. 38). This is a striking change in reporting and yet little is known about whether it reflects equally striking changes within corporations.

At its simplest corporate responsibility can be defined as a company operating in an economically, socially and environmentally sustainable manner or at least "considering, managing and balancing the economic, social and environmental impacts of its activities" (Parliamentary Joint Committee on Corporations and Financial Services 2006, p. xiii). There is a wide literature on the reasons why companies might take this approach: the business case for corporate responsibility is that it can improve corporate success through, amongst other things, improving reputation, motivating employees and reducing risk (Anderson 2005, p. 153; Corporations and Markets Advisory Committee 2006, para 2.3.3). Equally there are many sceptics of the concept who believe a company can only truly be responsible to one group and that this should be the shareholders (Jensen 2002). This view was famously put forward by Milton Friedman in stating "there is one and only one social responsibility of business – to use its resources and engage in activities designed to increase its profits so long as it stays within the rules of the game" (Friedman 1962, p. 133). Nevertheless, levels of reporting suggest a developing acceptance amongst large corporations that efforts towards improved corporate sustainability are not only expected but are of value to the business. However, the voluntary nature of this reporting, in a market that places strong emphasis on short-term share price, means a level of scepticism must be maintained.

## Challenges of corporate responsibility

Corporate responsibility faces many challenges both in practice and in theory. In many jurisdictions the traditional purpose of setting up a business in the form of a corporation is to limit personal liability and encourage investment through the selling of shares which hold the potential for future profit. Thus the first challenge for corporate responsibility is a rethinking of the theory behind the corporation to recognise more fully the contribution of all stakeholders and not just the shareholders. This theoretical debate is reflected in the law and regulation surrounding corporate behaviour which varies across different countries. Indeed, because the concept of corporate responsibility is in some ways contrary to the foundations of corporate law in many countries, as well as being very difficult to define, regulation in this area often takes the form of voluntary standards. The voluntary nature of corporate activity and reporting brings its own challenges of validity and legitimacy. Lastly, for companies who are choosing to embark on a more responsible future, there is the practical problem of how to implement and govern corporate responsibility in order to both integrate and institutionalise it across an organisation.

### Purpose of the corporation

Both the strategic purpose and objectives of the corporation and the nature of reporting on the achievement of these objectives remains tenuous and contested in terms of the law in many jurisdictions (Clarke 2013, Stout 2012). Many Northern European countries have built on their social-democratic traditions and have evolved strong stakeholder orientations based on the understanding that other groups, in addition to shareholders, make a contribution to the company's capital. However, some Anglo-Saxon jurisdictions have still not formally embraced the stakeholder concept in anything other than a very narrow sense (Keay 2007). Although the law in these countries can be interpreted to support the concept of corporate responsibility, it certainly does not mandate it. The issue is left to the discretion of corporate directors and there is a lack of clarity on how to implement corporate responsibility in practice and how to report on the topic. Despite this, most large companies say a great deal, publishing weighty reports on their achievements. This chapter examines the soft law influencing this behaviour and its role in improving corporate responsibility.

### Regulation through soft law

With the development and widespread voluntary uptake of international standards and frameworks for corporate responsibility such as the United Nations Global Compact (UNGC) and the Global Reporting Initiative (GRI), research into effective implementation is becoming more and more important (Baumann and Scherer 2010, Maon et al. 2009, Schembera 2012). These instruments provide broad principles and reporting frameworks but leave it up to the companies to decide how to implement these principles. The GRI has been adopted by companies world-wide as a means of reporting on corporate responsibility. Together with many other international, national and private sector initiatives, this has disseminated the knowledge and practice of sustainability and corporate social responsibility to a level of global significance (Gobbels 2006).

On the other hand, this proliferating range of sustainability standards and initiatives poses its own challenges of choice and legitimacy. Quite rightly there remains scepticism about corporate motivations surrounding corporate responsibility and whether reporting actually translates to positive action on the part of companies:

> This ability to implement policies founded upon a concept that remains ambiguous raises a number of questions regarding the definition employed by those who profess a commitment to CSR, why they have chosen to implement CSR policies, how they develop those policies and their value in terms of reducing the adverse impact of corporate activity.
>
> (Whitehouse 2006, p. 280)

Are these frameworks simply being used as window dressing or are they motivating real change? The development of corporate responsibility can be piecemeal and reactive (Yuan et al. 2011). Initiatives may be developed by companies as a response to the specific demands of external stakeholders or after a negative event in order to repair a company's reputation and regain the trust of customers or investors. The use of sustainability reporting in this way has been termed "greenwashing" and can be explained by the legitimacy theory of social disclosure:

> Based on this theory, companies facing greater exposure, as firms with poorer environmental performance are assumed to do, would be expected to provide more extensive off-setting or positive environmental disclosures in an attempt to address the increased threats to their legitimacy.
>
> (Cho and Patten 2007, p. 640)

In examining the response of managers to shareholder activism, David et al. concluded that "managers may opt for symbolic, rather than substantive, responses to external pressures" (2007, p. 98). For example, when it comes to environmental performance, Berrone and Gomez Meja point out that it might be easier for a company to set up a board environment committee than to actually reduce or eliminate toxic emissions (2009a, p. 120).

On the positive side, Douglas Branson has described the emergence of a "new corporate social responsibility movement, different from previous efforts because of its convergence with good corporate governance" (2001, p. 647). Corporate governance and corporate responsibility were for many years seen as different issues but the overlap between the two is becoming increasingly evident as corporate responsibility becomes more mainstream. Corporate responsibility has moved from being a marketing response towards being a key element of business strategy. This change requires leadership from the top and integration of corporate responsibility across all aspects of the business. In 2006, John Elkington, co-founder of SustainAbility, also wrote about the merging of corporate social responsibility with corporate governance: "The centre of gravity of the sustainable business debate is in the process of shifting from public relations to competitive advantage and corporate governance – and, in the process, from the factory fence to the boardroom" (p. 524). If CSR strategies and policies are to have real effect their implementation must be led and monitored by the board in the same way as other corporate strategies.

## Defining corporate responsibility

Corporate responsibility is a famously difficult concept to define (Whitehouse 2006, p. 279). Indeed, reviewing the multitude of definitions available has become a field of study in itself (Dahlsrud 2008, Moir 2001). The Australian Parliamentary Joint Committee on Corporations and Financial Services commented in its 2006 report on corporate responsibility that the terms "corporate responsibility", "corporate social responsibility (CSR)", "corporate social transparency", "triple bottom line", "corporate sustainability" and "social and environmental responsibility" are all used to refer to broadly the same concept (p. 4–5). In this chapter, the term "corporate responsibility" is used interchangeably with the terms "corporate sustainability" and "CSR", to include social as well as environmental aspects of acting responsibly. The working definition adopted by the PJC Report was:

> Corporate responsibility is usually described in terms of a company considering, managing and balancing the economic, social and environmental impacts of its activities. It is about companies assessing and managing risks, pursuing opportunities and creating corporate value, in areas beyond what would traditionally be regarded as a company's core business. It is also about companies taking an "enlightened self-interest" approach to considering the legitimate interests of a company's stakeholders.
>
> (Parliamentary Joint Committee on Corporations and Financial Services 2006, p. 4)

It is important when looking at CSR in a legal context to understand that it encompasses the voluntary aspects of corporate behaviour that go over and above a company's legal obligations. Carroll's pyramid of corporate responsibility developed in 1991 is still helpful in clarifying the scope of corporate responsibility. He placed economic viability at the base of the pyramid as the foundation for corporate activity. This is important as some opponents of CSR suggest that it is about compromising profits to do good. This is not the understanding taken in this chapter; rather, CSR is concerned with creating profits without causing undue harm.

The next layer of Carroll's pyramid comprises the need to comply with relevant law. Even Milton Friedman agreed that companies must play within the rules of the game (Friedman 1962). Every company must comply with relevant environment, employment and occupational health and safety laws, as well as laws that protect corporate creditors and consumers (Anderson 2005, p. 149). In fact many opponents of CSR claim that these specific laws are the correct way to protect society, and that the responsibility should remain on government (rather than companies) to implement protective legislation where necessary.

Next in Carroll's pyramid is the layer of corporate responsibility that this chapter is dealing with – voluntary activities that fall within the scope of ethical behaviour rather than compliance. Thus we are, by definition, not in the realm of hard law but that of soft law – recommendations, standards and guidelines. Carroll defines ethical responsibilities as "those standards, norms or expectations that reflect a concern for what consumers, employees, shareholders and the community regard as fair, just or in keeping with the respect or protection of stakeholders' moral rights" (1991,

p. 41). Immediately we have the introduction of the concept of stakeholders which is core to both the theory and practice of corporate responsibility. In practice, "corporate behaviour is socially responsible as long as it meets [stakeholders'] expectations regarding appropriate and acceptable corporate behaviour" (Campbell 2007, p. 950).

Thus the task of defining corporate responsibility is in the hands of each company's stakeholders, who in turn need to be defined and identified. A commonly used definition of corporate stakeholders is all those with an interest in the company's operations (Freeman 1994, Freeman and Reed 1990). This is usually taken to include shareholders, employees, customers, suppliers, regulators, government, local communities and groups representing the environment. It means that corporate responsibility will have a unique meaning for every company and is a dynamic concept that will change depending on the expectations of society and the operations of any particular corporation:

> It is important to reemphasize that corporate sustainability is fundamentally a complex problem and there are no approaches that universally apply. Corporations are faced with differing stakeholder demands, continually shifting priorities, and a multitude of alternatives to address their sustainability challenges.
>
> (Searcy 2012, p. 250)

Lastly, it is important to mention the top of Carroll's pyramid where he placed philanthropy to describe companies going further than ethics and positively contributing to social welfare. Philanthropy should not be classed as corporate responsibility for two reasons. Firstly, it can be a dangerous distraction from fundamentally irresponsible business practices: in the past companies may have attempted to balance the harming effects of their operations by donating profits towards charities that mitigate the effects of such harm. Secondly, there is a legal argument that donating profits to charities that have no connection with a company's operations has the potential to be contrary to directors' legal duty to act in the best interests of the corporation (Corporations and Markets Advisory Committee 2006, p. 37, Klein and du Plessis 2005). This chapter takes corporate responsibility as pertaining to the core operations of an organisation and the way in which these are carried out rather than peripheral activities.

## Regulating corporate responsibility

On the basis that CSR is a difficult concept to define it is not surprising that it is also a difficult concept to regulate. Indeed, if CSR is defined as voluntary behaviour, "the very idea that law might make business responsible for corporate social responsibility is paradoxical": it cannot be possible "for the *law* to make companies accountable for going *beyond the law*" (Parker 2007, p. 207). This has not stopped legislatures, courts and legal commentators from amending and/or interpreting the law to permit CSR as opposed to mandating it.

Sarre comments that the concept of CSR "is a rejection of the notion that prescribing minimum standards and enforcing them by law is an adequate form of regulation" (2002, p. 8). Instead it seems we are expecting companies to meet a wide variety of higher standards prescribed rather vaguely by a multitude of stakeholders. There are many influential organisations encouraging and influencing corporate behaviour through stock exchange listing requirements, institutional investment guidelines, reporting standards and market pressures. This is a new form of regulation that is steadily influencing our corporations, sometimes with little control or monitoring by government. In the United States, this style of contemporary regulation has been termed "new governance". Ford and Condon explain some of the elements agreed to be central to new governance including "a restructured and more collaborative relationship between the state and regulated entities based on the recognition that regulation may operate most effectively when it incorporates private actors' context-specific experience and relevant expertise" (2011, p. 450). Perhaps it is society's way of dealing with the deficiencies of law which tends to be reactive rather than proactive, slow and inflexible. These new regulatory frameworks mean it is not always a simple task to categorise a company's activities as voluntary or mandatory. As Martin comments, "the line between CSR and voluntary action and what the law requires is often rather thin. Many of the CSR voluntary activities are underpinned by a strong legislative framework and many follow directly from it" (Martin 2005, p. 91). Nevertheless, most of the regulation surrounding CSR reporting tends to fall on the more voluntary side of the equation. Indeed, although environmental, employment or occupational health and safety law may influence CSR activities, corporate law in Anglo-American jurisdictions is still relatively quiet on the issue.

### Australia

McConvill and Joy optimistically observed in 2003 that "the emerging trend is that social and environmental concerns will be incorporated into the legal framework which governs corporations" (p. 117). Despite much debate, this has still not occurred in Australia. In 2006 the results of two major inquiries into Australia's legal framework surrounding CSR were released, both focusing on the scope of directors' duties under the *Corporations Act 2001* as well as the framework for corporate reporting on CSR. The first was by the Corporations and Markets Advisory Committee (CAMAC Report) and the second by the Parliamentary Joint Committee on Corporations and Financial Services (PJC Report). Neither of these recommended any changes to the law, arguing that directors' duties could be interpreted to permit a stakeholder approach and whether or not to take such an approach should be left to the discretion of directors.

The relevant legal duties of Australian company directors are "to act in good faith in the best interests of the company" and "for a proper purpose". These duties exist both as fiduciary duties under the common law as well as being codified in sections 180 and 181 of the *Corporations Act 2001*. Until the 1980s these duties, especially the duty of care, were viewed as a relatively undemanding performance standard, used infrequently by shareholders in private actions against directors in circumstances of extreme neglect or obvious wrong-doing (Corbett and Bottomley 2004, p. 67). Only as companies have gotten larger and more powerful has it become obvious that the general public might also be concerned by the actions of directors.

There has been relatively little case law expanding on the detailed meaning of directors' duties although it was for many years understood that the "interests of the company" equated to the interests of its shareholders as a general group rather than the company as a firm (Farrar 2008, p. 109, Redmond 2012, p. 325, Kingsford Smith 2012, p. 400). This principle of "shareholder primacy" has been much debated in recent years in the context of whether companies and their directors should be more widely accountable, not only to shareholders but to local communities and the environment (Stout 2002).

Both Australian inquiry reports suggested there may be an implied duty on directors to take these factors into account on the basis that doing so is likely to be in the long-term interests of the company and its shareholders. The view was that the law permits flexibility and does not restrict directors from taking non-shareholder interests into account. As the CAMAC Report said: "The established formulation of directors' duties allows directors sufficient flexibility to take relevant interests and broader community considerations into account" (2006, p.7). Taking action to reduce damage to the environment or to treat employees equitably (to the extent this is over and above what is required by environmental or employment law) is therefore an optional choice for companies, motivated by a desire to improve corporate reputation and/or long-term sustainability (Sneirson 2009).

Recent case law on the topic supports this view. Justice Owen commented in 2008 that, although the established position is that "a reflection of the interests of the company may be seen in the interests of shareholders", this does not mean that "the general body of shareholders is always and for all purposes the embodiment of the company as a whole" (Marshall and Ramsay 2009, p. 10). In short, we are at a stage where directors are permitted to take different stakeholder interests into account but only to the point that this can be argued to be good for long-term shareholder wealth (Redmond 2012, p. 324). It would be hard for directors to make decisions that treat the well-being of employees or the environment as the primary cause for action (unless based on other legal obligations under employment or environmental law). Marshall and Ramsay state, "the extension of *duties* of directors has not been attended by the extension of *rights* for stakeholders" (2009, p. 16). Although the directors' duty to act in the best interests of the corporation has been interpreted to permit consideration of the interests of all stakeholders, there is no express legal requirement to do so and the extent to which this is done is at the discretion of the board. The argument against expanding directors' duties to expressly include all stakeholders is that it would leave them accountable to no one and struggling to determine priorities amidst conflicting interests. The CAMAC Report concluded

> that the proposed changes do not provide meaningful clarification for directors, yet risk obscuring their accountability.
>
> (2006, p. 7)

## United Kingdom

Nevertheless, several years ago the United Kingdom did exactly this and no accountability problems appear to have arisen (Keay 2007). Section 172(1) *Companies Act*

*2006* expressly includes the interests of a wide range of stakeholders as matters that directors must have regard to:

> A director of a company must act in a way that he considers, in good faith, would be most likely to promote the success of the company for the benefit of its members as a whole, and in doing so have regard (amongst other matters) to –
>
> (a) the likely consequences of any decision in the long term.
> (b) the interests of the company's employees.
> (c) the need to foster the company's business relationships with suppliers, customers and others.
> (d) the impact of the company's operations on the community and the environment.
> (e) the desirability of the company maintaining a reputation for high standards of business conduct.
> (f) the need to act fairly between the members of the company.

However there is little evidence at this stage that this restatement of directors' duties has in itself made a material difference to board decision-making in the UK (Keay 2010). Although this law better reflects the state of current norms on corporate responsibility, in a practical sense it still gives wide discretion to company directors, arguably entrenching shareholders as the priority group (Keay 2007, p. 592).

### United States

In the US, "constituency statutes" were enacted into the corporations law of more than 40 states from the 1980s onwards as a device to help protect companies faced with hostile predatory takeovers which were fuelled by junk bonds during the aggressive takeover era of the 1980s (takeovers in which all interests were often ignored other than those of the acquirer) (Clarke 1993). Though often portrayed as "stakeholder statutes" designed to protect wider corporate interests than simply shareholders, most of the statutes were concerned largely with what directors could do in the event of a takeover (Keay 2013, p. 190). The statutes in Arizona and Idaho went further and did require directors to consider the long-term interests of the company, while the Connecticut statute expressly empowered direction, empowering directors to consider stakeholder interests where control of the company was at issue:

> [A] director of a corporation shall consider, in determining what he reasonably believes to be in the best interests of the corporation . . . (3) the interests of the corporation's employees, customers, creditors and suppliers, and (4) community and social considerations including those of any community in which any office or other facility of the corporation is located.
>
> (Keay 2013, p. 189)

### Governing corporate responsibility

The governance of corporate responsibility remains a relatively unexplored field in terms of empirical investigation (Asif et al. 2011, Kolk and Pinkse 2010, p. 18, Lindgreen et al. 2008, p. 252; Russel et al. 2007, Runhaar and Lafferty 2009). As yet there is little published academic research in this area although it is a field of emerging interest (Aras and Crowther 2008, Baumann and Scherer 2010, Hansen and Reichwald 2009, Klettner et al. 2014, Kolk 2008, Kolk and Pinkse 2010, Morgan et al. 2009, Schembera 2012). Organisations such as the United Nations are leading the way in

Table 5.1 GRI Guidance on Governance of Sustainability

| GRI Guideline | Summary of Recommended Disclosures |
| --- | --- |
| **Engagement with Stakeholders** | |
| G4–24 | Provide a list of stakeholder groups engaged. |
| G4–25 | Report the basis for selection of those stakeholders. |
| G4–26 | Report the organization's approach to stakeholder engagement. |
| G4–27 | Report key topics and concerns that have been raised. |
| G4–37 | Report processes for consultation between stakeholders and the highest governance body on economic, environmental and social topics. |
| G4–45 | Report whether stakeholder consultation is used to support the highest governance body's identification and management of economic, environmental and social impacts, risks and opportunities. |
| G4–53 | Report how stakeholders' views are sought and taken into account regarding remuneration. |
| **Leadership of Sustainability** | |
| G4–34 | Identify any committees responsible for decision-making on economic, environmental and social impacts. |
| G4–36 | Report whether the organization has appointed an executive-level position with responsibility for economic, environmental and social topics. |
| G4–38 | Report the composition of the highest governance body and its committees by ... [amongst other things] competences relating to economic, environmental and social impacts. |
| G4–40 | Report the nomination and selection processes for the highest governance body and its committees and ... [amongst other things] whether and how expertise and competence relating to economic, environmental and social topics are considered. |
| G4–42 | Report highest governance body's and senior executives' roles in development ... of ... strategies, policies and goals related to economic, environmental and social impacts. |
| G4–43 | Report the measures taken to develop and enhance the highest governance body's collective knowledge of economic, environmental and social topics. |
| G4–44 | Report the processes for evaluation of the highest governance body's performance with respect to governance of economic, environmental and social topics. |
| G4–48 | Report the highest committee or position that formally reviews and approves the organization's sustainability report and ensures that all Aspects are covered. |
| **Implementation and Risk Management** | |
| G4–35 | Report the process for delegating authority for economic, environmental and social impacts from the highest governance body to senior executives and other employees. |
| G4–51 | Report how performance criteria in the remuneration policy relate to the highest governance body's and senior executives' economic, environmental and social objectives. |
| G4–45 to G4–47 | Report the highest governance body's role in the identification and management of economic environmental and social impacts, risks and opportunities. |

exploring how corporate sustainability ought to be governed. A June 2014 report by the UNEP Finance Initiative puts forward a model of integrated governance that "moves sustainability issues from the periphery of corporate strategy to the heart of it" (p. 5). The report aims to identify corporate governance practices that can be used to promote a durable culture of sustainability within corporations (2014, p. 6).

Looking at corporate responsibility from a change-management point of view, Doppelt has examined how the governance and leadership of an organisation can transform organisational culture and overcome resistance to change (2010, p. 96). He found that changes in governance structures and processes can provide much greater overall leverage for transformation to sustainability than implementation of specific sustainability initiatives. For example, installing better smokestacks or improving the sorting of waste are important steps towards sustainability but are not effective levers of change.

In the absence of hard legal rules on corporate responsibility, international standards have filled the gap. The fourth edition of the GRI guidelines makes a set of suggestions as to the governance of CSR issues termed "economic, environmental and social impacts" summarised in Table 5.1. Reflecting the importance of properly governing corporate responsibility, the GRI Guidelines have increased their recommendations on this topic from 10 in version G3.1 to 23 in the recently published G4. This reflects emerging practice in corporations and helps to entrench these norms of behaviour. Regulatory scholars have noted that norms and soft law are mutually reinforcing and tend to develop in parallel (Veasey 2001, p. 2189).

Although the GRI provides much guidance on sustainability reporting, the challenge for companies is how to integrate this with their financial reports in a meaningful way. In 2011 KPMG concluded that integrated reporting was the next step in the development of corporate reporting. In their 2008 survey KPMG found that only 4% of the 250 largest global companies had experimented with some form of integrated reporting whereas in 2011 the percentage had risen to 26% (KPMG 2011). The status of integrated reporting as the next stage of reporting was confirmed by the establishment in 2010 of the International Integrated Reporting Committee (IIRC) to lead the development of a globally accepted integrated reporting framework. The Committee defines an integrated report as a concise communication about how an organisation's strategy, governance, performance and prospects lead to the creation of value over the short, medium and long term.

The prototype integrated reporting framework encourages companies to report in relation to a broad range of "capitals" or resources used and created by the organisation. These include the traditional focus: financial capital but also: manufactured capital; human capital; intellectual capital; natural capital; and relationship (or social) capital. The IIRC see the integrated report as a concise document that may be supplemented by separate sustainability reports and financial statements.

## Stakeholder engagement

Although formal reporting through the annual report and sustainability report is a vital component of communication from a company to its stakeholders, there are many other methods of communication that a company can use both to provide information and, perhaps more importantly, to seek feedback. The GRI recommends that companies disclose: a list of stakeholders with whom they engage; the basis for identification and selection of those stakeholders; their approaches to engaging with stakeholders including their methods and frequency of engagement; and also: "key topics and concerns that have been raised through stakeholder engagement, and how the organization has responded to those key topics and concerns, including through its reporting" (GRI 2014, p. 30). Klettner et al. found that 54% of their sample of 50 large Australian companies reported against all or some of these GRI guidelines (2014, p. 155). The fourth edition of the GRI has developed this topic further, adding three more recommendations that deal with how the information gained from stakeholder engagement is fed into governance processes including board decision-making, risk management and remuneration policy (see Table 5.1).

Stakeholder engagement has to be a two-way process of engagement, communication, feedback and improvement involving a careful balancing process in the event that the interests of different stakeholders conflict. Ultimately, every company has to develop a sustainability strategy tailored to both internal and external contingencies which will be unique to the company concerned. Like corporate responsibility, academic understandings of stakeholder engagement tend to vary depending on the context or background from which research stems. Greenwood lists at least 20 different perspectives found in the literature including: risk management, knowledge appropriation, human resource management, legitimisation, participation and trust-building (2007, p. 319). Her point is that engagement in itself does not amount to responsibility unless the corporation actually acts on what is discovered and "balances the interests of legitimate stakeholders in a manner in keeping with justifiable moral principles" (2007, p. 322).

Klettner et al. found that of a sample of 50 large companies, 43 identified their stakeholders and, of these, 32 explained the methods used to engage with stakeholders (2014, p. 155). These methods illustrated increasingly sophisticated engagement processes such as customer focus groups, internal employee groups, investor briefings, initiatives with non-government organisations and input into government policy-making. However, research based on company disclosures has the risk of overly positive results. Using in-depth case studies as a methodology, Baumann and Scherer found that "external stakeholders are not integrated on a regular but on a case-by-case basis and most of the time interaction takes place in a situation of crisis" (2010, p. 30). This supports Mitchell et al.'s 1997 model of stakeholder salience which argues that stakeholder theory must account for power and urgency as well as legitimacy. It also supports Greenwood's theory that stakeholder engagement and management do not equate to corporate responsibility, rather are a process that may, or may not, lead to corporate responsibility (2007). Certainly there seems to be a move towards more meaningful engagement but both companies and stakeholders will need to see the value of this engagement if it is to continue to develop.

## Board leadership

Like any other aspect of corporate governance, implementing sustainability strategies requires clear leadership as well as structures and processes that ensure plans are properly developed, monitored and implemented. Academic research on the topic of leadership of sustainability, as opposed to leadership in general, is only in its early stages:

> . . . studies are only beginning to surface which identify real leadership practices, systems, and processes that organisations have used to effectively face the

challenges posed by moving towards more socially responsible business operations on a global scale. Most of the small body of existing research is qualitative,
exploratory, or case study research (e.g. Kakabadse and Kakabadse 2007). These
types of studies, often using grounded theory methods (Glaser and Strauss 1967),
are appropriate as we collectively begin to grapple with these questions, given that
we do not yet understand the nature of "socially responsible leadership" or even
whether effective leadership takes on new qualities or forms in a context of driving toward sustainability.

(Van Velsor 2009, pp. 3–4)

Leadership is essential if sustainability is to be truly integrated into core business
strategy and this is true both at board level and below:

For corporate citizenship to be effective – ensuring that a company minimizes
harm and maximizes benefits through its activities and, in so doing, takes account
of and is responsive to a full range of stakeholders – leadership is required at every
level of an enterprise. This places new demands on Boards of Directors to shape
and govern citizenship in companies and calls for robust management structures
and systems to integrate citizenship into the operations of a firm.

(Morgan et al. 2009, p. 40)

Interestingly, qualitative empirical work in this area shows that this may not be an
entirely new approach for boards. Marshall and Ramsay showed that 94.3% of their
sample of Australian directors believed that their duty was to take all stakeholders'
interests into account (2009, p. 36). Marshall and Ramsay conducted survey-based
research examining directors' perceptions of their duties. They asked directors to indicate whether they believed the law required them to act only in the interests of shareholders or whether it allowed them to consider a broader range of stakeholders (2009,
p. 35). The results showed very clearly that directors did not understand their duties
to require strict shareholder primacy:

A majority of directors understood that their primary obligation to act in the best
interests of the company meant that they should balance the interests of all stakeholders (55 percent). A further 38.2 percent believed that they must, by means of
acting in the interests of all stakeholders, ensure the long-term interests of shareholders. No directors believed that they were required to act in the short term interests of shareholders only and only a very small proportion (6.6 percent) believed
that they were required to act in the long term interests of shareholders only.

(2009, p. 35)

This shows that current moves towards corporate responsibility may simply amount
to a formalisation of what boards are already doing. Corporate governance codes
have been found to formalise and help entrench existing practices and the role of soft
law in CSR is likely to be the same (Klettner et al. 2010).

Nevertheless, the approach taken by a company has to be guided from the top
with clear strategic goals, policy frameworks and priorities. Morgan et al. found "that

while corporate Boards are assuming more responsibility for oversight of conduct and taking account of specific social and environmental issues, citizenship is not yet fully embedded into Boards or the operating structures and systems of most firms" (2009, p. 40). More recently Klettner et al. found increasing use of board and executive committees dedicated to CSR with 22 of Australia's 50 largest companies (44%) having a board committee dedicated to the issue (Klettner et al. 2014, p. 158). However in a wider sample of 3,512 companies, UNEP found only 56 companies with a non-executive director taking responsibility for sustainability, thereby concluding that "the governance of sustainability is still at an embryonic stage" (2014, p. 15).

Werther and Chandler outline a strategic approach to sustainability as involving four components:

- a sustainability perspective is incorporated into the strategic planning process;
- any actions taken on sustainability are directly related to core operations;
- stakeholder perspectives about social and environmental issues are incorporated; and
- the focus of activities is medium to long term, not short term.

(2011, p. 40)

To be truly strategic companies need robust governance structures and processes that permit sustainability-related information to flow into strategic planning at board and executive level. A committee dedicated to sustainability can provide a framework within which this can occur and can ensure that engagement processes (with both internal and external stakeholders) are relevant in the context of wider business strategy. The 2014 UNEP report confirms the value of a board committee in moving sustainability strategy to a leadership level but suggests that this is only a phase in the journey to integrated governance. Once sustainability is integrated in a truly holistic way, a separate board committee should no longer be needed because each board member and board committee will be integrating sustainability issues into their agenda (UNEP 2014, p. 6).

## Implementing corporate responsibility

Only a small strand of the extensive CSR literature deals with implementation of CSR often by putting forward process models for the integration of CSR into core business strategy (Asif et al. 2011, Castka et al. 2004, Kleine and von Hauff 2009, Yuan et al. 2011). Castka et al. (2004) put forward a process-based management system which has as its key, "the transformation of stakeholders' expectations into the operations of the organisations with continual monitoring of the impact". Kleine and von Hauff (2009) introduce an integrative sustainability triangle which deals with horizontal integration of CSR across different departments of an organisation. Yuan et al. (2011) take a comparative approach to CSR integration, identifying seven different ways by which organisations integrate CSR into their business, from embedding CSR into core business processes (patching) to simply removing practices that are detrimental to CSR (trimming).

The integration, mainstreaming and institutionalisation of corporate social responsibility is one of the latter stages of developing and implementing corporate responsibility (Maon et al. 2009). Firstly, companies need to audit existing sustainability norms, standards and practices and develop a company-specific integrated strategic plan. This then needs to be implemented, communicated, evaluated, improved and eventually institutionalised. Finally an integrated strategic plan needs to be supported by structures and processes such as:

> . . . designating a senior official or a committee responsible for overall corporate social responsiblity implementation, improving interfunctional coordination, building corporate social responsibilities into employees' job descriptions and performance evaluations, recruiting people knowledgeable in CSR with appropriate attitudes and skills, and developing regular forums in which to share issues and knowledge across the organization.
>
> (Maon et al. 2009, p. 81)

Although company leaders appear to be making progress towards defining and developing a more strategic approach to sustainability, to have any real effect their strategies must be put into action consistently throughout the organisation. One of the barriers faced by many companies is that they lack the governance frameworks through which to implement, measure and monitor a comprehensive approach. According to Lindgreen et al., this is the next big challenge:

> Specifically, practitioners lack guidance on various . . . sustainability . . . implementation issues including architecture; management; building and maintenance; repositioning; communication; and performance measures.
>
> (2009, p. 252)

Linking sustainability performance with remuneration is gaining attention as a way to fast track implementation. Morgan et al. in their 2009 study of 25 Fortune 500 companies across five industry sectors found "brief to no disclosure" on "employee compensation linked to corporate responsibility goals and targets" across all sectors, commenting:

> there is scant evidence in this sample that firms are linking citizenship into their performance appraisal and compensation systems. Interestingly, many feel that this is the missing component of the citizenship integration puzzle. Over 60 percent of respondents of an Ethical Corporation Magazine (2003) survey, for example, believe that management compensation linked to citizenship performance is among the top three strategies to more effective management of corporate citizenship.
>
> (2009, p. 45)

The UNEP report still finds very few companies linking executive compensation to ESG targets: only 7% of a sample of 600 companies (UNEP 2014, p. 45). However, the concept has been around for some time: in their interviews conducted in 2003–2004, Adams and Frost found one of their sample companies in the UK had,

". . . moved away from assessing managers' performance against financial KPIs and adopted a companywide balanced scorecard which has sixteen measures on it, three of the four quadrants of which relate to non-financial issues. Performance against these measures is linked to their remuneration" (2008, p. 295). More recently, Klettner et al. found that many Australian companies were taking this scorecard approach to assess short-term incentives, with several of the scorecard's metrics based on non-financial measures such as lost-time injury rates or customer satisfaction (2014, p. 160). Importantly, the proportion of overall short-term incentive (and of total remuneration) that these sustainability-related metrics made up was generally unclear making it possible that the figures were so small as to be only a very slight incentive towards implementation, if at all (Klettner et al. 2014). This was also noted in Adams and Frost's study:

> Occupational, health and safety targets are now built into the employee share plan based on the organisation meeting specific targets. Specific aspects of social and environmental performance are also built into the performance evaluation of the relevant managers, although the impact may be limited since profit remains the predominant determinant of the bonus.
>
> (2008, p. 297)

Berrone and Gomez Meja note that "the academic community has largely neglected the link between social issues and managerial pay" (2009b, p. 961) and this is still the case despite widespread belief that short-term compensation schemes contributed to the 2008 global financial crisis (Clarke 2010, Klettner 2012). This highlights an important area for further research: to identify the extent to which sustainability performance influences total remuneration. Such research would assist boards, shareholders and stakeholders in the development of more meaningful incentive and disclosure systems.

## Conclusions: the role of soft law

Corporate responsibility is not a static element of the organisation. Good practice has come about in large part because of poor publicity and action on behalf of various stakeholders, regulators and international organisations. This means that the practices of companies may improve or deteriorate depending on the level of volatility in their industry sector; the direction and calibre of their leadership; the degree of government intervention; and the level of stakeholder interest:

> More research is needed to explore to what extent CSR . . .[sustainability] efforts are initiated as a result of outside pressures, formal top down strategy setting, grass roots initiatives from employees or middle managers, or other sources, and what kinds of catalysts are most effective in creating culture and systems change.
>
> (Van Velsor 2009, p. 5)

Evidence is mounting that soft regulation can be very effective at encouraging social and cultural change rather than just compliance-oriented behaviour, by building on and entrenching emerging practices or norms. Soft regulatory techniques have the potential to encourage "a more meaningful process of corporate cultural reform than more traditional enforcement techniques" (Ford and Hess 2011, p. 513). They can and are being used to tackle complicated social problems related to corporate behaviour such as lack of women in leadership and wider issues of corporate responsibility and business ethics. As Hess states, "the challenge the law faces is to . . . support internal change initiatives that may be unique to any particular corporation" (Hess 2008, p. 452). These could be operational changes to improve corporate governance and risk management or cultural change to improve gender diversity, occupational health and safety or environmental performance.

Soft regulation has the capacity to institutionalise CSR moving it from the margins to the mainstream. The GRI has become an international standard for sustainability reporting and has influenced national policy making. Certainly evidence is emerging to support Bryan Horrigan's observation that "non-binding CSR standards can have a normative effect on corporate activity" (Horrigan 2010, p. 28). Kingsford Smith claims that the normative force of soft regulation can be seen from the fact that many companies follow its standards, believing it to have no legal effect but acknowledging in their public documents that they accept its obligations (2012, p. 403). Aguilera et al. argue that by building on emerging norms, soft regulation can encourage corporations to be "agents of social change" (2007, p. 848).

Although soft regulation can encourage and assist those companies keen to be responsible, the voluntary nature of disclosure still permits less ethical companies to report only the favourable numbers and retain any information that they consider might reflect badly on the organisation (Adams and Frost 2008, p. 297). True corporate accountability for sustainability may require tougher regulation or laws to ensure both good and bad information is revealed, or at least a statement by the CEO that disclosure is "true and fair" akin to that required for financial reporting. Certainly, this is an area where guidance and recommendations can lead to more consistent and comparable disclosures, as demonstrated by the GRI.

Even if soft regulation and corporate governance codes are ineffective in terms of disciplining certain behaviours they still have value in triggering dialogue and norm development (Fasterling 2011). Thus norms and soft regulation work in parallel each reinforcing the other. Soft regulation has a vital role in strengthening norms of behaviour and supporting change but it may struggle if put to contest against opposing share market norms such as the intense pressure to maintain short-term share price. It provides a tool for cultural change in circumstances where, on balance, wider institutional forces also support that change. Ntim et al. (2012) have explored corporate governance disclosures in South Africa separating them into shareholder and stakeholder disclosures. They find that disclosures aimed at stakeholders can improve firm legitimacy and facilitate access to critical resources (2007, p. 100).

Corporate responsibility remains a work-in-progress; and an ongoing challenge for companies to implement well and credibly. Companies need more guidance on how to lead and govern sustainability, including how to integrate this with existing corporate governance systems. Currently soft law, particularly international initiatives such as the GRI are filling the gaps left by domestic law, at least in Anglo-American jurisdictions. This soft law goes "further than law" to influence behaviour in the grey area of business ethics and social responsibility. It can delve into areas where prescriptive regulation would be inappropriate because of variation in the nature of companies and their operations. It assists companies to formalise their sustainability strategies by embedding them within existing corporate governance systems.

## Bibliography

Adams, C.A. and Frost, G.R. (2008), 'Integrating Sustainability Reporting into Management Practices,' *Accounting Forum*, vol. 32, pp. 288–302.

Aguilera, R.V., Rupp, D.E., Williams, C.A. and Ganapathi, J. (2007), 'Putting the S Back in Corporate Social Responsibility: A Multilevel Theory of Social Change in Organisations,' *Academy of Management Review*, vol. 32, no. 3, pp. 836–863.

Anderson, H. (2005), 'Corporate Social Responsibility: Some Critical Questions for Australia,' *University of Tasmania Law Review*, vol. 24, no. 2, pp. 143–172.

Aras, G. and Crowther, D. (2008), 'Governance and Sustainability: An Investigation into the Relationship Between Corporate Governance and Corporate Sustainability,' *Management Decision*, vol. 46, no. 3, pp. 433–448.

Asif, M., Searcy, C., Zutshi, A. and Fisscher, O. (2011), 'An Integrated Management Systems Approach to Corporate Social Responsibility,' *Journal of Cleaner Production*, vol. 56, pp. 1–11.

Corporations and Markets Advisory Committee (2006), *The Social Responsibility of Corporations*. Sydney: CAMAC.

Baumann, D. and Scherer, A.G. (2010), 'MNEs and the UN Global Compact: An Empirical Analysis of the Organizational Implementation of Corporate Citizenship'. Institute of Organization and Administrative Science, University of Zurich, IOU Working Paper No. 114.

Berle, A.A. (1931), 'Corporate Powers as Powers in Trust', *Harvard Law Review* vol. 44, pp. 1365–1372.

Berle, A.A. (1932), 'For Whom Corporate Managers Are Trustees: A Note,' *Harvard Law Review* 45.

Berrone, P. and Gomez-Mejia, L.R. (2009a), 'Environmental Performance and Executive Compensation: An Integrated Agency-Institutional Perspective,' *Academy of Management Journal* vol. 52, no. 1, pp. 103–126.

Berrone, P. and Gomez-Mejia, L.R. (2009b), 'The Pros and Cons of Rewarding Social Responsibility at the Top,' *Human Resource Management*, vol. 48, no. 6, pp. 959–971.

Branson, D. (2001), 'Corporate Governance "Reform" and the New Corporate Social Responsibility,' *University of Pittsburgh Law Review*, vol. 62, p. 605.

Carroll, A.B. (1991), 'The Pyramid of Corporate Responsibility: Toward the Moral Management of Organizational Stakeholders,' *Business Horizons*, vol. 34, no. 4, pp. 39–48.

Campbell, J.L. (2007), 'Why Would Corporations Behave in Socially Responsible Ways? An Institutional Theory of Corporate Social Responsibility,' *Academy of Management Review*, vol. 32, pp. 946–967.

Castka, P., Bamber, C.J., Bamber, D.J. and Sharp, J.M. (2004), 'Integrating Corporate Social Responsibility (CSR) Into ISO Management,' *The TQM Magazine*, vol. 16, no. 3, pp. 216–224.

Cho, C.H. and Patten, D.M. (2007), 'The Role of Environmental Disclosures as Tools of Legitimacy: A Research Note,' *Accounting, Organizations and Society*, vol. 32, no. 7–8, pp. 639–647.

Clarke, T. (1993), 'The Political Economy of the UK Privatisation Programme: A Blueprint for Other Countries?' In Clarke, T. and Pitelis, C. (eds.). *The Political Economy of Privatisation*. Routledge, London, pp. 205–233.

Clarke, T. (2010), 'Recurring Crises in Anglo-American Corporate Governance,' *Contributions to Political Economy*, vol. 29, no. 1, pp. 9–32.

Clarke, T. (2013), 'Deconstructing the Mythology of Shareholder Value,' *Accounting, Economics and Law*, vol. 3, no. 1, pp. 1–28.

Corbett, A. and Bottomley, S. (2004), 'Regulating Corporate Governance'. In Parker, C., Scott, C., Lacey, N. and Braithwaite, J. (eds.). *Regulating Law*. Oxford: Oxford University Press, pp. 60–81.

Dahlsrud, A. (2008), 'How Corporate Social Responsibility is Defined: an Analysis of 37 Definitions,' *Corporate Social Responsibility and Environmental Management*, vol. 15, pp. 1–13.

David, P., Bloom, M. and Hillman, A.J. (2007), 'Investor Activism, Managerial Responsiveness and Corporate Social Performance,' *Strategic Management Journal*, vol. 28, pp. 91–100.

Dodd, E.M. (1932), 'For Whom Are Corporate Managers Trustees?' *Harvard Law Review*, vol. 45, p. 1145.

Doppelt, B. (2010), *Leading Change Toward Sustainability: A Change-Management Guide for Business, Government and Civil Society*, 2nd edition. Greenleaf Publishing, Sheffield.

Elkington, J. (2006), 'Governance for Sustainability,' *Corporate Governance: An International Review*, vol. 14, no. 6, pp. 522–529.

Fasterling, B. (2011), 'Development of Norms Through Compliance Disclosure,' *Journal of Business Ethics*, vol. 106, no. 1, pp. 73–87.

Farrar, J. (2008), *Corporate Governance: Theories, Principles and Practice*. Oxford University Press, Victoria, Australia.

Freeman, R.E. (1994), 'The Politics of Stakeholder Theory: Some Future Directions', *Business Ethics Quarterly*, vol. 4, pp. 409–422.

Freeman, R.E. and Reed, W.M. (1990), 'Corporate Governance: A Stakeholder Interpretation', *Journal of Behavioural Economics*, vol. 19, no. 4, pp. 337–360.

Friedman, M. (1962), *Capitalism and Freedom*. University of Chicago Press, Chicago, IL.

Ford, C. and Condon, M. (2011), 'Introduction to "New Governance and the Business Organisation"'. Special Issue of Law and Policy *Law and Policy* vol. 33, no. 4, pp. 449–458.

Ford, C. and Hess, D. (2011), 'Corporate Monitorships and New Governance Regulation: In Theory, in Practice and in Context,' *Law and Policy*, vol. 33, no. 4, pp. 509–541.

Gobbels, M. (2006), 'Standards for Corporate Social Responsibility'. In Jonker, J. and de Witte, M. (eds.). *The Challenge of Organizing and Implementing Corporate Social Responsibility*. Palgrave Macmillan, New York, pp. 173–192.

Greenwood, M. (2007). 'Stakeholder Engagement: Beyond the Myth of Corporate Responsibility,' *Journal of Business Ethics*, vol. 74, pp. 315–327.

GRI (2011), *Sustainability Reporting Guidelines*, Version 3.1. Amsterdam: Global Reporting Initiative.

GRI (2014), *Sustainability Reporting Guidelines*, Version 4. Amsterdam: Global Reporting Initiative.

Hansen, E.G. and Reichwald, R. (2009), *CSR Leadership Study: Leading Corporate Responsibility in Multinational Corporations – A Study in Germany's Biggest Firms*. Report no. 01/2009 of the Institute for Information, Organization and Management, TUM Business School.

Hess, D. (2008), 'The Three Pillars of Corporate Social Reporting as New Governance Regulation: Disclosure, Dialogue and Development,' *Business Ethics Quarterly*, vol. 18, no. 4, pp. 447–482.

Horrigan, B. (2010), *Corporate Social Responsibility in the 21st Century: Debates, Models and Practices Across Government, Law and Business*. Edward Elgar Publishing, Cheltenham.

Jensen, M.C. (2002), 'Value Maximization, Stakeholder Theory, and the Corporate Objective Function', *Business Ethics Quarterly*, vol. 12, no. 2, pp. 235–256.

Keay, A. (2007), 'Tackling the Issue of the Corporate Objective: An Analysis of the United Kingdom's "Enlightened Shareholder Value" Approach,' *Sydney Law Review*, vol. 29, p. 577.

Keay, A. (2010), 'Moving Towards Stakeholderism? Constituency Statutes, Enlightened Shareholder Value, and All That: Much Ado About Little?' SSRN papers.ssrn.com/sol3/papers.cfm?abstract_id=115451.

Keay, A. (2013), *The Enlightened Shareholder Value Principle and Corporate Governance*. Routledge, London.

Kingsford Smith, D. (2012), 'Governing the Corporation: The Role of "Soft Regulation",' *University of New South Wales Law Journal* vol. 35, no. 1, pp. 378–403.

Klein, E. and du Plessis, J. (2005), 'Corporate Donations, the Best Interests of the Company and the Proper Purpose Doctrine,' *University of New South Wales Law Journal*, vol. 28, no. 1, pp. 69–97.

Kleine, A. and von Hauff, M. (2009), 'Sustainability-Driven Implementation of Corporate Social Responsibility: Application of the Integrative Sustainability Triangle,' *Journal of Business Ethics*, vol. 85, pp. 517–533.

Klettner, A. (2012), 'Corporate Governance and the Global Financial Crisis'. In Clarke, T. and Branson, D. (eds.), *The SAGE Handbook of Corporate Governance*. SAGE, London, pp. 556–584.

Klettner, A., Clarke, T. and Adams, M. (2010), 'Corporate Governance Reform: An Empirical Study of the Changing Roles and Responsibilities of Australian Boards and Directors,' *Australian Journal of Corporate Law*, vol. 24, pp. 148–176.

Klettner, A., Clarke, T. and Boersma, M. (2014), 'The Governance of Corporate Sustainability: Empirical Insights into the Development, Leadership and Implementation of Responsible Business Strategy,' *Journal of Business Ethics*, vol. 122, no. 1, pp. 145–165.

Kolk, A. (2008), 'Sustainability, Accountability and Corporate Governance: Exploring Multinationals' Reporting Practices,' *Business Strategy and the Environment*, vol. 17, no. 1, pp. 1–15.

Kolk, A. and Pinkse, J. (2010), 'The Integration of Corporate Governance in Corporate Social Responsibility Disclosures,' *Corporate Social Responsibility and Environmental Management*, vol. 17, no. 1, pp. 15–26.

KPMG, (2011), *The KPMG International Survey of Corporate Responsibility Reporting*. KPMG.

Lindgreen, A., Swaen, V. and Maon, F. (2008), 'Introduction: Corporate Social responsibility Implementation,' *Journal of Business Ethics*, vol. 85, pp. 251–256.

Maon, F., Lindgreen, A. and Swaen, V. (2009), 'Designing and Implementing Corporate Social Responsibility: An Integrative Framework Grounded in Theory and Practice,' *Journal of Business Ethics*, vol. 87, pp. 71–89.

Marshall, S. and Ramsay, I. (2009), *Stakeholders and Directors' Duties: Law, Theory and Evidence*, Working Paper. Revised and published as S. Marshall and I. Ramsay (2012), 'Stakeholders' and Directors' Duties: Law Theory and Evidence,' *University of New South Wales Law Journal*, vol. 35, pp. 291–316.

Martin, F. (2005), 'Corporate Social Responsibility and Public Policy'. In Mullerat, R. (ed.). *Corporate Social Responsibility: The Corporate Governance of the 21st Century*, International Bar Association, Netherlands, pp. 77–95.

McConvill, J. and Joy, M. (2003), 'The Interaction of Directors Duties and Sustainable Development in Australia: Setting off on the Uncharted Road,' *Melbourne University Law Review* vol. 27, pp. 116–138.

Mitchell, R.K., Agle, B.R. and Wood, D.J. (1997), 'Toward a Theory of Stakeholder Identification and Salience: Defining the Principle of Who and What Really Counts,' *The Academy of Management Review*, vol. 22, no. 4, pp. 853–886.

Moir, L. (2001), 'What Do We Mean by Corporate Social Responsibility?' *Corporate Governance*, vol. 1, no. 2, pp. 16–22.

Morgan, G., Ryu, K. and Mirvis, P. (2009), 'Leading Corporate Citizenship: Governance, Structure, Systems,' *Corporate Governance*, vol. 9, no. 1, pp. 39–49.

Ntim, C.G., Opong, K.K. and Danbolt, J. (2012), 'The Relative Value Relevance of Shareholder versus Stakeholder Corporate Governance Disclosure Policy Reforms in South Africa,' *Corporate Governance: An International Review*, vol. 20, no. 1, pp. 84–105.

Parker, C., (2007), 'Meta-Regulation: Legal Accountability for Corporate Social Responsibility'. In McBarnet, D., Voiculescu, A. and Campbell, T. (eds.), *The New Corporate Accountability: Corporate Social Responsibility and the Law*. Cambridge University Press, Cambridge, pp. 207–237.

Parliamentary Joint Committee on Corporations and Financial Services (2006), *Corporate Responsibility: Managing Risk and Creating Value*. Australian Parliament.

Redmond, P. (2012), 'Directors' Duties and Corporate Social Responsiveness,' *University of New South Wales Law Journal*, vol. 35, pp. 317–40.

Runhaar, H. and Lafferty, H. (2009), 'Governing Corporate Social Responsibility: An Assessment of the Contribution of the UN Global Compact to CSR Strategies in the Telecommunications Industry,' *Journal of Business Ethics*, vol. 84, pp. 479–495.

Russell, S., Haigh, N. and Griffiths, A. (2007), 'Understanding Corporate Sustainability: Recognizing the Impact of Different Governance Systems.' In Benn, S. and Dunphy, D. (eds.), *Corporate Governance and Sustainability: Challenges for Theory and Practice*. Routledge, London, pp. 36–56.

Sarre, R. (2002), 'Responding to Corporate Collapses: Is There a Role for Corporate Social Responsibility,' *Deakin Law Review*, vol. 7, no. 1, pp. 7–8.

Schembera, S. (2012), 'Implementing Corporate Social Responsibility: Empirical Insights on the Impact and Accountability of the UN Global Compact,' University of Zurich, Business Working Paper Series, Working Paper No. 316.

Searcy, C. (2012), 'Corporate Sustainability Performance Measurement Systems: A Review and Research Agenda,' *Journal of Business Ethics*, vol. 107, pp. 239–253.

Sneirson, J.F. (2009), 'Green is Good: Sustainability, Profitability, and a New Paradigm for Corporate Governance,' *Iowa Law Review*, vol. 94, no. 3, pp. 987–1022.

Stout, L.A. (2002), 'Bad and Not-so-bad Arguments for Shareholder Primacy,' *South California Law Review*, vol. 75, pp. 1189.

Stout, L.A. (2012), *The Shareholder Value Myth*. Berrett-Koehler, San Francisco, CA.

UNEP (2014), 'Integrated Governance: A New Model of Governance for Sustainability,' Asset Management Working Group of the United Nations Environment Programme Finance Initiative, June.

Van Velsor, E. (2009), 'Introduction: Leadership and Corporate Social Responsibility,' *Corporate Governance*, vol. 9, no. 1, pp. 3–6.

Veasey, N. (2001), 'Should Corporation Law inform Aspirations for Good Corporate Governance or Vice Versa?' *University of Pennsylvania Law Review*, vol. 149, pp. 2179–2191.

Wells, H. (2002), 'The Cycles of Corporate Social Responsibility: An Historical Retrospective for the Twenty-first Century,' *Kansas Law Review*, vol. 51, pp. 77–140.

Werther, W.B. and Chandler, D. (2011), *Strategic Corporate Social Responsibility: Stakeholders in a Global Environment*, 2nd Ed. SAGE Publications, London.

Whitehouse, L. (2006), 'Corporate Social Responsibility: Views from the Frontline,' *Journal of Business Ethics*, vol. 63, pp. 279–296.

Yuan, W., Bao, Y. and Verbeke, A. (2011), 'Integrating CSR Initiatives in Business: An Organizing Framework,' *Journal of Business Ethics*, vol. 101, pp. 75–92.

# Chapter 6

# Corporate citizenship, ethics and accountability

## The significance of the process of trust for corporate legitimacy in late modernity

*Jacob Dahl Rendtorff*

## Introduction

There is a close relation between integrity, accountability and trust as virtues of corporate citizenship (Mayer et al. 1995). Therefore we will in this paper discuss the significance of the process of trust for organizing accountability and why creating genuine trust relations are emergent foundations for values-driven management and ethics in organizational culture. We want to show that business ethics is the foundation for the popular dynamic process view of trust (Gehman et al. 2013, Langley and Tsoukas 2010, Langley et al. 2013, Möllering 2013). In the dynamic process view of trust as trusting Guido Möllering distinguishes between five important dimensions of trusting as: (1) continuing, (2) processing, (3) learning, (4), becoming (5), constituting (Möllering 2013). In a business ethics perspective a process of trust as trusting can be said to be an analysis of the ontological conditions of this conception of trust as trusting. As a foundation of trust as trusting, business ethics is considered as an interaction between stakeholders aiming at a common good for all implied parties.

Companies try to make a self-representation based on business ethics and codes of conduct in order to be trustworthy so that they create trust among consumers and customers. There is a dynamic interaction between the virtues of integrity, loyalty and trust in the sense-making and organizing of the concept of good corporate citizenship. This is indeed central in regard to development of social capital and prosperity in business organizations. Globalization of economic markets with lack of legal regulation and greater media awareness of corrupt business practices has increased awareness of the need for honest business. Such an importance of building trustworthy business practices in order to restore the integrity of the international business community is illustrated by recent scandals following the financial crisis concerning lack of transparency in international corporations.

In this context we should be clear about the unit of analysis and the topic. This is about the ethics of business, so businesses build trust by being trustworthy. Accordingly, consumers and other stakeholders respond by trusting. This means that businesses become trustworthy and this makes consumers and other stakeholders trust corporations. When corporations fail to create this kind of trust we face a social and political scandal. Some commentators even interpret such problems of corporate governance, accountability and transparency following business and financial scandals as a deep crisis of public trust and social acceptance of corporations (Bidault et al. 1997, DiPiazza Jr. and Eccles 2002).

Our argument is that trustworthy business practices are based on sense-making and organizing of ethical values. Organizing trust in business brand management expressed in the ethical interactions between employees and other stakeholders of the firm is viewed as an important social clue and the informal lubricant of business organizations and therefore it is an important concept for the constitution of corporate citizenship. Trust and trusting are necessary for accountability and integrity of corporations because no organization can survive on the basis of generalized mistrust and opportunistic behavior among employee, management and consumers and other stakeholders. Integrating trust in organizations through trustworthy business practices is central to internal unity and external legitimacy of corporations and therefore it is a key element in social capital of social relationships in business.

We will argue for an ethical definition of trust emphasizing that what is trustworthy sense-making in organizations is based on the accountability and responsibility of the firm. Authentic trust emerges as a result of authentic human relations and paradoxically it is the possibility of the experience of betrayal that lies behind the experience of authentic trust and trusting as an experience of freedom to act and choose in the world. This freedom of action in trust is also indeed the basis of capitalist systems where everyone is free to trust one another. In this sense there is a close relation between ethics and authentic trust (Solomon and Flores 2001, p. 11).

To trust someone means to hold that person or organization accountable over time believing that they will perform actions of integrity and honesty in the process of organizing. Trust is based on mutual expectations and promises for reciprocity and collaboration in the future. Such an idea of trust implies a close link between truth, honesty and transparency, which is illustrated by various degrees and cultures of trust in different corporations and societies. The process of emerging trust in organizations is closely connected to integrity and accountability of transparent business institutions and networks without corruption or social and economic crime.

### I Trust as a process of reduction of complexity in the social world

One important contribution to recent debates about trust and trusting has been the work of Ulrich Beck in *Risk Society* in which he argues that global society in late modernity implies a situation where those in power take more and more risks on behalf of the citizens in society (Beck 1986). The environment, the economy and the general culture of technological civilization and expert decision making emphasize the issue of the relations between uncertainty, risk and trust as emerging in the core of interactions among individuals in modern society. But we may also mention factors of globalization and the emergence of a complex network and virtual economy related to all kinds of e-businesses where there are few social relations and no direct physical link between the different actors as basis for increased need for trust rather than explicit contracts, written agreements, sanctions and rules in economic life (Beck et al. 1994). An increasing tendency in a global economy is that individuals have to make sense of trusting other people while being on shaking grounds. They must make choices and take risks based on limited knowledge and less personal frequentation of parties of interaction.

In risk society experts and highly qualified professionals have very specialized knowledge about different social issues and it is impossible for ordinary individuals to acquire all of this knowledge. Therefore, trust, accountability and transparency and the conditions for trusting professionals have emerged as essential processes in reflexive modernity. Trust and trusting is a response to distribution of power and functions as an acceptance of the power of certain individuals and authorities in risk society. This means that citizens, consumers and other stakeholders have no other choice than trusting authorities because they cannot understand all complexities of technical and organizational processes. So trust becomes an important instrument for creating social and organizational legitimacy. We can distinguish between generalized trust in institutions and social systems on the one hand and personal trust directed towards individuals on the other hand based on the knowledge about the behavior, knowledge, risk aversion and competence of those individuals and institutions.

The insecurity of risk society may explain the crisis of trust in business corporations. But trust is also important from the point of view of social ethics and it is considered as an important element for social capital (Field 2003, p. 62). Francis Fukuyama has contributed to the ethical understanding of trust as an inherent element of social capital (Fukuyama 1995, p. 26). This approach also contains a theoretical justification of the role of trust in the constitution of corporate citizenship. Economic action on fewer costs is founded on social capital in which mutual recognition, reciprocity and social bonds between individuals and groups in society constitute the cores of trust as the foundation of good corporate citizenship. Such civic relations based on a system of values constitute social capital and they are essential for economic development of society. Trustworthiness of social networks is based on their honorability and respectability.

What is especially important for economic prosperity is the ability to trust strangers. Low trust cultures may be characterized by strong family ties, but there is no strong civil public bond among members of community. While low trust cultures are poor of social cohesion there are strong ethical values and social bonds in families, civic associations and local communities in high trust cultures. This view of economics emphasizes the importance of ethics in community for social capital and progress of business. People trust each other because they are operating on the basis of a common set of norms (Fukuyama 1995, p. 27, Moon and Bonny 2001, p. 60). In high trust cultures like Japan or Western Europe trust has always been an ethical value that is a part of the morality and duty of work. One reason for this is that high trust societies rely on effective institutions that support cooperation between individuals and enforce agreements.

In this perspective the consequences of decline of trust in advanced countries can be very dangerous for economic prosperity. An important issue for present business relations is to avoid falling back into low trust cultures where there is less civic engagement and no culture of public trust. Instead our discussion on the role of trust for business ethics is motivated by the need of open and reliable civil communities as social basis for development of business and economic interactions. It has become a challenge for complex risk society to be used to "deal with strangers" that is to maintain and develop trusts cultures at economic markets and in business organizations with high levels of social recognition among economic trade partners who have no direct intimate relations with each others. That is why we need to focus on trust in business ethics (Govier 1997, p. 45).

In his studies of civic traditions in Italy and his analysis of the collapse of US civil society the US Sociologist Robert Putnam also contributes to this elaboration of the process of trust in business life. He draws attention to the importance of networks and shared values for people in organizations. Putnam argues for the importance of civic engagement and political stability for development of society. He analyzes the need for restoring social capital in modern society. Putnam agrees with the definition of trust as a part of social capital (Putnam 2000, p. 19). Because it develops values of reciprocity in social networks trust is one feature of social capital that can help to improve the efficiency of the economy. Egalitarian elements of strong civil bonds have democratic orientations and increases civic cooperation (Putnam et al. 1993). Therefore social capital implies that economic actors are not only determined by pure rational action, but also largely influenced by the strength of social networks and other social conditions for examples the ethical norms and values of particular organizations, networks and communities.

The German Sociologist Niklas Luhmann has developed an analysis of trust which helps us to get a profound understanding of the meaning of trust for social capital in risk society. He defines trust as tolerance of uncertainty, general reliance, belief and expectations of human beings to their social world (Luhman 1997, p. 22). This perspective can also be used to understand responsibility and legitimacy (Holmström 2004). In the perspective of functionalist analysis, looking at the possibilities of action in social systems, we can conceptualize trust as a basic element in systems of social interaction. Human action implies choices of interpretations and confrontations with the world, which presuppose basic reliance on many social facts and meanings. But trust is in particular an element of mutual commitment between human beings (Luhmann 1997, p. 43). The role of trust is reduction of complexity of ambiguities and of possibilities of action in social relationships (Luhmann 1997, p. 25).

In this context we could emphasize that trust is closely linked to the concept of "bounded rationality" in organizations where individual utility maximization is limited by the choices and actions of other individuals. We know that our knowledge is limited and that we need to generalize on the basis of fundamental existential and "ontological" trust in order to act and behave in the world. This condition is generalized from human individuals to be applicable to social, organizational and institutional interactions. Compared to the conditions in the pre-modern world, risk society is full of ambiguities and insecurities and trust is a way to cope with this complexity where we cannot have any evidence or security about how other people will behave towards us.

We can also consider ancient religious or ethical worldviews as ways of reducing the complexity of an unknown future (Luhmann 1997, p. 32). The unknown horizon of the future is conceptualized as an aspect of present expectations. Trust is reduction of complexity of an unknown future. Paradoxically, however, trust is also the ability that makes it possible for human beings to cope with an increasing complexity in the future. In the functionalist perspective trust is the capacity to deal with the increased number of unexpected events in a technological and scientific civilization. In the light of business economy we may add that creation of trust is the condition for the ability of corporations to act on increasingly sensitive markets where stakeholders have difficulties in perceiving ambiguities, for example in biotechnology production of genetically modified products where consumers have to rely on technological and corporate experts in evaluating the safety of products.

We can emphasize that trust is always indeterminate. Trust is based on the belief or expectation that person or entity in whom or which trust is placed is trustworthy and that there is sufficient information about trustworthiness to make successful choices and actions (Luhmann 1997, p. 32). Trust moves external insecurity to internal security. As reduction of complexity in systems of personal or social action trust reflects the contingency of the social world and the subjectivity of human expectations. To make the decision to trust someone in personal or organizational decision-making cannot be exclusively a problem of calculation of risk or rational planning, but is essentially a matter of absorption of insecurity. As generalized expectation between knowledge and ignorance trust is always in the end a matter of choice with no final rational foundation.

Moreover, from the process perspective trust and trusting is a learning process dependent on confirmation or rejection of trustful actions. Trust is also a matter of symbolic generalization and images. Consumers, managers or employees cannot conceptualize all aspects of the complexity of business organizations. Consequently they have to simplify their experiences of organizations, for example by relying on corporate mission statements, value expressions or codes of conduct.

Therefore we can distinguish between trusts in persons and trust in systems (Luhmann 1997, p. 48). Trust in persons is based on the recognition and expectation of the freedom of the other person. It is the belief that the other is free to act according to an infinite number of possibilities. In relations between persons trust depends on communication, self-representation and potentiality of action that increases as the subject expose trustful behavior. It is important to be aware of the institutional dimensions of personal trust in networks or organizations in which actions and human freedom are submitted to common an expectation that excludes deviant behavior. Interpersonal trust presupposes situations where subjects are willing to enter into a trust relationship. Such situations of personal trust communication are at the limits calculative exchange and imply exposure of vulnerability. In cases of successful trustworthy actions interpersonal trust is likely to increase the intimate relation and closeness between the subjects.

Even though such interpersonal trust is very basic to ethical relations of reciprocity among human beings in friendship, families and love relationship, personal trust is not a sufficient condition for trust in modern social systems (Luhmann 1997, p. 50). Rather trust does not only depend on personal elements but also on social systems and our trust in these social systems. System trust is different from person trust and is generated through our communication in social systems where what Luhmann calls "media" such as money, truth, love and power are functions of social systems that help to establish trustful relations among individuals. Communicative media in different systems – like money, which we intuitively value or truth that we recognize as an absolute value – function as symbols for trust, which help to reduce complexity and create stability in modern complex and highly differentiated societies. It is a general characteristic of risk society and the modern world that we have a tendency to go from personal trust to a somewhat diffuse system trust as the foundation for our lives in complex societies (Luhmann 1997, p. 53). A condition for our survival in complex societies is that we not only live in personalized life world with other people that we can trust, but also that we have to trust the many social systems in which we take part.

Self-representation of organizations in public space as good corporate citizens illustrates how corporations in a learning process of emergent trust contribute to the formation of public trust and increase their trustworthiness as business partners.

Formulation of corporate identity, branding and establishment of the organization in the public mind contribute to the symbolization of system trust. In cases of efforts to create genuine transparency and integrity in images of the organization such self-representation may manifest a reduction of complexity of the content of a social system, which is trustworthy for stakeholders of the corporation. This is realized by techniques of strategic public relations, for example appealing to the rhetorical figures: logos, ethos and pathos (Thyssen 2003, p. 46). Logos is about using factual language to create corporate legitimacy, ethos is about emphasizing normativity and pathos is about the good and serious intentions of the organization. In order to appeal to public trust rhetorical figures are used as a part of the expressive aesthetics of the organization. In presenting its values, virtues and self-understandings the organization constructs a symbolic picture of its own identity, which is a presupposition for the trust of its stakeholders.

This concept of system trust emphasizes the need to understand the process of trust at organizational and structural levels of institutional networks because of the need for reduction of complexity in technological society (Luhmann 1997, p. 58). System trust in the highly differentiated social systems of modernity expresses our trust in a generalized social order. This is emphasized by the fact that the understanding of complexity in modern business organizations and their functionality increasingly demands specified knowledge about economic markets, personalities of managers and employees and of decision making and production in economic systems. Control and understanding of systems require professional and practical knowledge and this is the reason why system trust to corporations may be very fragile in situations of risk and rapid social change. Moreover, in order to create corporate legitimacy according to social expectations system trust is essential in constituting corporations as good corporate citizens. Hence, even in the system perspective it is important to emphasize that this presupposes the relation between responsibility, accountability and integrity as constitutive elements of authentic trust and trusting (Mayer et al. 1995).

## 2 Trust as a dynamic movement of ethical accountability and responsibility

In this analysis of trust between persons and system trust we have relied on Luhmann's interpretation of Talcott Parsons' functionalist sociology in combination with phenomenological accounts of human intersubjectivity, intentionality and subjective relations to the world. Now we will analyze trust and trusting as a dynamic ethical movement of accountability and responsibility in business systems. We are close to the existentialism of the French philosopher Jean-Paul Sartre when we argue that trust, as reduction of complexity, is the way humanity deals with the possibility of chaos and anguish of nothingness beyond our human life-world (Rendtorff 1998, Sartre 1943). There is a kind of "bad faith" in our process of sense-making with trust because we refuse to deal with the contingency of the meaning of the social world.

Even though system trust is very different from personal trust similar conceptions seem to lie behind trust in social systems like organizations and business networks. As Kenneth Arrow has remarked trust process is "virtually every commercial transaction has within itself an element of trust, certainly any transaction conducted over a period of time" (Fritzsche 1997, p. 22). Among many definitions in theory of organizations trust is used as explanation of human action. Trust is based on individual's expectations of acceptable behavior of other people in situations of limited knowledge and uncertainty. Trust includes the elements of predictability, dependency and faith. This means that one relies so much on another person or institution that one takes the risk to expect that the other person or institution will behave in a certain way. Trust as opposed to opportunism indicates reduction of insecurity among agents in organizations. It is the reflective anticipation of a reliable behavior of possible opponents. Trust is defined as informal norms, which may have the same importance for organizational unity as the rule of law or ethical principles.

According to rational choice theory, trust and trusting can be reducible to self-interest (Ballet and Bry 2001, p. 266). Trust is described as a rational deliberation linked to personal choice. Therefore trust is at the same time a functional and also reflective instrument to calculate utility and risks of opportunism. Neither personal trust nor system trust can have any intrinsic importance. Opposed to this individualistic concept is the view of trust as based on solidarity and cooperation. In this perspective mutual reciprocity is the ethical foundation of trust as an important ingredient of building social institutions.

We would argue that the emergent trust in the processes of sense-making in organizing requires both elements of personal trust and of system trust and that this is an essential element in corporate citizenship. In this context, we see link between business ethics, trust and trustworthiness. This is an integrative model of trust that relies on the integrative paradigm of trust as accepted vulnerability, closely related to integrity (Rendtorff 2009). Here we go from aesthetics to ethics and use values in organizational culture to create social trust in organizations. One way to create symbols of social capital for organizations as an important element of corporate identity may seem to work with transparency and business ethics because these "media" and symbolization seems to appeal both at elements from personal and system trust. In order to establish a relation between these two dimensions of trust in regard to organizations we have to look at the ethical aspect of personal trust. When we extend the phenomenological perspective on trust as a component of human interaction and institution building we must admit that trust is fundamentally an ethical notion appealing to human moral autonomy, responsibility, transparency, accountability and integrity (Rendtorff 2011).

In the analysis of Luhmann's concept of trust we learned that personal trust in someone is to expose one's vulnerability to the other. This implies a philosophical and psychological notion of trust seeing the trust process as a sign of human interdependence and reciprocity and our ability to ignore and cope with risk in our lives because we have to trust each other (Govier 1997, p. 11). In this view the starting point may be the blind trust of the child relating unconditionally to the world without suspicion or distrust. But even though the trust of the child is engaging it is also an indication of the reflexivity of trust. Our argument for trust as choice of reduction of complexity emphasizes such reflexive aspects of trust. Experienced people decide whether to trust or mistrust in their existential confrontation with the world. Relating this concept of trust to institutions we may say that networks and organizations as the foundation for human actions, norms and decision-making are based on such a great vulnerability, complexity and ambiguity that we have to take the risk of trusting each other without having deep rational evidence or security to support our basic actions.

The Danish theologian K.E. Løgstrup has given the most comprehensive definition of the ethical foundation of trust, which can be argued to consider emergent trust as a process of sense-making. In his major work on ethics Løgstrup defines trust as human surrender to the conditions of existence (Løgstrup [1953] 1998, p. 74). He argues that one's expectation of the other, articulated in the act of trust, expresses an *ethical demand*. Rejected self-surrender expresses itself in moral accusations. Even in situations that have nothing to do with morality rejected hope of fulfillment of trust requirements may lead to conflict, moral disappointment and blame. In this view trust is a spontaneous expression of our belief in life and the world. We are basically confident and open to other people, for example in love relations and communicative encounters.

This is also the case when we relate to strangers. We suppose that they are reliable and that they are not going to hurt us. Trust and self-surrender to the other is a basic component of human existence. The ethical demand gives the other a basic ethical responsibility. In other words to trust the other person is to consider this trustworthy person as a person of integrity (Rendtorff 2011). Trust relies on expectations of ethical behavior because it has an open-ended character where we trust other persons without any basis in the natural, legal or other strong certainties. The essence of the sense-making in the trust process is the demand that the other person should fulfill our expectations. In our surrender we require that the person we have chosen to trust is responsible and accountable.

Accordingly, trust and trusting emerges in the mutual interdependence, reciprocity and interaction between human beings in a common social world. The ethics of trust implies the belief in the accountability of the other as compensation for our own vulnerability and fragility. Here the relation between trust and accepted vulnerability is important. It is based on the existential idea of facticity of human existence as "being in the world" where individuals in their situations of existential choice are open to the encounter of the other as subject for moral concern. In such a common world, human beings that are trustful are pictured as persons of accountability and integrity. Applying these ideas in business ethics we perceive that trust is a fundamental condition for good ethical relations among actors. A trustworthy person is someone who acts according to the Kantian concept of ethical and moral autonomy (O'Niell 2002). This idea is based on self-respect, dignity and integrity (Rendtorff and Kemp 2000). Respect for dignity presupposes reciprocity and mutuality, which extended in a process of interaction to relations with employees and customers or other stakeholders, becomes trust (Costa 1998, p. 231; Moon and Bonny 2001, p. 60). As a virtue of organizational and individual behavior integrity is very important for increasing good relations in process interactions among business partners. And trust is a part of the constitution of integrity when we meet these business partners who are like strangers from different cultures.

As we can deduce from the phenomenological perspective trust may be considered as the asymmetric opposite to responsibility, because the individual in trusting the other is committing oneself to the responsibility of the other. The idea is that by trusting somebody you allow yourself to be dependent on this person and this generates a responsibility for this person or entity to accept the challenges and requirements and not to abuse the trust relation. Therefore we can see a close relation between responsibility and accepted vulnerability. In this context trust and trusting indicate the ethical borderlines of economic theory where actors are vulnerable to risk. Business ethics is essential for the emerging trust relations in organizational sense-making and may help us to be aware of these challenges. Good faith and openness to the other is conceived as a fundamental basis for participating in economic life. In the end trust presupposes virtues of honest behavior and this can contribute to greater social coherence in community and better business opportunities.

In order to improve social capital in corporations we may draw the consequences of our ethical view of the process of trust for organizational sense-making in business life. The elements of organizational systems that help to create trust give organizations good images in public life. Active work with ethical values and business ethics helps to establish a trustful reputation of companies in the public. It is also very important to share knowledge and information with the public. A key element in trust is transparency that contributes to the belief of shareholders and stakeholders that the corporation is reliable for investing or purchase of products. A spirit of transparency includes that corporations do not hide controversial information about policies and corporate finance but include any important information in corporate reporting (DiPiazza Jr. and Eccles 2002, p. 4).

A different element of creation of public trust in business organization is to have a culture of accountability where organizations take responsibility for their actions and of lack of disclosure of information to stakeholders. Organizational accountability applies at all levels of the organization for managers, employees who should show their willingness to serve shareholders and stakeholders rather than exclusively pursuing their personal interests. Accountability and responsibility of corporations include compliance with all international standards, rules, regulations and codes of conduct. But this is not possible without people with integrity; individual managers or employees of the organizations who are committed to transparency, honesty, which implies to do the "right thing".

Accountability, integrity and moral responsibility manifest institutional symbolization appealing to the value of truth as the center of organizational commitment to be a good citizen in society. Therefore these values can be considered as the institutional basis for long-term sustainability and social capital of the corporation. The emergence of trust in organizations and more informal networks as social systems relates to the individual's expectation that a group of persons, a firm or an organization will act in accordance with basic ethical rules of the market system. This belief is fundamental for cooperation, because other firms in a complex environment without hard evidence must make a reduction of complexity and rely on the trust that other groups of persons, firms and institutions will not abstain from following fundamental values of accountability and moral responsibility for common action and economic exchange (Håkonsson and Johansson 1989).

To base a culture of trust on the accountability and responsibility of the organization can be explained by the concept of integrity in organizations. We can say that integrity is the other flip of the coin of the trust process of sense-making in organizations. Integrity in sense-making requires that the organization is honest and transparent about its policies and decisions, which is central to the institutional idea of organizational integrity (Paine 1994, 1996, 1997). In being honest and transparent an organization can appeal simultaneous to personal trust of its employees and to system trust in its self-representation in society and this initiates the trust process in organizational interaction. To be a good corporate citizen complying with rules and regulations and being transparent about decision-making in the public is the key to greater public trust.

Even though such ethical concepts of organizations may seem very plausible we have to deal with a problem of the normative dimensions of trust analysis. We have shown that ethics is an important presupposition for a sense-making perspective of both personal trust and system trust. It is therefore important to emphasize that there is a difference between the emphasis of ethics of trust and the dangers of explaining trust by moralizing that trust always will be good. One of the pitfalls of the ethical view of trust is to say that trust is always good. Even though we propose an ethical definition of trust we agree with Luhmann that we should be very skeptical of such possible moralization of the concept of trust (Luhmann 1997, p. 86).

We should not forget that it certainly is possible to find situations where mistrust would be better than trust for example when corporations use manipulative marketing campaigns to convince consumers about their products. There is no ultimate normative argument for trust, because it is very dependant on specific situations whether trust is good or bad. Trust cannot always be morally good, because it is dependent on specific situations of choice. Ethics must confront the many situations where trust is alienated, confused or deceived, for example when corporations use ethics programs and corporate reporting as a cosmetic instrument for hiding unethical behavior, financial problems or even criminal action. We can for example imagine large bureaucratic organizations where individuals blindly trust authorities without questioning their "evil" orders.

Therefore in order to be aware of the possible abuses of trust we can follow Luhmann in saying that it is important to work with the functionalist system theory when analyzing the role of trust processes in social systems. The fact that we think that ethics can help to build trust in organizations does not exclude the descriptive analysis of trust as the basis of decision theory inside and outside organizations. In emphasizing that trust is neither a prognosis, nor a mean, nor a goal in itself. We can say that trust is not the only element in social capital. Trust is only one among different functions and rationalities of sustaining complex organizations. Establishing trust relations as the basis for social capital gives the social system a certain institutional stability in different forms of formal and informal networks. Media such as money, truth, power or love help to build the organizational coherence in emergent trust processes. Such stabilization of social systems help to make them work more efficiently, but it also contributes to the differentiation of the system in regard to other systems and organizations. Trust and trustworthiness is one among different structures that help to reduce complexity and distinguish social systems from their social context and environment.

### 3 Trust as emergent social capital in organizational culture

We are now able to discuss the importance of trust and trusting as accountability for leadership, integrity in organizations and organizational culture as a way to create corporate citizenship as the basis for increased social capital. Trust is generally considered as a central informal element and condition of business ethics in modern society. How do we interpret this development? In terms of the work on the new spirit of capitalism of Luc Boltanski and Eve Chapello (1995) we can say that the new emphasis on values and trust expresses changing concepts of capitalism moving from stable bureaucracies to open process and project concepts of organizations.

According to them business ethics is a good example about how the vocabulary of the 1960s has moved into business. They say that the argument "ethics pays" from the ethics movement in the 1990s is an indirect way to introduce moral issues in business (Boltanski and Chapello 1995, p. 111). Managers want to expose themselves as people of trust and confidence in the emerging network economy and therefore they are motivated by business ethics. Business ethics is an element of the introduction of the logic of the private and domestic world into the business world and thereby an element of the introduction of network capitalism of the 1990s with its refusal of hierarchy, emphasis on change and flexibility, virtue, friendship. Luc Boltanski and Eve Chapello emphasizes that the management of the 1990s were trying to show themselves as persons of high ethical standards and integrity (Boltanski and Chapello 1995, p. 146). Business ethics is also response to the difficulties of managing persons in flexible network organizations, where people work in network far from central management. Therefore business ethics is a way to ensure compliance in organizing. This is the same thing with the concept of confidence or trust, which is becoming a new form of control.

Moreover, norms of reciprocity, respectability and trustworthiness help corporations to respond to social expectations by a good reputation in society. We could emphasize that a thoroughgoing lack of trust between business and its customers in the business environment simply would make it impossible to exchange goods. The functionalist view of trust based on the distinction between personal trust and more diffuse system trust may help us to conceptualize how corporations can increase external and internal trust relations. In a global network society with easy and very fast flows of information the need to build trustful images and reputation are important for the corporation in order to have stable customers and good employees. Without such fair arrangements of goods and interactions among members of organization are in danger of leading to corrupt and unequal power relations and mistrust opening for opportunistic behavior, which may generate discourses and relations of mistrust destroying the image and legitimacy of specific firms.

This need to express trustful character and identity is reflected in efforts of corporations to respond to demands of different stakeholders by engaging in organizational ethics, alternative reporting, efforts to relate in a socially responsible way to local community and also initiatives to reduce damage to the environment. To work with trust in leadership, values and corporate ethics indicate such an effort to make trust a part of organizational culture. Trust is important for work relations because it improves cooperation in changing and evolving organizations (Fairholm 1994, Kramer and Tyler 1996).

Trust is indeed an element in creating a sense of community and good citizenship among employees, which helps to cope with and other problems in the organization. Therefore building trust is a feature of leadership strategy because it reinforces the sustainability of the organization. We may consider trustworthiness as an element of the integrity of a good leader (Ciulla 2002). Leaders who are enjoying great loyalty cannot fake trustworthiness but have respect from employees due to their willingness to serve the common good. Such leaders with integrity are connective people who build up networks and social ties based on trust, but they are also people who are able to bridge between different value systems (Ciulla 2002, p. 348). And due to their ability to establish open trust relations, employees are willing to accept security and take more risk.

Moreover, motivated and educated employees cannot successfully be governed by strict control, and they are increasingly having the liberty to be free to organize their personal working life in order to make sense of their work in organizations. Building trust in organizations can help them to be more efficient, because it makes employees more tolerant for ambiguity. High trust organizations reduce the need for control and managers and employees can interact with their stakeholders dealing with a high degree of ambiguity, uncertainty and unexpected events. Interpersonal trust among organizational members improves the group cohesion and the culture of the organization (Fairholm 1994, p. 97). Reliability of stakeholders and other members of organizations improve cooperative action and possible success of organizational activities.

Simon Zadek shows us ways to build trust in his analysis of the civil corporation (Zadek 2001). In his view, trust functions not only an as image, but as a genuine concern to be ethical and care for stakeholders. This was for example the case when Levi-Strauss argued that it wanted to make a difference in improving people's lives and decided to improve its labor practices by joining the Fair Labor Association in 1999 (Zadek 2001, p. 39). Credibility and trust is based on individual citicens' visions and opinions about corporations, and trust in organizations is often based on reliance on particular individuals, for example leaders with high integrity have been a strong symbol of her firm's ecological value commitments. However, NGOs often experience greater trust than commercial firm because of their philanthropic commitments and this is an argument for the importance of business ethics and real commitment beyond economic greed in order to create corporate accountability (Zadek 2001, p. 44). Indeed, it is necessary to professionalize values-driven management and corporate reporting in order to expose the honest intentions of the firm. In these context efforts of external verification of triple bottom line auditing and accounting as required by companies like Shell, Novo Group is crucial for improving corporate credibility. However, external verification will not be sufficient without continuous will to improvement and stakeholder dialogue (Zadek 2001, p. 212).

The ethical definition of trust is a response to those who argue that not all reciprocity and cooperation may be good for society. What about the strong social ties of the Mafia? What about trust among members of corporations who do not obey the law? Here trust relations seem to reinforce inequality. What seems to be good for these corporations does not benefit society and it may have bad consequences for workers and consumers (Field 2003, p. 72). But the use of social capital in anti-social and amoral networks or organizations is in the long run not really efficient for the firm. Opportunistic manipulation with trust may create temporary beliefs in honesty and respectability of firms, but such a strategy is very dangerous and is likely to have negative consequences, because there is a close link between truth, moral integrity and trust.

In organizational culture reflective trust emerges in the tension between knowledge and ignorance, implying taking a risk in situations, where the search for full knowledge is impossible, irrational or very cost full for the social actor. With regard to interactions between individuals in institutions trust is very important for easy economic transactions. Establishment of expectations and habits of trust in organization put normative boundaries on individuals who are likely to act with pure selfishness with-out any cooperative efforts. In the perspective of game theory there also seems to exist very powerful strategic arguments for the advantage of cooperative trust relations where trusting the other after all is the most advantageous action of individuals who are maximizing rational self-interest (Govier 1997, p. 10). Cooperation is a game and going into collaboration with other individuals involves taking great risk (Axelrod 1984). Sometimes, however, the rational concept of trust is based on a too strong opposition between trust and distrust and makes us forget that there are different lev-els or degrees of trust. This is not always the case in practical reality of organization where there are many different levels of expectations of trust.

Further indication of the importance of trust as accountability for corporate citi-zenship and social capital in organizational culture is the complexity of the relations between power and responsibilities of employees, managers with regard to decision-making and practical judgment. Decision-making is required to be in accordance with values that reflect social expectations to the corporation. Mutual respect and trust is in this context a condition for collaboration in the community of the organiza-tion. We might say that the need of trust is motivated because of the vulnerability of managers and employees in organizations with regard to the stakeholders with whom they are dealing. Bad judgment and lack of integrity or simple errors may have fatal consequences for the collaborative efforts of community. Distrust may be the result of the inability to establish a common culture of trust to respect mutual vulnerabilities. Leaders both in private business and in public organizations need to establish trustful relations in order to keep their position in society. Not engaging in such trustful rela-tions makes risks emerge as a basis for decisions. Values of truth telling and promise keeping become central values in order to establish trustful relation among members of a particular organization.

What is needed is an institutional foundation for trust in the life world of institu-tions. Amartya Sen considers transparency guarantees where the individual can inter-act with others with stable expectations of what they can get as essential to capitalist freedom (Sen 1999, p. 39). Established rules of behaviour and knowledge about busi-ness partner's ethics are important non-economic conditions for development of mar-ket economics. One way to ensure this is to establish policies of values and sanctions at the institutional level so that there is special attention to fraud, dishonesty, corrup-tion and other deceptive practices at the institutional level. In this context ethics codes and policies of values-driven management may improve communication and branding for stakeholders and contribute to the reinforcement of trust between employees and managers and the external stakeholders. In this way professional self-regulation is a part of contributions to the common good at the social level. This work with values can be considered as ways to define this professional self-regulation. The ethics code is a device to determine action. It helps to show to the environment what is considered as good and trustful actions of the firm. The ethics codes help business individuals to be aware of what is good judgment and it can help to ensure compliance to ethics rules in the corporations. Ethical principles formulated in ethics codes are very important for the creation of a culture of trust in different organizations.

In this perspective we need trust and accountability as developed in business ethics and codes of conduct in order to build up social stability in economic interactions as a constitutive element of corporate citizenship. Economics is dependent on social relations based on common expectations, cultures, communities and strong social ties. Expectations of trust or mistrust contribute to the facilitation of social interaction. Trust is necessary because it stabilizes expectations to social actors in communication and exchange. External and internal relations of trust are the basis for integrating the firm in the civic traditions of society. This idea of embeddedness as developed by Karl Polanyi and Marc Granovetter imply that economic interactions cannot be separated from their embeddedness in civil structure of society (Granovetter 1985, Polanyi 1994). Due to the embeddedness of economic transactions in social structure, trust is also important in interactions between different companies. Moreover, firms have to communicate their capacity of institutional stability in a society of transformation with many different stakeholders. In this context we have analyzed trust as a contribution to the creation of reflexivity and self-observation of corporations.

## Conclusion

Thus, we can conclude that creating trust and trustworthiness is a part of the ethics and values of corporations that need to be institutionalized in order to create social acceptance and legitimacy of business firms. High levels of trust and trusting in organizational cultures are important for coherence of interactions in the firm. These internalization of common norms establish reciprocity and bounded solidarity in the firm, which will be the basis enlarging the institutional network of the firm in confident relations with its stakeholders. Accordingly we can argue that trust and accountability is important for the process of dynamic establishment of good corporate citizenship as an embedded factor of civic relations in society, responding to social expectations of consumers and citizens.

Our focus on the ethical idea of trust as based on integrity has demonstrated the need to see trustworthy business practices in the process perspective of creating good corporate citizenship and legitimacy with business ethics as the basis for trust and trustworthiness. When we analysed trust as a process of reduction of complexity in the social world we say that the business ethics is important for the creation of system trust as a necessary reduction of complexity in business institutions of the modern world. Here we say that the ethical culture of corporations creates good corporate citizenship that makes the business organization trustworthy. Trust is needed for institutional coherence both externally and internally in organiations. Trustworthiness and trust contributes to a process of reduction of complexity through sense-making by measures of ethical governance, values-driven management and corporate reporting. As a dynamic movement of accountability and responsibility creating trust through trustworthiness became an instrument for dealing with problems and complexity in business firms and organization.

By communicating trustworthiness through corporate citizenship corporations respond to social expectations and contribute to seeing themselves as good corporate citizens. Here, a firm creates trust and becomes trustworthy by responding to ethical norms and values. This is the dynamic movement of ethical accountability, integrity and responsibility where this relation is constitutive of authentic trust. This emergence of integrity contributes to the definition of trustworthiness as the result of the sense-making process in organization where organizational integrity emerges as a result of the efforts of making the corporation trustworthy. Social capital is created since the business corporation becomes trustworthy through business ethics performance that becomes an essential element and condition of trust in complex business systems.

Accordingly, from the ethical perspective trust, trusting and trustworthiness is an integrated part of business ethics in institutions that functions as an effort to improve the social legitimacy of business corporations. Business ethics activities creates trust and trustworthiness because the sense-making of the process of ethics include focus on accountability, integrity and responsibility which in general makes the corporation a trustworthy and legitimate institution and organization according to social expectations of society.

## Bibliography

Axelrod, Robert (1984), *The Evolution of Cooperation*, Basic Books, New York.

Ballet, Jerome and Bry, Françoise de (2001), *L'éthique de l'entreprise*, Éditions du Seuil, Paris.

Beck, Ulrich (1986), *Risikogesellschaft*, Suhrkamp, Frankfurt.

Beck, Ulrich, Giddens, Anthony and Lash, Scott (1994), *Reflexive Modernization*, Stanford University Press, Stanford.

Bidault, Jacques et al. (eds.). (1997), *Trust, the Firm and Society*, Macmillan, London.

Boltanski, Luc and Chapello, Eve (1995), *Le nouvel esprit du capitalisme*, Gallimard, Paris.

Ciulla, Joanne B. (2002) 'Trust and the Future of Leadership.' In Bowie, Norman (ed.). *The Blackwell Guide to Business Ethics*, Blackwell Publishers, Oxford, pp. 345–346.

Costa, John Dalla (1998) *The Ethical Imperative, Why Moral Leadership is Good Business*, Perseus Books, Reading, MA.

DiPiazza Jr., Samuel and Eccles, Robert G. (2002), *Building Public Trust*. John Wiley & Sons, London.

Fairholm, Gilbert W. (1994), *Leadership and the Culture of Trust*, Preager, London.

Field, John (2003), *Social Capital*, Routledge, London.

Fritzsche, David F. (1997), *Business Ethics. A Global and Managerial Perspective*, McGraw-Hill, International Editions, New York.

Fukuyama, Francis (1995), *Trust. The Social Virtues and the Creation of Prosperity*. Free Press, New York.

Gehman, Joel, Treviño, Linda K. and Garud, Raghu (2013), 'A Process study of the Emergence and Performance of Organizational Values Practices', *Academy of Management Journal*, vol. 58, no. 1, pp. 84–12.

Govier, Trudy (1997), *Social Trust and Human Communities*, McGill Queens University Press, Montreal.

Granovetter, Marc (1985), 'Economic Action and Social Structure: The Problem of Embeddedness', *American Journal of Sociology*, vol 91, pp. 481–510.

Håkonsson, H. and Johansson, J. (1989), *Corporate Technological Behaviour, Cooperation and Networks*. Croom Helm, London.

Holmström, Susanne (2004), *Grænser for ansvar – Den sensitive virksomhed i det refleksive samfund*. Skriftserie, Center for værdier i virksomheder, RUC 5.

Kramer, R.M. and Tyler, T.R. (eds.), (1996), *Trust in Organizations*, Sage, London.

Langley, Ann, Smallman, Clive, Tsoukas, Haridimos and Van de Ven, Andrew H. (2013), 'Process Studies of Change in Organization and Management: Unveiling Temporality, Activity, and Flow,' *Academy of Management Journal*, vol. 58, no. 1, pp. 1–13.

Langley, Ann and Tsoukas, Haridimos (2010), *Introducing "Perspectives on Process Organization Studies"*, Oxford University Press, Oxford.

Løgstrup, K.E. (1953), *Den etiske fordring*, Gyldendal, København (1998, 1953), Partly in English translation in Arne Johann Vetlesen: *The Ethics of Closeness*, Scandinavian University Press, Oslo, 1997, pp. 71–72.

Luhmann, Niklas (1997), *Trust and Power: Two Works by Niklas Luhmann*, With Introduction by Gianfranco Poggi, John Wilet and Sons, Chichester, New York, Brisbane, Toronto.

Mayer, R.C., Davis, J.H. and Schoorman, F.D. (1995), 'An Integrative Model of Organizational Trust,' *Academy of Management Review*, vol. 20, no. 3, pp. 709–734.

Möllering, Guido (2013), 'Process Views of Trusting and Crises.' In Bachmann, R. and Zaheer, A. (eds.) *Handbook of Advances in Trust Research*, Edward Elgar, Cheltenham.

Moon, Chris and Bonny, Clive (eds.) (2001), *Business Ethics. Facing Up to the Issues*, The Economist Books, London.

O'Niell, Onora (2002), *A Question of Trust*. Cambridge University Press, London.

Paine, Lynn Sharp (1994), 'Managing for Organizational Integrity', *Harvard Business Review*, Harvard, Cambridge, MA.

Paine, Lynn Sharp (1996), 'Moral Thinking in Management, an Essential Capability', *Business Ethics Quarterly*, vol. 6, no. 4, Reprinted by Harvard Business School Press

Paine, Lynn Sharp (1997), *Cases in Leadership, Ethics and Organizational Integrity. A Strategic Perspective*, Irwin, Chicago.

Polanyi, Karl (1944), *The Great Transformation*, Rinehart, New York.

Putnam, Robert D. (2000), 'Bowling Alone'. *The Collapse and Revival of American Community*. Touchstone, New York.

Putnam, Robert D., Leonardi, R. and Nanetti, R.Y. (1993), *Making Democracy Work*, Princeton University Press, Princeton, NJ.

Rendtorff, Jacob Dahl (1998), *Jean-Paul Sartres filosofi*, Hans Reitzels forlag, København.

Rendtorff, Jacob Dahl (2009), *Responsibility, Ethics and Legitimacy of Corporations*, Copenhagen Business School Press, Copenhagen.

Rendtorff, Jacob Dahl (2011), 'Corporate Citizenship as Organizational Integrity.' In Pies, Ingo and Koslowski, Peter (eds.). *Corporate Citizenship and New Governance: The Political Role of Corporations*, Springer, Dordrecht, Heidelberg, London, New York, pp. 59–91.

Rendtorff, Jacob Dahl and Kemp, Peter (2000), *Basic Ethical Principles in European Bioethics and Biolaw, Autonomy, Dignity, Integrity and Vulnerability, Vol I–II*, Center for Ethics and Law, Copenhagen and Barcelona.

Sartre, Jean-Paul (1943), *L'Être et le Néant*, Gallimard, Paris.

Sen, Amartya (1999), *Development as Freedom*, Anchor Books, New York.

Solomon, Robert C. and Flores, Fernanando (2001), *Building Trust in Business, Politics, Relationships, and Life*, Oxford University Press, Oxford.

Thyssen, Ole (2003), 'Det handler om tillid.' In Bordum, Anders and Barlebo Wenneberg, Søren (eds.). *Det handler om tillid*, Samfundslitteratur, København, pp. 163–175.

Zadek, Simon (2001), *The Civil Corporation. The New Economy of Corporate Zitizenship*, Earthscan, London.

# Part III

# Monitoring and reporting on sustainability

# Positioning of corporate social responsibility in media reporting

## The role of media setting

*Jamilah Ahmad and Suriati Saad*

Corporate social responsibility (CSR) has been a serious concern over the past three decades in media reports, public forums, academic debates and governmental policies, mainly because of the increasing careless corporate behaviours, poor and failed corporate governance practices together with continually rising social expectations and stakeholder pressures (Sun et al. 2010). However, issues like corporate fraud, greed, selfishness, short-termism, corporate failure and collapse, abuse of management power and the excess of executive remuneration would not have been so exacerbated and exposed

Media have a huge role in broadcasting corporate social responsibility (CSR) messages to the world at large. For corporations, it is not just about performing their effort for social causes but also to inform their stakeholders and publics so that others are inspired and they set an example for others to follow. Other than creating appealing and conscious advertisement, corporations must procure the cooperation and support of media in spreading awareness about CSR helping society look at the corporation beyond profits and hence the media (which is a guardian of public good) has a huge role to play in this endeavor.

The media can be used to seek volunteers from the society or the specific places where the corporations are launching their CSR initiatives. Further, they can be used to publish articles pertaining to the values and the mission of the corporation in promoting CSR. The way in which the social initiatives undertaken by corporations have been covered in the media speaks volumes about how well the corporation has managed its media coverage. Media function as an independent monitor for corporations and acts as a channel for corporations to communicate with public. How media tell their stories impacts public and policy makers' expectations, and influences decision making and business in socially responsible manner.

Apart from this, the media can also act as a conscience keeper by constantly reminding corporations about the need to give back to society and to look beyond profits. Internationally, *The Guardian* newspaper has been at the forefront of demanding accountability and transparency from the corporations. In India, *The Hindu* does a good job of publishing articles and editorials that exhort the corporations to be socially conscious. Finally, the media can also take a critical view of the CSR programs that a corporation claims to run and it can ensure that the corporation is not indulging in "Green Washing" which is the case where a corporation pretends to follow CSR but in reality does not do so.

## What is news?

The media play a critical role in influencing the reputation of companies (Einwiller et al. 2010, Jonsson et al. 2009, Kennedy 2009). By not covering negative corporate news or describing such events in a more positive light, editors and journalists can limit the damage caused by corporate scandals. While editors enjoy some discretion when selecting news stories, competition forces the media to provide content in which the audience has an interest (Gentzkow and Shapiro 2010). A common finding in empirical studies is that audiences want information that is relevant and new (Clayman and Reisner 1998). In our context, relevance implies that larger and more severe spills are more likely to be covered because they have a bigger impact on the natural environment and possibly human health. Similarly, events at larger firms are likely to find greater interest (Godfrey et al. 2009).

The news content of stories is a second dimension that is important to readers (Meyers 1997). There are many reasons why a faction of an audience may be interested in the CSR performance of a given corporation. Consumers, for instance, might prefer to buy products from socially responsible organisations (e.g., Casadesus-Masanell et al. 2009). Some investors enjoy owning firms that perform well on the CSR dimension (Rosen et al. 1991) and some are concerned that companies that disregard the social consequences of their actions will become the target of regulators and groups of activists, influencing their profitability in the future (Baron and Diermeier 2007, Lyon and Maxwell 2011). Because there are many sources of information about CSR programs – corporation reports, evaluations from independent organisations, as well as media coverage – the audience will have a prior assessment of the degree to which firms engage in CSR. An incident constitutes news if it has the potential to move that assessment.

## Corporate social responsibility (CSR)

CSR is defined as a "voluntary corporate commitment to exceed the explicit and implicit obligations imposed on accompany by society's expectations of conventional corporate behavior" (Falck and Heblich 2007, p. 247). For corporations, the adoption of CSR strategies can enhance their relationships with multiple stakeholders. Therefore, it is necessary to communicate CSR activities and use effective relationship management to satisfy stakeholders' expectations and achieve the expected goals of CSR initiatives (Clark 2000, Podnar 2008).

The general understanding is that CSR has three principles which represent environmental, social and economic dimensions (Kingston and Wagner 2004). The terminology for CSR also varies; some organisations refer to it as corporate responsibility, social responsibility, corporate citisenship, sustainability, or sustainable development (Overton 2004). Common definition of social responsibility refers to the obligations of businessmen to pursue social and sustainable policies to make which are desirable in terms of the objectives and values of our society (Carroll 1999).

In broad terms, CSR includes responsibilities of corporations to the communities and societies within which they are based and operate. Specifically, it involves a business or corporation identifying its stakeholders and incorporating their needs and values in its day-to-day decision-making processes and practices. Therefore,

CSR is the business commitment companies make to act ethically and contribute to the economic development of the community they do business within, while improving the community's well-being beyond what is legally required of them. Corporations should practice CSR engagement on a voluntary basis and involve in behaviours and actions beyond profit making that help improve the quality of life of the community and the individuals within that community to ensure sustainability of both that community and the corporation's long-term survival and well-being (Ahmad 2010).

Tsoutsoura (2004) described CSR as policies, practices and programs that are integrated into business operations, supply chains and decision-making processes throughout the organisation. These policies and practices usually emphasised on issues related to business ethics, community investment, environmental concerns, governance, human rights, the marketplace as well as the workplace. CSR is essentially a holistic concept whereby organisations decide voluntarily to contribute to a better society and cleaner environment (Vuontisjarvi 2006). CSR is a medium to integrate social and environmental concerns in their business operations.

The notion of CSR is an important concept and tool for corporations when responding to various concerns raised about their business or other practices in the globalised world they operate in today (Rampton 2004). Corporations and their public relations practitioners have tried to respond to criticisms aimed at them for not being good global citisens by conveying CSR messages to inform the world-at-large that they are in fact positively contributing to or giving back to society in various ways, both locally and globally (Prabu et al. 2005).

Meanwhile, corporate social responsibility reporting is referred to the provision of information about particular mass media (Kent and Monem 2008). Media are a major stakeholder in defining and promoting CSR, and media coverage of CSR sets the agendas for the public and to some extent, for corporations, by raising awareness about CSR issues and selectively emphasising certain aspects of CSR (Luo, 2012). Corporate social reporting or disclosure is, "the process of communicating the social and environmental effects of organisations' economic actions to particular interest groups within society and to society at large" (Gray et al. 1988). It is not a new trend. It has been traced back to 1880s practices of social disclosure by organisations (Guthrie and Parker 1990, Neu et al. 1998).

## CSR development in Malaysia

CSR as a common business practice has only recently established a foothold and is now an emerging trend in developing countries such as Malaysia (Ahamed et al. 2014). The degree of awareness and engagement in CSR is not at an ignorance stage (Lo and Yap 2011) due to the increasing number of companies which are actively practicing CSR (Azlan et al. 2013). According to Williams (2008), Malaysia is one of the leading countries in CSR among Southeast Asian countries due to the fact that CSR is part of the National Integrity Plan and the Government Linked Companies transformation programme. Based on research conducted on Malaysia companies, 97.5% of the 198 respondents agreed that Malaysian companies are involved in CSR activities (Lo and Yap 2011). Therefore, Khanifar et al. (2012) suggest that corporations have responsibilities to society that extend making profit.

CSR Malaysia is a network of corporate and academic organisations dedicated to improving responsible business practices (Jamilah and Suriati 2013). The goal of CSR Malaysia is to raise the level of CSR consciousness among corporations in Malaysia and to increase capability to tackle social issues aimed to promote responsible business. However, CSR in Malaysia is often perceived as philanthropic responsibility compared to legal obligation (Jamilah and Suriati 2011).

The origin of CSR can be traced back to developed countries and reflects the concerns of stakeholders in high income countries. It is reported that stakeholders in these parts of the world, including communities, are powerful and able to exert pressure on firms to behave appropriately, and they obtain more attention from firms (Kapelus 2002). It is well understood that CSR concepts were brought to Malaysia mainly through the practices of multinational companies.

## Media and corporate social responsibility

According to Zhang and Swanson (2006), media play an indispensable role in the dialogues round CSR. Tench et al. (2007) found that the media view organisations' engagement with CSR through one or more of five possible orientations which are Conformist, Cynic, Realist, Optimist and Strategic Idealist. CSR reporting in general and corporate environmental reporting in particular are in their infancy in Malaysia (Thompson and Zakaria 2004).

The reasons for the apparent low level of corporate environmental reporting in Malaysia is the referred to the lack of government and public pressure, lack of perceived benefits and the widely held view that companies do not significantly impact on the environment. Meanwhile, Bursa Malaysia has launched the CSR Framework for Malaysian public limited companies (PLCs) to adopt the practice of reporting their CSR initiatives. The guidelines for CSR framework and practices are developed based on the four important pillars pertaining: the environment, the community, the marketplace and the workplace as illustrated in Figure 7.1.

## Methodology

A study was conducted in two highest circulation newspaper publication in Malaysia for each language; Bahasa Malaysia (*Utusan Malaysia*) and English (*The Star*) for the period of one year starting from January 2013 to December 2013. A content analysis method was used in this study where news articles classified as an act of corporate social behaviour being analysed. The analysis includes types of coverage and how it was presented in the newspaper.

## Findings and discussion

Findings of the study indicate that CSR news are getting more attention by the news media. Figure 7.2 shows the number of CSR news coverage throughout the year by both newspapers. There is no significant pattern in the amount of coverage except it was lower in February and September. However, in terms of the type of news coverage, it was clear that social engagement and philanthropy initiatives dominate the type of news reported and indirectly relates to the kind of CSR initiatives taken up by most corporations. Figure 7.3 shows the different news associated to the four pillars of CSR initiatives.

*Figure 7.1* The Pillars of Corporate Social Responsibility

Source: Adapted from Bursa Malaysia 2006.

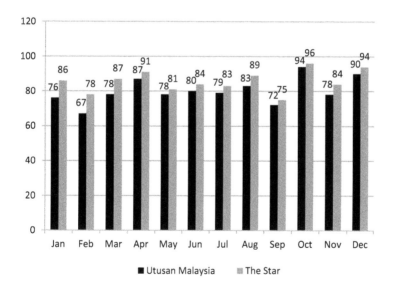

*Figure 7.2* CSR News Coverage by Month (Jan–Dec 2013)

Based on the content analysis CSR presented in the press begins with presenting an understanding of the context in which CSR is dealt with in the articles. This is done by the first analytic theme then classified into dominant themes. Thereafter, the classification of the dominant arguments presented in the articles that support the adoption of CSR. Corporations and the press use media space to express their views on what

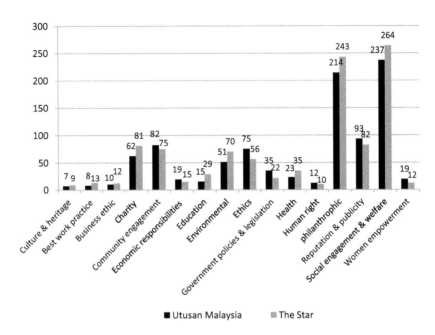

*Figure 7.3* CSR News by Category (Jan–Dec 2013)

CSR is, should be, and how CSR work should be implemented. Dominant themes in the news coverage of CSR are presented in relation to a limited number of themes (Figure 7.3).

Despite the vague and often rather complex nature of CSR, the articles report on issues and events that are straightforward and uncomplicated. The most covered issue is discussed in relation to corporate philanthropy projects and social engagement and welfare initiatives. Presenting social responsibility as corporate philanthropy is a traditional way of understanding business and societal relations, which had existed long before the label CSR was introduced (Vogel 2005). Most often, the press frames corporate philanthropy activities as individual, separate events; such as reporting about a local community project by a specific organisation or a donation to a program or project. These activities offer simplified and isolated events to report upon and are therefore also accessible for journalists and rather easy to turn into articles. Reporting on philanthropic activities also reduces the idea of understanding social responsibility as activities that corporations had been involved in, long before CSR has had its breakthrough.

The results of this study correspond with findings from a study on journalists' perception of CSR in the UK (Tench et al. 2007). In Tench et al.'s study, 50% of the responding journalists agree that CSR involves donations to social causes, and as many as 85% of the respondents stress that CSR is about community development. Corporate social responsibility is also frequently referred to and linked to discussions about rules regulating corporate responsibilities. In these articles, CSR is discussed both in terms of coercive regulations therefore making CSR mandatory for corporations. The news reporting focuses on soft regulation that concerns standards, directives, and guidelines that corporations can choose to follow in the area of CSR. This strengthens the idea of CSR as voluntary and something beyond the law.

The general public's view or opinion of a corporation and its image and reputation is mediated by advertising, the news, and information available in the media that includes the internet (Fombrun and Shanley 1990). Because news is selectively reported due to the process of gatekeeping by the media (Shoemaker et al. 2001) or any content creator at any point in time, and due to time and space constraints, there are always more stories that exist in society than the ones media do and can possibly cover (Carroll and McCombs 2003). Therefore, not all CSR activities of a corporation will be covered in the media at any given time or place. However, a corporation may use a series of strategies such as press releases to increase the chances of their CSR activities being covered in the media and thereby given media exposure and made known to their target publics (Shoemaker et al. 2001).

Previous studies typically investigated the impact of CSR using published news reports (Godfrey et al. 2009, Minor 2011). The results are best understood as describing the effects of CSR conditional on events being covered in the media. If selection is important, however, such media reports do not capture the full effect of CSR programs. To do so, scholars have to investigate the complete set of corporate events of a particular type in a given media market.

According to Einwiller et al. (2010), the media play a critical role in influencing the reputation of companies. By avoiding the coverage of negative corporate news or describing such events in a more positive or neutral light, editors and journalists can limit the damage caused to a corporation. Such practices can influence the process of agenda setting in favour of corporations. Due to media consonance where most leading news outlets report the same news stories and in similar ways (Eilders 2002) and the dependence on the same news wires or press releases by many news organisations, audience interest can be thwarted by the agendas set (Scheufele and Tewksbury 2007) by the main media outlets.

While editors enjoy some discretion when selecting news stories, competition can force the media to provide content in which the audience has an interest (Gentzkow and Shapiro 2010). In an era of highly concentrated cross-media ownership patterns seen across the globe, such a diversity of viewpoints, may not always be available to the general public to be well-informed or obtain a holistic view of events.

There are many reasons why a segment of an audience may be interested in CSR performances. For example, consumers might prefer to buy products from socially responsible organisations (Casadesus-Masanell et al. 2009). Some investors enjoy owning shares in firms that perform well on the CSR dimension (Rosen et al. 1991) and some are concerned that corporations that disregard the social consequences of their actions will become the target of regulators and groups of activists, influencing their profitability in the future (Lyon and Maxwell 2011). Generally, extensive media coverage of the financial crisis and the related corporate behaviour are usually associated with issues of business ethics. This would be a good example of CSR concept-coverage without the media employing the generally explicit term of CSR (Pomering and Dolnicar 2009).

## Role of media

It has been argued that scholarly research needs to pay attention to the role that media play in influencing management practices (Engwall and Sahlin 2007, Mazza and Alvarez 2000). It is also worth taking a look back to see how the often symbiotic business-media relationships came about. According to Argenti (2009), the expanded media, referred to as "the press" in earlier times, has always had a more antagonistic relationship with business, even in the American context. Therefore, it is useful to examine if this phenomenon still exists today especially in Malaysia.

The role of media as a creator and circulator of management ideas and behaviour is further strengthened by the massive development of business media over the past few decades. Business news has gained a prominent position as media are extensively covering corporate, financial and business news (Carroll 2010). Thereby, business media increasingly penetrate and shape corporate activities and vice versa by setting corporate agendas ascribing meaning to corporate events and activities (Hellgren et al. 2002), and creating and circulating management knowledge (Mazza and Alvarez 2000). Given the important role that media play in corporate life, scant attention has been paid to the role of media in the construction and popularisation of CSR – especially to examine if corporate agendas also influence media agendas.

Waddock (2002) indicate that "the main purposes of corporate news releases aimed at the media are to provide society with an accurate understanding of corporate activities and to carry out one's responsibility to inform the public". It underlines the notion that publicity is influenced by the power of the media. However, corporate press releases described as "information subsidies" (Griffin and Dunwoody 1995, Sweetser and Brown 2008, Zoch 2006) the media receives from corporations and used in producing news content, allow corporations to set or shape the media agenda and thereby the public agenda. This is more so with smaller news outlets, which depend largely on media releases to subsidise their newsgathering costs. The common argument being that in order for a corporation to proceed with its business, it is important to provide information about the organisation to the public via the media (with information subsidies), is balanced on the other hand by the question that such a dependence on media releases will undermine the independence and objectivity of the news reaching the general public. CSR initiatives are also interpreted as efforts by a corporation to gain free exposure in the media for the benefit of their clients.

## The symbiotic relationship between the media and CSR

According to the *CSR Digest* (2009), corporate social responsibility (CSR) and the media go hand in hand, with the media disseminating CSR activities and information to the public. But the question is what CSR really means to the media industry. There are also perceptions that the media reporting on CSR are often related to corporate philanthropy such as organisations donating to the poor, sponsorships for education and charitable activities that benefit the less fortunate, etc. However, some of this philanthropy could be good for entire communities as they can be projects aimed at environmental sustainability. For example corporate sponsorship of a mangrove plantation project by the Fishermen's Association in Penang helps fishermen to sustain their income because the healthy growth of mangroves increases biodiversity of the waterways they grow in by increasing the growth of fishes and other aquatic species. This eventually strengthens the livelihoods of the local community and by extension the country's socio-economic well being.

In order to encourage media to cover CSR activities in Malaysia, the prime minister's CSR Awards were launched by the Ministry for Women, Family and Community Development in 2007 (Ministry of Women, Family and Community Development 2012). This has encouraged more organisations to recognise the significance and value of integrating CSR into all aspects of their business operations and decision-making processes. As a result, communities should be seen as more than just a market for the roll-out of products and services for a corporation.

One could argue that there should also be a code for compliance in Malaysia, requiring media organisations to fulfill their own CSR obligations. This would ensure that media will disseminate accurate information on behalf of their stakeholders for the sake of good governance by government institutions, corporations, non-governmental organisations (NGOs), etc. Media should also able to play their role as a watchdog by freely critiquing organisations that use CSR simply for gaining free publicity for their organisations. CSR media reporting should be encouraged because CSR initiatives are a long-term engagement needed to maintain the sustainability of both organisations and communities. However, one could also argue that this is a responsibility already and traditionally entrusted to the media and their actual role today would be to make sure they do not get swayed by media subsidies when reporting corporate CSR activities.

Social media on the other hand provide alternative channels for CSR-related news dissemination and communication for corporations, NGOs and even state organisations, which can then bypass the traditional media gatekeepers (Weerakkody and Monaghan 2011). Social media is changing the way organisations report on CSR because it allows organisations to extend their efforts and CSR initiatives to new groups of stakeholders by communicating directly and interactively with them by receiving audience feedback on their activities. By proactively engaging in social media, corporations can gather more insight into the conversations or dialogues that take place on the blogosphere and understand stakeholder concerns and trends to help them better respond to new challenges (Suzanne 2009).

The news is selectively reported, a fuller understanding of the costs and benefits of CSR activities requires corporations to appreciate how investments in CSR influence the likelihood and quality of press coverage. Corporations' CSR records do in fact influence the probability that the media will pick up a story. Both leading corporations and CSR laggards experience increased media scrutiny. From our observation on media reporting throughout 2013, the results are consistent with prior research about news selection, which indicates that editors favor two types of stories: philanthropical and social engagement. An interesting question for future research is whether CSR can work as insurance for corporations in gaining better perception from stakeholders.

In previous studies of the popularisation of ideas about corporate behaviour, stakeholders are identified as pressure groups, thereby, playing significant roles in governing and influencing organisational behaviour and the adoption of ideas (e.g., den Hond et al. 2007, Peng and Lin 2008). In particular, it has been argued that research needs to pay attention to the role that media play in influencing management practice (e.g., Engwall and Sahlin 2007, Mazza and Alvarez 2000). For example, Alvarez et al. (2005) made inquires for studies addressing "the issue of how the media legitimatise and delegitimatises management practices".

This was supported by Deephouse and Heugens (2009) where they emphasise news media as a significant stakeholder when it comes to put pressure on corporations to change behaviour. The role of media as a creator and circulator of management ideas and behavior is further strengthened by the massive development of business media over the past few decades. Business news has gained a prominent position as media are extensively covering corporate life (Carroll 2010, Duval 2005, Grafström 2006, Kjaer and Slaatta 2007). Thereby, business media increasingly penetrate and shape corporate activities by setting corporate agendas (Carroll 2010, Carroll and McCombs 2003), ascribing meaning to corporate events and activities (e.g., Hellgren et al. 2002, Vaara and Tienari 2002), and creating and circulating management knowledge (Abrahamson and Fairchild 1999, Mazza and Alvarez 2000, Westphal et al. 1997). Given the important role that media play in corporate life, scarce attention has been paid to the role of media in the construction and popularisation of CSR (Tench et al. 2007). The article, thereby, contributes with insights on how corporate social behaviour is presented and mediated in the business press during which this idea has gained prominence. From the previous studies, we know that media matters in the business life. Media are not passive distributors of news, but rather they are active carriers that circulate and create knowledge and models (Mazza and Alvarez 2000, Sahlin-Andersson and Engwall 2002), and thereby influence the consumption of management knowledge (Abrahamson and Fairchild 1999, Alvarez et al. 2005). Media and business media in particular, influence corporate practice by distributing images and ideas on how corporations and corporate leaders should behave (Chen and Meindl 1991, Pollock and Rindova 2003). Business news media have an increasingly important role as agenda-setter (Carroll 2010, Carroll and McCombs 2003) and "sensemaker" by ascribing meaning to and legitimising corporate events and activities (e.g., Hellgren et al. 2002, Vaara and Tienari 2002). Findings from these studies have demonstrated how visibility in media influences the circulation and adoption of management ideas and models. Therefore, it is apt to assume that media also influence the adoption of CSR.

The interest of media for CSR influences corporate actors' interpretation and practice of the same concept. Media is an important stakeholder as media actors intermediate information, and stress that organisations are more likely to adopt social issues when they are paid attention to in the media. Deephouse and Heugens launch the concept infomediaries (information intermediaries) to highlight the role of information in the adoption processes of issues and ideas. Infomediaries, such as media, link organisational actors to societal issues (or ideas), and thereby contribute to the adoption of the same issues. Hence, among the groups of infomediaries, news media play a significant role in "creating linkages between putatively negative or dysfunctional situations in the form of social issues on the one hand, and responsible parties or focal firms whom control resources for issue resolution on the other" (Deephouse and Heugens 2009, p. 549). Media need to be addressed as a force influencing organisational and corporate life, rather than – as often has been the case in the organisational literature – be treated as an independent and unbiased recorder of news events. Media should not only be understood as a mirror of external events and actions, but as actors that frame and interpret practices, ideals, and events (e.g., Schudson 2003).

According to McCombs and Shaw (1972), the agenda setting theory has developed a framework for understanding media content as something that influences public knowledge and opinions. In short, the agenda-setting theory proposes that "the prominence of elements in the news influences the prominence of those elements among the public" (Carroll and McCombs 2003, pp. 36–37). The theory has developed into two levels of agenda-setting: whereas the first level of agenda setting concerns merely the media attention to certain events, issues, or actors, the second level is about how these events, issues, or actors are presented – what attributes are attached to them. Given the vague character of CSR, it is a concept that to a high degree is open for interpretations and reinterpretations in the business press. Schudson (2003) expresses it as "news is not a mirror of reality. It is a representation of the world, and all representations are selective."

Similarly, Chen and Meindl (1991) demonstrate how the popular press created and recreated the image of the corporate leader Donald Burr during his time at People Express. A comprehensive understanding of media must take into account their double roles: Media are both actors – as they construct ideas about CSR – and arenas – as they allow for stakeholders to present their views on CSR. Previous studies demonstrate that news production often takes place in interplay between media and other actor groups such as PR consultants, corporations, non-governmental organisations, and politicians (e.g., Ericson et al. 1989). Media content is hence not constructed in isolation at media organisations; rather, it takes form in constant interplay between various actors. There is a mutual dependence between media and other stakeholders as media are dependent on information from different sources to produce news stories (Deephouse and Heugens 2009), and stakeholders need to access media to further their ends (e.g., Deephouse 2000, Grafström and Pallas 2007).

Stakeholders are not equally visible in media; rather, media tend to rely on certain sources more than others (Danielian and Page 1994, Ericson et al. 1989, Gans 1979/2004). It is, therefore, reasonable to argue that certain actors have higher potential of reaching out with their views and interpretations on CSR than others. Therefore, media have the potential to influence interpretations as well as practices of CSR. By giving media space to CSR and presenting and framing the issue in a particular way, the business media have a potential to influence corporations' attitudes to CSR. Media participate in setting the corporate CSR agenda by deciding what issues become salient, and what attributes are highlighted, and by allowing certain actor groups to express their views on CSR.

## Conclusion

As CSR comes in many forms, researchers, practitioners, politicians, and representatives of the civil society have been searching for clarification and definitions of CSR (Carroll 1979, 1999, Garriga and Mele´ 2004); yet, there is no set definition. Frankental (2001, p. 20) even argues that the vagueness of CSR implies that it "can mean anything to anybody, and therefore is effectively without meaning". Although there are varying definitions and interpretations of the content and meaning of CSR, the adoption of the idea, broadly defined during the last decade, is impressive. It has become increasingly important for corporations to account for their behaviour, products, brands, and reputation in terms of social responsibility (McMillan 2007, Vanhamme and Grobben 2008, Vogel 2005).

Today more and more companies appear to be realising that in order to stay productive, competitive, and relevant in a rapidly changing globalised business world, they have to become socially responsible as well as be financially successful. Globalisation has also created fierce competition for skilled employees, investors, and consumer loyalty. Similarly, over the last decade, media have demonstrated a growing interest in CSR (Grasform 2011). The coverage of CSR activities in the media capture the varying forms of CSR and provide an understanding for how these issues are perceived in the corporate world. As the media coverage of CSR increases in a given media outlet or market, it draws attention to CSR and its positive effects on both the corporation and the community it serves. Therefore, it is important to make CSR an important aspect of any corporate agenda.

Ideally, in reporting a CSR-related story, journalists are required to fulfill certain guidelines consisting of some important factors that will vary depending on the industry, the corporation, and general context such as the culture of the location in which the corporation operates and other relevant issues.

Media contribute to the construction of meaning to CSR in corporate practice by creating links between:

- CSR and corporate activities
- CSR and media positioning
- CSR and news value

Each factor has several key elements that keen minds will automatically survey – particularly once within a specific framework. Therefore, CSR should be truly representing corporation's honesty and it has to be more than fulfilling the requirement.

The article consists of an overview of the CSR and media scenario to date as well as an insight to findings of a study analysis on analysed newspaper coverage on CSR in the two Malaysian newspapers. Both newspapers prominently highlight issues that illustrate the philanthropic and environmental concerns the corporation holds within a carefully hidden economic and legal agenda. CSR is being gauged and perceived by society and media as an organisation's activities/role to help the local community and society at large in addition to fulfilling its moral and ethical "duties and obligations" towards society.

CSR activities in Malaysia are merely a means for an organisation to receive publicity via the media attention the activities attract, while engaging in community relations activities. The media however will not distinguish between a corporation's CSR initiatives and community activities and there will be no significant relationship between the language used when reporting on CSR activities and others. Therefore, media is an essential aid to CSR development while becoming an important channel for providing of publicity for an organisation.

Media in Malaysia can be considered as CSR-friendly because any news under the CSR platform is usually taken as an organisation's efforts and initiatives towards society. Most of the time media in Malaysia do not cover any negative aspects of an organisation's CSR initiatives or critique the relevant CSR exercises and activities which also indicates it is community support, not critical media analysis that follows any CSR initiatives of an organisation.

## Bibliography

Abrahamson, E. and Fairchild, G. (1999), 'Management Fashion: Lifecycles, Triggers, and Collective Learning Processes,' *Administrative Science Quarterly*, vol. 44. pp. 708–740.

Ahamed, W.S., Almsafir, M.K., and Al-Smadi, A.W. (2014), 'Does Corporate Social Responsibility Lead to Improve in Firm Financial Performance? Evidence from Malaysia', *International Journal of Economics and Finance,* vol. 6, no. 3, pp. 126–138.

Ahmad, J. (2010), 'CSR in Malaysia: The Practices and Perception in Dealing with Corporate Social Responsibility in Malaysia and Indonesia.' In Aplikasi Corporate Social Responsibility (CSR) Perusahaan Malaysia dan Indonesia: Perspektif Komunikasi. Penerbit, FISIPOL UGM. Yogyakarta.

Alvarez, J.L., Mazza, C. and Pedersen, J.S. (2005), 'The Role of Mass Media in the Consumption of Management Knowledge,' *Scandinavian Journal of Management*, vol. 21, no. 2, pp. 127–132.

Amran, A., Zain, M.M., Sulaiman, M., Sarker, T. and Ooi, S.K. (2013), 'Empowering Society for Better Corporate Social Responsibility (CSR): The Case of Malaysia,' *Kajian Malaysia,* vol. 31, no. 1, pp. 57–78.

Argenti, P.A. (2009), *Strategic Corporate Communication: A Global Approach for Doing Business in the New India*. McGraw-Hill, New York.

Azlan, A., Mustaffa, M.Z., Maliah, S., Tapan, S. and Say, K.O. (2013), 'Empowering Society for better Corporate Social Responsibility (CSR): The Case of Malaysia', *Kajian Malaysia,* vol. 31, no.1, pp. 57–78.

Baron, D.P. (2008), 'Managerial Contracting and Corporate Social Responsibility,' *Journal of Public Economics*, vol. 92, no. 1, pp. 268–288.

Baron, D. P. and Diermeier, D. (2007), 'Strategic Activism and Nonmarket Strategy,' *Journal of Economics and Management Strategy*, vol. 16, pp. 599–634.

Buhr, H. and Grafström,. M. (2007), 'The Making of Meaning in the Media: Corporate Social Responsibility in the Financial Times, 1988–2000'. In Den Hond, F.G., De Bakker, A. and Neergaard, P. (eds.). *Managing Corporate Social Responsibility in Action: Talking, Doing and Measuring*. Ashgate Publishing, Hampshire. pp. 15–32

Bursa Malaysia (2006) Annual Report 2006 – Investor Relations retrieved from http://bursa.listedcompany.com/misc/ar2006.pdf.

Campbell, J.L. (2007), 'Why Would Corporations Behave in Socially Responsible Ways? An Institutional Theory of Corporate Social Responsibility,' *Academy of Management Review*, vol. 32, no. 3, pp. 946–967.

Carroll, A.B. (1999), 'Corporate Social Responsibility: Evolution of a Definitional Construct', *Business and Society,* vol. 38, No.3, pp. 268–295.

Carroll, C.E. (2010), *Corporate Reputation and the News Media: Agenda-Setting within Business News Coverage in Developed, Emerging, and Frontier Markets*. Routledge, New York and London.

Carroll, C.E. and Mccombs, M. (2003), 'Agenda-Setting Effects of Business News on the Public's Images and Opinions about Major Corporations,' *Corporate Reputation Review*, vol. 6, no. 1, pp. 36–46.

Casadesus-Masanell, R., Crooke, M., Reinhardt, F. and Vasishth, V. (2009), 'Households' Willingness to Pay for "green" Goods: Evidence from Patagonia's Introduction of Organic Cotton Sportswear,' *Journal of Economics & Management Strategy*, vol. 18, no. 1, pp. 203–233.

Chen, C.C. and Meindl, J.L. (1991), 'The Construction of Leadership Images in the Popular Press: The Case of Donald Burr and People Express,' *Administrative Science Quarterly*, vol. 36, no. 4, pp. 521–551.

Clark, C.E. (2000), 'Differences Between Public Relations and Corporate Social Responsibility: An Analysis', *Public Relations Review*, vol. 26, no. 3, pp. 363–380.

Clayman, S.E., and Reisner, A. (1998), 'Gatekeeping in Action: Editorial Conferences and Assessments of Newsworthiness', *American Sociological Review*, Vol 63 (2) pp. 178–199.

Cook, T.E. (1998), *Governing With the News: The News Media as a Political Institution*. University of Chicago Press, Chicago.

Danielian, L.H. and Page, B.I. (1994), 'The Heavenly Chorus: Interest Group Voices on TV News,' *American Journal of Political Science*, vol. 38, no. 4, pp. 1056–1078.

Deephouse, D. L. (2000), 'Media Reputation as a Strategic Resource: An Integration of Mass Communication and Resource-Based Theories', *Journal of Management*, vol. 26, no. 6, pp. 1091

Deephouse, D.L. and Heugens, P.P. (2009), 'Linking Social Issues to Organizational Impact: The Role of Infomediaries and the Infomediary Process,' *Journal of Business Ethics*, vol. 86, no. 4, pp. 541–553.

Den Hond, F. and De Bakker, F.G. (2007), 'Ideologically Motivated Activism: How Activist Groups Influence Corporate Social Change Activities', *Academy of Management Review*, vol. 32, no. 3, pp. 901–924.

Den Hond, F., Bakker, F. G. A. and Neergaard, P. (2007), Managing Corporate Social Responsibility in Action. Aldershot, Ashgate.

Duval, J. (2005), 'Economic Journalism in France.' In Benson, R. and Neveu, E. (eds.). *Bourdieu and the Journalistic Field*. Polity Press, Cambridge, pp. 135–155.

Eilders, C. (2002), 'Conflict and Consonance in Media Opinion Political Positions of Five German Quality Newspapers,' *European Journal of Communication*, vol. 17, no. 1, pp. 25–63.

Einwiller, S.A., Carroll, C.E. and Korn, K. (2010), 'Under What Conditions Do the News Media Influence Corporate Reputation?; The Roles of Media Dependency and Need for Orientation', *Corporate Reputation Review*, vol. 12, no. 4, pp. 299–315.

Engwall, L. and Sahlin, K. (2007), 'Corporate Governance and the Media: From Agency Theory to Edited Corporations.' In Kjaer, P. and Slatta, T. (eds.). *The Rise of the Nordic Business Press*. Copenhagen Business School Press, Copenhagen. pp. 265–284.

Ericson, R.V., Baranek, P.M and Chan, J.B.L. (1989), *Negotiating Control: A Study of News Sources*. Open University Press, Milton Keynes.

Falck, O. and Heblich, S. (2007), 'Corporate Social Responsibility: Doing Well by Doing Good,' *Business Horizons*, vol. 50, no. 3, pp. 247–254.

Flynn, T., Möller, C., Jönsson, R. and Lohmander, A. (2009), 'The High Prevalence of Otitis Media with Effusion in Children with Cleft Lip and Palate as Compared to Children Without Clefts,' *International Journal of Pediatric Otorhinolaryngology*, vol. 73, no. 10, pp. 1441–1446.

Fombrun, C.J. and Shanley, M. (1990), 'What Is in A Name? Reputation Building and Corporate Strategy', *Academy of Management Journal*, vol. 33, no. 2, pp. 233–259.

Frankental, P. (2001), 'Corporate Social Responsibility – A PR-Invention, Corporate Communications,' *An International Journal*, vol. 6, no. 1, pp. 18–23.

Gans, H. (1979), *Deciding What's News: A Study of CBS Evening News, NBC Nightly News, Newsweek, and Time*, Northwestern University Press, Evanston.

Garriga, E. and Mele´, D. (2004), 'Corporate Social Responsibility Theories: Mapping the Territory,' *Journal of Business Ethics*, vol. 53, no. 1/2, pp. 51–71.

Gentzkow, M. and Shapiro, J.M. (2010), 'What Drives Media Slant? Evidence from US Daily Newspapers', *Econometrica*, vol. 78, no. 1, pp. 35–71.

Godfrey, P.C., Craig, B. Merrill and Jared, M.H. (2009), 'The Relationship Between Corporate Social Responsibility and Shareholder Value: An Empirical Test of the Risk Management Hypothesis,' *Strategic Management Journal*, vol. 30, no. 4, pp. 425–445.

Grafstro, M.M. (2006), *The Development of Swedish Business Journalism: Historical Roots of an Organisational Field*. Unpublished doctoral dissertation, Uppsala University, Uppsala.

Grafström, M. and Windell, K. (2011), 'The Role of Infomediaries: CSR in the Business Press During 2000-2009,' *Journal of Business Ethics*, vol. 103, no. 2, pp. 221–237.

Grafström, M. and Pallas, J. (2007), 'The Negotiation of Business News.' In Kjaer, P. and Slaatta, T. (eds.). *Mediating Business: The Expansion of Business Journalism in the Nordic Countries*. CBS Press, Copenhagen, pp. 217–234

Gray, R., Owen, D. and Maunders, K. (1988), 'Corporate Social Reporting: Emerging Trends in Accountability and the Social Contract', *Accounting, Auditing & Accountability Journal*, vol. 1, no. 1, pp. 6–20.

Griffin, R.J. and Dunwoody, S. (1995), 'Impacts of Information Subsidies and Community Structure on Local Press Coverage of Environmental Contamination,' *Journalism & Mass Communication Quarterly*, vol. 72, no. 2, pp. 271–284.

Guthrie, J. and Parker, L.D. (1990), 'Corporate Social Disclosure Practice: A Comparative International Analysis', *Advances in Public Interest Accounting*, vol. 3, pp. 159–175.

Hellgren, A., Lennartson, B. and Fabian, M. (2002), 'Modelling and PLC-Based Implementation of Modular Supervisory Control', *Proceedings of the 6th International Workshop on Discrete Event Systems (WODES'02)*. Zaragoza, Spain.

Hirsch, P.M. (1986), 'From Ambushes to Golden Parachutes: Corporate Takeovers as an Instance of Cultural Framing and Institutional Integration,' *The American Journal of Sociology*, vol. 91, no. 4, pp. 800–837.

Jamilah, Ahmad and Suriati, Saad (2013), 'Beyond Theory and Practice: A Malaysian Case Study,' *Education and Corporate Social Responsibility: International Perspectives*, vol. 4, p. 267.

Jonsson, S., Greve, H. R., and Fujiwara-Greve, T. (2009), 'Undeserved Loss: The Spread of Legitimacy Loss to innocent Organizations in Response to reported Corporate Deviance,' *Administrative Science Quarterly*, vol. 54, no. 2, pp. 195–228.

Kapelus, P. (2002), 'Mining, Corporate Social Responsibility and the Community: The Case of Rio Tinto, Richards Bay Minerals and the Mbonambi,' *Journal of Business Ethics*, vol. 39, no. 3, pp. 275–296.

Kennedy, J.J. (2009), 'Maintaining Popular Support for the Chinese Communist Party: The Influence of Education and the State-Controlled Media,' *Political Studies*, vol. 57, no. 3, pp. 517–536.

Kent, P. and Monem, R. (2008), 'What Drives TBL Reporting: Good Governance or Threat to Legitimacy?'. *Australian Accounting Review*, vol. 18, no. 4, pp. 297–309.

Khanifar, H., Nazari, K., Emami, M. and Soltani, H.A. (2012), 'Impacts Corporate Social Responsibility Activities on Company Financial Performance,' *Interdisciplinary Journal of Contemporary Research in Business*, vol. 3, no. 9, pp. 583–592.

Kingston, P. and Wagner, J. (2004, 31 March), 'Sustainability and HSE/CSR Performance: The Role of Leadership'. In *International Conference on Health, Safety and Environment in Oil and Gas Exploration and Production*, pp. 1255–1264.

Kjær, P. and Slaatta, T. (2007), *Mediating Business: The Expansion of Business Journalism*. Copenhagen Business School Press, Copenhagen.

Lo, B.C.W. and Yap, K.L. (2011), 'Are Malaysian Companies Ready for Corporate Social Responsibility?,' *Labuan e-journal of Muammalat and Society*, vol. 5, no. 7, pp. 11–15.

Luo, J., Meier, S., and Oberholzer-Gee, F. (2012), 'No News is Good News CSR Strategy and Newspaper Coverage of Negative Firm Events,' *Harvard Business School Working Paper*, pp. 12–91

Lyon, T.P. and Maxwell, J.W. (2011), 'Greenwash: Corporate Environmental Disclosure under Threat of Audit,' *Journal of Economics & Management Strategy*, vol. 20, no. 1, pp. 3–41.

Mazza, C. and Alvarez, J.L. (2000), 'Haute Couture and Prêt-a-porter: The Popular Press and the Diffusion of Management Practices,' *Organization Studies*, vol. 21, no. 3, pp. 567–588.

McCombs, M. and Shaw, D.L. (1972), 'The Agenda- Setting Function of Mass Media,' *Public Opinion Quarterly*, vol. 36, no. 2, pp. 176–187.

McMillan, J.J. (2007), 'Why Corporate Social Responsibility: Why Now?.' In *The Debate Over Corporate Social Responsibility*. Oxford University Press, New York, pp. 15–29.

Minor, D.B. and J. Morgan. (2011), 'CSR as Reputation Insurance: Primum Non Nocere', *California Management Review*, vol. 53, no. 3, pp. 1–20

Morsing, M. and Langer, R. (2007), *Business Communication in the Business Press: Advantages of Strategic Ambiguity*, CBS Working Paper Series, No. 1 2007, Center for Corporate Values and Responsibility, Frederiksberg.

Meyers, M. (1997), *News Coverage of Violence Against Women: Engendering Blame*. Sage: Thousand Oaks, CA.

Minister Of Women, Family And Community Development (2012) , retrieved from http://www.jkm.simple.my/content.php?pagename=anugerah_corporate_social_responsibility__csr__perdana_menteri&lang=en.

Neu, D., Warsame, H. and Pedwell, K. (1988), 'Managing Public Impressions: Environmental Disclosures in Annual Reports', *Accounting, Organizations and Society*, vol. 23, no. 3, pp. 265–282

Overton, C. (2004, 29–31 March), 'Corporate Social Responsibility - Capturing the Value'. In the 7th SPE International Conference on Health, Safety, and Environment in Oil and Gas Exploration and Production', Calgary, Alberta, Canada

Peloza, J. (2006), 'Using Corporate Social Responsibility as Insurance for Financial Performance,' *California Management Review*, vol. 48, no. 2, p. 52.

Peng, Y.S. and Lin, S.S. (2008), 'Local Responsiveness Pressure, Subsidiary Resources, Green Management Adoption and Subsidiary's Performance: Evidence from Taiwanese Manufactures', *Journal of Business Ethics*, vol. 79, no. 1–2, pp. 199–212.

Podnar, K. (2008), 'Guest Editorial: Communicating Corporate Social Responsibility,' *Journal of Marketing Communications*, vol. 14, no. 2, pp. 75–81.

Pomering, A. and Dolnicar, S. (2009), 'Assessing the Prerequisite of Successful CSR Implementation: Are Consumers Aware of CSR Initiatives?' *Journal of Business Ethics*, vol. 85, no. 2, p. 285–301.

Pollock, T.G. and Rindova, V.P. (2003), 'Media Legitimation Effects in the Market for Initial Public Offerings,' *Academy of Management Journal*, vol. 46, no. 5, pp. 631–642.

Prabu, D., Kline, S., and Dai, Y. (2005), 'Corporate Social Responsibility Practices, Corporate Identity, and Purchase Intention: A Dual-process Model, *Journal of Public Relations Research*, vol. 17, no. 3, pp. 291–313.

Rampton, S. (2004), 'Corporate Social Responsibility and the Crisis of Globalization', *Center for Media and Democracy*, October 30. Retrieved from http://www.prwatch.org/node/273/print.

Rosen, B.N., Sandler, D.M., and Shani, D. (1991), 'Social Issues and Socially Responsible Investment Behavior: A Preliminary Empirical Investigation,' *Journal of Consumer Affairs*, vol. 25, no. 2, pp. 221–234.

Sahlin-Andersson, K., and Engwall, L. (2002), *The Expansion of Management Knowledge: Carriers, Flows, and Sources*. Stanford University Press, Stanford, CA.

Scheufele, D.A. and Tewksbury, D. (2007), Framing, Agenda Setting, and Priming: The Evolution of Three Media Effects Models,' *Journal of Communication*, vol. 57, no. 1, pp. 9–20.

Schudson, M. (2003), *The Sociology of News*, W.W. Norton & Company, New York.

Shoemaker, P.J., Eichholz, M., Kim, E. and Wrigley, B. (2001), 'Individual and Routine Forces in Gatekeeping,' *Journalism & Mass Communication Quarterly*, vol. 78, no. 2, pp. 233–246.

Sun, W., Pollard, D. and Stewart, J. (2010), *Reframing Corporate Social Responsibility*. Emerald, Bingley.

Suzanne, F. (2009), *New Social Media Channels for CSR Comunications*. Available from http://blogs.intel.com/csr/2009/05/new_social_media_channels_for/ (Accessed May 19, 2012).

Sweetser, K.D. and Brown, C.W. (2008), 'Information Subsidies and Agenda-building During the Israel–Lebanon Crisis,' *Public Relations Review*, vol. 34, no. 4, pp. 359–366.

Tench, R., Bowd, R. and Jones, B. (2007), 'Perceptions and Perspectives: Corporate Social Responsibility and the Media,' *Journal of Communication Management*, vol. 11, no. 4, pp. 348–370.

Thompson, P. and Zakaria, Z. (2004), 'Corporate Social Responsibility Reporting in Malaysia,' *Journal of Corporate Citizenship*, vol. 12, no. 13, pp.125–136.

Tsoutsoura, M. (2004), *'Corporate Social Responsibility and Financial Performance'*, Center for Responsible Business, pp. 6

Vaara, E. and Tienari, J. (2002), 'Justification, Legitimization and Naturalization of Mergers and Acquisitions: A Critical Discourse Analysis of Media Texts,' *Organization*, vol. 9, no. 2, pp. 275–304.

Vanhamme, J. and Grobben, B. (2009), ' "Too good to be true!". The Effectiveness of CSR History in Countering Negative Publicity,' *Journal of Business Ethics*, vol. 85, no. 2, pp. 273–283.

Vogel, D. (2005), *The Market for Virtue: The Potential and Limits of Corporate Social Responsibility*. Brookings Institution Press, Washington, DC.

Vuontisjärvi, T. (2006), 'Corporate Social Reporting in the European Context and Human Resource Disclosures: An analysis of Finnish Companies', *Journal of Business Ethics*, vol. 69, pp. 331–354.

Waddock, S. (2002), *Leading Corporate Citizens: Vision, Values, Value Added*. McGraw-Hill, New York.

Weerakkody, N. and Monaghan, R. (2011, January), 'Closed vs Open Corporate Social Networking Communities: A Case Study of the Victoria Police and Dairy Australia'. In *ISIT 2011: Proceedings of the 3rd International Conference on Information Technologies and Information Society: Social Media and Social Computing, Data Mining, Web Technologies*, pp. 1–6. [Information Technologies and Information Society].

Westphal, J.D., Gulati, R. and Shortell, S.M. (1997), 'Customization or Conformity? An Institutional and Network Perspective on the Content and Consequences of TQM Adoption,' *Administrative Science Quarterly*, vol. 42, pp. 366–394.

Williams, B. (2008), *CSR and the Financial Crisis: Taking Stock*. Available from http://csrinternational.blogspot.com/2008/11/csr-and-financial-crisis-taking-stock.html (Accessed June 23, 2014).

Zhang, J. and Swanson, D. (2006), 'Analysis of News Media's Representation of Corporate Social Responsibility (CSR),' *Public Relations Quarterly*, vol. 51, no. 2, p. 13.

Zoch, L.M. and J.C. Molleda (2006), 'Building a Theoretical Model of Media Relations Using Framing, Information Subsidies and Agenda Building.' In Botan, C. H and Hazleton, V. (eds.). Mahwah, NJ, Lawrence Erlbaum, pp. 279–309.

# Chapter 8

# A pathway to corporate sustainability – social accounting

*Douglas M. Branson*

## Introduction

A working definition of sustainability is a continued and sustained effort to ensure that institutions central to our lives benefit not only us in the short or medium term but are in existence to benefit our grandchildren and our grandchildrens' grandchildren. Rather than profit maximization or increasing shareholder wealth as the sole goal, the new teaching is that the corporation should balance risk-taking and profit-making goals with prudent risk management, leading, *inter alia*, to sustainability. An alternative, and perhaps fancier, exposition of the idea is that "[s]ustainability is defined as the persistence over an apparently indefinite future of certain necessary and desired characteristics of the socio-political system."

An important adjunct to sustainability is exemplary citizenship in communities of which the corporation is a part, namely, locales and regions where the corporation has its headquarters, other offices, plants, and other facilities. Many term this relationship to the communities and nations of which they are a part corporate social responsibility, often abbreviated as CSR (Cunningham 1999).[1] CSR has become, in the words of *The Economist*, "an industry in itself with full-time staff, newsletters, professional associations, and massed armies of consultants."[2] Yet even today, with corporate social responsibility having been at the fore at least since 1970 ("Earth Day") and probably earlier, no commonly accepted meaning of what social responsibility is or what it entails exists. Resembling beauty, social responsibility is in the eye of the beholder. "It means something but not always the same thing to everybody."[3]

Thus has developed the first virtue accorded social accounting: by selecting the processes and fields of outreach the corporation wishes to monitor and report upon, the company defines for itself what corporate social responsibility means or should be. I wrote the first major piece on corporate social accounting, in the US legal literature at least (Branson 1976).[4] To describe this possible benefit of social accounting, I drew upon the words of the Cheshire Cat in *Alice in Wonderland*, " 'Would you tell me please which way I ought to go from here?' 'That depends a good deal upon where you want to go' " (Branson 1976).

Current definitions of social accounting might include a perception of it as "the process of measuring, monitoring, and reporting to stakeholders the social and environmental effects of an organization's actions."[5] Tying the subject to firmer ground, another exposition reminds us that "[s]ocial accounting is first and foremost accounting. Similar to traditional accounting, it is a method of quantifying a company's performance."[6] Yet the degree to which the organization quantifies expenditures and results, let alone attempts to monetize them, varies widely: "the organization collects, analyses and interprets descriptive, quantitative and qualitative information in order to produce an account of its performance."[7]

Rather than attempt to measure the entire social impact of a corporation and its employees, with the aid of directors, managers, and employees, the corporation selects what the consensus values most, perhaps balancing that with a determination of in what areas can the corporation's effort have the maximum or a significant impact. In making determinations, the corporation may look in the rear view mirror, evaluating and selecting some areas of emphasis, but perhaps not all, from past endeavors. The corporation may change the mix from time to time. The auditing process and the directions in which it may point are not static. Missing from many accepted definitions of social accounting is this dynamic aspect. This is the process audit upon which I will expand upon in ensuing pages.

In business, a commonly encountered shibboleth is that "you manage what you measure." It is difficult to contemplate, then, how a firm or other organization can be serious about its social responsibility or about undertaking social responsibility measures without a great measure of accounting for expenditures and results and possibly with audits of those accounts to follow.

Being able to manage what you have and will continue to measure is only one benefit of corporate social accounting. There are many others. It is to that subject that I now turn.

## Benefits ascribed to corporate social accounting

### Identification of goals and objectives

The objectives in for-profit endeavor are not always maximization of revenues and profits. The "get big fast" phenomenon highlighted the primacy in some industries of grabbing market share, with the hope of becoming one, two, or perhaps three in a given industry or core area of its business, with an emphasis on profits left for another day (see e.g. Spector 2000). Perhaps share price, especially in comparison with historical prices and with share market prices of comparable companies, is a better measure of business success.

Debates about which indicator is a better measure of success has less relevance in the area of social responsibility. In fact, the point is that in the corporate responsibility area no set standards and goals or objectives are readily available. Social accounting, consistently applied, can provide those standards and goals, to an extent. Managers may use social accounting results to undertake historical comparisons as to expenditures and results, a vertical view back through past years.

A comparison to the right and to the left, a horizontal comparison, if you will, with other firms in the same and in similar fields, is not so easy, even with a commitment to social accounting (see e.g. Cunningham 1999).[8] To facilitate horizontal comparisons, social accounting would have to move past quantification to some sort of monetization. In the early days of social accounting, consulting firms and other entities attempted to do just that (Branson 1976, pp. 562–3, 565 and 574–75). Consultancy firms purported to be able to move past raw data, such as person hours expended, or pollution and other environmental degradation minimized or abated, to statements of those expenditures and results in dollar terms. Even beyond that, certain firms indicated an ability to measure and monetize entirely the expenditures and results, across the board, leading to a bottom line figure representing the net detriment or benefit a firm contributed to the society around it. For example, such an audit would purport to measure, quantify, and monetize the detriment a company imposed by its employees commuting to and from work individually rather than in car or vanpools (Branson 1976).[9]

Social auditing has evolved and matured over the years. One evident outcome in that maturation process seems to be a near universal cessation of attempts to monetize, or monetize comprehensively, social responsibility efforts. Evidence of this trend away from monetization inures in the more frequent use of the term "social responsibility reporting" rather than "social accounting" (see e.g. Toronto Dominion Bank 2013).

### Opening of dialogues with stakeholder constituencies

"Stakeholder" is relatively new term. In the United States, one early use of the term was by the National Cash Register Company (NCR) in the 1980s, in NCR's resistance to a takeover bid by American Telephone and Telegraph (AT&T). NCR published, in leading news magazines, a series of small print, highbrow advertisements asserting that NCR and its Board of Directors' responsibilities lay towards a number of constituencies, not solely to shareholders. Thus, in deciding whether and how strenuously to oppose a takeover, a board could consider, *inter alia*, the desires and interests of employees, consumers, suppliers, local communities where the company had substantial facilities or other presences ("a footprint"), regional economies, and local governments, stakeholders all.

Many US state legislatures permanently enshrined the stakeholder phenomenon in adopting non-shareholder constituency statutes (Bainbridge and Orts 1992). These statutes attempt to make clear a target company board's abilities to consider the interests of groups of stakeholders other than shareholders in defending against a takeover bid or other actions.

Today, the stakeholder movement has mushroomed into a worldwide development. Authoritarian corporate governance codes outline and urge cognizance of other stakeholder groups.[10] Positive law in some nation states go codes of best practices one better: corporate laws mandate corporate adherence to a stakeholder model (Aguilera and Jackson 2003).[11]

The social auditing process may well include the opening of a dialogue with various groups that do not have an everyday presence within the firm. In the course of that "stakeholder dialogue," both the firms and the group may express their desires and their priorities in changing or lessening the company's impact on the society of which it is part (Conley and Williams 2005, p. 13).

### Adjustment of social goals based upon changing circumstances

Again, financial measurements such as revenues, profits, earnings per share, year-to-year same store sales, order backlog, and the like, as measurement tools, or yardsticks, are relatively stable over time. From decade to decade, the emphasis my change. Financial analysts may key on one particular measure for a few years, changing to another in subsequent periods. Trends develop and, then, just as quickly, fall by the wayside. But financial performance and its measurement do not have the same chameleon natures as do corporate social responsibility and attempts at measurement of it.

Mixing metaphors, social responsibility is a moving target. What responsibilities a particular company may have and the emphasis that the company choses to put on a particular responsibility may change from locale to locale and over time as well. As to the later, global warming and a particular company's carbon footprint have come to the fore in the most recent decade. As another example, for a company such as Nike that manufactures footwear in the Peoples' Republic of China (PRC) and in Vietnam, supplier codes of conduct, auditing of compliance with the code, and enforcement of it seem an enduring concern but will abate somewhat. As wages rise and, as part of what is known as the plantation production phenomenon, factories and supply contracts shift, say, to Bangladesh or Myanmar from the PRC or Vietnam, problems and what social responsibility may dictate will differ.

Only by social auditing can a corporation track the shifts of, and the changing makeup of, its corporate social responsibility objectives.

### Consistent measurement of expenditures and results

Monetization may not carry over to social accounting but the requirement of consistency, as in "consistently applied," does. By its opinion letter, an auditor certifies that the financial statements have, among other things, been prepared in accordance with generally accepted accounting principles, "consistently applied."

That social responsibility and what it may entail tends to be a moving target adds to, rather than detracts from, the necessity that the units of measurement and the methods of deriving them remain essentially constant. There has to be some consistency in the latter to enable managers and directors to detect shifts in what may be required or the lack of return on certain expenditures of resources and efforts.

Note that notion is "consistently applied" rather than slavishly applied. Auditors and chartered accountants often do consent to changes in this or that accounting measure or principle, for example, the method by which a firm costs its inventory in computing profit from its turnover, or the choice the company makes from an array of choices in depreciating a newly acquired capital asset.

The first umbrella, and frequently forgotten, requirement is that the accounting measure chosen and the financial statements *in toto* present a true and fair view of the economic reality of what has been occurring within the firm. The second requirement is that financial statements and accompanying documents clearly disclose and explain reasons for any changes in accounting method or principle. In accord with the overriding principle of accounting conservatism, the third requirement is that changes in method or principle be infrequent and eminently justified.

Thus, in financial accounting, both footnotes to financial statements and statements of significant accounting policies in accompanying disclosure documents must evince consistency with those overriding meta-principles.

So, too, with social accounting. Social accounting, borrowing from financial accounting and its consistency requirement, along with a healthy dose of accounting conservatism, imposes a certain discipline and facilitates year-to-year comparisons of a company's social responsibility efforts and progress.

## Provide data with which to answer questions and criticisms from NGOs and other activist organizations

An executive active in the social responsibility area has spoken of "the 'language barriers' that can arise between NGOs, which speak an 'aspirational language,' and companies, which must speak a 'specific language of performance'" (Conley and Williams 2005, p. 10 (quoting an executive from Asia Pulp and Paper Co.). The executive further noted that "[t]he barrier becomes particularly daunting . . . with respect to the definition of success or failure."

Questions, criticism, and cynicism may come from a circle far wider than NGOs. The World Council of Churches, the Methodist, Episcopal, Uniting, and Presbyterian churches, various orders of Roman Catholic priests and nuns, Greenpeace, and environmental groups – all have been active in urging the social responsibility movement onward and in asking probing questions about CSR, social accounting, and social responsibility reports.

Well-thought out and well-constructed social audits and reports thereof can go a long way in lowering the communication barriers that may exist between companies and watchdog groups. If well-tuned social audits do not ameliorate the problem of language differences, at least a good quality social audit can highlight where disparities in language or methods of measurement exist.

## Deflection of allegations of insincerity and of "green washing"

Many critics state a "reason to be skeptical of corporate motives" as support for their view that corporations are insincere at heart. In social responsibility reporting, giving what amounts only to lip service to any responsibility or commitment to wider concerns, critics note that companies' "CSR activities rarely encompass 'core' activities." They further note that many companies never do "'scale up' social and environmental activities from the demonstration project level," further evincing the insincerity in involved with corporations' social responsibility efforts.

These criticisms of corporate social responsibility are long standing. In 1972, an early proponent of social accounting admitted that "[t]he reporting of corporate good deeds . . . has largely been confined to institutional advertising and annual reports showing the company in a favorable light." It amounts to "self-aggrandizement," pure public relations (Sethi 1973).

## Central to embedding social responsibility in a corporation's DNA

At certain corporations, compliance officers require employees with any connection to financial matters periodically to read and initial a copy of the corporation's code of ethics.[12] Human resources personnel make the initialed document part of the employee's permanent employment dossier.

At other corporations, HR personnel may require every employee to read and initial the corporation's mission statement, the aspirational "house on the hill" vision that attempts to encapsulate what the corporation is all about and to what it aspires. Similar exercises may take place with respect to safety codes or quality control efforts.

Many of these efforts may be seen as attempts firmly to implant, or embed, core values or objectives in manager and employee consciousness. What about the corporation's social responsibility? How can companies embed CSR in the corporate DNA?

The embedding, or inculcation, problem may transcend from a particular corporation to its suppliers, especially in today's global economy, with supply chains across vast oceans and more than halfway around the globe. It is difficult enough to translate stakeholder dialogue and CSR principles into the workplace. Implementation halfway around the globe may be geometrically more difficult.

In dialogues with Professors John Conley and Cynthia Williams, a CSR manager highlighted the situation a company may face with regard to its supply chain: "[A] socially responsible . . . buyer of Chinese goods might listen to its workers [and] stakeholders, impose a code of conduct on its suppliers, get their promised compliance, and even engage a third-party CSR auditor to perform monthly inspections, only to hear through back channels that the suppliers were reverting to business as usual the other 353 days of the year" (Conley and Williams 2005, p. 15). *The New York Times* reported that very same behavior in the Chinese toy manufacturing industry (Kahn 2003, A-1).

So cast, certain of these difficulties seem intractable. Conduct of good social audits, year-in and year-out would impress upon employees and others the corporation's seriousness of purpose when it came to its social responsibility. Evolution from audit results could produce a corporate code of social responsibility that corporations could attempt to center in management and employee consciousness similar to financial codes of ethics or lists of safety principles.

### Signaling to, if not establishing bonds with, interested investors, particularly institutional investors

In 1973, the Ford Foundation canvased 196 major US institutional investors and 115 responded. Well over a majority (57.4%) stated that they took social responsibility concerns into account both in selection and retention decisions on their investments (Longstreth and Rosenbloom 1972). Thirty nine institutions, or 33.9% of the respondents, surprisingly mostly banks and mutual funds (managed funds) rather than university endowments or foundations, stated a belief that "a correlation existed between socially responsible business enterprise and those that will produce a satisfactory return." A 1974 US congressional survey of banks and insurance companies resulted in similar findings (Branson 1976, p. 590). Corporations with classes of publicly traded securities, or a substantial number of them, want to ascertain who those potential investors in their company stock are and how activities and reports of them might be tailored to appeal to them.

Fast forwarding the mid-1970s to 1999, Professor Cynthia Williams made an argument for SEC mandated CSR disclosures, the same argument I made in a 1976 article.[13] One of Professor Williams's arguments was the growth trend in social investing, among whom were institutional investors who would value highly social as well as financial accounting results. "Today [1999] there are 144 'socially and environmentally responsible' mutual funds, comprising $96 billion in assets (up from $12 billion in 1995)" (Williams 1999, p. 1267, footnote omitted). She goes on to recite that the number of socially responsible investment companies (mutual funds) "increased eightfold from 1995 to 1997."

That trend appears to have slowed considerably since that time. The Forum for Sustainable and Responsible Investment lists only 204 such funds as of 2014, an increase of only 60 over a 15 or so year period. Moreover, the number of funds (204) pales in comparison with the mutual fund/managed fund industry as a whole: in 2014, there were 9,260 mutual funds in the US and 16,660 managed funds altogether (open-end and closed end funds, exchange traded funds, and unit trusts) (ICI 2015). Thus, social investment funds represented a mere 2.12% of the mutual fund total and 1.22% the managed funds overall.

Professor Williams plows on, painting perhaps an overly rosy picture. "Altogether, $1.185 trillion of the $13.7 trillion in funds under professional management in the United States (or about 9%) are invested using 'social screens' for either products to be avoided (tobacco, alcohol . . .) to practices to be encourage (intelligent environmental stewardship, for instance)" (Williams 1999, p. 1268). That number has grown a bit over five times in 15 or so years. The leading socially responsible investing trade ground reckons that "$6.2 trillion are held by 480 institutional investors and 880 community investment institutions [mostly public employee pension plans] that apply various environmental, social and governance screen to potential investments."[14]

There has been growth in the percentages of institutions of various stripes that have an interest in social responsible investing and would therefore be interested in social audit results and the reporting of them. But thought must be given to other investor categories whose CSR interests are minimal or non-existent. The US had 10,000 or more hedge funds (private wealth management vehicles for high net worth individuals) and 7,000 plus private equity firms (that utilize high net worth and investing institutions money to purchase majority or complete control in other companies). The incidence of socially responsible investing, or of interest in it, would be close to zero in both those groups.

Pension funds, once the fast growing sector of institutional investors, have seen a great slowing of their growth in recent years as corporate sponsors of retirement plans switch from defined benefit plans (professionally managed) to defined contribution plans (self-managed by the beneficiaries). Even among the defined benefit pension plans that remain, interest in socially responsible investment has strength only among subgroups, principally public employee and labor union pension plans. And a significant subgroup of those have no interest in promoting CSR or good governance: their managers feel strongly that their fiduciary duties to plan beneficiaries dictates that they focus on investment returns alone (see, generally, Rock 1991).

Corporations may undertake CSR accounting and reporting as a means of appealing to investor groups that apply CSR screens and search out socially responsible investments but, given the statistics, the idea seems to have been oversold. Companies that go down that path should be aware at least that, while not insignificant, the notion of winning the hearts and minds of great categories of investors through CSR activities and social accounting reports is somewhat remote.

### Staving off governmental intervention

Many NGOs, it has been reported, "believe that the CSR movement will stall without government involvement" (Conley and Williams 2005, p. 20). A recent text, published by the Cambridge University Press, is a thinly veiled volume of spadework for governmental mandates of gender, ethnic, and racial diversity on the boards of directors of publicly held companies in Canada and possibly the US, as well as elsewhere (Dhur 2015). Despite the "lopsided" nature of such supposedly scholarly efforts, they will win adherents for government intervention.[15]

Obviously, having as a primary objective of social accounting development of the wherewithal to forestall government intervention would render craven the entire accounting exercise at a particular company. That duly noted, however, having the social accounting exercise serving as a subsidiary, or incidental, role as a bulwark against further governmental intervention does not seem craven at all. Lessening the need for governmental action, if there is such a need at all, seems a natural outgrowth or by-product of consistent social accounting and reporting of accounting results.

### Essential step in managing what your measure

An excellent illustration of this bedrock principle can be found in the experiences of Deloitte Touche, the international accounting firm. By 1992, despite have great numbers of accounting professionals who were female, the firm still had less than 5% women partners (Crittenden 2001, p. 36). Thereafter, Deloitte devoted resources specifically to the advancement of women on the partnership track. The firm closely followed and kept records of those efforts and of women's progress toward partnership. Within a few years, the number of women partners at Deloitte grew from 5% to over 19% (Williams et al. 2004). You manage what you measure. Some sort of accounting is a first step in that process.

## Progress in the art of social accounting

Or has it been regression, albeit of a laudable sort, rather than forward progress (*regression* being a better word to describe what has occurred in the field over the last 40 years)? In 1976, from a review of the literature, I identified, or labeled, three gradations of social audits: progress audits, complete audits, and super social audits (Branson 1976, pp. 551–574).

In writing this chapter, I again surveyed the literature or, frequently in this day and age, the websites of several corporations, consultancy firms, and accounting firms.

In my survey, first, I found a marked propensity to pull back from attempts at monetization, especially monetization across the board. Second, I found the relegation of consultancy firms such as Abt Associates, or Arthur D. Little, Inc., to a secondary or even tertiary position. Major accountancy firms have staked out social accounting as a profit center, attempting to occupy the field and pushing the consultants aside a bit. Third, attempts at the super social audit, attempting to measure and often monetize every effect, no matter how small, a corporation has on the society that surrounds it, seem to have vanished, recognized as too difficult and unrealistic to accomplish, an exercise in false accuracy, or for a myriad other possible reasons. So, in certain ways, there has been a regression in the field.

Process audits are the simplest and oldest form of social accounting. They contemplate a limited range of subjects or accounts for audits rather than attempting to measure the total societal aspect of a company's activities. The process audit is not ambitious with respect to quantification, at least across the board.

[A] process audit would ascertain the following: the reason for undertaking a particular program, the goals of the program, the rationale for the action, a description of what actually is being done, and intermediate measures of performance if they are available (Bauer and Fenn 1972, p. 84).

In the mid-1970s, US corporations such as Bank of America, Quaker Oats, Dayton Hudson, Atlantic Richfield, DuPont, and General Motors began including process audits alongside financial data in their annual reports to shareholders (Branson 1976, p. 552–554).

The process audit is very much alive and, indeed, seems to flourish. PricewaterhouseCoopers (PWC), one of the "Big Four" international accounting firms, ballyhoos the process audit. On its website, PWC emphasize that "[w]e [focus] on responsible business, diversity and inclusion, community engagement and environmental stewardship."[16]

The complete audit attempts to measure the social impact of a corporation's activities across a broad spectrum, not merely to measure several processes or accounts. Measurements include those dealing with the detrimental effects, or social costs, inherent in day-to-day corporate activities as well as corporate programs in "do good" areas. So the failure to hire or promote minority group members, inadequate attempts to abate the company's carbon footprint, and any other shortcomings in a social sense would be offset against benefits the company bestows on society through social programs. Besides assessing the level of effort in all areas, the complete audit contemplates quantification as well as some monetization, arriving at some sort of bottom line (Linowes 1973).[17]

Dr. Clark Abt of Abt Associates, for starters, listed 20 accounts his firm stood ready to inventory, ranging from product safety and supplier selection and retention to sources of financing (Abt 1973).[18] In their book, accountants Raymond Bauer and Dan Fenn listed no fewer than 20 items, including charitable giving, support for artistic and cultural endeavors, and board of directors' composition (diversity) (Bauer and Fenn 1972, pp. 73–74). Before even reaching supplier relationships or other subjects, another 1970s publication list began with aid to the arts, employee programs related to health, employee programs related to safety, aids to employee self-development, minority group relationships, community related activities, and consumerism (Sethi 1973, p. 38).

Nowadays attempts at, or sales pitches for, complete social audits are frequent. In its annual social responsibility booklet, the international accountancy firm Deloitte proposes audit of 10 accounts on the subject of what it terms "responsible business practices": "organizational structure, leadership and governance, ethics, quality and risk management, independence, data privacy and security, talent growth and encouragement, diversity, physical security, and environmental sustainability." (Deloitte, 201, p. 19, upper case omitted). In its annual social responsibility report, Canada's Toronto Dominion Bank list 24 accounts to be inventoried and audited under five headings: customer focus, building an extraordinary workplace, being an environmental leader, strengthening our communities, and how we operate (TD Bank 2013, p. 3, upper case omitted).

The common law contained a doctrine that may add perspective to evaluating such "cover the waterfront" complete audits. The public duty doctrine stated that "a duty to all may be a duty to none." For instance, if a building collapsed, which the city or county had inspected and permitted, as statues had required the county agency to do, that duty to the public did not extend to persons injured by the building's collapse. The latter individual could not recover damages from the city, county, or state.

A corollary might be that a duty to many may lessen the duty perceived to be owed to any group or sub-group within the many. A number of other ways exist to communicate the criticism: a complete audit may result in social responsibility efforts being too thinly spread or, worse yet, may be an opportunistic attempt by the company to appear being socially responsible in the extreme without being really social responsible at all.

Next in the spectrum of social audits comes the super social audit, the attempt to measure, quantify, and monetize each and every effect, beneficial as well as detrimental, the corporation and its activities has upon society. What may have become clear is the spectrum represents a difference in quantity rather than in kind, spanning from the most focused (the process audit) to the more extensive (the complete audit) to the most extensive of all (the super social audit).

As noted elsewhere, a development of the last 40 years has been a near complete reduction in attempts to perform super social audits, attempting, as they purported to do, to measure what may well be immeasurable. So it is to other developments of those 40 years that this chapter now turns.

## Provision of social accounting services and reports

If one believes one major accounting firm's census, which it has conducted since the mid 1990's, social accounting and CSR reports have become ubiquitous, at least among major corporations. Beginning chronologically, the 2002 KPMG *International Corporate Sustainability Survey* reported that between 1999 and 2002 the percentage of *Fortune* Global 250 companies that rendered CSR reports increased from 35% to 45%, compared to only 10% in 1993 (KPMG International 2002, p. 9). External verification, in most instances by Big Four accounting firms, rose from 19% to 29% of the reports. The incidence of reporting was higher in many countries, at least among the 100 largest companies in the country: 72% in Japan, 49% in the UK, 36% in the U.S., and between 30% and 40% in the countries of the European Union (synthesized in Conley and Williams 2005, pp. 4–5 and note 26).

In 2014, KPMG issued another sustainability report, the eighth in 20 years, surveying the CSR reporting of the 100 largest companies in 41 countries, or 4,100 companies (KPMG, International 2013, p. 3). Countries included six the Americas, 11 in Asia Pacific, 19 in Europe, and five in Africa.[19] "Almost three quarters (71 percent) of the 4,100 companies surveyed" now report on CSR activities.[20] The comparable figure for G250 companies is now 82%, up from a mere 10% in 1993 and 35%–45% in 2002. "Over half (59 percent) of the G250 companies that report CSR data now invest in external assurance," that is, some form of audit of social accounting reporting and results.[21]

In its survey, KPMG then moves on to an analysis that leads to "quality scores" for CSR reporting, although how precisely the KPMG accountants compute such scores remains a mystery. Overall, the quality score for the G250 is 59 out of a possible 100. Ten international firms achieved a score over 90: Maersk of Denmark; BMW and Siemens of Germany; Cisco Systems, Ford Motor and Hewlett-Packard of the US; ING of the Netherlands; Nestle of Switzerland; Repsol of Spain; and Total of France. The KPMG report is rather opaque, or coy, about how it derives these "quality scores." A suspicion arises that KPMG does not wish to disclose too much about the inner workings of its black box, lest it lose business to other providers.

What does a review of the major accounting firms, their websites, and some major firms' CSR reporting activities reveal? First, a review of, or report on, progress demonstrates that CSR reporting, whether constituting mere lip service or meaningful efforts, is an upward trend toward universality, at least among larger incorporated entities.

Second, since 1990 or so, the major accounting firms have occupied the field. By contrast, a very unscientific review of consultancy firms' websites indicates that social auditing has disappeared from their lists of primary services offered. KPMG's latest report on CSR reporting is 20 pages, the latter part of which is a sales pitch, listing KPMG's social auditing point persons in various countries along with telephone numbers and email addresses. Another major firm, PWC, maintains a Center for Corporate Social Responsibility that has tentacles reaching throughout the global firm.[22] The Deloitte Touche Tohmatsu Limited (Deloitte) CSR reporting report is 57 pages in length, setting forth "numerous examples of the great work member firms around the world are doing in this area" (Deloitte 2007, p. 5 [letter from Barry Salzberg, Deloitte CEO]).

Not to be outdone by KPMG, Ernst and Young publishes its own survey of top firms. Highlights include the statistic that 86% of the companies surveyed "said that sustainability was embedded in their firms strategy" (what else would they say?) while 61% said that consumers' agendas were "the primary driver in implementing corporate special responsibility practices" (*Ernst and Young Report*, Blue and Green Tomorrow 2013).

Third, some of the major accounting firms' seeming occupation with the field produces some uneasiness. The outlook the accounting firms urge upon corporations seems to have regressed from a responsibility toward society as a whole to a more parochial accountant's perspective, namely, painting corporate social accounting as conducive to preserving or improving the corporation's bottom line (profits). The firms espouse a shareholder-centric model and fealty to it as the principal role social accounting plays. Thus, the KPMG pitch is that "CSR reports should [identify] the CSR issues with the greatest potential impacts on the business itself and shareholders" and that CSR reporting is an "essential management tool" (KPMG International 2014, pp. 7 and 9). Increasingly, Deloitte's CEO states, corporate executives are "recognizing corporate responsibility as a driver of business strategy" (Deloitte 2011, p. 5).

Fourth, corporate CSR reporting has become denser and denser simultaneously expanding to extra ordinary lengths. The Toronto Dominion Bank (TD) CSR report is 117 pages (TD CSR Report 2013). The British American Tobacco (BAT) document is "a dense sprawling report with 58 pages of compact text" (Conley and Williams 2005, pp. 27–28). One of Exxon Mobil's CSR reports was 41 pages in 2003 and 76 pages in 2014 (ExxonMobil 2003, 2014).

Fifth, accessibility of these reports is quite mixed. Only approximately half of the largest corporations include CSR reporting in their annual reports sent to shareholders (KPMG International 2013).[23] The other half promulgate lengthy reports that are, however, accessible only to those individuals and organizations who know of the report's existence and either request a copy from the company's headquarters, or who access the report on the Internet, assuming the company has posted the report on the web.

## Conclusion

This chapter's aim has been to give the reader the 10,000-foot (3,048-meters) view of corporate social accounting and how it has developed over the last 40 years. There exists a plethora of lower-altitude and ground-level views of corporate social accounting, how to set about doing it, auditing of accounting results, and the services various accounting and consultancy firms offer. The danger of becoming immersed in the ground-level literature, though, is that the reader will lose sight of the bigger picture, that is, lose sight of the forest while dealing with individual trees. The tenor of this piece has been to paint a picture, or take a snapshot, if you will, of the forest, or at least what has become a prominent copse, on the accounting, reporting, and sustainability landscape.

## Notes

1 Lawrence Cunningham (1999) terms this the "horizontal aspect" of corporate governance.
2 Staff, *The Economist* (2004) "London is now awash with PR consultants, social auditors, firms providing verification or 'assurance' for companies' social and environmental reports, and bespoke investment analysts, all vying for business."
3 Id.
4 Other early works include Raymond A. Bauer and Dan Fenn (1972); and Thomas J. Schoenbaum (1972).
5 Social Accounting Network, http://socialaccounting.org.
6 Innovation and Social, http://innov8social.com/2011/09/what-is-socail-acounting (accessed August 21, 2015).
7 Social Accounting Network (SAN), http://socialaccounting.org/ (accessed August 21, 2015).
8 Supra note 2.
9 Page 570 and note 82 (Abt Associates super social audit).
10 See e.g. OECD, §§ 60–67, at 20–22 ("The Role of Stakeholders in Corporate Governance").
11 See e.g. comparing European with UK/US stakeholder requirements and models.
12 Sarbanes-Oxley Act §406, "Code of Ethics for Senior Financial Officers": "The Commission shall issue rules to require each issuer . . . to disclose whether or not, and if not, the reason therefore, such issuers has adopted a code for senior financial officers [including the principal financial and accounting officers] . . ." (2002).
13 *Compare* Branson (1976) *with* Cynthia A. Williams (1999).
14 The Forum for Sustainable and Responsible Investment (2014, p. 12).
15 See generally Douglas M. Branson, Book Review, *Women on Corporate Boards: Challenging Homogeneity or Dictating Heterogeneity*, Canadian Bus Journal (forthcoming 2015).
16 Http://www.pwc.com/gx/en/corporate-responsibility/ (accessed September 2, 2015).
17 Contains a schematic for and urges use of complete audits.
18 Abt, *Management Decisions Made Better with Social Audits; Social Audit Aids to Corporate Decision Making* at 2 (unpublished pamphlet, Abt Associates, 1973).
19 Id., p. 5.
20 Id., p. 10.
21 Id., p. 11.
22 PricewaterhouseCoopers Center for Corporate Social Responsibility, available at http://www.gsom.spbu.ru/en/researc/csr (accessed September 2, 2015).
23 "[O]ver half of the reporting companies worldwide (51 percent) now include CR information in their annual financial reports", p. 10.

## Bibliography

Abt Associates (1973), *Management Decisions Made Better with Social Audits; Social Audit Aids to Corporate Decision Making* at 2 (unpublished pamphlet).

Aguilera, R.V. and Jackson, G. (2003), 'The Cross-National Diversity of Corporate Governance; Dimensions and Determinants,' *Academy of Management Review*, vol. 28, pp. 447–465.

Bainbridge, S.M. and Orts, E.W. (1992), 'Beyond Shareholders: Interpreting Corporate Constituency Statutes,' *George Washington Law Review*, vol. 61, pp. 305–308.

Bauer, R.A. and Fenn, D. (1972), *The Corporate Social Audit*. Russell Sage Foundation, New York.

Blue and Green Tomorrow (2013), *Ernst & Young Report Has Sustainability at the Top of Corporate Agendas*. Available from http://blueandgreentomorrow.com/2013/05/08/erns-young-report (Accessed September 2, 2015).

Branson, D.M. (1976), 'Progress in the Art of Social Accounting and Other Arguments in Favor of Disclosure on Corporate Social Responsibility,' *Vanderbilt Law Review*, vol. 29, pp. 539–684.

Branson, D.M. (2007), *No Seat at the Table: How Governance and Law Keep Women Out of the Boardroom*. New York University Press, New York.

Conley, J.M. and Williams, C.A. (2005), 'Engage, Embed, and Embellish: Theory Versus Practice in the Corporate Social Responsibility Movement,' *Journal of Corporate Law*, vol. 31, pp. 1–38.

Crittenden, A. (2001), *The Price of Motherhood*. Metropolitan Books, New York.

Cunningham, L. (1999), 'Commonalities and Prescriptions in the Vertical Dimension of Corporate Governance', *Cornell Law Review*, vol. 84, pp. 1133–35.

Deloitte (2007), *Corporate Responsibility Inaugural Report*. Available from http://public.deloitte.com/media/0146/ar/08_cr_report.pdf.

Deloitte (2011), *Corporate Responsibility Report*. Available from http://www.econsense.de/sites/all/files/dttl_cr_2011_crreport.pdf.

Dhur, A.A. (2015), *Challenging Boardroom Homogeneity*, Cambridge University Press, New York.

The Economist (2004), 'Two-Faced Capitalism', *The Economist*, January 22. Available from http//www.economist.com/PrinterFriendly.cfm?Story_ID=2369912.

ExxonMobil (2003), *Corporate Citizenship Report*. Available from http://www.exxonmobil.com/files/corporate/Corporate Citizenship (accessed September 2, 2015).

ExxonMobil (2014), *Corporate Citizenship Report*. Available from http://www.exxonmobile.com/en/community/corporate-citizenship-report (accessed September 15, 2015).

The Forum for Sustainable and Responsible Investment (US SIF) (2014), *Report on US Sustainable, Responsible and Impact Investing*. Available from http://www.ussif.org (accessed September 15, 2015).

ICI (2015), *Investment Company Fact Book*. Available from http://www.icifactbook.org/fb-ch1.html (accessed September 15, 2015).

Kahn, J. (2003), 'Ruse in Toyland: Chinese Workers' Hidden Woe'. *N.Y. Times*, December 7. Available from http://www.nytimes.com/2003/12/07/world/ruse-in-toyland-chinese-workers-hidden-woe.html?pagewanted=all.

KPMG International (2002), *Survey of Corporate Sustainability Reporting*. Available from http://old.gppi.net/fileadmin/gppi/KPMG2002.pdf.

KPMG International (2013), *Survey of Corporate Sustainability Reporting*. Available from https://www.kpmg.com/Global/en/IssuesAndInsights/ArticlesPublications/corporate-responsibility/Documents/kpmg-survey-of-corporate-responsibility-reporting-2013.pdf.

Linowes, D.F. (1973), 'Let's Get on With the Social Audit: A Specific Proposal', *Business and Society Review*, no. 4, pp. 39–42.

Longstreth, B. and Rosenbloom, D.H. (1972), *Corporate Social Responsibility and the Ethical Investor*. Praeger Publishers, New York.

OECD (2014), The Role of Stakeholders in Corporate Governance. *OECD Principles of Corporate Governance*. Available from http://www.OECD.org/daf/ca/OECD-Principles-CG-2014-Draft.pdf (accessed September 15, 2015).

Portney, K. (1994), 'Environmental Justice and Sustainability,' *Fordham Urban Law Journal*, vol. 21, pp. 827, 832–39.

Rock, E. (1991), 'The Logic and (Uncertain) Significance of Institutional Shareholder Activism,' *Georgetown Law Review*, vol. 79, pp. 445–506.

Schoenbaum, T.J. (1972), 'The Relationship Between Corporate Disclosure and Corporate Responsibility,' *Fordham Law Review*, vol. 40, pp. 565–594.

Sethi, S.P. (1972), 'Getting a Handle on the Social Audit,' *Business and Society Review/Innovation*, vol. 4, pp. 31–38.

Spector, R. (2000), *Amazon.com – Get Big Fast – Inside the Revolutionary Business Model That Changed the World*. Harper Business, New York.

Toronto Dominion Bank (2013), *Corporate Responsibility Report 2013*. Available from http://content.yudu.com/A2t2sg/2013CorpResReport/resources/index.htm?referrerUrl=http%3A%2F%2Fcontent.yudu.com%2FhtmlReader%2FA2t2sg%2F2013CorpResReport%2Findex.html.

Williams, C.A. (1999), 'The Securities and Exchange Commission and Corporate Social Transparency,' *Harvard Law Review*, vol. 112, pp. 1197–1999.

Williams, J., Thomas, C., and Green, H. (2004), 'Better on Balance? The Corporate Counsel Retention Project: Final Report,' *William and Mary Journal of Women and the Law*, vol. 10, pp. 367–452.

# Chapter 9

# ESG matters in the boardroom

*Alison L. Dempsey*

## Introduction

The role of boards of directors has attracted increasing scrutiny over the past two decades leading to heightened standards of accountability and expectations of responsibility to a broadening constituency of interests. In addition to their traditional core oversight of strategy, financial performance, risk management, internal controls and executive compensation, these higher standards and expectations are extending the board's function in relation to the non-financial dimensions of corporate activity.

While many of the changes in the board governance function stem from increased regulation and legal requirements aimed at preventing or reducing the incidence of corporate misconduct, not all of the shifts in the evolving board mandate have been in response to formal legal or regulatory intervention. Instead, many reflect changing normative and cultural expectations, as well as the emergence and escalation of new and non-traditional risk factors that directly reflect changes in attitudes toward corporate social, ethical and environmental impacts and influences.

Companies around the world face an operating environment in which environmental, ethical, social and governance issues and risks have an increasing impact on present and future business and market value, strategy, operations and practices alongside financial and economic considerations.

Many constituents and participants in the broader economic and capital market sphere – including regulators, internal and external stakeholders, business partners, providers of capital and finance, consumers and the investment community – have been or are turning their attention to these environmental and social considerations, scrutinising and raising the standards for corporate non-financial as well as financial conduct.

Around the globe, state-based law makers and regulators are introducing new and more explicit disclosure and reporting requirements in corporate and securities laws relating to corporate environmental and social impact and activity.

Current and future employees, as well as customers and those in charge of procurement and supply chains, are expressing their preference for companies that are responsible and accountable for the manner in which they conduct business and careful in their choices of business and supply chain partners.

In financial markets, a growing number of individual stock exchanges provide a platform for voluntary, and in a few cases mandatory, disclosure of corporate environmental, social and governance information. Internationally, there is cooperation in the form of the United Nations Sustainable Stock Exchange Initiative to advance the case for new mandatory listing standards that explicitly address environmental, social and governance matters.

Institutional and long-term investors now look to a company's successful management of these factors as a long-term value driver in recognition of a wider set of considerations that can have significant implications for an organization's financial and competitive as well as reputational, environmental and societal standing (Deutsche Bank Group 2012, Soyka and Bateman 2012).[1]

Combined, these market forces are driving increased board level attention to the environmental and social dimensions of corporate activity, their attendant responsibilities and risks and the implications for governance oversight and corporate accountability.

This chapter focuses on the pertinence of environmental and social dimensions of corporate governance to board members. It pays particular attention to the role that investor attention to and demand for non-financial information is influencing how public companies understand their reporting and disclosure responsibilities and the means by which they fulfill those responsibilities.

## Responsibility, risk and reputation

A company's relationships and interdependencies extend well beyond those given formal definition in law and contract. In recent decades, awareness of the need to attend to a broader set of connections, impacts and interests arising from business activity around the globe has increased along with the very real experience of the risks and costs – direct and indirect – associated with failing to take them into account.

System wide shocks such as those emanating from the recent financial crisis along with specific issues such as: the impact of uncertain and unpredictable weather patterns; concerns over resource consumption and constraint; the advent of carbon emissions regulation and carbon pricing; the adverse consequences of social and economic instability; and physical and technological threats to security have served to accelerate and elevate the discussion of environmental and social dimensions of development and growth.

If these were not sufficient to attract boardroom level attention, headlines covering the spectrum of corporate transgressions from worker health and safety, environmental harm, fraud and corruption, to tax practices and supply chain weaknesses show that the price of getting things wrong can be high. The attendant costs of such transgressions and of overlooking the broader impacts of corporate activity are not limited to one-off fines, penalties and advisor fees that can be absorbed or justified as a so-called price of doing business. Instead, they continue in the forms of often lengthy litigation, more rigorous regulatory and public scrutiny, higher thresholds to – or exclusion from – procurement, increased transaction costs, lost business opportunity, damaged reputation and loss of trust.

Considering that it is generally estimated that up to 80 percent of a company's market capitalization is made up of intangibles such as brand and license to operate, companies can ill afford these kinds of mistakes at the best of times, let alone in an uneven and competitive economy where news of the slightest transgression can spread in seconds in a world of 24/7 instant communications (Deloitte 2013).[2]

One need only contemplate the US$18.7 billion dollars oil giant BP has agreed to pay in settlement of all US federal and state claims in addition to the over US$40 billion in legal and clean-up costs resulting from the Deepwater Horizon oil spill into the Gulf of Mexico in 2010 (Gilbert and Kent 2015). In 2013, Walmart faced investigation by the US Justice Department, the SEC and foreign officials following allegations made public in a *New York Times* exposé of possible bribery overseas and labour rights practices in Brazil, India and China. The 2013 tragedy of the Rana Plaza factory collapse in Bangladesh shed the spotlight on retailers and their failures of responsibility in ensuring safe working conditions in their supply chains.

Also in 2013, Starbucks encountered very public disapproval following revelations of the company's tax practices in the United Kingdom while others, including Amazon, Apple and Google have been publicly criticised for using secretive jurisdictions, royalties and complex company structures for tax purposes (Barford and Holt 2013). In the case of Amazon, the scrutiny prompted a policy change such that the company will report revenue in a number of European jurisdictions rather than routing almost all of its revenue through Luxembourg to take advantage of a low tax agreement. Proving sector and size are no barrier to scrutiny, in May 2015 six global banks faced more than $5.6 billion dollars of fines in connection with allegations by regulators in the United Kingdom and United States that the banks had rigged foreign exchange markets.

As seen in the past, such failures are often precursors to formal policy and regulatory developments as well as informal and market driven shifts that have increased the level of responsibility as well as the administrative, financial and oversight burden for all companies, good and bad.

For example, in the United Kingdom, a series of business scandals that caused considerable damage to public and market confidence in the honesty, accountability and value of public companies led to corporate governance reforms in the early 1990s. Those reforms, following the recommendations made by the Cadbury Committee, were based on the principles of openness, integrity and accountability and are generally considered to have influenced the course of modern corporate governance and board responsibilities and practices in over 28 countries and institutions such as the World Bank (The Cadbury Committee 2002).[3]

Australia, similarly established a committee of representatives from business and the professions in 1990 at least partly in response to damaging publicity arising out of the malpractices of a small number of prominent companies in the 1980s that included HIH and One.Tel.[4] The Bosch committee's resulting guidelines for directors of Australian companies *Corporate Practices and Conduct* had the main objective to "improve the performance and reputation of Australian business by encouraging and assisting the general adoption of the highest standards of corporate conduct" (Bosch 1995, Foreword).

In the United States, the series of high profile corporate accounting and governance scandals early this century and the financial crisis in 2008 led to the passage of the *Sarbanes Oxley Act* in 1992 and the *Dodd-Frank Wall Street Reform and Consumer Protection Act* less than a decade later, both of which introduced substantial new law and regulation.[5]

Almost inevitably, the proliferation of new rules leads to increased compliance costs. A 2013 survey conducted in the United States of 128 large companies in the United

States placed the cost of maintaining documentation to respond to potential requests from regulators alone at more than US$40million per company a year with a similar cost burden on mid-sized and smaller companies (Hubbard 2014). These kinds of costs are not immaterial to investors: according to an Ernst and Young survey in 2013 of 163 institutional investors, analysts and portfolio managers around the globe, one of the two most important non-financial issues of concern was the business impact of regulation (Ernst and Young 2014).

For boards of directors, the advent of new and more stringent regulation and practices over the past few decades has led to a greater proportion of time spent on the procedural and technical aspects of compliance. Arguably, this attention has detracted from their more substantive strategic, risk and oversight function.

## Attending to shareholders' interests

With clear evidence of the material financial implications of corporate failure to address the ethical, environmental, social, and governance (ESG) aspects of their operations and practices, the distinction between the financial and so-called non-financial dimensions of business is becoming blurred.

In recent years, some of the most forceful impetus for this blurring of the lines has come from the investment community. For this constituency, particularly those with long-term investment mandates or horizons, taking into consideration performance against a broader set of performance indicators functions as a proxy for the quality of corporate management and boards and their ability to steer a sustainable course in a resource constrained world (Soyka and Bateman 2012).[6]

No longer reserved to specialist socially responsible investment funds, the integration of ESG into mainstream investment practice has direct implications for those in the board rooms of publicly listed companies where the interests of shareholders and providers of capital have long been a dominant if not exclusive focus. This is particularly the case in jurisdictions that have traditionally followed the so-called shareholder primacy corporate model that has traditionally emphasized the rights and interests of shareholders at times at the expense of other stakeholders, including communities and the environment.

Historically, this focus on shareholders' interests – reinforced by legal and fiduciary obligations – has directed the attention of boards to the financial dimensions of corporate accountability, particularly with respect to matters of equity risk and returns, deployment and management of capital, debt and economic performance. This bias toward economic objectives is in turn reflected in the information provided to, and the presumed information needs of shareholders, prospective investors and other financial stakeholders.

The foremost sources of corporate information for capital markets are regulatory filings and ongoing disclosures. Corporate disclosures made pursuant to annual reporting requirements such as Form 10-K and Regulation S-K in the United States, and similar corporate disclosure and reporting obligations in other jurisdictions like Canada's National Instrument 51–102 *Continuous Disclosure Obligations*.

For reporting issuers, formal corporate disclosure obligations are based on the concept of materiality. The term "materiality" has a very particular interpretation in the context of financial reporting that does not necessarily translate or accord with how the term is used outside that context. From an accounting standpoint, for financial reporting purposes the threshold test for determining the materiality of an issue is based on an assessment of the significance of information to a user in their decisions based on financial information about the reporting issuer (IASB and FASB 2010). For continuous disclosure purposes, pursuant to securities regulation the test focuses on the economic or investment decisions of users, particularly shareholders such as whether or not to buy, sell or hold a security (FRC 2013, SEC 2000).[7] According to the OECD *Principles of Corporate Governance,* "material information can be defined as information whose omission or misstatement could influence the economic decisions taken by users of information. Material information can also be defined as information that a reasonable investor would consider important in making an investment or voting decision" (OECD 2015, p. 41).

In all of these, the assessment, despite its object, is largely made by corporations and their advisors from a corporate-centric perspective. In practice, this assessment has tended to a predominant focus on matters directly related to corporate financials – backward-looking and near term results – rather than a broader understanding of the range of issues that growing numbers of investors and shareholders are now considering significant in their calculations as to corporate future as well as short-term prospects, value and risk. That is, the emphasis is on a narrow quantitative understanding of materiality rather than a quantitative and qualitative assessment that takes into account factors such as a company's industry, location, type, size and circumstance.

The result is that much of formal corporate financial reporting does not commonly extend to information on many of the wider concerns and risks associated with the changing environmental and social context in which businesses operate and that are coming within investors' wider focus. Issues associated with environmental impact, resource useage, corruption, market abuse, supply-chain risk, tax practices, diversity, social and income inequality have been commonly perceived and treated as externalities and therefore outside the scope let alone a material risk for the purposes of corporate financial reporting obligations.

In the 1970s, the United States SEC considered investor interest in the ethical, environmental and social dimensions of corporate activity following a series of cases and shareholder requests for broader disclosure in the 1960s and 1970s. The purpose was to ascertain whether such interest could be viewed as that of the "reasonable investor" for the purpose of establishing materiality (Schwartz 1971).[8] At the time, the percent of stocks and bonds invested according to what were then characterized as ethical principles was only a fraction of the total market value. Similarly, the level of support for shareholder proposals on environmental and social issues was considered insufficient to establish a baseline for determining reasonable investor interest.[9]

Such an assessment made in today's context might well yield quite different results. Of the respondents to the Ernst & Young 2013 global survey of investors, analysts and portfolio managers, nine out of ten stated that non-financial performance had played a pivotal role in their investment decision making in the past 12 months.[10] In 2014, a study conducted by PwC found that the majority of investors surveyed now incorporate sustainability issues into their investment strategy and proxy voting (PwC 2014).

Yet the underlying challenge – the lack or inadequacy of information on environmental and social issues available to investors – continues with formal corporate reporting still failing to provide the breadth of information sought by investors. Most of those who responded to the 2014 PwC survey reported being dissatisfied with sustainability related disclosure, with over 60 percent dissatisfaction with current levels in all regions except Europe (*Ibid*).

It is important to note that the prevailing focus on a narrow set of financial information points and inadequate or incomplete disclosure on other economically relevant information not captured in corporate financial statements is not a function of regulatory requirements. In fact, the disclosure based system is premised on the importance of providing information to investors to enable informed decision making and exercise of voting rights in fair, orderly and efficient capital markets.

For example, in the United Kingdom, *The Companies Act* 2006 mandates that companies listed on the London Stock Exchange disclose in their annual Business Review information on environmental, workplace, social and community matters "to the extent that they are important to understanding the company's business."[11] In South Africa, since 2009 all South African companies and, as of 2010, all companies listed on the Johannesburg Stock Exchange are required to describe financial, social and environmental factors within the report and to disclose "material matters," including sustainability risks, in a timely manner (King III 2009).

In the United States, *Securities Act* Rule 408 and *Exchange Act* Rule 12b-2 require the disclosure of:

> such further material information, if any, as may be necessary to make the required statements, in light of the circumstances under which they are made, not misleading.[12]

These rules, in essence, mean that companies failing to make honest, truthful and complete disclosure of material information that a reasonable investor would consider significant when deciding whether to buy, sell or hold a stock are acting unlawfully. This includes companies that make some disclosure on, say, compliance with existing environmental regulations but omit relevant information relating to additional regulation such as the introduction of more stringent emissions controls since the omission leads to an incomplete picture of changes to operating conditions, costs and potential legal and regulatory risks.

Furthermore, securities regulators explicitly assert issuers' obligations to recognize and report on material environmental factors alongside financial and governance matters as part of their established continuous disclosure. In 2010, securities regulators in both the United States and Canada provided specific guidance to issuers in relation to environment related disclosures.[13]

There are five key disclosure requirements in Canada's National Instrument 51–102 *Continuous Disclosure Obligations* that directly relate to environmental considerations. These are: environmental risks; trends and uncertainties; environmental liabilities; asset retirement obligations and financial and operational effects of environmental protection requirements. The information about each of these factors, when material, is important to gain a complete understanding of a company's risk profile.[14]

In the United States, Regulation S-K Item 101 expressly requires disclosure on the costs of complying with environmental laws. Item 103 requires the description of material pending legal proceedings, while Item 503 (c) requires a discussion of the most significant risk factors to an investment in the company. The disclosure under Management's Discussion and Analysis of Financial Condition and Results of Operations (MD&A) is required to provide a full context for companies' financial information, financial condition and prospects including textual disclosure on companies' future prospects (SEC 2010).

However, despite this guidance, the level of reporting on environmental and sustainability related issues such as climate change continues to be inadequate under existing mandatory disclosure requirements.

A 2014 Ceres report, *Cool Response: The SEC and Climate Change Reporting*, based on a survey of more than 40,000 SEC comment letters sent to companies over four years and an analysis of state of reporting on climate disclosure by S&P500 companies through the end of 2013 found that financial reporting on climate change in the majority of company filings is too brief and largely superficial, and that most companies are failing to meet the SEC's disclosure requirements (Ceres 2014). Even when these issues are identified as business risk factors in corporate annual reporting, companies are not required and tend not to provide information on how the risks are being addressed (*Ibid*).[15]

With formal reporting falling short of demand, those who seek information on the non-financial aspects of corporate activity and performance are doing so outside the traditional corporate reporting and disclosure mechanisms where such information currently may not be contained in – or readily discernible from – the financial information conventionally provided in formal disclosures.

## Market demand for ESG information

Recent decades have seen a perceptible shift toward a more explicit recognition of ESG factors in investment decisions. Those making the decisions – current shareholders and prospective investors – accordingly are taking into consideration more than narrow calculations of financial risk, return and liquidity, especially when assessing prospective returns and performance over the mid to longer term.

With growing evidence of a clear relationship between effective management of ESG risk and long-term financial value, investment decisions made without due consideration of important "non-financial" factors such as environmental, social and governance issues fail to recognize and fully account for longer-term risk and opportunity factors that are potentially financially material. In particular, a narrow or overly short-term focus may overlook many environmental and social issues and risks that can no longer be considered external to, or separate from, the companies responsible for them.

Furthermore, it can fail to recognize that the risks and costs of companies' mismanagement or mistakes in relation to ESG factors are increasing, with significant implications for economic and competitive as well as reputational, environmental and societal standing.

As a consequence, information about corporate governance, policy, strategy, management and performance in relation to non-financial matters is increasingly important to shareholders, investment fund managers and prospective investors, as well as other stakeholders. Accordingly, they require and are seeking ways to access reliable, clear, comparable and meaningful disclosure about companies' ESG policy and practices in sufficient detail for them to assess the quality of board oversight, corporate management and strategy and make informed decisions about risk, valuation, competitiveness and capacity to operate and adapt successfully in the face of change (Ernst and Young 2014).[16] All of these are factors that impact asset selection, capital allocation and ownership decisions, stewardship and the voting of shares.

There are numerous compelling indicators of the increase in the demand and expectations for ESG related information.

According to the *Global Sustainable Investment Review 2014* produced by the Global Sustainable Investment Alliance, at the start of 2014 the value of assets in the global sustainable investment market reached $21.4 trillion. This represented an 8.7 percent increase over two years in professionally managed assets in Europe, the United States, Canada, Asia, Japan, Australasia and Africa and translates into a growing share of the market (Global Sustainable Investment Alliance 2014).

North America represented two of the three fastest growing regions for sustainable investment in the two-year period of the study. In that time, the sector in Canada increased by 60 percent to $945 billion and in the United States it grew to nearly 18 percent of professional managed assets representing $6.57 trillion considering ESG factors in investment decisions or actively engaging on ESG issues through their shares in publicly traded companies. In the United Kingdom, the sustainable investment market is estimated to be growing at 32 percent a year. In Europe, the region with the largest growth, more than half of assets under professional management actively incorporate environmental, social and governance criteria.[17]

While a long-established approach for those specialising in socially responsible investment (SRI), factoring these ESG considerations into the investment thesis is rapidly becoming part of mainstream investment strategy and practice.

The main institutional investors in the OECD – pension funds, insurance companies and mutual funds – are estimated to hold over $71 trillion in assets. These are shareholders with ongoing future liabilities and obligations that are seeking consistent, sustainable economic returns over the long term. Given the potential significant future ESG costs, such as those associated with, for example, environmental remediation, resource scarcity, carbon pricing, changing and extreme weather, and social impacts, those whose duty it is to invest prudently for current and future beneficial interests are arguably compelled to assess their investment thesis and approach in this light. Accordingly, such large investors along with public and private trust, foundation and endowment funds are increasingly adopting and integrating ESG related criteria, principles and standards to the selection, allocation and retention of assets (IIRC 2012, Johnson 2014, UNEP FI [October 2005]).

In a 2013 survey of pension funds by the National Association of Pension Funds (NAPF) in the United Kingdom, 82 percent of respondents agreed that ESG factors can have a material impact on their fund's investments in the long term (UKSIF 2014).

For such long-term investors, and the asset managers who work with them, the motivation to consider and integrate ESG information may be driven by fund or institutional mandates, investment principles or approaches, or by virtue of legal requirements in addition to economic considerations. For example, pension fund trustees in the United Kingdom have been required to disclose the extent to which they have taken ESG considerations into account in their investment decisions since 2000 when the British Parliament introduced the first legislative requirement in the world for socially responsible investing reporting by occupational pension schemes (HMSO 1999).[18]

Similar requirements were introduced in France, Sweden and other European countries, along with Australia between 2001 and 2005. Recently, the Canadian province of Ontario introduced legislation requiring pension plan administrators from January 2016 to disclose in their filed Statements of Investment Policies and Procedures (SIPPs) whether and the extent that ESG factors are incorporated into the SIPP and how they are addressed in the plan's investment strategy.[19]

Public and social responsibility also has a significant role to play in light of heightened pressure from clients and beneficiaries to be responsible, ethical stewards of assets – for example the high profile campaign for trustees of public funds and endowments to divest from fossil fuel investments (Ansar et al. 2013).[20] In 2014, Norway's $900 billion State Pension Fund sold its stakes in 49 companies, mainly in coal and gold mining, on sustainability grounds and in June 2015 sought a mandate from the Norwegian Parliament to fully divest from coal. These moves away from fossil fuel are informed by economic as well environmental considerations since performance indicators suggest that fund performance does not suffer and can outperform without these types of assets and may be at risk by holding them (IEEFA 2015, HSBC Global Research 2015).[21]

In all cases, taking account of the ESG dimension is or is becoming an integral part of portfolio risk management. A similar development is also evident among other providers of finance as, for example, in the Equator Principles launched in 2003, just over a decade ago. The EP signatories, in 2014 numbering 80 financial institutions in 34 countries according to the EP website, commit to determining, assessing and managing environmental and social risk in connection with project finance and advice.

The increased interest and focus is also evident in the various ways that investors are articulating and engaging on these issues with companies. Specifically, the call for corporate environmental, social and governance information is increasingly explicit and public.

Interestingly, this call for information is coming not only from individual investors, but also taking the form of collective action the scale of which is increasingly hard to overlook either by companies and their boards or the policy makers that set the formal frameworks within which businesses operate.

For example, in 2012, the Corporate Sustainability Reporting Coalition backed by the UN Global Compact and comprising over 70 organizations, primarily institutional investors managing in excess of $2 trillion, proposed that UN member states develop an international convention requiring all listed and large private companies to integrate sustainability issues within their annual report and accounts, or to explain why they are not doing so.

At the beginning of 2015, the United Nations supported Principles for Responsible Investment (PRI), numbered over 1,300 signatories globally representing over US$45 trillion assets under management.[22] These signatories work together to understand and incorporate consideration of sustainability and ESG issues in investment strategy, decision making and ownership practices.

In late 2015, the PRI released a significant report on fiduciary duty, ESG integration and long-term responsible investment. The report makes the case that long-term investors' fiduciary duty to beneficiaries and clients necessitates analysis and action on

ESG issues, tackling head on the contested interpretations and variable legal landscape around what the duty entails (Sullivan et al. 2015). The report advances the ground-breaking position on fiduciary duty taken a decade ago in the Freshfield Report that "it may be a breach of fiduciary duties to fail to take account of ESG considerations that are relevant and to give them appropriate weight, bearing in mind that some important economic analysts and leading financial institutions are satisfied that a strong link between good ESG performance and good financial performance exists" (UNEP FI 2005, p. 100).[23]

Over 820 institutional investors globally representing assets of US$95 trillion have signed The Carbon Disclosure Project (CDP) which collects climate change-related information from over 5,000 companies. The CDP's special focus Water Program and Forest Program have the support, respectively, of approaching 620 institutional investors representing US$63 trillion in assets, and nearly 298 institutional investors representing US$19 trillion in assets.

Active direct engagement with companies on ESG issues has also seen a dramatic increase with the number of environmental, social and governance issues put forward in shareholder resolutions doubling within a decade to a record 417 shareholder resolutions filed in the 2014 proxy season in the United States. As of February 2015, another record number of 433 proposals were filed in the United States on ESG related matters for the 2015 proxy season, with the largest proportion relating to environmental issues with a particular focus on climate change and energy related risks (Welsh and Passoff 2015). Of these proposals, 15 sought greater board diversity, 14 related to board oversight of ESG with 8 of those requesting the establishment of board committees for the supervision of human rights and sustainability, and 30 requested sustainability reports.[24]

The proxy resolution process provides tangible indications of a growing belief on the part of institutional investors that a company's environmental and social policies correlate strongly with its approach to risk management and potentially, therefore, to its financial performance.

Not only are levels of support for these proposals increasing year on year, but their impact is being felt. In early 2015, Royal Dutch Shell under pressure from activist shareholders supported a resolution on climate change filed by 150 of its investors that requires the oil company to test its business model against a 2°C limit to global warming. BP faced similar pressure from its shareholders concerned with climate change with 98 percent of its investors voting for a climate resolution ordering the company to disclose more information on the risks.[25]

In May 2015, both Exxon Mobil and Chevron faced shareholder resolutions urging the companies to establish goals for greenhouse gas emission reduction and to evolve their business models to demonstrate responsible corporate governance in the face of climate change related risks. The proposals filed by 46 shareholders in the case of Exxon Mobil and 13 shareholders in the case of Chevron cite regulatory and financial risks arising from global and domestic climate related policy and associated technological change.

Shareholders and prospective investors are increasingly voicing their concerns for and interest in the non-financial as well as financial dimensions of their investment in companies around the world amid shifting fortunes and market uncertainty for the foreseeable future. Companies and their directors that are not already doing so would do well to consider how all aspects of their businesses affect investment choices and where their current and prospective shareholders are accessing that information.

## Reporting – beyond the financials

While for the present there is a disconnection, or tension, between corporate mandatory reporting and the expanded information needs of market actors, this is a changing circumstance. In fact, the test of materiality for the purposes of financial reporting that is determined by reference to the interests of shareholders allows for the kind of evolution in the perspectives of investors and shareholders that is now occurring and by extension the information that companies must disclose to satisfy existing as well as new reporting requirements.

Currently, in the absence of uneven or limited ESG information available in corporations' regulated financial disclosure particularly the environmental and social aspects, the market – investors, analysts, corporate stakeholders – look to other sources beyond corporate financial reporting to meet their information needs. This includes information disclosed by companies under voluntary ESG and sustainability reporting frameworks and standards.

Much of this reporting is voluntary with information that can vary in coverage, quality and substance. To address this concern, internationally recognized voluntary reporting frameworks provide both reporters and consumers of sustainability information with more robust, comparable and transparent platforms.

The most influential of these include the Global Reporting Initiative (GRI) now in its fourth generation and the leading voluntary ESG reporting framework and the UN Global Compact both of which encompass a broad range of environmental, social and governance issues.

Other leading frameworks focus on particular dimensions of sustainability. These include ISO 26000 which provides guidance on how organizations can operate in a socially responsible way and the carbon disclosure project (CDP), which seeks enhanced disclosure on environmental issues such as GHG emissions, water usage and forestry practices.

These frameworks are serving to fill an information gap for the growing body of capital market actors who factor ESG dimensions of corporate activity, strategy and performance into their asset allocation decisions, such as the signatories to the UN Principles for Responsible Investment (PRI) and the Equator Principles.

Voluntary reporting frameworks and initiatives have seen rising recognition and acceptance at both ends of the reporting process in recent years: from the growing numbers of companies that voluntarily submit reports in accordance with disclosure guidelines, to the public and private stakeholders, institutional investors, shareholders and capital markets worldwide that use the information in those reports to inform policy, decisions and action.

As widely accessible information platforms, they are also largely responsible for the availability of ESG data – policies, practices, metrics, opportunities and risks – that is in turn contributing to and informing a rapidly-changing ESG regulatory environment for issuers, investors and their stakeholders.[26]

In growing numbers, companies for their part are applying the principle that disclosure, accountability and transparency enhances credibility to the reporting of what is regarded as "non-financial" information. In recognition and in response to market-driven momentum toward mainstreaming sustainable business practices, steadily increasing numbers of companies are reporting on these so-called "non-financial" dimensions of their businesses.

In 2013, according to KPMG's Survey of Corporate Responsibility Reporting, 93 percent of Global Fortune 250 companies and 86 percent of the largest companies in the United States report on corporate responsibility. The research found that ESG reporting is a global trend. Reporting rates for companies in the Americas, Europe, and Asia Pacific were 76 percent, 73 percent and 71 percent respectively. In some of the fastest growing emerging markets, the number of companies reporting has shown significant increase up by 16 percent in China and by 53 percent in India from 2011–2013 (KPMG 2013).

The numbers of companies in the influential S&P 500 Index found to have published a sustainability or corporate responsibility report saw a three-fold increase from 20 percent in 2011 to more than 72 percent in 2013.[27]

In 2014, the Global Reporting Initiative (GRI) an internationally recognized framework for corporate sustainability reporting numbered over 7,000 reporters and more than 8,000 companies adhere to the commitments of the Global Compact.

While these are considered non-regulatory, or voluntary, conduct and reporting they are a growing influence on how companies communicate to the market. As a consequence, they are becoming, if not already, key elements in determining what matters to and demands the attention of boards of directors.

Not only do these voluntary reporting mechanisms serve the information needs of investors as well as other financial, regulatory and public stakeholders that are currently unevenly met in the regulated disclosure space, they also enable comparison between companies across sectors, industries and regions and encourage best practices and transparency.

From a company standpoint, they provide a means to assess, develop, evaluate, track and compare management of ESG considerations with peers, differentiate themselves from competitors and inform current and prospective shareholders. For example, from January 1, 2016, companies reporting under the GRI pursuant to the latest reporting framework – G4 – will do so according to a new materiality principle developed as with previous versions through a multi-stakeholder process. This materiality principle is the basis for establishing those aspects of an organization, its operations and impacts that are sufficiently important to be included in the report: aspects that "reflect the organization's significant economic, environmental and social impacts; or substantively influence the assessments and decisions of stakeholders" (GRI, G4 2015).

The process of identifying Material Aspects for the purposes of preparing and reporting under G4 necessitates that organizations have both discipline and focus in undertaking the material, qualitative analysis, quantitative assessment and discussion with stakeholders necessary to ensure completeness, accuracy and reliability of reported information. With this elevated threshold, the process is no longer one that can be undertaken solely at the operational level.

The intention with G4 to engage those at the highest levels of the organization is made clear with the requirement that final reports include a strategy statement from the most senior decision-maker of the organization such as CEO, chair, or equivalent senior position. The statement is expected to address the relevance of sustainability to the organization, the organization's short-, medium- and long-term vision and strategy for addressing sustainability with attention to its significant economic, environmental and social impacts or those linked to its activities.

Furthermore, as new legislated standards, like the recent mandatory ESG reporting requirement for companies in the EU, import these voluntary frameworks for companies to satisfy their reporting requirements there is an obvious advantage to companies that are already voluntarily reporting under these frameworks.

The introduction of what is arguably a competing materiality standard to that which has long governed corporate disclosure under securities regulatory regimes in the US and Canada and major markets around the world is potentially problematic for reporting issues and the markets that depend on clear, reliable and consistent information. However, on closer analysis it may well be that this is a sign of the need for formal as well as functional convergence in what is understood to be important and increasingly material to corporate shareholders, investors and the market generally.

## Regulatory change

Recent developments have also seen formal and regulated standards advancing the ESG agenda.

In 2013, a proposal was formally submitted to the World Federation of Exchanges to engage member stock exchanges on a uniform ESG-related reporting standard. Exchanges like the Johannesburg Stock Exchange and Brazil's BM&F BOVESPA already have mandatory ESG listing requirements and there are 24 partner exchanges of the United Nations Sustainable Stock Exchanges Initiative (SSEI), including NASDAQ, the London Stock Exchange and NYSE, working toward the introduction of sustainability related disclosure requirements.[28] In September 2015, the SSEI released its inaugural *Model Guidance on ESG Reporting to Investors: A Voluntary Tool for stock Exchanges to Guide Issuers*. The guidance is intended to assist stock exchanges around the globe in developing broadly consistent expectations for, and engaging their issuers on, voluntary reporting on ESG issues and related data.

Policy developments in countries in Europe, the UK, South Africa, Australia, the US and in some developing economies already have or are adopting explicit requirements for environmental and social as well as financial and governance related disclosures by companies in regulated markets. As of 2014, 19 members of the G20 had at least one regulation in place requiring that companies disclose at least some social and/or environmental metrics (SSEI 2014).

One leading example is the 2014/95/EU *Directive of the European Parliament and of the Council amending Directive 2013/34/EU as regards disclosure of non-financial and diversity information by certain large undertakings and groups*. Pursuant to the Directive, companies with more than 500 employees in the European Union will be required to disclose in their annual reports "relevant, useful information" necessary for an understanding of such companies' environmental, social, employee, human rights and anti-corruption and bribery matters. These companies will also be required to disclose board diversity matters. The disclosure is to focus on the companies' governing policies in relation to these matters, related risks and the management of such risks. This requirement adopted by the European Parliament on September 29, 2014 and in the process of being transposed into national legislation will affect approximately 6,000 companies although some to a lesser degree such as those in EU countries where there are already ESG disclosure requirements such as the United Kingdom, Denmark, France, Spain and Sweden.

The new directive will also impact companies that are EU exchange-listed and, potentially, those with a presence in an individual Member State significant enough for that Member State to designate the company as an entity subject to the reporting requirements. As noted above, companies in the EU can satisfy their formal reporting obligations through their voluntary disclosure in accordance with recognized disclosure frameworks such as the GRI or the Global Compact.

Also, while still early in its evolution, the concept of integrating ESG and financial information in corporate reporting is expected to advance as a result of the recognition and demand for information that presents a more holistic view of a corporation. The International Integrated Reporting Council (IIRC) published the first integrated reporting framework in December 2013.[29] Over 80 businesses and over 30 investors are currently involved in the IIRC Pilot Programme.[30]

In the US, the Sustainability Accounting Standards Board (SASB) an independent non-profit organization launched its development of standards for the integrated reporting of material sustainability issues and sustainability accounting standards in October 2012. Although not affiliated with the official financial accounting standards board in the United States, FASB, or the International Accounting Standards Board (IASB), the organization's stated goal is to develop standards for the reporting of material non-financial information in mandatory SEC filings such as the Form 10-K and 20-F for 80 industries in ten sectors drawing from evidence based research and broad stakeholder participation.[31]

These moves toward closer integration of reported financial and non-financial information are impetus to changes to corporate disclosure practices potentially as significant as the move toward international accounting rules a decade ago.

In parallel, formal regulatory expectations and requirements are expanding and becoming more explicit with broad based acknowledgement of the need to respond to issues associated with natural resource depletion, carbon emissions, climate change, corruption, social inequity, supply chain and worker safety among others that pose risks to businesses as well as society as a whole.

Legislation in effect in the United Kingdom under the 2011 *Bribery Act*, in the United States under Section 1502 of the *Dodd Frank Wall Street Reform And Consumer Protection Act* (the Conflict Minerals reporting requirement), in Canada under the *Extractive Sector Transparency Measures Act* and being implemented across the European Union under the *Resource Extraction Payments Disclosure Law*, 2015, and in Australia and other OECD countries advances a global effort to combat bribery and corruption through transparency.[32] These measures require companies engaged in or controlling entities engaged in the extractive industries, specifically oil, gas or minerals, to report payments made to all levels of domestic and foreign governments. While there are concerns about the quality of disclosure and the information being reported under the new requirements, over time the goal is that the companies that are most credible and transparent in their reporting of the measures they take to ensure a supply chain free of corruption will be able to distinguish themselves from industry peers (Amnesty International 2015).[33]

Most recently, the new *G20/OECD Principles of Corporate Governance* released in September 2015, include new specific reference to the disclosure of non-financial information that companies may be required to make, for example in their management reports, or do so voluntarily. Principle V Disclosure and transparency, at A.2 states that: "companies are encouraged to disclose policies and performance relating to business ethics, the environment and, where material to the company, social issues, human rights and other public policy commitments" (OECD 2015).

Together, these various developments are effectively re-defining the baseline standard for how corporate strategies for effective oversight and management of environmental and social impacts and risks are identified and evaluated alongside and ultimately as part of the financial and governance dimensions of their business.

## Performance and reward

Companies and the boards of directors that oversee them would not be doing their job if they failed to consider the impact of these changing operating conditions and market expectations on performance.

In the past, the drive to increase corporate profit and externalise costs influenced much of the understanding of capitalism, particularly in the dominant US marketplace where responsibility for decisions or actions beyond those within the narrow lens of financial performance was perceived as inconsistent with the primary obligation to maximize shareholder returns. This perception and the associated narrative are changing with indications that broader responsibility is not inconsistent with better performance.

Data supporting the link between sustainable business practices and performance is increasingly available and persuasive for companies as well as their shareholders, prospective investors and stakeholders. A growing body of research from such varied sources as Deloitte, Goldman Sachs, McKinsey and the US Department Energy as well as the academic community have been exploring the link between sustainability and corporate performance.[34] The most compelling of these focus on environmental, social and governance factors that have potentially significant and material impacts on the long-term risk and return profile of a company.

What is interesting and perhaps most promising is that these studies also reveal considerable opportunities and benefits to be realized by companies that actively and successfully direct and manage their operations to minimize negative impacts while working toward developing and achieving sustainable business goals. In combination they make a clear link between effective ESG management and both short- and long-term shareholder value and value creation.

The greater attention to these issues – far from being ancillary to or inconsistent with the purpose of business – is increasingly recognized as important, if not critical, to the ability for companies to operate profitably as well as ethically and in a sustainable way in the future.

Policy makers, capital market participants, civil society and members of the business community express growing concern about potential under-recognized and accordingly under-reported risk to current and future valuations in light of mainstreaming of responsible and sustainable business practices – directly through competitive, operational and resource pressures, and indirectly through regulation and shifting market expectations.[35] At the same time there is under-recognized and as yet under valued competitive advantage for companies with or who are developing sustainable business practices in light of shifting market and regulatory operating conditions and expectations (CDP S&P 500 2014).[36]

Closely linked to issues of performance is the long-standing corporate governance battleground of executive compensation and reward.

For years, boards have been challenged to attend to the linkage between corporate performance, shareholder return and management reward amidst greater public and shareholder focus on executive pay and regulatory requirements for increased transparency around the composition and determinants of compensation.

As part of the Board of Director's responsibility to the company, shareholders, and stakeholders to direct and govern for sustainable value creation, compensation committees that are not already doing so will find that increased scrutiny of corporate non-financial performance will necessitate evaluation of the components and structure of executive compensation with a view to integrating key ESG metrics into the design of compensation and reward arrangements.

As well as aligning with shareholders' evolving expectations for corporate governance, strategic and management oversight, boards now need to ensure that executive and management incentives focus on and address the full spectrum of risks to present and future corporate value and valuation associated with "extra-financial" factors. Compensation arrangements that do not incorporate performance elements relating to the environmental, social and governance dimensions of a business run the risk that management is not attending to factors that can impact everything from product and supply lines, to headlines and bottom lines.

In June 2012, The UNPRI published guidance for investors and companies on integrating environmental, social and governance issues into executive pay stating that ". . . the inclusion of appropriate Environmental, Social and Governance (ESG) issues within executive management goals and incentive schemes can be an important factor in the creation and protection of long-term shareholder value" (UNPRI 2012, p. 1). The 2015 proxy season in the United States saw 11 shareholder proposals requesting executive pay links to sustainability metrics.[37]

In the aftermath of the recent financial crisis, insight into the role of incentives in encouraging unacceptably risky behaviour has drawn attention to the nature and combination of performance measures used and the types of behaviour and levels of risk that such measures encourage. It is now widely acknowledged that the inherent conflict between short-term share price performance and longer-term sustainable value is exacerbated by performance metrics and compensation that focus solely on the former at the expense of the latter. Consequently, the elements and measures of performance incorporated in compensation will need to provide clear direction and incentive for management to focus on a broader set of drivers aimed at sustainable business success.

Boards are encouraged to work with shareholders and internal and external stakeholders to understand and choose the ESG metrics that are most relevant to the nature of the business, its particular set of challenges and risks to as well as opportunities for long-term success.

Measures may include strategic and operational goals based on, for example: legal and regulatory compliance; supply chain integrity; reducing negative environmental impacts; meeting and exceeding worker health and safety standards; improving

shareholder and stakeholder relations. For many businesses, the development of strategies for energy efficiency, conservation and resource productivity and adaptation
to changing demographic, climate and weather patterns are increasingly important
in view of rising energy and commodity costs, carbon pricing and stricter emissions
regulation.

With the heightened interest, scrutiny and activism around ESG issues, boards have
an opportunity to incorporate and report proactively on the combination of financial
and non-financial metrics that will challenge management to find a sustainable balance between the near and longer term, to operate effectively and efficiently and to be
positioned to anticipate, manage, mitigate and profit from the changes to their present
and future operating environment.

## Conclusion

In today's and tomorrow's operating environment purely economic measures of performance do not encompass the full extent of factors that companies need to "get
right" to ensure corporate success. As the accounting scandals of just over a decade
ago and the recent global financial crisis evidenced, in today's business environment
*how* profits are made matters.

In the past, companies may have overlooked the full extent of their business conduct and reporting obligations in relation to so-called "non-financial" matters. Now,
however, there is both a market driven and a compliance imperative. Whatever the
motivation, corporate boards together with management need to evaluate regularly
how they think about, undertake and arrive at their strategic, operating, oversight
and reporting decisions in relation to a wider set of non-financial as well as financial
dimensions and risks affecting their business.

Ultimately, adding the E&S to the Financial and Governance matters on the board
agenda is therefore about recognizing that these increasingly pressing issues go to the
core of what companies do, how they are governed and held accountable for the consequences and risks, as well as opportunities that flow, and whether or not they will
meet the unprecedented challenges ahead successfully.

## Notes

1 Recent research includes: "Sustainable Investing – Establishing Long Term Value and
  Performance," Deutsche Bank Group, June 2012; and the IRRC Institute funded –
  "Finding Common Ground on the Metrics that Matter," by Peter A. Soyka, Mark E. Bateman (February 2012).
2 A 2013 Deloitte Touche Tomahatsu Ltd. report of a survey of 300 executives around the
  world conducted by Forbes Insights found that reputation ranks as the top strategic risk
  concern for most individual industries as well as across industries in large part due to the role
  of social media in publicising corporate activity. Deloitte, *Exploring Strategic Risk* (2013),
  http://www2.deloitte.com/us/en/pages/governance-risk-and-compliance/articles/exploring-
  strategic-risk.html (accessed May 14, 2015).
3 The Cadbury Committee, *The Report of the Committee on the Financial Aspects of Corporate Governance*, Gee, London, 2002 (*The Cadbury Report*). The draft report was issued
  in May 1992 and the final report in December 1992. Online at: http://www.jbs.cam.ac.uk/
  cadbury/report/index.html.

4  HIH is the largest collapse in Australian corporate history and the subject of an A$40 million Royal Commission (HIH Royal Commission). The Commissions findings were published in April 2003 HIH Royal Commission, Commonwealth of Australia, The Failure of HIH Insurance (2003), http://www.hihroyalcom.gov.au/finalreport/index.htm.

5  The Sarbanes–Oxley Act of 2002 (Pub.L. 107–204, 116 Stat. 745, enacted 30 July 2002), also known as the Public Company Accounting Reform and Investor Protection Act (in the Senate) and Corporate and Auditing Accountability and Responsibility Act (in the House) and commonly referred to as the Sarbanes–Oxley Act, Sarbanes–Oxley or the acronym SOX. Dodd–Frank Wall Street Reform and Consumer Protection Act (Pub.L. 111–203, H.R. 4173).

6  Peter E. Soyka, Mark A. Bateman, *Finding Common Ground on the Metrics that Matter*, IRRC Institute (February, 2012), p. 7.

7  In Canada, Form 51–102F1 *Management's Discussion and Analysis* Part 1(f) and Form 51–102F2 Annual Information Form Part 1(e).

8  For example: *NRDC v. SEC*, 389 F. Supp. 689, 693–694 (D.D.C. 1974). Campaign GM, a proxy proposal form GM shareholders requesting more information from the company on environmental and civil rights performance and on safety and design issues.

9  Commission Conclusions and Rule-Making Proposals, Securities Act release No. 5627, Exchange Act Release No. 11773, [1965–1976 Transfer Binder] Fed. Sec. L. Rep (CCH) 80, 820 at 85, 719–720 (Oct. 14, 1975).

10  Ernst and Young, Tomorrow's investment rules: global survey of institutional investors on non-financial performance, supra note 10.

11  *Companies Act 2006* (c. 46).

12  17 CFR 230.408 and 17 CFR 240.12b-20. There is also 17 CFR 240.10B-5 Employment of Manipulative and Deceptive Devices that similarly makes it unlawful to omit or withhold information if doing so makes the disclosed information untrue or misleading.

13  CSA Staff Notice 51–333 *Environmental Reporting Guidance*, October 27, 2010; OSC Staff Notice 51–717 Corporate Governance and Environmental Disclosure, 2009.

14  CSA Staff Notice 51–333 *Environmental Reporting Guidance*, supra note 23 at p.8.

15  http://www.sec.gov/answers/reada10k.htm.

16  EY, *Tomorrow's investment rules: global survey of institutional investors on non-financial performance* (2014, EYGM Limited) supra-note 10.

17  *Ibid*. Supra-note 27.

18  *SRI Pension Disclosure Regulation 2000* amendment to the UK *Pensions Act 1995*. HMSO (1999). The Occupational Pension Schemes Amendment Regulations 1999: Statutory Instrument 1999 No. 1849. Now, The Occupational Investment Schemes (Investment) Regulation: Statutory Instrument 2005 No. 3378.

19  Ontario Regulation 235/14 under *Pensions Benefits Act*, R.S.O. 1990, C.P.8.

20  For example the 2012 Fossil Fuel Divestment Campaign launched by the United States based civic organization 350.org. Atif Ansar, Ben Caldecott, James Tilbury, *Stranded assets and the fossil fuel divestment campaign: what does divestment mean for the valuation of fossil fuel assets?*, Smith School of Enterprise and the Environment Oxford University (October, 2013) p.11.

21  http://www.bankofengland.co.uk/pra/Pages/supervision/activities/climatechange.aspx#.

22  See: http://www.unpri.org/about-pri/about-pri/ (last accessed May 15, 2015).

23  United Nations Environment Programme Finance Initiative [UNEP FI] (2005), *A Legal Framework for the Integration of Environmental, Social and Governance Issues into Institutional Investment* (UNEP FI, Nairobi), p. 100 [commonly referred to as "the Freshfields Report"].

24  *Proxy Preview 2015*, supra-note 38.

25  www.ShareAction.org.

26  These voluntary reporting frameworks are being referred to in some newly enacted ESG mandatory and voluntary regulation as "approved" guidelines for reporting under these regulatory regimes.

27  Governance & Accountability Institute.

28  The United Nations Sustainable Stock Exchanges Initiative (www.sseinitiative.org) was launched in 2009 by the UN Secretary General Ban Ki-moon and is co-organised by UNC-TAD, the UN Global Compact, the UN-supported Principles for Responsible Investment and the UNEP Finance Initiative.

29  http://integratedreporting.org/.

30  http://integratedreporting.org/companies-and-investors/.

31  http://www.sasb.org/.

32  Find OECD Anti-Bribery and anti corruption legal instruments, guidance and resources at http://www.oecd.org/corruption/keyoecdanti-corruptiondocuments.htm. (accessed September 8, 2015).

33  Note that while the US conflict minerals reporting requirement came into effect in 2014, at time of writing, certain provisions are subject to legal challenge in US Court.

34  See for example, "Sustainable Investing – Establishing Long Term Value and Performance", Deutsche Bank Group, June 2012; "Sustainability Pays: Studies That Prove the Case for Sustainability", Natural Capital Solutions, December 2012. www.natcapsolutions.org/businesscasereports.pdf.

35  See for example, http://www.bankofengland.co.uk/pra/Pages/supervision/activities/climatechange.aspx#.

36  A recent report by CDP found that S&P 500 firms that disclose their environmental data and set strong carbon reduction goals had higher financial profitability, stability, and returns to shareholders than peers. See *CDP S&P 500 Climate Change Report 2014*, November 2014, https://www.cdp.net/CDPResults/CDP-SP500-leaders-report-2014.pdf.

37  *Proxy Preview 2015*, supra-note 26.

## Bibliography

Amnesty International (2015), *Digging for Transparency; How U.S. Companies are only Scratching the Surface of Conflict Minerals Reporting*. Global Witness, April 22. Available from https://www.globalwitness.org/campaigns/democratic-republic-congo/digging-transparency (accessed May 15, 2015).

Ansar, A., Caldecott, B. and Tilbury, J. (2013), *Stranded Assets and the Fossil Fuel Divestment Campaign: What Does Divestment Mean for the Valuation of Fossil Fuel Assets?* Smith School of Enterprise and the Environment Oxford University. Available from http://www.smithschool.ox.ac.uk/research-programmes/stranded-assets/SAP-divestment-report-final.pdf.

Barford, V. and Holt, G. (2013), Google, Amazon, Starbucks: The Rise of Tax Shaming, *BBC News Magazine*, March 21. Available from http://www.bbc.com/news/magazine-20560359 (accessed May 24, 2015).

Bosch, H. (1995), *Corporate Practice and Conduct*. 3rd Ed. Woodslane Pty. Ltd, Sydney, Australia.

The Cadbury Committee (2002), *The Report of the Committee on the Financial Aspects of Corporate Governance*. Gee, London.

Ceres (2014), *Cool Response: the SEC and Climate Change Reporting* (February). Available from http://www.ceres.org/resources/reports/cool-response-the-sec-corporate-climate-change-reporting/view.

Deloitte (2013), *Exploring Strategic Risk*. Available from http://www2.deloitte.com/us/en/pages/governance-risk-and-compliance/articles/exploring-strategic-risk.html (accessed May 14, 2015).

Deutsche Bank Group (2012), *Sustainable Investing – Establishing Long Term Value and Performance*. Available from https://institutional.deutscheawm.com/content/_media/Sustainable_Investing_2012.pdf.

Ernst and Young (2014), *Tomorrow's Investment Rules: Global Survey of Institutional Investors on Non-Financial Performance*. Available from http://www.ey.com/GL/en/Services/Specialty-Services/Climate-Change-and-Sustainability-Services/EY-Tomorrows-investment-rules-a-global-survey#.VVT4HMvbJVd (accessed May 14, 2015).

Financial Reporting Council (FRC) (2013), *International Standard on Auditing (UK and Ireland) 320: Materiality in Planning and Performing an Audit*. Available from https://www.frc.

org.uk/Our-Work/Publications/Audit-and-Assurance-Team/ISA-700-(UK-and-Ireland)-700-(Revised)-File.pdf.

Gilbert, D. and Kent, S. (2015), BP Agrees to Pay $18.7 Billion to Settle Deepwater Horizon Oil Spill Claims, *The Wall Street Journal*, July 2. Available from http://www.wsj.com/articles/bp-agrees-to-pay-18–7-billion-to-settle-deepwater-horizon-oil-spill-claims-1435842739 (accessed September 9, 2015).

Global Reporting Initiative (GRI) (2015), *G4 Sustainability Reporting Guidelines – Reporting Principles and Standard Disclosures*. Available from https://www.globalreporting.org/resourcelibrary/GRIG4-Part1-Reporting-Principles-and-Standard-Disclosures.pdf (accessed August 22, 2015).

Global Sustainable Investment Alliance (2014), *Global Sustainable Investment Review 2014*. Available from http://www.gsi-alliance.org/members-resources/global-sustainable-investment-review-2014.

HIH Royal Commission, Commonwealth of Australia (2003), *The Failure of HIH Insurance*. Available from http://www.hihroyalcom.gov.au/finalreport/index.htm.

HSBC Global Research (2015), *Stranded Assets – What Next?* Available from http://www.businessgreen.com/digital_assets/8779/hsbc_Stranded_assets_what_next.pdf (accessed May 15, 2015).

Hubbard, W.H.J. (2014), *Preservation Costs Survey*. Final Report. Available from http://www.ediscoverylaw.com/files/2014/02/Hubbard-Preservation_Costs_Survey_Final_Report.pdf (accessed May 14, 2015).

IASB and FASB (2010), *The Conceptual Framework for Financial Reporting*, September. Available from http://www.ifrs.org/Current-Projects/IASB-Projects/Conceptual-Framework/Objectives-and-qualitative-characteristics/Documents/CFFeedbackStmt.pdf.

IEEFA (2015), *MSCI ACWI Fossil Fuels Index*. Institute for Energy Economics and Financial Analysis (IEEFA) Report. Available from https://www.msci.com/resources/factsheets/index_fact_sheet/msci-acwi-ex-fossil-fuels-index-gbp-gross.pdf.

IRRC Institute (2012), *Environmental, Social and Governance Investing by College and University Endowments in the United States*. Tellus Institute, July. Available from http://www.irrcinstitute.org/wp-content/uploads/2015/09/FINAL_IRRCi_ESG_Endowments_Study_July_2012.pdf.

Johnson, K. (2014), 'Introduction to Institutional Investor Fiduciary Duties', *Institute for Sustainable Development Report*, February. Available from http://www.reinhartlaw.com/Documents/art140402%20RIIS.pdf.

King III (2009), *The King Code on Corporate Governance for South Africa*. The Institute of Directors in Southern Africa, September. Available from http://www.iodsa.co.za/?page=KingCopyright.

KPMG (2013), *Survey of Corporate Responsibility Reporting*. Available from kpmg.com/sustainability.

OECD (2015), *G20/OECD Principles of Corporate Governance*, September. Available from http://www.oecd.org/g20/topics/financing-for-investment/Corporate-Governance-Principles-ENG.pdf (accessed September 8, 2015).

PriceWaterhouseCoopers (PwC) (2014), *Investor Survey*. Winter/Spring Series, May. Available from http://www.pwc.com/en_US/us/pwc-investor-resource-institute/publications/assets/pwc-sustainability-goes-mainstream-investor-views.pdf.

Schwartz, D.E. (1971), 'The Public-Interest Proxy Contest: Reflections on Campaign GM,' *Michigan Law Review*, vol. 69, no. 3, pp. 419–538. Available from http://www.jstor.org/stable/1287435.

Securities and Exchange Commission (2010), 'Commission Guidance Related to Disclosure Regarding Climate Change,' *Federal Register*, vol. 75, no. 25, February 8.

Soyka, P.A., and Bateman, M.E. (2012). *Finding Common Ground on the Metrics that Matter*. Available from http://papers.ssrn.com/sol3/papers.cfm?abstract_id=2013594.

Sullivan, R., Martindale, W., Feller, E., Bordon, A., and Garcia-Alba, J. (2015). *Fiduciary Duty in the 21st Century*. UNEP, UNPRI. Available from http://www.unepfi.org/fileadmin/documents/fiduciary_duty_21st_century.pdf.

Sustainable Stock Exchanges (SSEI) (2014). *Report on Progress*. Sustainable Stock Exchanges Initiative. Available from http://www.sseinitiative.org/wp-content/uploads/2012/03/SSE-2014-ROP.pdf (accessed May 22, 2015).

UKSIF (2014), *Attitudes to Ownership 2014: Exploring Pension Fund and Public Opinion on Ownership and Stewardship Issues*. March. Available from http://ownershipday.co.uk/wp-content/uploads/2014/03/Attitudes-to-Ownership-Report.pdf (accessed May 22, 2015).

UNEP Finance Initiative (2005). *A Legal Framework for the Integration of Environmental, Social and Governance Issues into Institutional Investment*. Asset Management Working group. Freshfields Bruckhaus Deringer, October. Available from http://www.unepfi.org/fileadmin/documents/freshfields_legal_resp_20051123.pdf (accessed May 22, 2015).

UNPRI (2012). *Integrating ESG Issues into Executive Pay. Principles for Responsible Investment*. Available from http://2xjmlj8428u1a2k5o34l1m71.wpengine.netdna-cdn.com/wp-content/uploads/IntegratingESGissues.pdf.

US Securities and Exchange Commission (SEC) (2000). *Regulation on Fair Disclosure (Regulation FD)*, October. Available from http://www.sec.gov/rules/final/33–7881.htm.

Welsh, H., and Passoff, M. (2015). *Proxy Preview*. As You Sow. Available from www.proxypreview.org (accessed May 22, 2015).

# Part IV

# The requirements for implementation of sustainability

# Chapter 10

# The drivers of change

*Suzanne H. Benn*

## Introduction

This chapter examines the key issues that are driving organizational change for sustainability. It is only in recent decades that we have become aware of the extent to which the dynamics of natural systems make them vulnerable to human intervention. But in that relatively short period in the history of industrialization, it has become increasingly evident that the damage wrought to the planet is such that without dramatic change in the behaviour of business organizations and our individual behaviour as consumers, life on the Earth as we know it is unsustainable. For the sake of the ecosystem upon which we all depend for the ultimate source of much of our aesthetic understanding of beauty and for what is left of the remaining great wilderness areas of the planet (Mittermeier et al. 2002), we must question what we mean by business development. If we stop to reflect on what will be left for the next generation of nature in all its wonder, we can come to recognise that it is business that we must rely on for change, not just through the greening of a single organization but through the role it can play in interaction with other stakeholders (Jamison 2000). This chapter sets out more specifically the reasons why business and its networks need to come on board.

## Dynamic natural environment

### Climate change

In 2008, UN Secretary-General Ban Ki-moon warned that climate change is the "defining challenge of the era"(UN News Centre 2008). Four years later, the OECD Environmental Outlook to 2050 (OECD 2012a) provided more evidence of the urgency with which action is needed on behalf of global ecological limits. It emphasized that without more ambitious policies than those in force today, greenhouse gas emissions will increase by another 50 per cent by 2050 – primarily due to a projected 80 per cent increase in global energy demand and economic growth in key emerging economies. Global average temperature increase is projected to be 3°C to 6°C higher by the end of the century, exceeding the internationally agreed goal of limiting it to 2°C above pre-industrial levels. Temperature changes will be likely to be unevenly distributed but increases will be sufficient to alter precipitation patterns, melt glaciers, cause sea-level rise and intensify extreme weather events to unprecedented levels. They might also exceed some critical "tipping-points", causing dramatic natural changes that could have catastrophic or irreversible outcomes for natural systems and society. In 2015, in the run up to COP21, another OECD report (2015) notes that the support for fossil fuels still remains high and that the time is ripe for change. Regional attempts to improve energy intensity that are evident in emerging economies such as Brazil and Russia are not likely to address the increasing energy demand worldwide. So, while greenhouse gas emissions from land use and forestry are expected to decrease, that will not be enough to counterbalance the expected increases overall.

The implications of climate change are evident in economic scenarios that indicate that companies reliant on fossil fuel face major issues of long-term risk management. For instance, recent studies have shown that the benefits of a radical rethinking of our energy sources far outweigh the economic cost (Stern 2010). Research from Carbon Tracker and the Grantham Research Institute on Climate Change and the Environment at the London School of Economics published in the report "Unburnable Carbon 2013: Wasted Capital and Stranded Assets" has revealed that fossil fuel reserves already far exceed the carbon budget to avoid global warming of 2°C. Yet "$674 billion was spent last year to find and develop new potentially stranded assets". The research report "calls for regulators, governments and investors to re-evaluate energy business models against carbon budgets, to prevent a $6 trillion carbon bubble in the next decade" (Carbon Tracker and the Grantham Research Institute 2013).

### Other environmental impacts

The report *Natural Capital at Risk – The Top 100 Externalities of Business*, from the Economics of Ecosystems and Biodiversity (TEEB) Coalition (TEEB 2013), produced valuations of direct environmental impacts (that is, those produced by a company's own operations per sector and region). Examples of this work are in Table 10.1. The report notes that indirect impacts (from sources upstream in supply chains or downstream from product use or disposal or investments) are also crucial to understand. Even in the one industry sector there are differences across regions. Indirect impacts can be very high in some sectors such as the consumer goods sector, where impacts may be hidden upstream in the supply chain.

*Table 10.1* Total Direct Environmental Damage as a Percentage of Revenue for an Illustrative Selection of Primary, Manufacturing and Tertiary Sectors, Using Global Averages

| Sector | Total Direct Impact Ratio (Natural Capital Cost as % of Revenue) |
| --- | --- |
| Cattle ranching and farming | 710 |
| Wheat farming | 400 |
| Cement manufacturing | 120 |
| Coal power generation | 110 |
| Iron and steel mills | 60 |
| Iron ore mining | 14 |
| Plastics material and resin manufacturing | 5 |
| Snack food manufacturing | 2 |
| Apparel knitting mills | 1 |

Source: Modified from TEEB, Natural Capital at Risk – The Top 100 Externalities of Business, TEEB 2013.

The TEEB Coalition also found that the global top 100 environmental externalities are costing the economy worldwide around US $4.7 trillion a year in terms of the economic costs of greenhouse gas emissions, loss of natural resources, loss of nature-based services such as carbon storage by forests, climate change and air pollution-related health costs (TEEB 2013).

The findings of the 2012 World Wide Fund for Nature (WWF) *Living Planet Report* (2012) further demonstrate the extent to which existing policies have failed to deal with the other planetary impacts of industrialization and globalization. The Living Planet Index measures the ecological health of the planet. While the Index for high-income countries shows an increase of 7 per cent between 1970 and 2008, that for low-income countries has declined by 60 per cent, a finding likely to be due to the differing capacities of high- and low-income nations to purchase and import resources. These figures indicate a potential catastrophe for biodiversity, for people living in certain regions of the world and for the planet as a whole. The text below shows the five greatest pressures on the planet according to this report.

## The five greatest direct pressures on the planet

- *The loss, alteration and fragmentation of habitats* – mainly through conversion of natural land for agricultural, aquacultural, industrial or urban use; damming and other changes to river systems for irrigation or flow regulation
- *Overexploitation of wild species' populations* – harvesting of animals and plants for food, materials or medicine at a rate higher than they can reproduce
- *Pollution* – mainly from excessive pesticide use in agriculture and aquaculture, urban and industrial effluents, mining waste and excessive fertilizer use
- *Climate change* – due to rising levels of greenhouse gases in the atmosphere, caused mainly by the burning of fossil fuels, forest clearing and industrial processes
- *Invasive species* – introduced deliberately or inadvertently to one part of the world from another; they then become competitors, predators or parasites of native species.

(Source: Living Planet Report 2012, online. Available HTTP:
<http://awassets.panda.org/downloads/lpr_2012_
summary_booklet_final.pdf>, page 12
(accessed 4 March 2014)

For example, recent figures indicate:

- Nearly a quarter of all mammals and a third of all amphibians are threatened with extinction.
- Coral reefs are worth US $172 billion a year to the human economy, but they are on the verge of extinction.
- Deforestation contributes to between 15 and 20 per cent of the world's carbon dioxide emissions (New Economics Foundation 2013).

This chapter argues that business can and should be playing a leadership role in redressing these impacts on the natural world. Business can design more efficient production systems and more sustainable products. It can educate consumers to be more ecologically conscious and discriminating in their purchasing. It can work with governments and other stakeholders to develop viable and sustainable ways of delivering human and ecological sustainability so that landmark achievements associated with human development are not at the expense of our precious ecosystems.

For example, while the average life span in China has risen from 35 to 74.9 years in just over five decades, rising 3.43 years between 2000 and 2010 (English.news.cn 2013), China's leadership now publicly recognizes that environmental impacts will impede the continuing economic development of that country. A joint research report by a team from the World Bank and the Development Research Center of China's State Council argues that the current model of growth will not continue and that future growth and employment will rely upon China promoting innovation and green growth along with expanding health and education services. The compelling argument is that green growth can be stimulated in China through better design and enforcement of regulations to complement market incentives, such as taxes, fees, tradable permits and quotas, and eco-labelling (World Bank 2013).

The destructive environmental and social side-effects of the combination of population growth and increased consumption have contributed to these challenges of global survival. The 2012b OECD (p. 353) report states the situation bluntly that:

> Humanity has witnessed unprecedented growth and prosperity in the past decades, with the size of the world economy more than tripling and population increasing by over 3 billion people since 1970. This growth, however, has been accompanied by environmental pollution and natural resource depletion. The current growth model and the mismanagement of natural assets could ultimately undermine human development.

## Globalization

Hence the forces of globalization are another key driver for corporate change. Globalization has opened markets, dispersed capital and grown investments and has been endorsed by most leaders of developing and developed countries. Recent figures show that the value of world merchandise exports increased by 20 per cent in 2011 while exports of commercial services grew by 11 per cent (World Trade Organization 2012). The impact on human development is remarkable; the 2013 United Nations Development Programme Human Development Report (UNDP HD Report) shows increasing convergence between nations, so that no nation had a lower Human Development Index (HDI) value in 2012 than in 2000. Yet the report also highlights the still uneven progress within and between nations. Globalization, while lifting many from poverty, is simultaneously contributing to the reinforcing and extending of inequities in human living standards as well as exacerbating climate change and other negative impacts listed above. As noted in previous HD Reports, the lower HDI nations will be most impacted by negative effects of climate change and in some areas of the world such effects are already manifest in drought, water shortages, floods and diminishing food security.

Pointing to shifting power differentials and sustainability risks and opportunities, key areas of development are in the South – Brazil, China and India. In these countries, development is being driven by new business relationships between nations of the South and most obviously, by technological advances, suggesting that the future impact of globalization depends on how technology is utilized for human and ecological sustainability. Some writers have long advocated greening of business models which work within the current model of capitalism and democracy and support continuing technological innovation and economic growth (von Weizsacker et al. 1997). Others argue that this approach merely encourages the continuing exploitation of ecological resources, rather than guiding us towards a more harmonious relationship with nature (Ehrenfeld 2000). There is a long tradition in the literature of criticism for a reliance on technical solutions for sustainable development and their diffusion to the countries of the South. In the view of these critics, this represents just another exploitative, special-interest-based relationship between North and South, although this situation is now changing with the huge upsurge in growth of South–South relationships (Sachs 1993, Shiva 1993).

Clearly managing for sustainability is a matter of relationship building, whatever approach us taken. Of great importance is how relationships between business, civil society and government are harnessed for sustainable outcomes, countering risks from terrorism, nuclear warfare and social, environmental and financial instability (UNDP 2013). As Ulrich Beck put it – we are embedded in the conditions of "the world risk society" where we are becoming increasingly concerned with the impacts of the modernization we have ourselves driven (Beck 1999).

### *"Globalization from above"*

Two sets of actors have emerged on the global stage in reaction to these adverse social and environmental effects of globalization and industrialization. Qutoing Falk, Beck argues that at one level, there is "globalization from above", which represents groupings at the level of nation-states and international organizations. "Globalization from below", on the other hand, represents groupings for local action that include citizens and not-for-profits (Beck 1992). So, from above, government representatives are negotiating international agreements, alongside with business, such as the response to diminishing world oil reserves, the nuclear non-proliferation treaties, General Agreement on Tariffs and Trade (GATT), the World Economic Forum, the World Trade Organization and intergovernmental agreements on the environment. The ineptness of national governments to date in dealing with climate change demonstrates the extent to which they experience difficulties in cooperating in the implementation of intergovernmental agreements concerning sustainability for various reasons, including unemployment, economic conditions and the activities of various interest groups. This puts the onus on multinational corporations to take more responsibility for their actions, confronting the hitherto dominant understanding of what should be regarded as business priority. Does the business world defend and take part in this system that contributes to social and environmental problems or does it shift mind-set and activities to become part of the solution?

To understand the countervailing pressures associated with "globalization from above" we need to look at how sustainability has been interpreted in its global context. Sustainability can be defined as that *state* that results from the *process* of sustainable development (Benn and Kearins 2012). Sustainable development is that which "meets the needs of the present without compromising the ability of the future generations to meet their own needs" (World Commission of Environment and Development [WCED] 1987). The WCED report, *Our Common Future*, was the first attempt by an intergovernmental body to promote global dialogue on sustainability and sustainable development. This view of appropriate and sustainable development was promoted at the Second United Nations Conference on the Environment and Development (UNCED), held in 1992 in Rio de Janeiro. At the time, it was the largest-ever Heads of Government meeting, with more than 170 countries represented. The Conference endorsed the major action plan, Agenda 21, since widely taken as a blueprint for the implementation of sustainable development and the integration of economic growth with environmental responsibility. Along the way since 1992, the international community has developed a range of treaties and agreements which are designed to monitor "progress" largely according to this definition. A number of global treaties and hundreds of regional and bilateral agreements have since been negotiated.

In the decades since Rio, the discourse of sustainable development has also been embedded within many governmental and intergovernmental documents and agreements. For example, the key concepts of sustainable development, interpreted as Education for Sustainability principles, are now espoused by many higher education institutions and enshrined in the UN Decade for Education for Sustainable Development. Also manifesting in the corporate sector, the World Business Council for Sustainable Development emerged post Rio as a CEO-led alliance of some of the world's biggest and most influential companies across sector and region claiming to pursue sustainable development and has since been involved in numerous multi-stakeholder arrangements that purport to address sustainability.

Given the extent to which business is clearly not internalizing environmental costs, one has to question the effectiveness of the top-down global-level approach in terms of what is lacking and what are possible improvements. Arguably, recent meetings conducted under the umbrella of the United Nations Framework Convention on Climate Change (UNFCCC) have exposed the limitations of existing global institutional arrangements for managing environmental impacts such as climate change (Bluhdorn 2011). Agreements or conventions that are largely constitutional, as with UNFCCC, face the problem that they are not designed to address compliance matters, and function largely as governance models. The Kyoto Protocol, on the other hand, from the outset included mandatory requirements concerning greenhouse gas emissions. According to Bodansky and O'Connor (2012), stringency, participation and compliance are the factors necessary for intergovernmental arrangements to be effective, and neither UNFCCC or the Kyoto Protocol meet all three. The problem is how to balance these characteristics so that the international standards and agreements are participatory, yet offer some commitment to setting standards of achievement.

Environmental agreements in particular are associated with tensions between national legislation and international agreements, largely related to the fact that environmental issues are inherently transboundary. Birds, fish and plants do not recognize those boundary lines we humans draw across the globe. World Heritage areas such as the Great Barrier Reef, for example, may be internationally protected, but threatened by local development which is quite lawful according to Australian legislation. Swedish Lapland, the last great European wilderness, could similarly be threatened by the Swedish extractive industry in neighbouring areas.

Many treaties and other cross-national arrangements do not result in effective action and often preserve existing inequities that favour the interests of the already privileged nations. Corporate and government irresponsibility and equity issues in the development of treaties and agreements are putting business under pressure to implement voluntary sustainability measures to supplement the international agreements. Numerous voluntary codes, principles and agreements have been developed by industry organizations, multi-stakeholder arrangements and individual organizations in order to restore their credibility (Benn et al. 2014).

At the World Economic Forum in Davos in 1999, UN Secretary-General Kofi Annan challenged business to support a Global Compact which he called "Globalization with a Human Face". The Compact is intended to promote human rights, just labour standards and good environmental practices and marks an attempt by the UN to lead both the private and public spheres in the direction of a more equitable and ecologically sustainable model of development. As of 2015, figures for the number of participants show that the initiative has grown to include over 8,300 businesses in 162 countries around the world. Linked in through UN action is the Global Reporting Initiative (GRI), a highly structured set of performance indicators to assist companies to report on sustainability performance.

Other sustainability related guiding principles for companies that could be described as "globalization from above" include the Valdez Principles, the US Business Principles for Human Rights of Workers in China and the Business Charter for Sustainable Development. The Principles of Responsible Investment and TEEB have both emerged through the agency of the UN Environment Program, with the latter a multi-stakeholder entity also supported by G8. TEEB activities focus on raising awareness of the business case for natural-capital accounting, research and supporting the development of harmonized methods for measuring, managing and reporting environmental externalities in business.

Twenty years on from Rio, the Rio +20 Conference, a three-day summit attended by 189 states and held in Brazil, produced the document titled "The Future We Want". Although criticized for not going far enough in terms of gaining agreement around key measures such as phasing out subsidies for fossil fuels, the conference did provide some gains with particular implications for business sustainability. For example, the concepts of "green economy" and "integrated reporting" were endorsed and support groups were developed around these concepts.

Overall, despite some advances, it seems that the ongoing inability of such global structures to deal effectively with blatant sustainability problems, reflects an apparent impasse around the participatory and holistic principles upon which sustainability rests (Rio Declaration 1992: Principles 3, 4 and 10). They are well meaning, but are they so ambiguous, slippery, contested and readily politicized as to be inoperable? (Tregidga et al. 2013). The discourse has been criticized, on the one hand, as being inherently weak, in fact legitimating development by the wealthier countries of the North (Banerjee 2003), while questioned on the other hand, in terms of the costs of attempting to balance environmental, social and economic development (Lomborg 2001). On a more positive note, however, it could be the very openness and breadth of the concepts of sustainability and sustainable development that allow a broad range of stakeholders to the table. This is evident in a parallel trend that has been labelled "globalization from below" (Beck 1992).

### *"Globalization from below"*

Powerful forces are swelling up from below to pressure corporate change. Organized by transnational NGOs and spread largely on the Internet, "globalization from below" is an initiative directed against the perceived self-seeking manipulations of elite nation-states and transnationals driving "globalization from above" (Beck 1999). Work done by Inglehart and Welzel (2010) indicates a shift in industrialized countries towards what they term a self-expression society, concerned with environmental issues, freedom for self-expression and a high value placed on creativity, argued as the key qualities needed for democracy to be effective. The most overt demonstration of this polarization between survival and self-expression is the Occupy Movement. This leaderless, global and still emergent phenomenon is represented in its website refrain:

> We are the 99 percent. We are getting kicked out of our homes. We are forced to choose between groceries and rent. We are denied quality medical care. We are suffering from environmental pollution. We are working long hours for little pay and no rights, if we're working at all. We are getting nothing while the other 1 percent is getting everything. We are the 99 percent.
>
> (Occupy Wall St 2013)

The aims of "globalization from below" are diffuse and the vision for the future is not clearly specified. But the message is clear. The "globalization from below" movement has spread from a criticism of Western "imperialism" in the form of developmentalism, to a wider dissatisfaction with how global capitalism and lax national standards are contributing to destructive environmental and social conditions at the local level. It is not just a protest in Wall Street. In China, for example, pollution has replaced land disputes as the main cause of social unrest. China now sees 30,000 to 50,000 so-called mass incidents every year. Chen Jiping, a former leading member of the Chinese Communist Party's Committee of Political and Legislative Affairs, has claimed that increased use of mobile phones and the internet has allowed protesters to show their anger more effectively.

### *Networks and alliances for sustainability*

"Globalization from below" highlights two important issues for corporations that are driving the change agenda. First, globalization and the information revolution have also given the general public the means for self-critique and self-transformation. As awareness of the limitations of our traditional institutions spreads, we have continued to move towards what Hazel Henderson termed more than a decade ago "the networked society". Henderson noted then the emergence of a political trend in the form of citizen organizations. They are now a distinct third sector in the world, holding the private and public sectors more accountable. More access to information has helped to empower citizens, consumer choice, employees and socially responsible investors. "The information society has created new winners", as Henderson once said (Henderson 1999), but what is now clear is that it has also created new losers. Examples abound of the power of viral networks in attacking corporate brands. In 2010 Greenpeace targeted Nestlé's famous KitKat product over concerns about the use of palm oil and the resulting impact on the habitats of orangutans. A viral advertising campaign led Nestlé to announce that it would stop using ingredients that may be sourced as a result of rainforest destruction (KPMG and Institute of Chartered Accountants in Australia [ICAA] 2011). The Occupy Movement has utilized its crowd-sourcing mobilizing techniques to target major corporates such as the Bank of America. In Australia, NGOs such as Animals Australia and Voiceless have organized campaigns. Some, such as those alleging cruelty against the methods used for butchering Australian cattle in some Indonesian abattoirs, have gone viral. The impact of these campaigns can be enormous – for instance, exposure of the conditions in some Indonesian abbatoirs caused the Australian government to temporarily call a halt to all live cattle exports until conditions were reviewed. The second factor provoking business response is that manifest increased public awareness of sustainability issues and diminishing public trust in both corporations and governments are creating market expectations for more responsible corporate behaviour and sustainable products and services. A 2015 Globescan survey showed that national governments and global corporations are the least trusted institutions, with more than half respondents believing companies are not transparent and have improved little over the last five years (Globescan Radar 2015).

Alliances and networks forming around single issues such as climate change are now including social and natural scientists, business, local government, community and other social actors whose allegiances cross established disciplinary and role boundaries. Communities of practice formed between sustainability professionals from very different disciplinary backgrounds, working in very different sectors, are increasingly common and are forged by concepts or discourses acting as boundary objects across the different knowledge worlds of the participants (Benn and Martin 2010). The media, information systems and ad hoc coalitions of opposites, such as those between NGOs and business organizations discussed below, are increasingly influential in all aspects of society. The GRI, for instance, gathers input from environmental, human rights and industry association NGOs.

Consumer action and mass boycotts and protests, such as those targeted over the years at Nike, Apple, IKEA and BP, are forcing corporations to defend their actions. The Australian company heavily involved in the woodchipping industry in some of the old growth forests in Tasmania, for example, has now gone out of business, unable to finance its operations after massive public campaigns led by a range of NGOs. The open-ended nature of the sustainability ethic gives it the power to bring together, at least at the discussion table, people and groups with very different political and ideological perspectives.

Alliances or collaborations around sustainability can be grouped according to their participants:

- Company–company collaborations such as between Toyota and Ford around new hybrid technology for light trucks and SUVs
- Multi-industry collaborations formed around a single issue such as the Plant PET Collaboration Initiative
- Company–NGO collaborations such as between Coca-Cola and WWF, and between Starbucks and Conservation International
- Single-industry collaborations such as the Sustainable Apparel Coalition and the Sustainable Steel Certification Scheme in Australia

Dynamic partnerships between different stakeholders can provide learning opportunities that have the potential to change corporate attitudes and practices. The networking opportunities provided by the GRI, for example, are assisting thousands of companies around the world to measure their progression to sustainability. Although costs associated with prescriptive standards may preclude smaller companies taking it up (Tuxworth 2013), there appear to be advantages in taking up opportunities and overall risk management. In another example of a productive learning partnership, the NGO Global Forest Watch provides maps indicating the whereabouts of old-growth forests and other data for the IKEA corporation to enable purchasing of forest products according to sustainable criteria. Similarly, the partnership formed between the WWF and Unilever, at the time the world's largest supplier of frozen fish, aims to develop incentives to support sustainable fishing. The Marine Stewardship Council emerged as a result of this alliance. WWF has also partnered with Coca-Cola to reduce water consumption, with measureable benefits (Giddens 2011).

---

### The Play Fair Alliance

Play Fair is a global campaign coordinated by international trade union federations and NGOs, namely, the International Trades Union Federation (ITUC), the International Textile, Garment and Leather Workers' Federation (ITGLWF), the Building and Wood Workers' International (BWI) and the Clean Clothes Campaign (CCC). The campaign calls on those who organize and profit from sports events to take specific steps to ensure that workers making sporting goods and building venues are not exploited, and that international labour standards are respected in the workplace as well as in the stadium. Campaigns began with the 2004 Athens Olympics and have continued across the 2008 Beijing Olympics, the 2010 Vancouver Winter Games and the 2010 South Africa World Cup. Campaigns aimed at event organizers, construction companies and sport-goods brands include the Ukraine and Poland European Championship, the London 2012 Olympics and the Sochi 2014 Winter Games. In an example of the activities of such alliances, research conducted in association with the Playfair London 2012 campaign found breaches of every one of the nine standards of the ethical code embraced by London Organising Committee of the Olympic Games and Paralympic Games (LOCOG) in factories in China producing official merchandise bearing the London 2012 Olympic Games logo (Playfair 2012).

---

Networks and alliances that include corporations, state and local governments are addressing the lack of action by national governments on climate change. In Canada, the Network for Business Sustainability claims to move beyond disciplinary and organizational silos so that different aspects of society can work together. Influential reports and networking events emanating from such centres in many countries are pushing against corporate resistance.

### Supply chains as networks

While sustainability has been largely the domain of big business, small- to medium-size enterprises (SMEs) are now taking some action because of pressures and requirements along supply chain networks. As mentioned above, major indirect sustainability impacts exist in some sectors and numerous sustainability advocacy bodies, consultancies and not-for-profits are working with companies to improve sustainability performance along their supply chains. For instance, the long-established advocacy organization CERES, with wide experience in working towards sustainable business, has estimated that up to 60 per cent of a manufacturing company's carbon footprint is in its supply chain. For retailers it is perhaps as much as 80 per cent – with an equally high supply-chain exposure to human rights and social issues (CERES 2013). Examples of how companies are working with CERES and other NGOs and stakeholders to implement sustainable supply chain measures are PepsiCo establishing a policy on the human right to water; the footwear and apparel industry's "Eco-Index", a shared platform for companies to evaluate the environmental impacts of the design and manufacturing of their products; and the Electric Utility Sustainable Supply Chain Alliance, including the organization of a process to obtain multi-stakeholder input into the group's scope, criteria and disclosure mechanisms. Procter and Gamble exerts control over its supply chain through a sustainability scorecard against which it assesses its suppliers in terms of environmental factors such as waste management (Worldwatch Institute 2013).

Despite the establishment of such structures and claims that sustainable supply-chain management can deliver business gains in the form of reputational risk management, productivity and efficiency gains, clearly some organizations in certain industry sectors have major problems in managing their global supply chain according to these standards. Disasters in the Bangladeshi garment factory include the Rana Plaza collapse which claimed the death of more than 1,200 workers, allegedly producing garments for such brands as Walmart, C&A, Benetton and Mango. The dependence of the Bangladeshi economy on this industry has made change difficult: it comprises some 3,500 export-oriented factories which generate over 80 per cent of the nation's export earnings and employs more than 4 million mostly female workers. Recent initiatives supported by the Swedish Government and the International Labour Organization (ILO) aim to improve industrial relations and worker conditions across the sector.

## Evolving forms of regulation

### User pays

The "user pays" principle is now a well-established regulatory approach easily applied through legislation that is driving corporate change by ensuring that those who create the risks pay for them. Taxes such as consumer fees for the disposal of appliances (applied in Japan), legislation for producer responsibility (in Sweden and the Netherlands) and pollution taxes in many countries are examples. Incentives-based and polluter-pays strategies include load-based licensing and tradable permits to encourage reduction of pollution. In load-based licensing, companies are charged licence fees which vary according to the amount of pollution they discharge. Other economic policy tools include tradable rights to natural resources to encourage efficient resource management, innovative design and cleaner production. Examples of such incentives include vehicle emission quotas, landfill taxes and "green taxes", such as carbon taxes (as in Denmark), congestion taxes (as in Singapore) and vehicle-return bonuses.

## Co-regulation

As defined by the European Economic and Social Committee, co-regulation means that government entrusts the attainment of various legislative objectives to "parties which are recognized in the field (such as economic operators, the social partners, non-governmental organizations, or associations)" (European Economic and Social Committee 2013). Since the Brundtland Report and the 1992 Rio Conference, business has been increasingly drawn into a system of co-regulation, where government, business and community are all expected to play a part in sustainable development. Over the years it has become evident that command-and-control forms of governance lack effectiveness in terms of changing behaviour and that beyond the setting of minimal standards, regulation needs to be a more participatory and reflexive process. Co-regulatory forms that have the potential to deliver on these requirements include legislation that incorporates a role for community consultative committees. Such arrangements are frequently used to enable community response in legislation pertaining to mining operations, for example.

Porter and van der Linde's (1995) early argument that regulation can force or "enlighten" corporations to employ the environment as a "competitive opportunity" has held up over the years, having been successfully deployed by governments in Northern Europe and Japan. These governments have initiated policies geared to encourage the emergence of a specific sector that focuses on the development of green technology, or environmental services. This approach is an example of what has been termed "ecological modernization", a policy approach which sees scientific and technological advances as an answer to the dilemma of how to provide for continued economic growth without negatively impacting on the environment. The key argument is that we do not have to create a new political economy so as to achieve sustainability. It is enough to ensure that innovative environmental goods and services become a source of profit (Dryzek 2005). This approach is also co-regulatory, its proponents arguing that market, government and NGOs all have a role to play in industrial transformation incorporating more ecologically friendly principles (eg Mol 1997). Indeed, many of the governments which have been most successful in shifting the economy away from a dependency on unsustainable production technology and towards green production technology, such as Japan, Sweden, Norway and Germany, have a tradition of close associative relations between industry, business and government (Mason 1999).

## Codes of conduct

The emergence of multiple forms of corporate codes is a relatively recent "regulatory" phenomenon, where industry associations, individual firms or certain supply chains develop documents that set out specific standards of behaviour. Codes of conduct usually focus on ethical or socially responsible issues and are an example of the self-regulation of industry (Benn and Bolton 2011). While voluntary, such codes are increasingly acting as de facto regulation, with some also having reporting requirements. In later chapters, we explore a range of codes of conduct and how they are becoming an instrumental form of regulation requiring compliance according to these standards. Although codes of ethics have a long history in business (Jensen et al. 2009), it is only relatively recently that corporate sustainability and corporate social responsibility (CSR) have been addressed comprehensively in such codes. Examples include the Nike Code of Conduct and voluntary sector-specific agreements such as the Responsible Care programme of the chemicals sector.

### New reporting requirements and concepts

Accompanying the push for greater regulation in one form or another, is increased pressure on corporations to employ better assessment and measurement techniques in activities relevant to sustainability. Companies are increasingly expected to report against non-financial as well as financial criteria. Pressure is coming from not-for-profit organizations such as the Carbon Disclosure Project (CDP), which leverages market forces including shareholders, customers and governments to motivate companies to reveal their carbon and other environmental impacts and manage risks associated with climate change, deforestation and water scarcity. CDP investor initiatives – backed in 2015 by more than 822 institutional investors representing an excess of US$95 trillion in assets, provide information for investors into companies' greenhouse gas emissions, water usage and strategies for managing climate change, water and deforestation risks. In another instance of the growing importance of reporting, at Rio +20 a group of countries (Brazil, Denmark, France and South Africa) joined with GRI and UNEP to champion integrated reporting which combines financial data with information on organizations' performance on environmental, social and governance issues.

Recent research indicates that sustainability reporting not only increases transparency but can also change corporate behaviour. In one study, researchers applied an econometric model to data from 58 countries regarding laws and regulations that mandate a minimum level of disclosure on environmental, social and governance matters. They found that: mandatory disclosure of sustainability information leads to a) an increase in the social responsibility of business leaders, b) a prioritization of sustainable development, c) a prioritization of employee training, d) more efficient supervision of managers by boards of directors, e) an increase in the implementation of ethical practices by firms, f) a decrease in bribery and corruption, and g) an improvement of managerial credibility within society (Ioannou and Serafeim 2014).

This paper notes a widespread increase in reporting of non-financial information, mostly on a voluntary basis, over the preceding decade. According to the GRI, only 44 firms followed GRI guidelines to report sustainability information in 2000. According to the GRI database, by 2015, the number of reports produced according to GRI guidelines had grown to more than 20,000.

## New technologies and business models

### Innovation and technology

Aside from policy-focused recommendations, such as setting economy-wide greenhouse gas (GHG) mitigation targets to guide policy and investment decisions and setting a price on carbon, innovation is clearly one way to avoid further irreparable damage – presenting a clear role and opportunity for business (OECD 2012a). However, business needs to collaborate with government and the not-for-profit sector in order to take up these opportunities.

For example, the leading environmental organization WWF has numerous partner-ships with business and information gathered through such collaborations has assisted in the identification of six key solutions to the challenge of meeting global energy demand without damaging the global climate:

1   Improving energy efficiency
2   Stopping forest loss
3   Accelerating the development of low-emissions technologies
4   Developing flexible fuels
5   Replacing high-carbon coal with low-carbon gas
6   Equipping fossil fuel plants with carbon capture and storage technology

(WWF 2007)

According to the prominent NGO Worldwatch Institute, new technologies embed-ded in advanced automotive, electronics and buildings systems will allow a substan-tial reduction in carbon dioxide ($CO_2$) emissions, at negative cost once the saving in energy bills is taken into account. The savings from these measures can effectively pay for a significant portion of the additional cost of advanced renewable energy technolo-gies to replace fossil fuels, including wind, solar, geothermal and bioenergy.

### New business models

A range of new business models are also emerging in response to the evident negative social and environmental impacts of global capitalism. Shared value, Business at Base of the Pyramid, Fair Trade, natural capitalism, industrial ecology, biomimicry, col-laborative consumption – these are just some of the new ways of doing business that are emerging in practice. Some are incremental and based in efficiency measures, while others are more transformative and reflect a company working to ensure long-term value for society and the environment as well as for its shareholders (Benn et al. 2014).

On a positive note, some world and corporate leaders are showing that they are willing to push for development which is more cautious, self-reflective and support-ive of sustainable business as a means to foster learning and capacity building in local communities. For example, the major cleaning products company SC Johnson is integrating local farmers into its supply chain according to the Business at the Base of the Pyramid model (Tieman 2012). Leading business academics are proclaiming the need for business to shed an outdated understanding of value and to build shared value with society so that, by rethinking products and markets and building relation-ships along its supply chains and at and around its locations a company can not only reduce its externalities but build value for wider society (Porter and Kramer 2011).

While there have been academic attempts to explode the "myth of the ethical con-sumer" (Devinney et al. 2010), new models of consumerism are offering more sophis-ticated approaches to purchasing that have less-negative social and environmental impact in the long term. According to the exponents of collaborative consumption, renting and sharing resources, or using services such as eBay, reflects a new trend in business, one based on communication where the use-value of objects or services is shared and where trust is an important aspect of the business equation (Botsman and

Rogers 2010). In this model, individuals act as brokers for goods and services that consumers would normally purchase from retailers – examples include the peer-to-peer rental services of various types, such as cars, landspace, rental rooms and tools. Benefits for the future are seen as breaking the consumer mind-set and reducing the environmental impact of our production systems.

### Natural capitalism: the business advantage

As a business model, natural capitalism is based on the win–win business logic of increasing the productivity of natural resources. Key principles are: profiting from increasing the productivity of natural resources, closing materials loops and eliminating waste, shifting to biologically-inspired production models, providing their customers with efficient solutions and reinvesting in natural capital, they can gain a commanding competitive advantage (Lovins, Lovins and Hawken 2008). Proponents argue tracking material and energy flows over the whole producer–consumer cycle reduces the likelihood of suboptimal solutions and unintended consequences (Ehrenfeld 2000).

At Hewlett-Packard (HP), for example, its Environmental Strategies and Solutions programme was established based on acceptance of the fact that the planet is a closed system which will eventually face limits and hence sustainability does offer companies a strategic competitive advantage (Preston 2000). When these limits are reached, the firm would be in a new social and economic situation, and would have to deal with the challenges of a new business environment. According to Gabi Zedlmayer, Vice President, Sustainability and Social Innovation: HP's commitment to environmental sustainability helps guide the direction of our company, positions us as a leader in our industry, and drives the innovation of new products and solutions that make a positive impact in the world (Hewlett Packard 2013).

Associated historical achievements at HP noted include a 20 per cent reduction in 2011 GHG emissions for HP operations, as compared with 2005. In 2014, HP claims it became the first global IT company to set greenhouse gas (GHG) emissions reduction goals for our entire value chain: suppliers, operations, and products and solutions (Hewlett-Packard 2013, 2015).

### Cost avoidance and risk management

The most obvious internal pressures on managers driving corporate change for sustainability are cost avoidance and risk management. But the firm now needs to consider potential costs to its reputation in the eyes of its employees as well as of external stakeholders such as shareholders, suppliers and consumers.

Being competitive means reducing costs. As we have indicated, governments are still experimenting with measures to ensure increased sustainability. As we have shown above, most governments impose penalty measures for non-compliance. Corporations which do not address social and environmental requirements face fines, workers' compensation cases, criminal convictions and payment of clean-up costs. The potential for damage liability can make non-compliance a significant business risk and the costs of non-compliance can be devastating for corporations.

Some examples:

- The Deepwater Horizon oil spill in the Gulf of Mexico in 2010, when 11 men died, huge losses and damage to wildlife occurred and many fishermen went out of business, cost BP US$18.7 billion (Robertson et al. 2015).
- The recent scandal involving Volkswagen where it admitted cheating emissions tests in the US is another case in point. The company installed devices in diesel cars so that emissions were reduced under test conditions but when on the road, the devices turned off and nitrogen emissions were discovered to be polluting at more than 40 times the legal limit. According to a BBC Report, the company will need to set aside €6.5 billion to cover costs. But the EPA has the power to fine a company up to US$37,500 for each vehicle that breaches standards – a maximum fine of about US$18 billion This is just in the US alone with wider impacts as yet unclear. Although the CEO has resigned, it is still unclear where the actual guilt in the company's management lies (Hotten 2015).
- In the USA, the total corporate liability costs for asbestos-related diseases have been estimated at US$30 billion, far more than the product ever earned its manufacturers. According to "UK Asbestos: the Definitive Guide", in the UK the estimated future cost to the UK insurance industry of asbestos-related claims is £4–£10 billion (GIR Seminar 2010).
- Costs to Tokyo Electric Power Co. of the Fukushima nuclear disaster in Japan in 2011 are estimated to be at least 11 trillion yen (US$137 billion) and may be as high as three times that. Environmental and human costs are huge, with more than 150,000 people evicted from their homes and more nuclear material being discharged into the ocean than ever in history (Environmental Health Policy Institute 2013).

Management of intangibles and associated performance measurement is emerging as a key driver of organizational sustainability. The Sustainability Balanced Scorecard, for instance, is an instrument that builds on the well-established Balanced Scorecard, adding social and environmental perspectives to the existing financial, customer, business process and learning and development perspectives and linking the perspectives with cause-and-effect chains (Wagner and Schaltegger 2006).

Key trends in risk management now include:

- The need for public trust
- The need for a partnership approach
- The role of personal leadership and workforce involvement
- The use of the law as a lever for safety management
- The public demand for a risk-free world

(Brinded 2000)

Business models that incorporate such risk management, and other approaches such as the natural capitalism and eco-efficiency models, are targeted at change according to the efficiency stage of the sustainability phase model. Other more transformative approaches look to a radical reconfiguration of what we value in business, with much more emphasis on recognition of the costs of natural capital and business performance, as well as on the value of community and employee relations to the long-term success of the company.

The costly effects of climate change are increasingly being recognized as an aspect of company value. However, the potential risks and opportunities associated with environmental impacts are not straightforward and differ markedly from sector to sector. Again referring to the "Unburnable Carbon 2013: Wasted Capital and Stranded Assets" report, Professor Lord Stern comments:

> Smart investors can see that investing in companies that rely solely or heavily on constantly replenishing reserves of fossil fuels is becoming a very risky decision. The report raises serious questions as to the ability of the financial system to act on industry-wide long term risk, since currently the only measure of risk is performance against industry benchmarks.
>
> (Carbon Tracker and the Grantham
> Research Institute 2013)

### Pressure from investors

Accordingly, risk management for large investors of necessity now includes sustainability assessment. In April 2006, United Nations Secretary-General Kofi Annan was joined by the heads of leading institutional investors managing combined assets worth more than US$2 trillion to launch Principles of Responsible Investment. More informed shareholders are demanding a role in corporate decision making. Not only can shareholder activism be extremely damaging to the reputation of the corporation, but shareholders are now using sustainability as a measure of financial success. In 2014, the Global Sustainable Investment Alliance (GSIA) released a report showing that "the global sustainable investment market has continued to grow both in absolute and relative terms, rising from US$13.3 trillion at the outset of 2012 to US$21.4 trillion at the start of 2014, and from 21.5 percent to 30.2 percent of the professionally managed assets in the regions covered" (GSIA 2014). Clearly, financial markets are requiring more information on standards of accountability and the financial services industry is now under considerable pressure to provide for ethical investment.

### The knowledge-based organization

In the information-based economy, corporations are looking to long-term survival through the development of knowledge systems, stores of social capital and a culture of innovation. These aspects of human sustainability in turn enable the firm to take a position of more environmental responsibility. A position of corporate sustainability requires a firm both to be responsible to employees and to look to its own needs for long-term survival. The bringing together of the corporate virtues of innovation and sustainability is the positive angle of change for sustainability – displayed already in the actions of leading organizations such as GE, Novo Nordisk, Natura and Unilever, but now being taken up by smaller players – and implemented along their supply chains.

Knowledge management is also drawing attention to the value of an organization's human resources. Motivation, qualifications and commitment, when combined with a significant store of "corporate memory", are a major asset to the corporation. Companies are long recognised dependent on employees who can work cooperatively and contribute to the social capital of the organization (Sagawa and Segal 2000). Social capital is fundamental to the successful working of the new organizational forms such as the network organization and communities of practice.

As prized employees hunt for the firm with a strong sense of values, there are real rewards in becoming an employer of choice. Firms need employees who can give high levels of customer service and who are sufficiently motivated by the company's mission and prospects to stay and aspire to higher levels of productivity. The importance of teamwork, loyalty and skills is becoming doctrine in almost every industry.

Recent work also indicates a relationship between human resource policies, the successful implementation of the Environmental Management System (EMS) and its maintenance as a strategic business- and risk-management tool. Our own research shows a causal link between participation in EMS and employee commitment, connected with perception of good environmental performance by the organization (Benn e al. 2015).

### A culture of innovation

Managers are also recognizing the links between an organizational culture of innovation and one designed to deliver sustainability. Practices designed to enhance human sustainability and social capital within the organization (such as empowerment, teamwork and continuous learning) are linked to the capacity to innovate and escape from rigid models of operation and production. Arguably, implementing more sustainable practices creates an organizational culture that facilitates both resource productivity and product differentiation.

A number of companies have been successful in employing a strategy of environmental product differentiation. Such a strategy will be successful if consumers are prepared to pay more, if the benefits can be communicated readily and if the innovation is unique long enough for a profit to be made (Reinhardt 2000). Corporations face an accelerating rate of change and an increasingly complex society. For these business conditions, innovation depends on cultural and structural characteristics of the organization. Both sets of characteristics are linked to the organization's capacity to engage with sustainability. Cultural factors such as those associated with the learning organization also underpin a culture of precaution. Structural factors such as an internal network culture, employee participation and the capability to develop community partnerships also support human sustainability. In other words, innovation, business concept redesign and sustainability can be readily linked in a dynamic relationship aimed at delivering long-term business advantage.

Importantly, such qualities enable the corporation to be more responsive to the external drivers of change. An organization geared to innovation is ready to take up government incentives for ecological modernization; that is, it can readily translate social and moral issues into market issues and can exploit the potentially huge market that ecological sustainability, in particular, represents. Such an organization can more critically reflect on the possibilities of new relationships between nature, society and technology that will mark a new, more sustainable age.

### Conclusion

This chapter began by asking why organizations are moving to address the challenges of human and ecological sustainability. In large part, the answer is that the new reality for managers is that business success and sustainability are inextricably linked. Social and environmental health are essential aspects of corporate survival. Some managers are reacting primarily to the reputational and litigious risks associated with the increasingly global reach of corporations, to the actions of internationally mobilized human rights and environmental activists and to international and national agreements and regulations concerning environmental protection and social and environmental justice. International and national governments are experimenting with a variety of policy incentives and models of governance to ensure corporate accountability.

But many other managers are also taking proactive measures in the struggle to conserve resources, minimize waste and contribute to social and ecological renewal. More companies are moving beyond compliance with government regulations to accreditation under voluntary schemes such as ISO 14001. This delivers benefits from recognition by the community, customers and other stakeholders. Importantly, corporations are increasingly influenced by new alliances being formed across the range of corporate stakeholders. Community representatives and NGOs are working with firms to develop the knowledge and social capital required for the shift to sustainable products and processes.

Shareholders and investors are also looking to more than financial success in the assessment of performance. Their selection of investments increasingly takes into account reputation and performance on the longer-term factors of social and ecological sustainability. Investors are also placing more value on the human capabilities and commitment that the organization has built. In the new economy the building of knowledge systems, social capital and other strategies designed to increase and sustain human capability is vital to corporate performance.

More and more employees have strong expectations of workplace safety and heightened environmental awareness; they are searching for more meaningful work, particularly for work that makes a social and ecological contribution as well as providing an income.

In this context, the principles of community, interconnectedness and cooperation can be seen as a model for the way forward for corporations wishing to move towards sustainability. They provide a framework for new levels of resource productivity and generate new strategic directions. More importantly, they serve as a way of understanding the corporation as a moral entity (White 2009).

But we also need to recognize that there are countervailing forces tending to maintain the status quo, i.e. business as usual:

1   Public lack of awareness of environmental (ecological and social) crises
2   Difficulty of tracking and measuring sustainability improvements and difficulty in evaluating risks of inattention to sustainability
3   Public cynicism about the ability of individuals to influence the course of events; moral disengagement, particularly in sections of the corporate world
4   Corporate disinformation campaigns (lies) around environmental issues led by those corporations with a strong stake in the status quo, particularly oil and mining companies; direct and indirect lobbying of governments at all levels
5   Political coalitions around the politically conservative, particularly the fundamentalist religious right antagonistic to scientific knowledge on climate change
6   Adherence to a capitalistic core belief that "economic growth" (meaning increasing material consumption) is good
7   Government distortion of resource markets, particularly energy, by subsidies, e.g. for carbon-based energy production, coal export etc.

While there are increasing pressures to move toward a more sustainable world, we must never underestimate the power of the forces with an interest in the status quo. As the crisis increases, we can expect an increasing political reorientation and intensification of conflict; the old political division between capital and labour is already shifting to a division between those for maintaining "business as usual" based on the old wasteful economic growth paradigm and those who stand for a sustainable economy based on alternative energy and remanufacturing and recycling.

Finally, we again make the point that energy is society's critical master resource (Dixon 2006). We need it for everything we do. Therefore it is vital that we move rapidly to a carbon-neutral economy.

We also must recognize that increasing connectivity in global society leads to multiplier effects and the possibility of synchronous failure as problems occurring across interrelated systems coalesce, as, for example, with the Global Financial Crisis (GFC). Therefore we need to build resilience at all levels (e.g. nations and organizations) through buffering and redundancy. Combined energy, climate and pollution shocks challenge traditional capitalistic assumptions. Systems adaptation may still be possible, but it is a race against time. We need economic redirection as well as economic recovery.

The sustainability of cities will be an increasing issue. As seas rise, some cities and coastal communities will have to be relocated in whole or part; country communities built on flood plains will also need relocation as extreme weather conditions increase in frequency and scope (as is already happening in some regions across the world). Feeding city populations will also be an increasing problem as the costs of transportation rise with rising oil costs.

Our wealth has been funded on the exploitation of non-renewable resources and too-rapid use of potentially renewable resources. Many of the crises we have discussed are signals (Wrong Way: Go Back). We must green our economy, and in this, corporations, as powerhouses of economic change, must play a vital role. Fortunately, when we shift paradigms to think in terms of a sustainable future, we can plan corporate transformation that eliminates waste and increases productivity as well as preserving a world fit for human habitation for future generations. We need a working model for a truly sustainable global society and knowledge of how to create the transformative processes that will bring this about. What clearly we need to understand is the role of corporations in this transformative process.

## Bibliography

Banerjee, S. (2003), 'Who Sustains Whose Development? Sustainable Development and the Reinvention of Nature,' *Organization Studies*, vol. 24, no. 1, pp. 143–80.

Beck, U. (1992), *Risk Society: Towards a New Modernity*, Sage Publications, London.

Beck, U. (1999), *World Risk Society*, Polity Press, Cambridge.

Benn, S. and Bolton, D. (2011), *Key Concepts of Corporate Social Responsibility*, Sage Publications, London.

Benn, S., Dunphy, D. and Griffiths, A. (2014), *Organizational Change for Corporate Sustainability*, 3rd edn. Routledge, New York, and London.

Benn, S. and Kearins, K. (2012), 'Sustainability and Organizational Change.' In Boje, D., Burnes, B. and Hassard, J. (eds) *Handbook of Organizational Change*. Sage Publications, London, pp. 535–551.

Benn, S. and Martin, A. (2010), 'Learning and Change for Sustainability Reconsidered: A Role for Boundary Objects,' *Academy of Management Learning and Education*, vol. 9, no. 3, pp. 397–412.

Benn, S., Teo, S. and Martin, A. (2015), 'Working for the Environment and Intention to Stay, the Informal Economy,' *Personnel Review*, vol. 44, no. 4, pp. 492–510.

Bloomberg News (2013), *Chinese Anger over Pollution Becomes Main Cause of Social Unrest*, Bloomberg News, Beijing, [Online]. Available from http://www.bloomberg.com/news/2013–03–06/pollution-passes-land-grievances-as-main-spark-of-china-protests.html (accessed April 22, 2013).

Bluhdorn, I. (2011), *The Sustainability of Democracy*. [Online]. Available from http://www.thenewsignificance.com/2011/07/12/ingolfur-bluhdorn-the-sustainability-of-democracy/ (accessed April 26, 2013).

Bodansky, D. and O'Connor, S. (2012), *The Durban Platform: Issues and Options for a 2015 Agreement*. [Online]. Available from http://www.c2es.org/docUploads/durban-platform-issues-and-options.pdf (accessed April 25, 2013).

Botsman, R. and Rogers, R. (2010), *What's Mine Is Yours: The Rise of Collaborative Consumption*, HarperCollins. [Online]. Available from http://www.wired.co.uk/news/archive/2011–10/13/rachel-botsman-wired-11 and http://www.sustainablebrands.com/news_and_views/behavior_change/what-are-most-effective-ways-drive-changes-consumer-behavior (accessed April 20, 2013).

Brinded, M. (2000), *Perception Versus Analysis: How to Handle Risk*. Speech to the Royal Academy of Engineering, London, May 31, 2000.

Carbon Disclosure Project (2015), [Online]. Available from https://www.cdp.net/en-US/WhatWeDo/Pages/investors.aspx (accessed September 30, 2015).

Carbon Tracker and the Grantham Research Institute, Unburnable Carbon 2013: Wasted Capital and Stranded Assets, LSE, London. [Online]. Available from http://www.carbontracker.org/report/wasted-capital-and-stranded-assets/ (accessed September 28, 2015).

Carbon Tracker and the Grantham Research Institute, Unburnable Carbon 2013: Wasted Capital and Stranded Assets, Foreword by Lord Stern, 7.

CERES (2013), *Sustainable Supply Chains*. [Online]. Available from http://www.ceres.org/issues/supply-chain (accessed April 28, 2013).

Devinney, T., Auger, P. and Eckhardt, G. (2010), *The Myth of the Ethical Consumer*. Cambridge University Press, Cambridge.

Dixon, T.H. (2006), *The Upside of Down*, Text Publishing, Melbourne.

Doha Climate Change Conference (2012), [Online]. Available from http://unfccc.int/meetings/doha_nov_2012/meeting/6815.php (accessed October 8, 2013).

Dryzek, J. (2005), *The Politics of the Earth*, 2nd Ed. Oxford University Press, Oxford.

Ehrenfeld, J. (2000), 'Industrial Ecology: Paradigm Shift or Normal Science,' *American Behavioural Scientist*, vol. 44, no. 2, pp. 229–244.

English.news.cn (2012), *Life Expectancy Rises in China*, China: Xinhua, english.news.cn. [Online]. Available from http://news.xinhuanet.com/english/china/2012–08/09/c_131773481.htm (accessed April 20, 2013).

Environmental Health Policy Institute (2013), Costs and Consequences of the Fukushima Daiishi Nuclear Disaster. [Online]. Available from http://www.psr.org/environment-and-health/environmental-health-policy-institute/responses/costs-and-consequences-of-fukushima.html (accessed May 3, 2013).

European Economic and Social Committee (2013), Key Definitions. [Online]. Available from http://www.eesc.europa.eu/?i=portal.en.self-and-co-regulation-definitions-concepts-examples (accessed April 28, 2013).

Giddens, A. (2011), *The Politics of Climate Change*, Polity Press, Cambridge.

GIR Seminar (2010), "UK Asbestos – The Definitive Guide". [Online]. Available from <www.actuaries.org.uk/system/files/documents/pdf/Lowe_0.pdf> (accessed May 3, 2013).

Global Sustainable Investment Alliance (GSIA) (2014), *Global Sustainable Investment Review 2014*. Available from http://www.gsi-alliance.org/wp-content/uploads/2015/02/GSIA_Review_download.pdf (accessed September 29, 2015).

Globescan Radar (2015), *Trust, Expectations and Leadership: Global Societal Trends on Perception of Business*. Available from http://www.globescan.com/images/Reports/Radar/GlobeScan_Radar_Webinar_18June2015.pdf (accessed October 1, 2015).

Henderson, H. (1999), *Beyond Globalization: Shaping a Sustainable Global Economy*, Kumarian Press, West Hartford, CT.

Hewlett-Packard (2015), *About Environmental Progress*. Available from http://www8.hp.com/us/en/hp-information/environment/sustainability.html#.UYS3OpFaef8 (accessed September 30, 2015).

Hewlett-Packard (2013), *About Environmental Sustainability*. [Online]. Available from http://www8.hp.com/us/en/hp-information/environment/sustainability.html#.UYS3OpFaef8 (accessed May 4, 2013).

Hotten, R. (2015), *Volkswagen: the Scandal Explained*. Available from http://www.bbc.com/news/business-34324772 (accessed September 29, 2015).

HP Policy Position, [Online]. Available from <http://www.hp.com/hpinfo/abouthp/government/ww/pdf/SER_Climate_Change.pdf> (accessed March 5, 2014).

ILO (2015), *Garment Worker's Rights and Voice in Bangladesh Given Boost*. Available from http://www.ilo.org/newyork/news/WCMS_408360/lang--en/index.htm (accessed September 28, 2015).

Inglehart, R. and Welzel, C. (2010), *Modernization, Cultural Change and Democracy*, Cambridge University Press, New York.

International Business Times (2013), BP Gulf of Mexico Oil Spill: Counting the costs. [Online]. Available from <http://www.ibtimes.co.uk/articles/462933/20130430/bp-deepwater-horizon-oil-spill-cost.htm> (accessed May 3, 2013).

Ioannou, I. and Serafeim, G. (2014), *The Consequences of Mandatory Corporate Sustainability Reporting*, Harvard Business School Working Paper, 11–100, Harvard Business School, August 2014. [Online]. Available from <http://www.hbs.edu/faculty/Publication%20Files/11–100_35684ae7-fcdc-4aae-9626-de4b2acb1748.pdf> (accessed September 30, 2015).

Jamison, A. (2000), *The Making of Green Knowledge*, Cambridge: Cambridge University Press.

Jensen, T., Sandstrom, J. and Helin, S. (2009), 'Corporate Codes of Ethics and the Bending of Moral Space,' *Organization*, vol. 16, no. 4, pp. 529–545.

KPMG and Institute of Chartered Accountants in Australia (ICAA) (2011), *20 Issues on Building a Sustainable Business*, Business Briefing Series, The Institute of Chartered Accountants in Australia and KPMG, Sydney.

Lomborg, B. (2001), *The Skeptical Environmentalist*, Cambridge University Press, Cambridge.

Lovins, A., Lovins, L. and Hawken, P. (2008), *Road Map for Natural Capitalism*, Back Bay Books, New York.

Mason, M. (1999), *Environmental Democracy*, Earthscan Publications, London.

Mittermeier, R., Mittermeier, C., Pilgrim, G., Fonseca, J., Konstant, G. and Brooks, T. (2002), *Wilderness: Earth's Last Wild Places*. University of Chicago Press, Chicago.

Mol, A. (1997), 'Ecological Modernization: Industrial Transformations and Environmental Reform.' In Redclift, M. and Woodgate, G. (eds.), *The International Handbook of Environmental Sociology*, Edward Elgar, Cheltenham, 138–149.

Network for Business Sustainability (2013), *News and Events*. [Online]. Available from http://nbs.net/category/news-events/ (accessed April 26, 2013).

New Economics Foundation (2013), *Our Work: The Environment, 2013*. [Online]. Available from http://www.neweconomics.org/issues/entry/environment (accessed September 21, 2015).

Occupy Wall Street (2013), [Online]. Available from <http://occupy wallst.org/> (accessed May 2, 2013).

OECD (2012a), *The OECD Environmental Outlook to 2050*, OECD Publishing, p. 8. [Online]. Available from <http://www.oecd.org/environment/oecdenvironmentaloutlookto2050the consequencesofinaction.htm> (accessed May 1, 2015).

OECD (2012b), *The OECD Environmental Outlook to 2050: The Consequences of Inaction.* [Online]. Available from <http://www.oecd.org/env/indicators-modelling-outlooks/oecdenvi ronmentaloutlookto2050theconsequencesofinaction.htm> (accessed March 4, 2014).

OECD (2015), News Release *Support to Fossil Fuels Remains High and the Time is Ripe For Change*, OECD News Release, for the Launch of the Report *OECD Companion to the Inventory of Support Measures for Fossil Fuels 2015*. September 21, 2015, Available from http://www.oecd.org/environment/cc/cop21.htm, (accessed September 28, 2015).

Play Fair (2012), *Toying with People's Rights, A Report on Producing Merchandise for the 2012 London Olympic Games*. [Online]. Available from <http://www.ituc-csi.org/IMG/pdf/play_fair_en_final.pdf> (accessed April 26, 2013).

Porter, M. and Kramer, M. (2011), 'Creating Shared Value,' *Harvard Business Review*, January 2011. [Online]. Available from <http://hbr.org/2011/01/the-big-idea-creating-shared-value> (accessed May 3, 2013).

Porter, M. and van der Linde, C. (1995), 'Towards a New Conception of the Environment-Competitiveness Relationship,' *Journal of Economic Perspectives*, vol. 9, no. 4, pp. 97–118.

Preston, L. (2000), 'Sustainability at Hewlett-Packard,' *Financial Times*, June 2, 2000.

Reinhardt, F. (2000), 'Bringing the Environment Down to Earth.' In Starkey, R. and Welford, R. (eds.). *Business and Sustainable Development*, London: Earthscan Publications, pp. 53–64.

Rio Declaration on Environmental Development (1992). *Agenda 21 : programme of action for sustainable development ; Rio Declaration on Environment and Development ; Statement of Forest Principles: The final text of agreements negotiated by governments at the United Nations Conference on Environment and Development (UNCED), 3–14 June, Rio de Janeiro, Brazil*. New York, NY: United Nations Dept. of Public Information, 1993.

Robertson, C., Schwartz, J. and Pérez-Peña, R. (2015), BP to Pay 18.7 bn for Deepwater Horizon Oil Spill. July 2, 2015. Available from http://www.nytimes.com/2015/07/03/us/bp-to-pay-gulf-coast-states-18–7-billion-for-deepwater-horizon-oil-spill.html?_r=0. (accessed September 29, 2015).

Sachs, W. (1993), 'Global Ecology and the Shadow of Development.' In Sachs, W. (ed.). *Global Ecology*, Zed Books, London, pp. 3–21.

Sagawa, S. and Segal, E. (2000), 'Common Interest, Common Good: Creating Value Through Business and Social Sector Relationships,' *California Management Review*, vol. 42, no. 2, pp. 105–123.

Shiva, V. (1993), 'Greening of the Global Reach,' In Sachs, W. (ed.) *Global Ecology*, Zed Books, London, pp. 149–156.

Stern, N. (2010), *The Stern Review: Economics of Climate Change*. [Online]. Available from <http://webarchive.nationalarchives.gov.uk/+/http://www.hmtreasury.gov.uk/stern_review_report.htmreport> (accessed April 20, 2013).

TEEB (2013), *Natural Capital at Risk – The Top 100 Externalities of Business*, Trucost Plc, London.

Tieman, R. (2012), 'Sustainable Business,' *Financial Times*, April 24, 2012, p. 2.

Tregidga, H., Kearins, K. and Milne, M. (2013), 'The Politics of Knowing "Organizational Sustainable Development",' *Organization & Environment*, vol. 26, pp. 102–129.

Tuxworth, B. (2013), GRI: A New Framework?. *Global Sustainable Business Blog*. [Online]. Available from <http://www.guardian.co.uk/sustainable-business/global-reporting-initiative-updates> (accessed April 22, 2013).

UNDP (2013), *Human Development Report 2013*, UNDP. [Online]. Available from http://hdr.undp.org/en/media/HDR2013_EN_Summary.pdf> (accessed April 25, 2013).

United Nations (2015), UN Global Compact, 2015. [Online]. Available from <https://www.unglobalcompact.org/ > (accessed September 28, 2015).

UN News Centre. (2008), 'Climate Change Poses "Defining Challenge" of Our Time, Ban Says'. [Online]. Available from <http://www.un.org/apps/news/story.asp?NewsID=28458#. UX-kwJFaef8> (accessed September 29, 2015).

Von Weizsacker, E., Lovins, A. and Lovins, L. (1997), *Factor 4: Doubling Wealth – Halving Resource Use*, Earthscan Publications, London.

Wagner, M. and Schaltegger, S. (2006), Mapping the Links of Corporate Sustainability. In *Managing the Business Case for Sustainability*, Greenleaf Publishing, Sheffield, pp. 108–127.

White, J. (2009), 'Moral Accountability in the Corporate World,' *Accountability in Research*, vol. 16, no. 1, pp. 41–74.

World Bank. (2013), *China 2030: Building a Modern, Harmonious, and Creative High-Income Society*, The World Bank, Washington, DC.

World Business Council for Sustainable Development (WBCSD) (2012), *Analyses of the Rio+20 Outcome Document "The Future We Want"*. [Online]. Available from <http://www.wbcsd.org/rio-20/rio20.aspx> (accessed November 23, 2013).

The World Commission of Environment and Development. (1987), *Report of the World Commission on Environment and Development: Our Common Future*, United Nations, 1987, p. 43. [Online]. Available from <http://www.un-documents.net/our-common-future.pdf> (accessed May 4, 2013).

World Trade Organization (2012), *World Trade Statistics*, WTO. [Online]. Available from <http://www.wto.org/english/res_e/statis_e/its2012_e/its12_highlights1_e.pdf> (accessed April 21, 2013).

World Wide Fund for Nature (WWF) Living Planet Report (2012), [Online]. Available from <http://awassets.panda. org/downloads/lpr_2012_summary_booklet_final.pdf>, p. 12 (accessed March 4, 2014).

Worldwatch Institute (2013), *State of the World 2012: Moving towards Sustainable Prosperity*, Worldwatch Institute Report.

WWF (2007), *Climate Solutions, WWF's Vision for 2050*. [Online]. Available from <http://wwf.panda.org/about_our_earth/top_5_environmental_questions/what_is_climate_change/> (accessed April 19, 2013).

WWF (2013), History. [Online]. Available from http://worldwildlife.org/about/history (accessed September 8, 2013).

Chapter 11

# From ego to eco – theoretical challenges and practical implications of a "next generation" responsible leadership as a collaborative endeavor[1]

*Elke Fein, Jürgen Deeg and Jonathan Reams*

## 1 Introduction: responsible leadership – questions and challenges

The idea and concept of responsible leadership (RL) has gained increasing public and academic attention over the past years (e.g. Doh and Stumpf 2005, Freeman and Auster 2011, Maak and Pless 2006, Voegtlin et al. 2012, Waldman and Balven 2015, Waldman and Galvin 2008). This can be attributed to several factors and developments. On the one hand, environmental and corporate scandals have shown extensively that narrow-minded, short-term business strategies can have rather destructive outcomes on their social and ecological environments. On the other hand, worldwide media coverage of similar occurrences, as well as a general trend towards greater awareness of global systemic interconnections have put sustainability issues up front on public political, educational and corporate agendas. On this basis, the topic of responsible leadership has become an essential and logical requirement to sustainable governance in and outside of the corporate world. But what exactly does responsibility and responsible leadership mean in this context? And how can we come up with a definition of RL that is grounded in research rather than just normative ideals?

If we take the notion of sustainability seriously in the basic three dimensions of the term (economic, ecological and social), it becomes obvious that there is no separate space outside of responsibility on a shared planet, in particular since economy and business are no independent realms outside of society. Rather, they are embedded in multiple complex social and ecological contexts. In this perspective, so-called externalities can therefore not be externalized anymore in a globalized world, even though this is still part of more traditional economic theories and business strategies. This is why conventional views assuming individual rational agents are increasingly challenged by RL literature (Sonenshein 2007).

On this background, we argue that the challenge of RL has two dimensions which, we claim, are of equal importance and closely connected. In view of (re-)conceptualizing RL in a way that meets the demands of sustainability in our age of globalization we propose to focus on the interconnections between structural features of both the systemic and the consciousness dimensions. In recent times, facts such as the limited resources and regeneration potentials of planet Earth and the multiple, complex interdependences between economy and ecology have become evident. Also, we observe and increasing awareness of the huge and still underestimated impacts of human economic thinking and, as a result, consumer behavior on the eco-system (Meadows 1972). Moreover, many of our current ecological problems have been consequences of living and implementing certain values on individual, organizational, social and political levels. At the same time, we observe that different human actors have different outlooks on their own economic – and thereby ecological – behavior, as well as on issues of sustainability and responsibility in general. In other words: people are conscious of their own "ecological footprint" to varying degrees due to cultural, educational, motivational and other factors and influences.

We therefore claim that a RL successfully serving the demands of sustainability in a global world involves understanding the relationship between, on the one hand, internalized structures of meaning making (consciousness) and how they influence decisions, behaviors activities etc. that impact the above mentioned externalities. On the other hand, our meaning making is also influenced and shaped by our external environment, in other words by the structures of the economic, ecological, political and other systems constituting the context of economic, political and leadership behavior. So how can a responsible leadership practice address the challenges of global complexity adequately and how can leadership scholarship and education enhance the consciousness necessary for doing this in a responsible way? In view of answering these questions, the chapter takes a twofold approach and makes two essential arguments accordingly. First, in a theoretical part, we discuss how the concept of RL has been conceived of so far and how it can be refined and developed further in order to meet the needs of an interconnected, globalized world. In this part, we propose a meta-theoretical, developmental lens drawing on adult development theory and inspired by Otto Scharmer's formula calling for a transformation of personal, socio-cultural and political consciousness "from ego to eco system perspectives". On this basis, we claim that RL essentially needs leaders who are able to transcend their individual/ego perspectives in favor of broader, more encompassing notions of responsibility (Vincent et al. 2015, p. 239). While consciousness development essentially happens on an individual level, late stages of development tend to view responsibility as a shared, collective challenge (Commons and Sonnert 1994, Kohlberg 1973). In this sense, in a globalized world, individual responsible leadership tends to become a contradiction in itself.

In the second part we discuss what collective ways of responsible leadership can look like, which actually take into account the requirements of the broader, more encompassing notions of responsibility outlined before. Our basic claim here is that **responsible leadership needs to be radically collaborative**. This has at least two practical implications. First, performing such collaborative RL makes certain cognitive demands, for example on perspective taking and stakeholder awareness etc. of the involved individuals. Second, multiple and multi-level stakeholder engagement must be a core element of this kind of "next generation" RL. Collaborative leadership therefore needs to be based on methods which allow for co-creating shared visions and thus, a powerful common, collective purpose. By systematically transcending particularistic, interest-based perspectives, collaborative RL can prevent "externalities" from happening in the first place by the very framing of the process of decision making. To illustrate this suggestion, we present a number of practical examples and experiences which the concept and practice of collaborative RL can draw on.

## 2  Redefining responsible leadership – theoretical and conceptual remarks

### 2.1  Reviewing the state of the art: developments and shortcomings of current literature

When reviewing current literature on RL, a number of theoretical developments can be observed, as well as several shortcomings connected to them which, we argue, can be overcome by a more collaborative notion of RL. The following list of observations is not a comprehensive overview of general theory development in the field, but rather highlights those aspects which we think a more resilient, more sustainable and thus, more responsible concept of RL needs to address. Some of these aspects are actually mentioned in parts of the literature – however, in our view, without always receiving the substantial and systematic attention they deserve.

- RL is still mostly discussed in terms of **compliance with CSR and other standards** (Sarbanes Oxley, Global Compact etc.; Waldman 2014). Doing leadership responsibly is thus defined in terms of extrinsic motivations rather than as an aim in itself and/or a necessity by its own right (Voegtlin et al. 2012; for a positive exception see Pless's portrait of Anita Roddick's leadership behavior, Pless 2007). Extrinsic motivations, however, do not appear to be sufficient to achieve RL especially in contexts of low compliance cultures or leadership styles, and, as noticed by Scherer and Palazzo (2011), in times where the previous division of labor between business and the state is no longer functioning.
- As a result of the compliance focus, reference is often made to **morals/morality and ethics** as desirable qualities of a responsible leader. Leadership concepts such as "transformational", "servant", "ethical", "value-based", "spiritual" and "authentic leadership" (Brown and Treviño 2006) can be seen as expressions and examples of this normative approach to RL. However, in our view, there are two problems with a normative definition of RL. First, similar concepts often do not seem to be aware of the constructed and thus culture dependent nature of their own normative ideals of responsibility (Miska et al. 2014, Pless et al. 2012, Waldman and Balven 2015). Rather they sometimes seem to implicitly assume that there is one "right" definition of responsibility – thereby disregarding Waldman and Galvin's much quoted truism that "responsible leadership is not the same concept in the minds of all" (Waldman and Galvin 2008, p. 328). Second, for this reason, similar normative ideals and demands do not necessarily meet the actual "moral competencies or capacities" of empirical actors (Cook-Greuter 1999, Kegan and Lahey 2009, Rooke and Torbert 1998). Therefore, moral qualities cannot be discussed adequately as standards of behavior without a systematic developmental perspective looking at the structures of meaning making of the actual leaders and their followers one is talking about which is often missing in this literature though.
- While there is some awareness of **developmentally based criteria of responsibility and RL** such as in Waldman, Siegel and Javidan's study on CEOs' CSR engagement (2006), in Pless's (2007) discussion of Roddick or in the two dimensions mentioned by Miska et al. 2014 (degree of stakeholder inclusion and scope of

responsibility) and those proposed by Pless et al. 2012 (breadth of des constituent group focus and degree of accountability toward others), this developmental basis is in fact not systematically discussed on a conceptual level. In other words those dimensions are seemingly treated as *types* of thinking and/or behavior rather than as hierarchical levels of complexity in thinking, implying a higher or lesser degree of responsibility depending on their respective (developmental) degree/scope/breadth of focus and awareness.

- Similarly, while different perspectives of leaders are rightly explained as expressions of value and belief systems (Pless et al. 2012), those systems are not systematically distinguished and analyzed in terms of their **developmental complexity**. Even though the authors cautiously make the assumption, for example, that "the *opportunity seeker* orientation could be an evolution from a traditional economic orientation to a, more enlightened perspective" (Pless et al. 2012, p. 60), they do not discuss the rest of their findings in these terms. For instance, despite a valuable description of an "integrative" leadership orientation, the latter is presented as a mere *type* rather than as a more complex worldview and logic of thinking and acting based on a more developed ego concept (which in our perspective is the reason for its significantly greater power and effectiveness). This reluctance to consider the developmental basis of "integrative" leadership behavior also explains why those authors do not draw sufficient consequences from these observations in terms of training and development.

- Also, while discussing RL in terms of personal qualities rather than of underlying cognitive and cultural structures, two important theoretical developments of social science but also of leadership research in the past three decades are neglected (Carey 1992, Reams 2010). Besides the basic insight into the constructed nature of linguistic and normative concepts such as leadership and responsibility themselves, this also concerns the question who is the **subject of leadership**. Conceiving of leadership as an individual phenomenon in particular neglects more recent theory development in leadership studies such as the concepts of "shared", "distributed", "collective" or "leadership in the plural" (Denis et al. 2012). While authors like Pless et al. (2012) do suggest that RL should "best be viewed as shared" or even go beyond organizations (Waldman 2014), they fall short of giving convincing reasons why this is not just a question of taste but an important condition of its success and efficiency in a global sustainability perspective.

- The importance of **stakeholder dialogs** is indeed widely stressed (Maak and Pless 2006, Voegtlin et al. 2012, Waldman and Galvin 2008, Waldman and Siegel 2008). At the same time, while some authors do view stakeholder inclusion as a gradual challenge (Miska et al. 2014, p. 350), other parts of the literature still view the latter either as polar opposites to shareholder-based concepts or as external, somehow fashionable "nice-to-have" attributes of the respective businesses or their leadership style (Waldman and Galvin 2008). In general, RL literature does not necessarily view stakeholder dialogs as something to be integrated into the very core modes and missions of doing business. Even though parts of the literature propose "an understanding of responsible leadership in the sense of deliberative processes" (Voegtlin et al. 2012, p. 3), we do not consider the emphasis on either rational discussion or individual intuition (Sonenshein 2007) alone as appropriate avenues in this regard (see Joiner and Josephs 2007).

- The importance of **vision and purpose** is acknowledged in much of the literature, but those are often not considered as something which can and actually has to be co-created collectively, i.e. collaboratively, if they are to gain sufficient motivational power and thus to be of sustainable, or even transformative value. Instead, important parts of the literature still talk about vision and purpose as something to be (only) collectively "implemented", seemingly presupposing that in the first place, they are pre-defined by some leading body or person (Waldman and Galvin 2008, p. 338) who then let their knowledge "flow" to stakeholders (Waldman and Balven 2015, p. 22, quoting Doh and Quigley). For example, Voegtlin et al. (2012, p. 6 and 10) claim that "leaders exert influence by fostering an active stakeholder dialog" and that as change agents, sense givers and "managers of meaning (they) can influence the perceived 'CRS character' of an organization by sensitizing their employees for possible social and environmental consequences of corporate actions". – In other words, it is the (individual) leaders who are in charge and who make sure their organizations move into the "right" direction. To some extent, this is also true for Maak and Pless (2006) who, despite their legitimate claim that "in an interdependent and turbulent world (RL) cannot be achieved in isolation by the 'great man' alone or the charismatic leader", still focus on a detailed description of that individual leader – now portrayed as an integrative being combining multiple roles in him- or herself (p. 106).

In sum, many of the shortcomings of current RL discourse can be attributed to the still influential mainstream business paradigm claiming that businesses need to strive for "being the best *in* the world", i.e. to optimize their respective (own) profile in order to be successful in a competitive environment. In contrast, a more resilient and thus more likely sustainable and responsible paradigm would need businesses to strive for "being the best *for* the world" (Muff 2013). This would eventually also imply questioning some of the fundamental assumptions of our current economic model (Scherer and Palazzo 2011) and require a paradigm shift from competition to cooperation on a broader scale. So how can RL be redefined in order to overcome the shortcomings mentioned above in theory, consciousness and practice?

## 2.2 Responsible leadership viewed from a developmental perspective

*"Leadership is not a science or an art, it is a state of consciousness."*
(Chatterjee 1998, p. 24)

Waldman and Galvin (2008, p. 327) call for "a comprehensive definition" of RL, acknowledging that "people in (positions of leadership) often view responsibility in a narrow or incomplete manner". The authors consequently ask important questions: "To whom or to what should leaders be responsible, and how will responsibility be demonstrated?" If leaders are responsible to intra- or extra-organizational others, then "who are these 'others', and how exactly does a leader show responsibility toward them?" Waldman and Galvin thereby rightly recall that "definitions can vary depending on one's perspective" and that "responsible leadership is not the same concept in the minds of all" (Waldman and Galvin 2008, p. 328). Moreover, in a changing universe of science and practice, we argue that a comprehensive description of RL is equally unlikely to exist. On these grounds, we rather propose to strive for a *more* comprehensive definition and to identify convincing criteria for mapping the *degree* of comprehensiveness of RL definitions. To do this, we first take a closer look at how different perspectives shape different notions of RL, and what criteria could be helpful for evaluating the validity of each perspective. If they are not equally valid, the question arises which perspective is more valid, or more adequate in times of global interconnection, complexity and crisis and on what grounds.

In view of answering these questions we propose a concept of RL which is systematically informed by constructivist adult development theory, focusing on the cognitive prerequisites and demands of RL. Using a broad sense of the term "cognition" (including rationality, emotions, intuition etc.) we hold several core dimensions of consciousness development to be relevant to leadership performance some of which have been studied intensively by AD research. While namely the "level of moral development" (Kohlberg 1981) is indeed sometimes referred to as a factor influencing RL (Voegtlin et al. 2012, p. 13; Brown and Treviño 2006) we argue that putting cognitive developmental factors as such into the center of attention is a promising strategy for redefining RL on conceptually more solid grounds.

In a nutshell, constructivist developmental theories from Baldwin (1895, 1904, 1906), Piaget (1932, 1954, 1970) and Mead (1934) to Case (1993), Commons (Commons et al. 1998, Dawson 2002), Fischer (1980, and Fischer and Bidell 2006), Mascolo and Fischer (2010) all show that cognitive and cultural structures of meaning making, together with the structures of perception, perspective taking, self/ego and identity development (Cook-Greuter 1999, 2005, Kegan 1979, 1994, Loevinger 1976) potentially develop from less complex to more complex structures. This can happen not only all through childhood and adolescence, but also throughout adulthood (Cook-Greuter 1999, Robinson 2013). In this context, structural complexity is defined in terms of the number, quality, kind and degree of interconnectedness of variables of a given "reality" which the person can perceive, differentiate, distinguish, process and integrate in a specific area of consciousness development (for example social perspective taking, moral judgment or self/identity). This essentially means that more complex structures of perception, perspective taking and meaning making (on individual and collective levels) are better prepared to deal with complex challenges and to handle the existing complexity of reality and change in an adequate way (Commons et al. 2011, Reams 2005, Rooke and Torbert 1998, Vincent et al. 2015, Vygotsky 1978). For as the complexity/development of consciousness increases, the degree to which a person projects incomplete (under-complex) and thus biased and inadequate concepts, expectations and demands upon other (complex) real life actors in and outside of organizations decreases (Kegan 1994, Rooke and Torbert 1998, Torbert et al. 2004).

As a result, leaders operating from more complex levels of consciousness are more likely to find adequate, i.e. effective and mutually acceptable, ways of addressing conflicts and/or adaptive challenges because they have the "capacity to cognitively seize, process and assess complex situations, problems and developments from different stakeholder viewpoints" (Maak and Pless 2006, p. 104). In other words, they are able to respond to more "others" in a way which suits their respective perspectives and world views and thus, the "mental language" of those complex others as their own cognitive complexity (and, accordingly, empathy) grows. In fact, long-term studies

(Rooke and Torbert 1998, Torbert et al. 2004) have demonstrated that the success of organizational transformation efforts was dependent upon the level of consciousness of leadership (for an overview on research exploring the relationship between consciousness development and leadership, as well as more practical impacts of higher, post-conventional levels of consciousness development in leaders (see Vincent et al. 2015, p. 241).

Two models can illustrate the gains of a developmentally informed perspective on RL. Figure 11.1 (the "I-We-All-of-Us"-model) is a very simple, even simplistic illustration of how a growing awareness of reality comes with more complex and more encompassing perspectives. Note that Miska et al. 2014 also model a connection between scope of perspective and degree of responsibility, yet they don't link these dimensions to consciousness and ego development, thereby underestimating the relevance of this connection.

While an I-lens (in Miska et al. 2014: "agent view") purely perceives its own ego interests and goals, the We-lens takes into account certain collective bonds and interests which are typically defined by families, peer groups, ethnic groups, religious associations, nations or, in an organizational context, teams or whole organizations as distinguished from (and competing with) other teams/organizations. The All-of-Us-lens transcends both I and We perspectives, as well as the notion of competition between them. By asking which solutions serve the interest of all, it integrates the perspectives of all relevant stakeholders regardless of particular group affiliations they might have. In an even wider definition this lens also includes bio- and ecosphere perspectives and interests. The process of widening one's perspective on the world by gradually transcending a more narrow or incomplete ego-perspective in favor of the next more complex perspective has been described by Robert Kegan as a change of a person's "subject-object-balance". Kegan speaks of this process as a process of objectification during which the subject de-identifies with its formerly held image of self (identity) and learns to reflect upon it from a meta-type perspective which turns the former subject-identity into an object of critical reflection and self-observation. At the same time it is integrated into the new and wider, more encompassing perspective (Cook-Greuter 2005, Kegan 1979). In this sense, these perspectives form a clear hierarchy, since more encompassing views can be expected to be more successful in integrating more stakeholder concerns. This is because growing awareness of and respect for the world outside our own private concerns results in a contextualization and thereby, grounding of particularistic interests and endeavors in a more balanced, more

Figure 11.1 The "I-We-All-of-Us" Model

realistic, more solid analysis of things – and, most likely in more sustainable and more responsible actions. This claim also hooks up with Otto Scharmer's call for a paradigm shift from ego- to eco-system perspectives as an essential element of a "next generation" leadership model.

The second, more differentiated and more focused model we draw on shows the connections between different complexity levels of self-development, one of the core dimensions of leadership behavior, and how they affect specific leadership understandings, styles and practices. These connections have been elaborated in a study conducted by Putz and Raynor (2004), building on more fundamental research by Kohlberg, Kegan, Loevinger, Cook-Greuter and others. On this basis, Table 11.1 gives a more precise description of how, as self-image and self-understanding of a leader develop, their notions and practices of leadership gradually shift from more egocentric goals and desires to more encompassing ways of serving the interest of a broader group, organization or system as a whole.

While it is beyond the scope of this chapter to give a more detailed account of structuralist adult development theories and their relevance for leadership here (see McCauley et al. 2006, Reams 2014, Vincent et al. 2015), our core concern is to show that they do provide us with clear criteria for analyzing the level of complexity of different conceptions of leadership. What's more, on this basis, we can also evaluate their likeliness to be able to respond to complex challenges in an adequate way and thus, their quality as RL concepts. This does not mean that lower complexity self and leadership conceptions are less valuable per se (Table 11.1 also shows that strengths and weaknesses exist on each level). However, a complexity developmental approach makes clear that while an egocentric structure of reasoning might, for example, well be sufficient to defend the interests of a business against a competitor, trying to solve complex challenges involving multiple stakeholders by an egocentric approach is bound to fail (see also Elliot Jaques's conception of the "requisite organization", Jaques 1997 and Jaques et al. 1994). In other words, we claim that leadership practices can be more or less adequate, more or less responsive, and therefore more or less capable to solve specific challenges, depending on their developmental complexity.

On this basis, we argue that accordingly, leaders' **notions of responsibility** also undergo gradual change with increasing self development. A more complex self/identity will generally adopt a more encompassing idea of both leadership and responsibility. This means that the questions on RL which have been quoted above from Waldman and Gavin are likely to be answered differently by leaders on different levels of consciousness and personality development. As a matter of fact, we argue that they can nevertheless be described rather precisely in a theoretically informed way, namely as ideal types of meaning making and behavior grounded in particular concepts of self and identity and their respective reasoning and value structures. Table 11.2 illustrates how outlooks on responsibility and RL change on different levels of self development.

So what does this mean in view of answering our initial question? How RL can be defined in a more comprehensive way? First, as outlined above, a (more) comprehensive definition of RL has to acknowledge the fact that different structures of reasoning and meaning making will always have different definitions of responsibility. Consequently, there cannot be one single definition that is valid for all and for all times. Second, if we conceptualize RL as "the effectiveness in establishing consensual solutions that are accepted as legitimate by all affected parties" (Voegtlin et al. 2012, p. 5)

Table 11.1 Levels of Self Development and Leadership

| Level of Self Development | Subjective Self-Understanding | General Leadership Style | Leadership Strengths | Leadership Weaknesses |
|---|---|---|---|---|
| 1) Impulsive | "I" am my impulses (like a very young child) and unable to take the perspective of others | No leadership possible | None | Leaders not found at this level of development |
| 2) Egocentric | "I" am my needs and desires -able to manage my impulses and to take the perspective of others, but motivated solely by my own needs and desires | Strong, "great men", leader-centered. His/her wishes are orders; heroic leadership | Aggressive, "can do" personality | Destructive to teamwork and initiative ("my way or the highway") |
| 3) Interpersonal | "I" am defined by my relationships and social roles — what is "right" is defined by rules, regulations and proper authority (chain of command) | "Good boss" who cares and is in charge, paternalistic leadership, governed by relations of loyalty versus authority | Strong team player and supporter of organizational vision | Independent thinking, mediating competing relationship demands, e.g., boss, family, subordinates |
| 4) Autonomous (in Kegan: institutional self; Loevinger: experts/achievers) | "I" create my own identity, inclusive of but not defined by my roles, relationships and the expectations of others | Transactional leadership, inviting followers to give their best, incentives versus good performance | Better able to take independent action and mediate competing relationship demands, e.g., boss, subordinates | Rigid self-identity that is associated with current success and threatened by fundamental change |
| 5) Integral (in Kegan: interindividual self, Loevinger: strategist) | "I" am a continually evolving person who is aware of development in myself and others; "I" have a flexible sense of identity that embraces complexity and paradox on a personal level (not just intellectually) but nevertheless has clear values and boundaries | Transformative leadership, shared/ distributed leadership, inviting followers (team members) to follow their purpose and make a meaningful contribution to the overall success of the whole | More adaptive to fundamental change without threat to personal identity; better able to support the self-development of others, and understand oneself in a multi-paradigmatic way | Flexible self-identity may be confusing or threatening to subordinates; might push others to grow before they are ready |

Source: Adapted from Putz and Raynor 2004, published first in Reams 2005, p. 129.

*Table 11.2* Notions of Responsibility and Responsible Leadership on Different Levels of Self Development

| Level of Self Development | What Does/Can Responsibility Mean and How Is it Generally Demonstrated? | Who Are the "Others" that Leaders Are Responsible to (In or/and Outside of Organizations)? | How Exactly Does a Leader Show Responsibility Toward Them? |
|---|---|---|---|
| 1) Impulsive | — | No-one, no concept of separate others | — |
| 2) Egocentric | Not an important category | No-one, only themselves and their interests | — |
| 3) Interpersonal | Respecting rules and obligations, building good relationships, keeping promises, being and holding accountable | The surrounding group (team, organization, business; nation/ state) | Paternalistic, offering protection, in response demanding loyalty and obedience |
| 4) Autonomous (in Kegan: institutional self; Loevinger: experts/ achievers) | Truthfulness to important values, principles and/ or ideas of how things (should) work, contributing to success of own projects | "Higher" ends and goals such as growth, profit, quality, being the best in a certain field (or beyond); shareholders | Try as hard as possible to meet goals, encourage/expect subordinates/teams to do the same, offer incentives |
| 5) Integral (in Kegan: interindividual self, Cook-Greuter, Torbert: strategist) | Serving a greater purpose, making a meaningful contribution to a good, just society, using resources thoughtfully, reflecting potential consequences of own actions on others (in a broad sense) | Team members, stakeholders (including shareholders), society, the larger social and ecological environment | Inviting stakeholders to share concerns, invite team members to contribute to co-creative processes, facilitate spaces for the enactment of purpose |

we have to acknowledge that this is a definition stemming from a rather complex, context-sensitive level of meaning making which can therefore not be generalized or expected to find consensus across different complexity levels of reasoning. Third, the developmentally informed theoretical lens proposed here, together with empirical evidence supporting it, make clear that stages of cognitive development impact what is even possible in terms of such conceptions and their respective reasoning structures, and also how they influence the interpretation of both public discourse and the use of various popular terms that gain traction in the academic and other communities (Reams 2010). Moreover, they show that "establishing consensual solutions . . ." is an issue and a goal only on interpersonal and higher levels of self and leadership complexity in the first place. Leaders who fall short of this level (according to Cook

Greuter 2005, p. 2, 10 percent of the US population score below; according to Rooke and Torbert 1998, p. 14, only 10 percent of leaders reach this level) will not have consensual problem solving as an aim on their agendas at all – unless very precise and tangible personal gains or advantages are connected to it (Joiner and Josephs 2007). And leaders on levels 3 and 4 (in Tables 11.1 and 11.2) will have different understandings of the scope of their responsibility than leaders on level 5.

As our models show, leadership tends to become more responsible in itself as the complexity of self development increases, in the sense that it gradually responds to larger groups of interested or concerned individuals, while only the most complex levels conceive of responsibility as a commitment generally going beyond attaining particular(istic) organizational goals and interests. Only they will therefore be capable and prepared to involve broader numbers of extra-organizational stakeholders without perceiving this as a threat to their personal or organizational identity. In other words, there are varying degrees of both responsibility and RL, depending on the extent to which the respective leader is able to transcend and contextualize his/her (organization's/business') primary needs and interests and see the latter as part of a larger context, i.e. of the social or even eco-system the respective organization is part of. Karen Litfin therefore suggests to talk about "respons*ability*" due to the "wider expanse of reality (. . .) and capacity to respond" (Litfin 2003, p. 51).

In the second part of this chapter, we will explore this claim in more detail. We will show that as complexity requirements increase, successful RL becomes less and less a matter of "enlightened individuals" possessing the "right" personal traits and qualities but rather a matter of **ongoing collaborative inquiry** and effort. In fact, this claim is in line with late Lawrence Kohlberg's assumption that his **6th order** of moral reasoning was likely to go beyond a mere individual competence – which also explains why it is so hard to spot in studies using an individual-centered methodology (Commons and Sonnert 1994, Kohlberg 1973). Indeed, the nature of collective intelligence and wisdom is different from both the participating individuals' intelligences and the sum of all of them (Atlee 2003, Rowson 2008). It therefore needs different methods, tools and procedures to be captured, harvested and cultivated in order to develop their full potential.

## 3 Theory and practice of collaborative responsible leadership

> We need to "grasp the phenomenon (of leadership) as the field of awareness rather than a personality trait or mental attribute."
>
> (Chatterjee 1998, p. 24)

### 3.1 What is collaborative leadership?

In a **recent literature review**, Denis et al. (2012) have distinguished four "streams" of theorizing "leadership in the plural" which they have grouped around the concepts of "collective", "distributed", "shared" and "relational leadership" (Denis et al. 2012, p. 213). These streams of research, it appears, have been neglected by important parts of RL literature so far, or have at least not been systematically integrated into RL discourse. While all of the streams identified by Denis et al. (2012) somehow look at the phenomenon of leadership as operated by several people, the way in which this is done differs across the four streams. While "collective" and "distributed leadership" approaches do not question more traditional outlooks according to which leadership is a quality or property which can be attributed to particular people, and while they therefore conceive of some people as leaders and some as followers, the other two approaches have a stronger focus on mutuality. While in the first group of approaches, leadership is pooled or distributed differently but still "remains the privilege of an elite group" (Denis et al. 2012, p. 269), the latter two streams rather conceive of leaders and followers as essentially the same people, based on the idea that group members implicitly or explicitly "lead *each other* within a closed interacting group" (ibid.). And while the first two streams are therefore less interesting and less relevant for our purpose, the concepts of shared and relational leadership provide important insights into the workings of a leadership concept "beyond the individual" which we call "collaborative" here (for similar uses of the term see also Drath et al. 2008, and Vincent et al. 2015). This is because they focus on emerging new forms of collaboration and, in the case of relational leadership, on the conditions which are necessary in order to bring them about.

In these views, leadership is redefined as transcending individual actors and their respective personal properties (either in the singular or in the plural) and rather conceived of as a social phenomenon, a process, a collective and emergent characteristic of collective entities such as organizations. In this perspective, actors are present, enacting leadership, but are not containers of/for leadership themselves (see Denis et al. 2012, pp. 261, 263). This conception is "fundamentally more about participation and collectively creating a sense of direction than it is about control and exercising authority" (Denis et al. 2012, p. 254). Moreover, "leadership occurs when leaders abandon the need to control and dominate", and it "emerges within the dynamic interactions of daily organizational existence" (Follet 1924, quoted after Denis et al. 2012, p. 255). The quasi ontological shift which this depersonalized view of leadership constitutes as compared to more traditional approaches has been described in more detail by Drath et al. (2008).

At the same time, there are both commonalities and some (substantial) differences between shared leadership (in the sense of good teamwork) and the concept of collaborative leadership as proposed here. What both concepts have in common is, first, to stress that sharing leadership brings forward and helps to access complementary talents and capabilities across firms and organizations, that it ensures a deep and broad search for ideas and mobilizes diverse skills from within team dynamics in view of getting things done in a better way. Second, they both stress that, on this basis, sharing leadership helps to focus on and converge forces around common goals and directions. In the context of shared leadership this is mainly regarded through the lens of team effectiveness.

However, while shared leadership approaches tend to limit themselves to describing the dynamics within teams which are often seen as democratic ideals and discussed within respective normative discourses, relational approaches are also concerned with the conditions under which new qualities of collaboration within teams emerge. Emergence is understood here as "the development of complex, organized configurations" of whatever kind (Van Dijk 2014, p. 7). So relational leadership approaches for example study, on the one hand, social relations and their respective influence processes through which emergent coordination happens, in other words through which evolving social order is constructed, produced and changed (see for example Uhl-Bien's relational leadership theory 2006). On the other hand, they ask how specific leadership behaviors can support and foster those processes (Denis et al. 2012, p. 263). On this basis, the question arises what the conditions of successful collaborative emergence are and how specific individuals and groups can develop the behaviors necessary to bring them about.

In this chapter, collaborative leadership is understood as a form of collaboration which aims to access and make use of the realm of collective intelligence within a group by systematically going beyond individual views and perspectives in order to enact broader and deeper collective purposes and potentials. In fact, this idea is not new but rather has plenty of intellectual "ancestors". It has been spelled out by Peter Senge (1990) who identifies shared vision as one of the "five disciplines" of leadership. It also draws on Bohm's notions of dialog (Bohm 1996), in which shared meaning is revealed, and the collective intelligence, or "how we think together" comes as a prior conception to how individuals partake in and enact meaning. In order for collective intelligence and wisdom to successfully emerge and inspire collaborative action, we argue that there are at least two preconditions which need to be met. In a nutshell, it needs a field of awareness which opens up spaces of communication and cognition beyond both conventional ego-awareness and more traditional particularistic We-spaces as described by Wheatley (1996, Wheatley and Frieze 2011). Moreover, those spaces need to be constructed as "landing strips" (to use Otto Scharmer's term) for desirable futures whereby "desirable" implies desirability from a maximum broad all-of-us-perspective.

Therefore, contrary to the assumption voiced by some relational leadership theorists that "any individuals can develop these behaviors" (Denis et al. 2012, p. 263) we hold that, first, individuals and groups need to be well enough prepared to engage in collaborative inquiry and meaning making. This generally means that in order to host similar processes they should have run through certain experiences of personal growth and transformation themselves. For only then are they open and flexible enough to cognitively admit and allow collective intelligence to appear and to take the place of previously held individual convictions as well as, eventually, to seize, harvest and implement solutions coming from that level. Going through a developmental trajectory of structural decentering and self-transcendence can in fact happen both on individual and collective levels.

As has been shown in the models above, higher levels of complexity of reasoning and self development by definition tend to become more self-transcending and, at the same time, more inclusive in their perception of self, others and the world around them (provided that the respective developmental trajectory has not lead to more complex "shadows" interfering with good collaboration). This of course also impacts the way individuals on those levels act as leaders (Vincent et al. 2015). Once leaders have reached higher (in the model above: integral, in Kegan: inter-individual, in Commons: meta-systematic) levels of self-reflection and meaning making, they have embraced a global, systemic perspective and are likely to show rather sophisticated and differentiated ways of reasoning. At this point, they are also able to become aware of, for example, how certain systems of meaning making, as well as current individual and collective action based on them, actually co-create many of the problems we are facing on societal and global levels today. On this basis, leaders are thus also likely to recognize that none of them is capable individually to make significant, i.e. systemic changes on their own. It becomes increasingly clear to them that first, others also have other modalities of being, including a subjective world of values etc. of their own. On this basis, second, they see that "a plurality of leaders is needed because no single individual alone could conceivably bridge the sources of influence, expertise, [wisdom] and legitimacy needed to move a complex social system forward constructively" (Denis et al. 2012, p. 272, Rowson 2008). They rather see that they need the support of both the members of their own organizations and the collaboration of other leaders/organizations in various key areas of the systems that are related to the problems in question in order to make far-reaching, cross-sectoral or even systemic changes serving all who are concerned (see Grint 2005, Van Dijk 2014, p. 6).

In other words, leaders who are familiar with complex systemic thinking and have developed the respective levels of personal and cognitive growth and complexity are a **first precondition** for collaborative leadership based on collective intelligence. – But does collaborative leadership occur automatically once a bunch of sufficiently prepared leaders come together?

As a **second precondition** for collective intelligence to emerge, besides sufficiently conscious leaders, we claim, that successful collaborative endeavors also require adequate framing and scaffolding. In other words, the setting needs to be based on suitable forms of organization, a culture, and a set of tools and practices able to create and provide the safe spaces that are necessary for deeper, more conscious and thus more responsible kinds of communication to happen. What then could similar **settings** look like? How can they be (co-)created? Which practices enable collaborative inquiry into the realms of collective intelligence in view of more integrative and therefore both more sustainable and more responsible solutions to burning societal and leadership problems to emerge?

In view of answering these questions we must distinguish at least two different cases and scenarios. Collaborative RL can be practiced, first, within existing organizations and, second, in wider contexts designed to bridge different organizations, sectors, interest groups, domains or even cultures by arranging broader stakeholder dialogs in order to address issues which go beyond narrow individual group or organizational concerns. At the same time, successful collaborative RL seems to be characterized by very similar traits and principles in both cases.

Collaborative forms of leadership in organizational settings have recently been described in some detail by Pless (2007) in her description of The Body Shop, by Kegan et al. (2014) and, in particular, by Frederic Laloux. In his bestselling book *Reinventing Organizations* (2014), Laloux conceives of what we propose here as an innovative, because more comprehensive and more encompassing kind of responsible leadership as the expression of a **new paradigm** of leadership and collaboration in organizations altogether. And similar to what has been argued above, Laloux reconstructs and theorizes it as emerging from a new level of complexity of consciousness and culture. Moreover, his analysis underpins the assumption that the types of organizations we as cultural beings invent, and the ways of collaboration going with them, are always "tied to the prevailing worldview and consciousness" (Laloux 2014, p. 14), more precisely, to their degree of complexity. This means that transitions from more narrow ego- to broader and more responsible eco-system perspectives require appropriate, i.e. sufficiently wide and complex structures of cognition, meaning making and practices derived from them (Scharmer and Kaeufer 2013). As those wider and more complex mental "operating systems" gain momentum they will eventually change our approaches to both leadership and organization on a broader societal scale as well. This is actually already happening as Laloux has found in a dozen cases pioneering those "next generation" ways of doing collaborative responsible leadership in organizations.

Laloux's study of new, what he calls "evolutionary" ways of organizing was inspired by, on the one hand, personal observations and frustrations and, on the other, by empirical data backing up Peter Drucker's famous quote that "so much of what we call management consists in making it difficult for people to work" (cited after Laloux 2014, p. 288). According to a survey by Tower Watson from 2012 only "a third of people are engaged in their work (35 percent); many more (. . .) are 'detached' or actively 'disengaged' (43 percent)" and "the remaining 22 percent feel 'unsupported' " (Laloux 2014, p. 62). Laloux himself equally observed that in many organizations, including businesses, at present, employees experience a "deep inner sense of emptiness" and sometimes "quiet suffering" which, he claims, is often only poorly covered by "frantic activity", "façade" and "bravado" (Laloux 2014, p. 4). Based on these observations he went to look for "concrete ways to run organizations from a higher stage of consciousness" in order to create "soulful workplaces (. . .) where our talents can blossom and our callings can be honored (. . .), free of the pathologies that show up all too often" (Laloux 2014, p. 8, 13; see also Benefiel 2005, Bolman and Deal 1995, Chopra 2010, Rabbin 1998).

As a result of his short trip through the history of leadership and organization, Laloux argues that the dominant models have so far been based primarily on skeptical views of human potentials, or even on fear (engendering the need to either authoritative rule, detailed planning and/or strict control of others' behaviors) rather than on trust. At the same time only the latter breeds responsibility, intrinsic motivation, engagement from a sense of meaning and ownership of one's work and, ultimately, joy and happiness in people. Laloux's detailed analysis of about a dozen leading innovators in collaborative leadership around the globe identifies three core principles and a number of necessary traits and conditions which all organizations in his survey proved to have in common. As a matter of fact, Kegan et al. (2014), starting from a developmentally informed perspective, have found very similar characteristics in what they call "deliberately developmental organizations (DDOs)". In a nutshell, they are based on an attitude of trust and stem from the fundamental insight that "no-one is as smart as everyone" (together)[2] and that it thus needs more than just a good leader in charge at the top to make an organization thrive. Moreover, to manifest the best of potentials, it needs the joint collective intelligence of the whole team.

The three principles described by Laloux are self-management, the quest for wholeness and a commitment to what he calls "evolutionary purpose", i.e. a strong common yet flexible and dynamic sense of direction. All three connect strongly with a qualitatively **new kind of collaborative leadership** and management where teamwork not only becomes joyful, effortless and much more effective, but also allows for peak moments of collective genius to take over the lead. This is because all three principles draw on the maximum (breadth and depth) of knowledge, intelligence, wisdom and potential accessible within the respective team or organization (Drath et al. 2008). They do this by

- Integrating the maximum number of people (everyone working in an organization) into decision making processes (self-management)
- Inviting those people (staff, members and external stakeholders) to show up and to bring themselves in as whole persons, including their interpersonal, emotional and spiritual competences, i.e. valuing them not only their mental and cognitive competences as experts for specific topics or tasks
- Aligning the organization's work, energy and development to the long-term overall goals it is serving, i.e. putting its common purpose ahead of short-term concerns

In order to fill these principles with life the essence of collaborative (responsible) leadership has been translated into practices supporting and enabling the following ideas on a daily basis:

- All involved individuals (workers, external stakeholders etc. participating in a collaborative project) are trusted to make valuable contributions to overarching goals. At the same time, these overarching (group, team, organizational or project) goals and purposes are given priority over more narrow and particularistic individual concerns by the very framing of the setting and process.
- On this basis, power and leadership can be more widely dispersed and distributed among group, team or organizational members and external stakeholders, trusting that leadership lies not in individual people but in their relations or interstices (Denis et al. 2012, p. 253).
- The concept of power, as well as the mental models of how to exercise power and how to achieve success and effectiveness (this is true for both workplaces and other projects, see below) thus change from power-over (others) to power-with, i.e. from a coercive power to a jointly developed, co-active one. In this conception, it is not commands that are important, but social relationships which facilitate and can be facilitated in order to match and support processes of co-creating the group's purpose, identity and actions. (This concept of power and collaborative leadership has been spelled out in more detail by Hannah Arendt in "Vita Activa", 1960, and by Mary P. Follet in "Creative experience" as early as 1924.)

As a result:

- Power and authority "continually shift and morph" between different teams and roles to match the needs of the situation as it evolves (see Van Dijk 2014). Moreover, leadership spreads from one individual to all members of the respective team or project each of whom is empowered and trusted to make the best contribution they can by filling their respective role.
- Leadership can give up control, surrender to the process of co-creation and limit itself to holding the space for collective learning and transformation to occur.

- This means that this type of leadership is characterized above all by a very high degree of trust, flexibility and reflexivity on both individual and collective levels. Because it recognizes what kind of conditions or incentives are needed in a specific context, it can establish a direct and ever changing link between the nature of a specific issue and the corresponding leadership style. Moreover, it can subsequently create the necessary conditions and practices (Van Dijk 2014, p. 3). Heifetz (1994) has therefore described it as "adaptive leadership".

The main leadership tool in view of achieving this flexibility to adapt to complex dynamics, is the Self, i.e. the state of mind of the leader(s) who need(s) to cultivate "an awareness of the total situation" coming from a specific "way of being-in-the-world" (Denis et al. 2012, pp. 260, 265), or, in Otto Scharmer's words: "a deeper attention structure characterized by an open mind, heart, and will" (Scharmer 2007). Moreover, by adopting adequate cultures and practices of communication, all participating individuals and teams can grow towards the competence of holding and creatively making use of collaborative spaces themselves. It is therefore not surprising that Kegan et al. (2014) have coined the term "deliberately developmental organizations (DDO)" for what they describe in very similar terms.

On these grounds, the pioneering organizations studied by Laloux have turned into **communities of collaborative practice**. And since many of them have integrated a notion of service to a broader group of stakeholders into their company purposes, a comprehensive notion of responsibility towards the larger society is an almost trivial part of those organizations' self-understanding – so how can this kind of collaborative RL be practiced in other contexts? How can these new "operating systems" and the practices which go along with them be translated and adopted to contexts extending beyond single organizations?

### 3.2 Collaborative RL beyond organizations: examples from collaboratories

> At Moral Stage 6, morality itself becomes societal. At this stage, individuals realize that they cannot be moral in isolation and that discursive processes are necessary to achieve satisfactory moral solutions. (. . .) Moral stage 6 paradigmatic coordination cannot be monologically determined, because it depends on the agreement of the participants of the coordination. It changes and evolves as participants exchange arguments.
>
> (Commons and Sonnert 1994, pp. 9, 11)

One of Laloux's observations was that holding the space for collaborative ways of doing leadership inside organizations proved to be easier, the larger the number of people capable of displaying a level of awareness necessary to support the collaborative endeavor. This finding is true especially in organizations the members of which have previously not been used to similar, non-hierarchical cultures of collaboration. It is also crucial for collaborative projects beyond single organizations. This has been shown based on community leadership development programs in Australia (Vincent et al. 2015). It can also be illustrated by experiences from experiments in collaborative leadership undertaken by the currently active EU project "Leadership for Transition (LiFT)" in which the authors of this chapter are involved.

LiFT is a Grundtvig Learning Partnership run by five organizations from different European countries, all of which are specialized in either leadership, adult education and development and/or societal transition (LiFT project 2013, www.leadership-for-transition.eu). The partners have gathered around the general vision and purpose of bringing together "innovative researchers, practitioners and citizens engaged in the fields of leadership, education and societal transition to promote more integrative, more effective and thus more sustainable ways of living in Europe and beyond". One of the core assumptions of the project rationale is that "for the first time since the beginning of modernity, technical solutions are clearly not sufficient anymore" for solving the problems today's world is facing and that therefore, it is necessary "to make radical changes in our ways of thinking and behaving". LiFT's goals therefore are:

- "to empower individuals and society at large to take over responsibility for working towards the common good" and thereby,
- to help putting into practice "large scale eco-system transitions" which are held to be necessary to meet "the challenges facing European and world societies in both socio-economic and ecological realms", in times of multidimensional crisis (LiFT project rationale 2013).

On these grounds, LiFT started by asking two questions:

1   How can larger groups of people beyond single organizations successfully accomplish meaningful things together?
2   How can co-creative collaborative processes be framed and scaffolded in order to support this?

In view of answering these questions, LiFT has worked with the principles of collaborative leadership as outlined above on two levels at the same time. First, as a rather loose network of partnering organizations, gathered around an ambitious purpose, yet within the limits and constraints of a temporary, two year project, it had to go through a process of shaping and defining its own identity and potential scope of action. Second, the challenge was to look for ways to implement some of the principles of collaborative responsible leadership in order to serve and realize the aforementioned goals within the limits of the given project.

In fact, LiFT found itself implementing most of the elements, principles and practices of collaborative leadership based on the experiences of pioneering organizations. This is not surprising, since a number of consequences naturally follow from transcending purely egocentric concerns by more complex conceptions of responsibility and leadership. The latter are therefore characteristic of all "post-heroic" leadership concepts (Fletcher 2004, p. 656, cited after Denis et al. 2012, p. 266), in and outside organizational contexts.

The following section tells the story of how the essence of collaborative leadership has been translated into concrete actions and practices by the LiFT project – and to what extent this has actually required a collaborative approach.

*Co-creating collective purpose/starting from a blank page*

Besides the rather broad and general goals of the project cited above, there was no a priori or strategic goal to be met, no specific deliverables other than the formal requirement to conduct about five workshops in two years. – But there was a strong desire of all involved staff members (= the core group) to do something meaningful, i.e. something that would have a positive impact on larger society.

This "something" took shape in result of a process of collectively sensing "into the void" (of the "blank page") which the project was in the beginning, in order to grasp what contribution it could actually make in view of the general vision and purpose. While this might have felt a bit unusual even to some of the leadership "high potentials" within LiFT, the group started working from an "empty space" in the center without a clear-cut plan or strategy of what to do. However, it turned out that this made all the difference. By sharing ideas, visions, hopes and dreams concerning the overall idea of "leadership for transition" in a safe space of mutual trust and respect, a more specific purpose gradually unfolded in the course of several sessions of collective sensing in. Combined with brainstorming for gathering ideas, experiences and competences the different participating organizations and their staff could bring in, a more clear-cut working program for LiFT successively emerged.

*Defining tasks, roles and responsibilities in a flexible, adaptive way*

On these grounds, fine-tuning followed easily from this process. Based on the extent to which each member of the core group felt able to contribute due to individual potentials, time restrictions and the degree of commitment they were willing to make, the distribution of tasks, roles and responsibilities "fell into place" quite effortlessly, without needing extensive discussion or negotiation. In result (and in line with the overall funding regulations), the core group set out to host a series of public workshops in different places in Europe, each of which was being designed to address a particular challenge of today's society.

So far, LiFT has conducted three collaborative stakeholder workshops in 2014, either taking up burning issues in the particular hosting context (LiFT Sweden), digging deeper into the overall topic of leadership as such (LiFT Norway) or in a world of changing organizational realities in particular (LiFT Austria). These workshops were essentially prepared and organized by the LiFT partner in the respective country, while other staff roles and constellations circulated between all partners. Moreover, roles were defined flexibly according to local, methodological and thematic needs, and, of course, the specific competencies of the staff members. Note that at each event, the local host was liberated from the duty to facilitate the main part of the event, thereby distributing burdens and responsibilities onto several shoulders.

*Collaborative stakeholder engagement*

In the center of each public workshop, LiFT hosted a so-called *Collaboratory* session, attracting between 30 and over 100 participants at each event.

The "Collaboratory" had been developed earlier by one of the LiFT partners (Muff 2014) as a powerful format combining a number of communication methods and tools for involving a large number and range of stakeholders around burning topics in need of collective action. While the specific topics of each LiFT workshop had been selected by the local partner in charge, the collaborative process was prepared and put into practice as a joint effort, based on the central elements and principles described by Laloux and others, namely:

- Broad stakeholder engagement around a common question, purpose or goal
- An atmosphere of trust inviting participants to show up as whole persons
- A facilitation designed to allow for flexibility and for achieving tangible outcomes at the same time

### Holistic framing and facilitation

The *collaboratory* template follows a certain, though not strictly dogmatic format. In fact, each collaboratory has an individual setting, framing, schedule and facilitation. However, the core elements were similar or even the same in all of them. Starting with a well chosen opening, the purpose and overall frame of the event is defined. After setting the stage, facilitators devote considerable time to welcoming all participants as whole persons. This is done by inviting them to bring themselves into the process with their whole body of personal experience, knowledge, motivation and wisdom, and by making sure that the overall atmosphere is one of trust, dialog, and cooperation, instead of disguise, showing off, and competition.

### Facilitating increasing levels of collective awareness and intelligence

Facilitation then runs the group through a process which roughly follows the stages of increasing awareness as defined, for example, in Otto Scharmer's "Theory U" (Scharmer 2007). In a nutshell, the most important elements of the collaborative process are:

- Inviting a broad range of perspectives and expertise to speak out about the issue in question
- Reflecting on these perspectives individually and in smaller groups
- Developing a common vision of how things could look like if the respective issue or problem was solved
- Looking for practical steps and ideas which help to get closer to the common vision
- Translating some of those steps into clear-cut projects and tangible results
- Designating concrete individuals committed to make sure the agreed upon projects are implemented within a period of 2–3 months

During the collaborative process, the main responsibility of facilitation is first, to hold a strong focus on the initial purpose of the overall event without becoming dogmatic about it, and second, to hold the collaborative space, making sure the atmosphere of collaboration, creativity, playfulness and respect is preserved.

While LiFT held the first event with only a single, highly experienced facilitator, reflecting this experience within the core group made clear that distributing roles between a facilitation team of several members is a better strategy for channeling the plurality of a large and diverse group of stakeholders, as well as for generating adequate coherence for trust, creativity, and vision to emerge. In a situation where the self of the leader(s) is the most important leadership tool, sensing into the needs of a large group at every moment becomes easier, more effective and more powerful if several, equally well prepared leaders bring their respective personal experiences, resources and capabilities into the process. This happened during LiFT workshops 2 (Sweden) and 3 (Austria).

One of the learnings voiced by members of the core group during the internal debriefings of the last two workshops was the experience of a qualitative transformation of the mode of collaboration. When the original "owner" of the collaboratory method handed it over to LiFT, the project took on a new dynamic of its own, driven by its purpose. At the same time, the collaborative method and the partnering organizations turned into stewards serving the enactment of this purpose. The power and dynamic of this shift, from leading collaboration to co-creating simplicity in complexity, was a groundbreaking experience to the whole team.

As a result, LiFT so far saw several local projects take shape and develop independently, as well as one of its partner organizations engage in a fundamental transformation inspired by the LiFT workshop it had hosted before.

## 4 Discussion and implications

So how does the perspective on leadership proposed here go beyond current theorizing on RL? And to what extent do collaborative qualities add a new dimension to this? The essence of our contribution can be summarized by Otto Scharmer's formula that transitions "from ego to eco systems" require similar transitions from ego to eco system thinking and acting. In contrast, less than integral approaches are not sufficient to address the complex problems and challenges our societies and the world at large are currently facing, but rather tend to reproduce them. This has immediate implications for the way responsibility in general and responsible leadership in particular are conceived of. In more detail, we have made the following arguments:

- While authors like Ciulla (1998), Solomon (1999), George (2003) claim that "having a good character and being a moral person are at the core of being a responsible leader" (Maak and Pless 2006, p. 105), we argue that this normative, values-based concept is (maybe) necessary, but not sufficient for defining RL in a more comprehensive, and more sustainable way. This is because concepts like morality tend to be understood differently by different structures of reasoning, cognitive development and meaning making. In contrast, a meta-level perspective uncovering the structures of meaning making themselves offers clear criteria for evaluating the degree to which the respective morality is adequate for and compatible with the demands of responsibility in and for a global economy and society: the wider the scope of cognition, the more likely does it respond in adequate and sustainable ways.
- Authors like Maak and Pless (2006) rightly stress that good, responsible leaders need both moral and relational qualities, defining the "purpose of leadership (. . .) as to build and cultivate sustainable and trustful relationships to different

stakeholders inside and outside the organization and to co-ordinate their action to achieve common objectives . . .". At the same time, when describing the leader as "a cultivator of these relationships" (Maak and Pless 2006, p. 103f.), these authors still focus on the single leader as "one integrative being" who is more or less in charge and in control of the above mentioned processes (Maak and Pless 2006, p. 107). In contrast, we argue that in times of multiple crises, only collaborative leadership, based on direction, alignment and commitment (Drath et al. 2008) is sufficiently prepared to provide responsible outcomes.

- While Maak and Pless, for example, correctly describe many preconditions of successful stakeholder dialog processes, such as cultivating good relationships with all stakeholders and "creating a holding environment" for those processes (p. 112), they apparently do not theorize them based on a concept of leadership "in the plural". However, our experience is that in order to successfully respond to current global challenges, collaborative leadership needs to abandon what Drath et al. call a "tripod ontology" of leadership, in favor of a more integrative, more pragmatic ontology, transcending particularistic concerns by putting collective purpose into the center of attention.
- We agree with Maak and Pless's claim that in order "cognitively seize, process and assess complex situations, problems and developments from different stakeholder viewpoints . . .", leaders need to "practice introspection", including taking a critical perspective on themselves. Yet, we believe that responsible leadership for a more sustainable age needs to go beyond both merely rational and merely individual self-reflection, and should systematically establish spaces, cultures and practices of collaborative, co-creative self- and meta-reflection focusing on broader common purposes and outcomes.

Moreover, we suggest that the actual "relational innovation" of a more comprehensive, integral concept of RL is the leaders' ability to engage in radical decentering which means self-transcending, giving up control (cf. Rowson 2008, Rowson and Reams 2015, Varela 1999 and Varela and Scharmer 2000), and rather trusting (and scaffolding) carefully framed processes of emerging collective wisdom. This also implies that individual leaders cease to be as important, as compared to the overall setting, practices, process and purpose. Ultimately, for leadership to become a truly collaborative, sustainable and responsible endeavor, collective intelligence and wisdom need to be put "in the driver's seat".

While existing literature does acknowledge the importance of collaboration, stakeholder engagement and processes of co-creation, it mostly falls short of proposing more specific answers as to what this means in practice, what a more collaborative leadership based on collective intelligence can look like, which demands it makes, and which methods and tools can be used to implement it (Scherer and Palazzo 2011, p. 920). Since this kind of approach is still fairly new, the relation between theory and practice generally remains undiscussed. However, strong communities of practice seem to be one of the most important tools and conditions for implementing RL as a collaborative endeavor. In our view, the essence of collaborative responsible leadership, able to address today's "big, wicked issues", is a practice of joint listening into the "void" and then follow what wants to emerge from a deeper kind of awareness. The responsible leadership we need is then able to co-create adequate conditions, settings and processes to let more sustainable answers and solutions emerge.

Therefore, we argue that RL theory needs to make a paradigmatic "quantum leap" and move from individualistic conceptions such as the "tripod ontology" towards acknowledging that sustainable RL needs to unite creativity around collaborative ideas of a desirable future.

## Notes

1 This chapter is based on a conference paper submitted to the 31st EGOS Colloquium, "Organizations and the examined life: Reason, reflexivity, and responsibility", Athens 2015 (Sub-theme 57: Responsible Leadership: Addressing Social, Environmental and Business Implications of Leadership). **Corresponding author:** Elke R. Fein, fein.elke@gmail.com.
2 See also Gary Hamel's statement that "the ideology of leadership and management that underpins large-scale human organizations today is as limiting to organizational success as the ideology of feudalism was limiting to economic success in the 16th and 17th centuries" (Hamel, quoted after Laloux 2014, p. 285).

## Bibliography

Arendt, H. (1960), *Vita Activa oder Vom tätigen Leben*, Kohlhammer, Stuttgart.

Atlee, T. (2003), *The Tao of Democracy. Using Co-intelligence to Create a World that Works for all*, The Writer's Collective, Cranston, RI.

Baldwin, J. Mark. (1895), *Mental Development of the Child and the Race*. Macmillan, London.

Baldwin, J. Mark. (1904), 'The Genetic Progression of Psychic Objects,' *Psychological Review*, vol. 11, pp. 216–221.

Baldwin, J. Mark. (1906), *Social and Ethical Interpretations in Mental Development*. Macmillan, New York.

Benefiel, M. (2005), *Soul at Work*. Veritas Publications, Dublin, IR.

Bohm, D. (1996), *On Dialog*. Routledge, New York.

Bolman, L. and Deal, T. (1995), *Leading With Soul. An Uncommon Journey of Spirit*. Jossey-Bass, San Francisco.

Brown, M.E. and Treviño, L.K. (2006), 'Ethical Leadership: A Review and Future Directions,' *The Leadership Quarterly*, vol. 17, pp. 595–616.

Carey, M.R. (1992), 'Transformational Leadership and the Fundamental Option for Self-Transcendence,' *The Leadership Quarterly*, vol. 3, no. 3, pp. 217–236.

Case, R. (1993), 'Theories of Learning and Theories of Development,' *Educational Psychologist*, vol. 28, no. 3, pp. 219–233.

Chatterjee, D. (1998), *Leading Consciously. A Pilgrimage Toward Self Mastery*. Butterworth-Heinemann, Boston.

Chopra, D. (2010), *The Soul of Leadership: Applying Spiritual Intelligence to Business and to Life*. Harmony/Random House, New York.

Ciulla, J. (1998), *Ethics. The Heart of Leadership*. Praeger, Westport, CT, London.

Commons, M.L., Ross, S.N. and Bresette, L.M. (2011), 'The Connection Between Postformal Thought, Stage Transition, Persistence, and Ambition and Major Scientific Innovations'. In Hoare, C. (ed.). *Oxford Handbook of Adult Development and Learning*. New York: Oxford University Press, 2nd Ed, pp. 287–301.

Commons, M.L. and Sonnert, G. (1994), 'Society and the Highest Stages of Moral Development,' *Politics and the Individual*, vol. 4, no. 1, pp. 31–55.

Commons, M.L., Trudeau, E.J., Stein, S.A., Richards, F.A. and Krause, S.R. (1998), 'Hierarchical Complexity of Tasks Shows the Existence of Developmental Stages,' *Developmental Review*, vol. 18, pp. 237–278.

Cook-Greuter, S. (1999), *Postautonomous Ego Development: A Study of its Nature and Measurement*. Harvard University, Boston, MA.

Cook-Greuter, S. (2005), *Ego Development. Nine Levels of Increasing Embrace*, Available from scookgreuter@ii.org.

Dawson, T.L. (2002), 'A Comparison of Three Developmental Stage Scoring Systems', *Journal of Applied Measurement*, vol. 3, no. 2, pp. 146–189.

Denis, J.L., Langley, A. and Sergi, V. (2012), 'Leadership in the Plural,' *The Academy of Management Annals*, vol. 6, no. 1, pp. 211–283.

Doh, J.P. and Stumpf, S.A. (eds.) (2005), *Handbook on Responsible Leadership and Governance in Global Business*. Edward Elgar, Cheltenham.

Drath, W., McCauley, C., Van Velsor, E., O'Connor, P. and McGuire, J. (2008), 'Direction, Alignment, Commitment: Toward a More Integrative Ontology of Leadership,' *Leadership Quarterly*, vol. 19, no. 6, pp. 635–653.

Fischer, K. (1980), 'A Theory of Cognitive Development: The Control and Construction of Hierarchies of Skills,' *Psychological Review*, vol. 87, pp. 477–531.

Fischer, K. and Bidell, T. (2006), 'Dynamic Development of Action, Thought, and Emotion'. In Damon, W. and Lerner, R. (eds.). *Handbook of Child Psychology: Theoretical Models of Human Development*. New York: Wiley, pp. 313–399.

Fletcher, J.K. (2004), 'The Paradox of Postheroic Leadership: An Essay on Gender, Power, and Transformational Change,' *Leadership Quarterly*, vol. 15, no. 5, pp. 647–661

Follet, M.P. (1924), *Creative Experience*. Longmans, Green, New York.

Freeman, R.E. and Auster, E.A. (2011), 'Values, Authenticity and Responsible Leadership,' *Journal of Business Ethics*, vol. 98, pp. 15–23.

George, B. (2003), *Authentic Leadership: Rediscovering the Secrets to Creating Lasting Value*. San Francisco, CA, Jossey-Bass.

Grint, K. (2005), 'Problems, Problems, Problems: The Social Construction of Leadership,' *Human Relations*, vol. 58, no. 11, pp. 1467–1494.

Heifetz, R.A. (1994), *Leadership Without Easy Answers*. The Belknap Press/Harvard UP, Cambridge/MA; London.

Jaques, E. (1997), *Requisite Organization: Total System for Effective Managerial Organization and Managerial Leadership for the 21st Century*. Gower, London.

Jaques, E., Clement, S.D. and Lessem, R. (1994), *Executive Leadership: A Practical Guide to Managing Complexity*. Blackwell Publishing, Oxford.

Joiner, B. and Josephs, S. (2007), *Leadership Agility: Mastering Core Competencies for Handling Change*. Jossey-Bass, San Francisco.

Kegan, R. (1979), 'The Evolving Self: A Process Conception for Ego Psychology,' *The Counseling Psychologist*, vol. 8, no. 2, 5–34.

Kegan, R. (1994), *In Over Our Heads. The Mental Demands of Modern Life*. Harvard University Press, Cambridge, MA.

Kegan, R. and Lahey, L. (2009), *Immunity to Change. How to Overcome It and Unlock Potential in Yourself and your Organization*. Harvard Business Press, Boston, MA.

Kegan, R., Lahey, L., Fleming, A., Miller, M. and Markus, I. (2014), Deliberately Developmental Organizations. Extended Whitepaper, Online. Available from http://www.waytogrowinc.com/#!resources/cfvf.

Kohlberg, L. (1973), 'The Claim to Moral Adequacy of a Highest Stage of Moral Judgment,' *Journal of Philosophy*, vol. 70, no. 18, pp. 630–646.

Kohlberg, L. (1981), *Essays on Moral Development, Vol. I: The Philosophy of Moral Development*. Harper & Row, San Francisco, CA.

Laloux, F. (2014), *Reinventing Organizations. A Guide to Creating Organizations Inspired by the Next Stage of Human Consciousness*. Nelson Parker, Brussels.

Litfin, K. (2003), 'Towards an Integral Perspective on World Politics: Secularism, Sovereignty and the Challenge of Global Ecology,' *Journal of International Studies*, vol. 32, no. 1, pp. 29–56.

Loevinger, J. (1976), *Ego Development: Concepts and Theories*. Jossey-Bass, San Francisco.

Maak, T. and Pless, N. (2006), 'Responsible Leadership in a Stakeholder Society: A Relational Perspective,' *Journal of Business Ethics*, vol. 66, no. 1, pp. 99–115.

Mascolo, M.F. and Fischer, K.W. (2010), 'The Dynamic Development of Thinking, Feeling, and Acting Over the Life Span'. In Overton, W.F. (ed.), *Biology, Cognition, and Methods across the Lifespan* (Vol. 1). Wiley, Hoboken, NJ, pp. 149–194

McCauley, C.D., Drath, W.H., Palus, C.J., O'Connor, P.M.G. and Baker, B.A. (2006), 'The Use of Constructive-developmental Theory to Advance the Understanding of Leadership,'. *The Leadership Quarterly*, vol. 17, pp. 634–653.

Mead, G.H. (1934), *Mind, Self, and Society*, University of Chicago Press, Chicago.

Meadows, D.H. (1972), *The Limits to Growth: A Report for The Club of Rome's Project on the Predicament of Mankind*, Universe Books, New York.

Miska, C., Hilbe, C. and Mayer, S. (2014), 'Reconciling Different Views on Responsible Leadership: A Rationality-based Approach,' *Journal of Business Ethics*, vol. 125, no. 2, pp. 349–360.

Muff, K. (2013), 'Developing Globally Responsible Leaders in Business Schools: A Vision and Transformational Practice for the Journey Ahead,' *Journal of Management Development*, vol. 32, no. 5, pp. 487–507.

Muff, K. (ed.) (2014), *The Collaboratory. A Co-creative Stakeholder Engagement Process for Solving Complex Problems*. Greenleaf Publishing, Sheffield.

Piaget, J. (1932), *Moral Judgment of the Child*. Free Press, New York.

Piaget, J. (1954), *The Construction of Reality in the Child*. Basic Books, New York.

Piaget, J. (1970), *Structuralism*, Trans. C. Maschler. Harper&Row, New York.

Pless, N. (2007), 'Understanding Responsible Leadership: Role Identity and Motivational Drivers,' *Journal of Business Ethics*, vol. 74, no. 4, pp. 437–456.

Pless, N.M., Maak, T. and Waldman, D.A. (2012), 'Different Approaches Toward Doing the Right Thing: Mapping the Responsibility Orientations of Leaders', *The Academy of Management Perspectives*, vol. 26, no. 4, pp. 51–65.

Putz, M. and Raynor, M. (2004), *Integral Leadership: Overcoming the Paradox of Growth*. Unpublished manuscript.

Rabbin, R. (1998), *Invisible Leadership: Igniting the Soul at Work*. Acropolis Books, Lakewood, CO.

Reams, J. (2005), 'What's Integral about Leadership? A Reflection on Leadership and Integral Theory,' *Integral Review*, vol. 1, pp. 118–132.

Reams, J. (2010), 'Leading the Future', *Futures*, vol. 42, pp. 1088–1093.

Reams, J. (2014), 'A Brief Overview of Developmental Theory, or What I Learned in the FOLA Course,' *Integral Review*, vol. 10, no. 1, pp. 122–152.

Robinson, O. (2013), *Development though Adulthood: An Integrative Sourcebook*. Palgrave Macmillan, New York.

Rooke, D. and Torbert, W.R. (1998), 'Organizational Transformation as a Function of CEO's Developmental Stage,' *Organizational Development Journal*, vol. 16, no. 1, pp. 11–28.

Rowson, J. (2008), *From Wisdom-Related Knowledge to Wise Acts: Refashioning the Conception of Wisdom to Improve Our Chances of Becoming Wiser*. PhD Thesis, University of Bristol, Bristol, UK.

Rowson, J. and Reams, J. (2015), 'Wisdom, Spirituality and the Virtuality of Self: An Interview with Jonathan Rowson,' *Integral Review*, vol. 11, no. 2, 79–102.

Scharmer, O. (2007), *Theory U: Leading from the Future as it Emerges*. The Society for Organizational Learning, Cambridge, MA.

Scharmer, O. and Kaeufer, K. (2013), *Leading From the Emerging Future. From Ego-System to Eco-System Economies. Applying Theory U to Transforming Business, Society, and Self*. Berett-Koehler, San Francisco.

Scherer, A.G. and Palazzo, G. (2011), 'The New Political Role of Business in a Globalized World: A Review of a New Perspective on CSR and its Implications for the Firm, Governance, and Democracy,' *Journal of Management Studies*, vol. 48, no. 4, pp. 899–931.

Senge, P.M. (1990), *The Fifth Discipline: The Art and Practice of the Learning Organization*. Currency, Doubleday.

Solomon, R.C. (1999), *A Better Way to Think about Business*. Oxford University Press, New York, Oxford.

Sonenshein, S. (2007), 'The Role of Construction, Intuition, and Justification in Responding to Ethical Issues at Work: The Sensemaking-intuition Model,' *The Academy of Management Review*, vol. 32, no. 4, pp. 1022–1040.

Torbert, W.R. & Associates (2004), *Action Inquiry: The Secret of Timely and Transforming Leadership*. Berrett-Kohler, San Franscisco.

Uhl-Bien, M. (2006), Relational Leadership Theory: Exploring the Social Processes of Leadership and Organizing. In: *The Leadership Quarterly*, vol. 17, no. 6, S. 654–676.

Van Dijk, G. (2014), *Organisational Ecology: Simplicity in Complexity*. Paper based on the inaugural lecture at the Tilburg University, March 21, 2014.

Varela, F. (1999), *Ethical Know-How: Action, Wisdom and Cognition*. Stanford University Press, Stanford.

Varela, F. and Scharmer, C.O. (2000), *Dialog on Leadership. The Three Gestures of Becoming Aware*. Available from http://www.iwp.jku.at/born/mpwfst/02/www.dialogonleadership.org/varelax2000.html.

Vincent, N., Ward, L. and Denson, L. (2015), 'Promoting Post-conventional Consciousness in Leaders: Australian Community Leadership Programs,' *The Leadership Quarterly*, vol. 26, pp. 238–253.

Voegtlin, C., Patzer, M. and Scherer, A.G. (2012), 'Responsible Leadership in Global Business: A New Approach to Leadership and its Multi-level Outcomes,' *Journal of Business Ethics*, vol. 105, pp. 1–16.

Vygotsky, L.S. (1978), *Mind in Society. The Development of Higher Psychological Processes*. Harvard University Press, Cambridge, MA.

Waldman, D.A. (2014), 'Bridging the Domains of Leadership and Corporate Social Responsibility. Chapter 25'. In Day, D. (ed.). *The Oxford Handbook of Leadership and Organizations* Oxford University Press, Oxford, pp. 539–555.

Waldman, D.A. and Balven, R.M. (2015), 'Symposium. Responsible Leadership: Theoretical Issues and Research Directions,' *The Academy of Management Perspectives*, vol. 29, no. 1, pp. 19–29.

Waldman, D.A. and Galvin, B.M. (2008), 'Alternative Perspectives of Responsible Leadership,' *Organizational Dynamics*, vol. 37, no. 4, pp. 327–341.

Waldman, D.A. and Siegel, D. (2008), 'Defining the Socially Responsible Leader,' *The Leadership Quarterly*, vol. 19, no. 1, pp. 117–131.

Waldman, D.A., Siegel, D.S. and Javidan, M. (2006), 'Components of CEO Transformational Leadership and Corporate Social Responsibility,' *Journal of Management Studies*, vol. 43, no. 8, pp. 1703–1725.

Wheatley, M. (1996), *Leadership and the New Science: Discovering Order in a Chaotic World*. Berrett-Koehler, San Francisco.

Wheatley, M. and Frieze, D. (2011), 'Leadership in the Age of Complexity: From Hero to Host,' *Resurgence Magazine*, Winter 2011, 1–5, [Online]. Available from http://www.margaretwheatley.com/articles/Leadership-in-Age-of-Complexity.pdf.

Wilber, K. (2000), *Integral Psychology. Consciousness, Spirit, Psychology, Therapy*. Shambhala, Boston, MA.

# Chapter 12

# Valuing corporate governance – a way out of the current impasse?

## Changing the leadership focus to behaviours and values rather than codes and compliance

*Bob Garratt*

## The current failures of corporate governance

"Corporate Governance" addresses an irresolvable dilemma for boards – how do we drive our organisation forward to ensure its continuing success whilst also ensuring that it is under prudent control? Boards of directors are ultimately responsible for the answer to both questions. Internationally, corporate governance is accepted as crucial in ensuring the leadership efficiency and effectiveness of all of our organisations – private, public and not-for-profit. This is because our organisations are the cement that holds modern societies together. Yet, after 25 years of lukewarm promotion by politicians, regulators and some business leaders the current concept of "corporate governance" is running aground in many of the world's leading countries. It is seen increasingly as merely a compliance tool leading only to risk-aversion and bounded by increasing bureaucratic and costly irrelevancies. Corporate governance in its currently accepted form is ineffective. If it is the cement of our society, why should this be so?

Why in a time of a deep international political and financial leadership crisis should so powerful a concept as corporate governance be discounted by so many directors, managers, politicians and the general public? I find this odd as my view is more positive. I see effective corporate governance rather as Portia saw her small candle – as "a shining light in a naughtie world"; a counter to the incompetence, ignorance and corruption that is undermining our organisations and societies. Matters are made worse by so few of those affected having any idea or language by which such reforms can be made.

With so many unconvinced of its effectiveness it is time to reconsider the essence of corporate governance and to create a new mind-set to restore its relevance and our long-term survival.

I argue that there is one main causes of the current problem and suggest a very different mind-set to resolve it.

## Corporate governance being sold by politicians as the silver bullet to an over-expectant, under-educated and gullible public

It is noticeable increasingly just how many times governmental, judicial and international agencies' reports on organisational failures strongly demand better corporate governance. This is true for business, the public sector, government and charities. Yet little effective action is then taken other than public wailing and increasing the number of regulations. This seems odd until one pauses to think about it more. Rather than repeat the increasingly frequent "something must be done on the governance front" mantra of the politicians, media and the public, deeper analysis reveals that little can be done for the simple reason that those making the most noise know little of what effective corporate governance means in practice. They rely increasingly on prescriptive regulations rather than go deeply into its societal cement function. It is similar to the anti-racism pressure groups who thought that by banning the offensive words this would stop offensive thoughts. This has not proved so in either case. Something deeper is needed. So the players affected retreat to a "don't blame me" position. But the pressures for something to be done continue. So the politicians use the only real weapon that they have and seek public approval by increasing legislation. They move from good intentions and public pressure to pushing the regulators first to produce Guidelines then Codes, then to increase the Codes until they achieve the Dogma of "comply or be found guilty" and ultimately through reducto ad absurdum to a zero sum game.

This is not a learning system as politicians do not increase their understanding of the issues but create a "them-and-us" culture. Regulators cannot try to solve deep human issues of behaviours and values by increasing the number of compliance codes. It is not just politicians and regulators that fall into this trap but the majority of owners who try to use structural interventions by board and executive changes to solve all too human problems. Sadly, too many directors do not see the societal need to develop consciously their care, skills and diligence to fulfil even their primary legal duties. These are rarely assessed or enforced. It is odd that the very legislators demanding compliance to the Codes are those that passed the more powerful primary laws that they do not then bother to enforce.

Each of the four main parties with responsibilities for effective corporate governance – owners, directors, legislators and regulators – then blames the others. This is unwise. Frustrations abound on all sides. And few actions are taken in any systematic manner by any party to learn how to resolve the erosion of the leadership of our organisations. So the whining, whimpering and buck-passing continues. Yet few can complain as they are so ill-educated in the ways of organisational and financial life that they cannot articulate their needs for a future improved system of corporate governance. Is there another way?

## Towards a future corporate governance system that builds on learning systems, human behaviours and values rather than increasing compliance

"Corporate Governance" only arose in the business mind following the UK's *1992 Cadbury Report on The Financial Aspects of Corporate Governance* (Cadbury 1992). Before that it was more an academic discipline made manifest by the publication of Bob Tricker's *Corporate Governance* (Tricker 1984). Since 1992 the Cadbury Report has become the international default document for anyone interested in the direction and control of businesses. It was a radical insight into a world previously hidden from the public, and many directors. It went well beyond its initial "financial aspects" remit to shed light on the roles of boards of directors and suggested structures and processes by which the outside world could begin to assess the performance and compliance of boards.

Yet it had two major limitations. Its main sponsors were the Institute of Accountants of England and Wales and the International Stock Exchange of London. Its major foci were, therefore, financial accountancy and audit, and only companies listing on the London Stock Exchange. Although these are powerful in the national economy they are only a fraction of the registered organisations that exist in the private, public and not-for-profit worlds. Subsequent unthinking acceptance of the Cadbury Code and its renewals by the majority of organisations in these sectors has led to many organisations trying to fit into increasingly inappropriate, onerous and complex compliance rules. It is always easy to grab at pre-digested food but it is rarely appropriate for specific dietary needs. At a time when the politicians are out to get the bankers and big business it is especially dangerous for other organisations to follow slavishly anything but the basic principles.

## Conduct, codes and national cultures

Easy acceptance of inappropriate structure and processes is nonsense for two reasons. First, The Cadbury Code was posited as a very British response in part to counter the development of US legal "extraterritoriality" imperialism – the concern was of the global imposition of US law and its fixation with rules and draconian penalties. The worry was that corporate governance could become globally a US lawyers' paradise with much litigation and an ever-increasing set of rules. It was, and is, a route to corporate bureaucracy and risk aversion with no guarantee of company success. The US system does not encourage discretion, explanation or risk-taking with the agreement of the owners. It is anti-liberal capitalism.

The UK argued for a more flexible *Principles-Based* Code than rigid US *Rules-Based* compliance. This reflected national cultures. The UK argued for the use of discretion by a board to suit its particular circumstances. If its actions were seen to be outside the governing code yet within the primary law, then the board must set this before the owners at an AGM or EGM and seek approval. This also had immediate attractions for non-listed companies in the UK and Commonwealth cultures. However, the UK Codes are moving into areas of management rather than directing, becoming increasingly prescriptive and rules-based egged on by politicians ignorant of corporate governance and organisational leadership. Worryingly they are being pushed into areas such as Remuneration, HR Policies and Culture where their prescriptions are against the very nature of a principles-based approach.

This is a consequence of the continuing pubic fury at the Western Economic Failure of 2008. Yet most directors are neither venal nor bankers and do not work in listed companies. We need a broader and more diversity-embracing approach towards effective corporate governance to restore public trust in corporate governance and organisational leadership as a national asset. This must involve human values and behaviours. It is beyond the world of accountants.

## Corporate governance and culture

It is worth noting that in the two nations, the UK and South Africa, seen to be most effectively advocating effective corporate governance the innovators focus on developing two distinct areas; *Stewardship* between the board and the owners and *culture* as a learning system. Much has been said about stewardship recently (Tomorrows Company 2011) so I want to focus on "culture" here. I argue strongly that this is not the territory of the regulators. It is the territory of our directors and managers to develop constructive and honest cultures, emotional temperatures, in their organisations. This requires consistent internal organisational rewards and behaviours, not external regulation.

In the 2014 *Developments in Corporate Governance and Stewardship*, published by the UK's Financial Reporting Council, the new chairman, Sir Win Bischoff, comments:

> *The governance of individual companies depends crucially on culture. Unfortunately we still see examples of governance failings. Boards have responsibility for shaping the culture, both within the boardroom and across the organisation as a whole and that requires constant vigilance. This is not an easy task. Our recent guidance on risk management highlighted the need for boards to think hard about assessing whether the culture practised within the company is in line with what they espouse. Boards should consider what assurance they have around culture. Are performance drivers and values consistent? How can culture be maintained under pressure and through change? Is the culture consistent throughout the business? We will be working to promote best practice in these areas during 2015.*

I think that asking such questions and asking individual organisations to respond is as far as a regulator can go. These are impossible areas to assess using most current business tools. Any attempt by regulators to specify and measure an organisation's culture will likely lead to more rules, risk-aversion and ineffective compliance. This is happening already in the Risk Assessment areas. Rather organisations need to develop transparent systems of assessment, rapid feedback for the owners' scrutiny and have processes for both development and sanctions to grow their unique culture.

Do such tools exist? Yes, but they are not considered "normal" business tools. They are interdisciplinary and involve psychology and anthropology which are currently beyond the syllabus of traditional business schools. We have to look to these "soft" and "wimpish" areas like social psychology, board dynamics and culture to get help. But many directors and managers see themselves as "hard" and macho and so have an inbuilt aversion to such disciplines. More fool them. If they dipped a toe in the water they would see quickly that the concepts of the short-term "emotional climate" of an organisation and the subsequent development of its long-term "culture" are key measures of current organisational health and the development of *continuing* success. So boards need to track their trends over time. This is invaluable information for directors and managers. Yet they rarely have it. So they often pontificate on the necessity of developing and changing culture without have any experience of so doing.

## A hierarchy of culture

What is the framework within which it is possible to develop such measures? I argue that it is necessary for any leader to understand a simple, five-level hierarchy that ranges from instantly observable *behaviours* to deeply held, and often unconscious, *beliefs*:

Behaviours
Opinions
Attitudes
Values
Beliefs

Social psychology, especially group dynamics and its analytical tools, is helpful in measuring and understanding the more visible levels of Behaviours, Opinions and Attitudes. Anthropology – *the study of man, his origins, institutions, religious beliefs and social relationships* – analyses the less visible Values and Beliefs often at an intensely personal level. Beliefs are the anchors of an individual's life. That is why, especially if held unconsciously, they are so difficult to change. Aggregated they form the organisation's culture.

We know this in day-to-day organisational life. "Culture" is often flippantly described as "the way we do things around here" or, more alarmingly for board members, "what we do when no-one is looking". Most boards only discover the latter when there is a crisis, by which time it is often too late. There are many tools available, particularly rigorous and well-designed emotional climate surveys which can be tracked over time by boards and top management to warn of visible and invisible values blockages. Yet they rarely form part of a board's dashboard. So insidious behaviours and values often erode the organisation's espoused values.

A "value" is a belief in action. It defines a moral principal in which a person believes. Reward systems are rarely created with measurable emotional climates and values in mind. Indeed in most businesses "value" has a primarily financial meaning rather than as a moral belief. In many organisations "value" tends to be much more closely related only to accountancy practice rather than anthropological analysis. Yet the tools to avert this reductionist stand-off exist and I argue should be part of any future director's kitbag. From the board's viewpoint a more anthropological understanding of their organisation's Values and Beliefs will improve their leadership effectiveness greatly.

This will be resisted by the macho many. It amazes me still how many directors see their organisations as purely impersonal and mechanical with simple and guaranteed command-and-obey linkages and processes. This defies reality. I have worked with so many organisations of all types where both the Chairman and Chief Executive have admitted privately that "when I pull the levers of power I have no idea if they are connected". Feedback mechanisms are slow. Learning is slower. Messages passing upwards are modified to protect the incompetent or guilty and organisational learning is either non-existent or negative. The rate of organisational learning is not equal to, or greater than, the rate of environmental change to ensure the continuing success of the organisation.

As the Board is the only body charged legally with the oversight and leadership of the total organisation it is crucial for the directors to transcend their inbuilt managerial/operational mind-set to understand the positive and negative dynamics of the "culture" that they have created. When working with a board I have found a quotation from

Clifford Geertz (1973) immensely powerful to study and then work with, even though they often find the words hard initially:

> *Culture is an historically transmitted pattern of meaning embodied in symbols; a series of inherited conceptions expressed in symbolic forms by means of which men communicate, perpetuate, and develop their knowledge about and attitudes towards life . . . Man is an animal suspended in webs of signification he himself has spun. I take culture to be those webs, and the analysis of it to be therefore not an experimental science in search of law, but an interpretive one in search of meaning.*

This is very practical, if taken in bite-sized chunks. And if you don't like the intellectual language then just go to any company reception area, look and listen. The way in which you are greeted, the colours and shapes of the space and the general posture of those employed tells you all you need to know about the emotional climate of that organisation. When this is repeated constantly throughout the organisation it becomes their symbolic Values which over time determine their behaviours and inevitably shape their long-term Culture. It tells you what you can, and cannot, do in this organisation, who gets rewarded and who punished, who stays and who goes.

## The value of values

I was taught that the basic moral values of effective leadership and, so, of Corporate Governance, are Accountability, Probity and Transparency. These are the building blocks of leadership and corporate governance. They are measurable in both personal and organisational terms. So trends can be tracked over time to see the emergent patterns and dimensions of an organisation's developing culture. The Abrahamic religions of Judaism. Christianity and Islam may dispute many things but their underlying moral values have been similar and clear for millennia. Starting with *Thou shalt not kill* these are made manifest in, for example, the Seven Deadly Sins and their opposite, The Seven Virtues:

| Greed | vs | Charity |
|-------|-----|------------|
| Lust | vs | Chastity |
| Gluttony | vs | Temperance |
| Sloth | vs | Diligence |
| Wrath | vs | Patience |
| Fury | vs | Kindness |
| Pride | vs | Humility |

My worry is that as business regulators try and extend their territory into "Culture" they have not read Geertz or anyone like him. What is worse is that they will ask some soulless bureaucrats or committee to create a Code that specifies the clauses and subsets by which moral values can be beaten into a compliance code. I argue that we do not need a code, just ways of ensuring full implementation of these millennia-tested values.

We even have values built into our primary law but few seem to be aware of know this, including the regulators. The UK's 2006 Companies Act listed the Seven Basic Duties of a director:

1 To act within their powers (constitution)
2 To promote the success of their company
3 To exercise independent judgement
4 To exercise reasonable care, skill and diligence
5 To avoid conflicts of interest
6 Not to accept benefits from third parties
7 To declare interests in proposed transactions.

If the politicians and regulators ensured a climate of self-enforcement of these well-tested behaviours and values we would not need increasingly dense Codes that battle against human nature and enterprise.

## What do Alan Greenspan and Gillian Tett have in common?

In this essay I have argued that the four major players of corporate governance – the boards, owners, regulators and legislators do not act as an integrated system of learning on behalf of the nation. There is little oversight of each of them and none see themselves as a key to developing effective national leadership as an asset to stabilise and develop our society. The solutions to designing such a learning system would need another essay to espouse.

Here I want to look at the current continuing failures of moral purpose and values seen following the 2008 Western Financial Crisis. In so many nations there are many examples of leadership inadequacies in the media, courts, politicians, boards, the police, health managers, local government and charities. And those are only examples that I have taken from the last two days' UK newspapers.

What on earth went so wrong that the social revolution of the Swinging Sixties gave way to the Corrupt Noughties leading to the Austerity Era and the rise of public fear, growing authoritarianism and terrorism? I argue strongly that it was a lack of understanding of the moral purpose of organisations combined with a lack of personal courage to say "no" to corrupting pressures which allowed two attitudes to affect our Western world. First, that it is wrong to query any action on moral grounds. So challenges ranging from the support of the Paedophile Exchange to the IRA or ISIS were made socially non-discussable. This was reinforced strongly by the rise of "politically correct" language with the expectation that banning certain words in public would guarantee that enduring public problems would be erased. The opposite is happening and the consequent lack of public debate is eroding the social cement, the explicit values and behaviours, which held our organisations, family and personal mental health together.

Second, such international dynamics as the financial "Big Bang" changed our perceptions of what are acceptable behaviours and values in our organisations. Many employees and some managers saw them already as impersonal machines or psychic prisons. Now they were free to see them also as personal financial aggrandisement vehicles where you took what you could grab and devil take the hindmost. Effective corporate governance went out of the window eroded by greed, lust and gluttony. Executive remuneration soared despite rewarding the majority for mediocre performance at best. Such thinking was backed, especially in financial services, by the rise of impersonal digital technology so that "players" could "game" the system instantly and without concern for the effect on others. This is the realm of psychopaths.

I had not realised quite how bad things were until I read *the Map And the Territory* (2013), the memoire of Alan Greenspan, previously the Chairman of the US Federal Bank and so one of the most powerful people in the world – The Master of the Masters of the Universe.

It makes you weep that such power was wielded in such a narrow and inhuman way. In the book and subsequent interviews when asked why such a global financial crash happened his answer is "our models did not work. We had 250 PhDs working on them and they were tuned to the neo-classical economic concept that markets will always return to equilibrium given time". When they did not, and with the global financial system crashing around them, no-one really knew what to do because we had not factored in two powers which were then spooking the markets. First, was the nature and speed of market dynamics (sic) and second was "people" and their unpredictable emotions (even "sic-er"). It is mind boggling that the human and emotional aspects of our wealth and existence had not been seriously considered important enough to be in The Model. They did not consider seriously the powerful driving emotions of greed and fear in people. When this was then transmitted through instantaneous global communication systems we all suffered and continue to suffer the results. We are now poorer but not much wiser as our leaders have not yet shown the contrition to the public that they need to gain their forgiveness to be able to create the new emotional climate in which to learn. Reputations were rubbished and neo-classical economics, especially macro-economics, has suffered a continuing nervous breakdown. Behavioural economics and "nudging" is the new hot trend.

What has this to do with Gillian Tett (2013), US Editor of the *Financial Times*? She is a trained anthropologist and her regular writings demonstrate this rigorously. She is very helpful on organisational and moral purpose. She wrote a devastatingly insightful interview of Alan Greenspan and his book (Greenspan 2013). He was marginally contrite but did admit that he now needed in retirement to study a discipline the importance of which had previously eluded him – anthropology! He needed to know much more about people and their values. He has enrolled to do so. Is this a way forward for leadership and effective corporate governance where we all spend less time on Codes and more on understanding human nature, beliefs, enterprise and their effects on the dynamics of markets? I hope so.

## Bibliography

Cadbury, A. (1992), *The Financial Aspects of Corporate Governance*. The Cadbury Committee Report. Gee & Co, London.

*Developments in Corporate Governance and Stewardship* (2014), UK Financial Reporting Council, London. Available from https://www.frc.org.uk/Our-Work/Publications/Corporate-Governance/Developments-in-Corporate-Governance-and-Stewardsh.pdf.

Geertz, Clifford (1973), *The Interpretation of Cultures*. Basic Books, New York.

Greenspan, Alan (2013), *The Map and the Territory: Risk, Human Nature and the Future of Forecasting*. Allen Lane, New York.

Tett, Gillian (2013), 'An Interview with Alan Greenspan', *The Financial Times Weekend Magazine*, October 25. Available from http://www.ft.com/intl/cms/s/2/25ebae9e-3c3a-11e3-b85f-00144feab7de.html.

Tricker, R.I. (1984), *Corporate Governance*. Oxford: Oxford University Press.

Tomorrow's Company (2011), *Why Stewardship Matters*, Tomorrow's Company Limited, London. Available at: tomorrowscompany.com/why-stewardship-matters-pdf.

# Chapter 13

# Defining and achieving good governance

*Shann Turnbull*

## 1 Introduction

The purpose of this chapter is to identify how some widely accepted governance practices are not necessarily consistent with the objectives of good governance. One reason for this inconsistency is that there is little agreement as to what are the objectives of generic good governance, be it in the public, private or non-profit sectors. The objective of good governance suggested for all sectors in this chapter is the ability of an organization to further its purpose for its existence without imposing costs, harms and risks on society while acting equitably and ethically. In this way Corporate Social Responsibilities (CSRs) become integrated into corporate governance while minimizing the extent, cost and need for government laws, regulations, regulators, legal actions and codes (Turnbull 2014d).

However, many laws, regulations and codes accepted, promoted and even imposed by some regulators and governance-rating agencies include unethical counter productive conflicts of interests. Examples are identified with suggestions on how corporate constitutions could be amended to remove and/or ethically manage commonly accepted problems on a creditable basis by separating governance powers from management. A separation of powers facilitates stakeholder engagement to obtain feedback and correction on any costs, harms and risks introduced by the organization while obtaining intelligence for achieving operating benefits with good governance (Turnbull 2014b).

A fundamental problem is that regulators, governance rating agencies and experts who formulate governance codes have not articulated the objectives of generic good governance. Without an objective of where you want to be it does not matter where you head. As a result practices have been introduced that are assumed to promote good governance are neither supported by theory or compelling empirical evidence. On the other hand empirical evidence, common sense or the "science of governance" (Turnbull 2002b; 2008a; 2012) provides evidence why many current practices promoted as good governance have been the cause of unethical behavior, fraud, financial losses and firm failures.

Good governance described in this chapter requires organizations to further their self-governance (Turnbull 2014a). Self-governance is ubiquitous in nature to allow creatures with little intelligence to reproduce in dynamic, complex unknowable environments. This chapter describes how the laws of nature can be used to design the constitutions of organizations to follow the compelling success of simple creatures (Turnbull 2007, 2013c, 2014d).

However, the theory and practices of self-regulation is poorly recognized by social scientists including economists and lawyers who populate regulatory authorities and advise legislators. Legislators with knowledge of the science of control and communication, described as "cybernetics" (Weiner 1948), or those with common sense are required to become involved to provide direction and leadership for furthering the common good by reforming corporate governance practices. The involvement of such individuals is assumed to be required because unethical counter productive practices have become so widely accepted by governance experts, rating agencies and entrenched in codes and even laws (Romano 2004).

Governance is fundamentally concerned about the exercise of power. But as noted in Lord Acton's dictum: "All power, corrupts and absolute power corrupts absolutely". The solution to the corruption of absolute power is a division of power to introduce checks and balances. Modern nation states typically introduce a division of power in their constitutions. However, few democracies require these principles to also be embedded into the constitutions of organizations be they in the public, private or non-profit sectors.

To provide a focus for analysis this chapter limits its discussion to the constitutional architecture of Publicly Traded Corporations (PTCs). Reform of public sector organizations is considered in Turnbull (1994, 1995) and non-profit organizations in Turnbull (2013b).

However, firms that are not PTCs need to be considered to provide evidence on how a separation of powers into two or more boards can provide competitive advantages. The term "Compound Board" will be used to describe: "Two or more control centres, whether or not they are required by law, the constitution of the firm or are created by relationships external to the firm" (Turnbull 2000c, p. 27). Compound boards create "network governance" (Turnbull 2000c, p. 76).

A global survey of stakeholder-controlled firms indicated that without exception, network governance was a condition for their ability to survive and thrive over generations of managers (Bernstein 1980). The existence of network-governed firms in many jurisdictions around the world provides evidence that no changes in law are required to introduce compound boards. High profile examples that possess over a hundred boards are the John Lewis Partnership in the UK, the Mondragón Corporation Cooperativa (MCC) in Spain and VISA Inc in the US from its formation in 1970 until it became a PLC in 2008.

In some jurisdictions, PLCs may be required to possess three of more boards (Analytica 1992). These "control centres" could include a Supervisory and an Audit Board elected by shareholders, a Works Council elected by employees, and an Executive Board appointed by the Supervisory Board. As a major shareholder is a "control centre" of a firm and is "created by relationships external to the firm" they become part of a compound board. La Porta et al. (1999) found that "relatively few firms" around the world did not have a major shareholder. The surprising result is that the phenomenon of compound boards is a global norm rather than an exception.

Not surprising is how suppliers of finance form a compound board as a condition of their providing funds. Venture Capitalists (VCs) typically require a shareholder agreement to transfer a number of governance power to them like the appointment and remuneration of directors, appointment and control of the auditor, strategic direction of the business including major capital investment, the payment of dividends, etc.

Similar requirements are introduced by Leverage Buyout Organizations (LBOs) that Jensen (1993, p. 869) states represent "a proven model of governance structure". Loan agreements with bankers also introduce, but to a lesser degree, the sharing of power to create a compound board.

Major shareholders can act in a similar way to a supervisory board that appoints the executive board and auditor, determines the remuneration of both, and the strategic direction of the firm. However, English-speaking scholars have under-researched the phenomenon of multiple boards because it is considered to be a feature restricted to Europe.

Research has also been limited because a methodology for analyzing complex organizational forms is not well known. The methodology described as "Transaction Byte Analysis" (TBA) subsumes "Transaction Cost Economics" (TCE) developed by Williamson (1985). This is achieved by replacing the social construct of cost in TCE that is used as the unit of analysis with perturbations in nature described as "bytes" (Turnbull 2000c, Table 7.1). As a result the operating and/or competitive advantages of compound boards has been little understood. Besides introducing checks and balances, network governance also introduces the decomposition of decision-making labor to improve the management of complexity. TBA provides a basis to explain what Clarke (2010) describes as the "Recurring crises in Anglo-American Corporate Governance".

Evidence of a systemic deficiency in Anglophone corporate governance is that "one company in two in the S&P 500 index of America's most valuable listed firms has had a big activist fund on its share register" (*The Economist* 2015, p. 9). *The Economist* goes on to say that: "activists fill a governance void that afflicts today's public companies". Private equity funds and activist shareholders have invested over $100 billion to fill the void created by directors obtaining excessive powers not subject to meaningful review. This indicates how significant wealth could be added to the economy by the checks and balances introduced by network governance. Network governance would also introduce additional benefits by reducing the cost regulation discussed later.

Compound boards create a more economic, effective, efficient, timely and sensitive way to systemically fill the governance void with counter balancing influences. Network governance replaces the expensive and problematic competition for corporate control through stock markets with competition for power within the firm as described by writers like Bernstein (1978), Dallas (1997), Guthrie and Turnbull (1995), Jensen (1993), Hatherly (1995), Pound (1992; 1993a, b), Tricker (1980) and Turnbull (2000a, b, c; 2002a; 2013a, b, c; 2014a, b, c, d, e).

Financial institutions have provided the focus of the crises in Anglo-American corporate governance. It is these large systemically important financial institutions in the UK and the US that lack a major shareholder to provide oversight to introduce checks and balances. However, regulators seem blind to the problem of PLCs directors possessing absolute power to corrupt themselves and their business with serious harms imposed on the economy both locally and internationally. It would seem that regulators either lack the common sense of Lord Acton for the need to avoid concentrated power to mitigate corporate excesses, hubris, mistakes, fraud, unethical, or reckless behavior. One is forced to conclude that UK and US regulators have allowed their common sense to be overwhelmed by a belief that compliance to so called "good" corporate governance practices provides adequate safeguards.

It is for this reason that this chapter recommends that the common sense of legislators be involved to force reform of current views of so called "good governance" in English speaking jurisdictions. Evidence is provided below that compliance to so-called "good governance" practices could well contribute to, rather than inhibit, corporate excesses, hubris, mistakes, fraud, unethical or reckless behavior.

Economists Shleifer and Vishny (1997, p. 2) defined corporate governance as "the ways in which suppliers of finance to corporations assure themselves of getting a return on their investment". This statement is only relevant when the "suppliers of finance" cited above require the sharing of power. The Shleifer and Vishny definition is not appropriate for financial institutions or PLCs generally when they become self-financing. As outlined in the next section the Shleifer and Vishny view is not supported by history of how current corporate governance practices evolved.

The third section reviews systemic director conflicts. Defining good governance and its competitive advantages are considered in the fourth section. Some of the natural laws of governance are outlined in section five followed by concluding remarks.

## 2  How did "good governance" practices become toxic?

This section reviews the evolution of corporate governance over recent centuries. It reveals how some practices that were developed to further private interests in the US or the UK were exchanged between jurisdictions to produce unintended negative consequences. Company directors and regulators initiated the problems, not "suppliers of finance".

One result is that corporate governance laws, regulations and codes failed to prevent the Global Financial Crisis of 2008. The US Government *Financial Crisis Inquiry Report* (FCIR 2011, p. xviii) concluded "dramatic failures of corporate governance and risk management at many systemically important financial institutions were a key cause of this crisis". Yet the 57 US banking institutions that required government assistance were more compliant with governance standards than other firms (Adams 2012). The *UK Parliamentary Commission into Banking Standards Report* (PCBSR 2013, p. 142) reported that the regulator "was not so much the dog that did not bark as a dog barking up the wrong tree". The inconvenient truth is that many practices accepted or enforced by regulators create toxic problems – rather than providing solutions.

It is inconvenient because it undermines many powerful reputations.[1] It also undermines much of the lucrative and extensive corporate governance compliance industry developed since the Cadbury Report of 1992 as reported by Rose (2006).

The Cadbury recommendations promoted conflicted unethical relationships between directors and auditors that were identified two years earlier in a House of Lords judgment (Caparo 1990).[2] The conflicts arose from Cadbury recommending the US practice of forming audit committees of directors instead of *shareholders*. US audit committees developed in the 1920s when stock exchanges did not even require firms to publish a balance sheet (O'Connor 2004, p. 40). US audit committees were formed to protect directors not investors (Guthrie and Turnbull 1995, Turnbull 2008b).

In the 1920s directors became personally liable for corporate liabilities if management did not use the cash obtained from lenders in ways approved by the lender. This led directors to hire a public accountant to check if management had used borrowed funds according to the loan agreement. The task was much simpler than auditing company accounts required today.

In the Caparo case, Lord Justice Oliver stated that the purpose of an external auditor was:

> . . . to provide shareholders with reliable intelligence for the purpose of enabling them to scrutinise the conduct of the company's affairs and to exercise their collective powers to reward or control or remove those to whom that conduct has been confided.
>
> (Caparo 1990, p. 17)

The Caparo case determined that UK audits were not prepared for investors but for members of a company to carry out their *governance* functions. Members of UK companies may have their liabilities limited by guarantee or by shares. However, in the US audits are not undertaken for shareholders but for *investors*. When the SEC was established in 1933 its initial concerns were limited to the issue of *new* shares across state borders. Quite reasonably the US followed the 1929 UK prospectus practice for *new* issues of shares where the auditor is appointed by the directors and reports to the directors (O'Connor 2004, p. 51).

However, the statutory auditor arrangements in the UK, Australia and some other former colonies are quire different. The auditor is appointed by shareholders to report to shareholders – not the directors as in the US. Unfortunately the SEC Act of 1934 for *existing* shareholders inappropriately followed the UK practice for *new* share issues. As all four leading global audit firms are based in the US they have inappropriately insinuated the toxic US practice on the rest of the world. It is toxic because auditor becomes a paid agent of directors whose accounts he or she is judging. This unethical relationship creates a conflict for both the judge and those being judged a discussed below citing: Bazerman et al. (1997); Caparo (1990, p. 11); Hatherly (1995); Hayward (2003); O'Connor (2004, p. 62); Page (2009); Romano (2004); Shapiro (2004) & Turnbull (2008b).

Auditing by UK shareholders was first prescribed in the Company Clauses Act of 1846. The government paid a shareholder to act as the auditor and then invoiced the company to recover their cost (O'Connor 2004, p. 14). The UK audit cannot be for economic reasons as the law applies also to corporations without shares whose liabilities are limited by the guarantee of its members.

The UK 1862 Company Act published a model optional corporate constitution that established a *shareholder* audit committee as found in some European jurisdictions today.[3] At that time many companies were family controlled with family members on the board. So it is understandable why families with impeccable reputations like those of Sir Adrian Cadbury would consider it was not the directors that an external auditor needed "to scrutinise" but just their managers like in the US.

However, company law requires directors to avoid conflicts of interest. As auditors are appointed to judge if the directors' accounts are true and fair, a toxic systemic unethical conflict of interest is created when those being judged control the judge. No law court judge could accept such a conflict. As pointed out by Shapiro (2004), those "who pay the auditor call the tune". As all directors are being judged it makes no difference if some are described as "independent".

However, accounting standards allow auditors to attest when they co-sign the directors' accounts that they are "independent". But if the ordinary meaning of the word "independent" were applied it would represent a lie. That audits are "not independent at all" has been confirmed by a former big four UK audit partner (Hayward 2003). Bazerman et al. (1997) have pointed out "The impossibility of auditor independence". O'Connor (2004, p. 62) states:

> Thus, the American accountant/auditor is placed in the untenable position of the agent serving many masters with conflicting interests. In such an imbroglio, is it any wonder that the group who hires, fires, and sets compensation for the auditor becomes the *de facto* client?

"Agents cannot successfully serve two principals with potentially adverse interests" (O'Connor 2004, p. 3). The purpose of having an audit is because of the possibility that the interests of directors are different from those of the shareholders as noted by Lord Bridge cited in footnote 2. Milgram (1974) first identified the general nature of this problem of "good people" doing bad things, even like torture and genocide from peer group pressures.

The Sarbanes Oxley Act (SOX) makes legal directors having counterproductive conflicts in controlling the external auditors. SOX was described as "Quack Corporate Governance" by Romano (2004) who stated:

> The learning of the literature, which was available when Congress was legislating, is that SOX's corporate governance provisions were ill-conceived. The political environment explains why Congress would enact legislation with such mismatched means and ends.

UK regulators have forced directors of UK banks and their auditors to accept this counterproductive unethical relationship. This is inconsistent with the ethical aims of the UK Financial Conduct Authority and Australian regulators.

## 3 Systemic director conflicts

Directors who form board nomination and remuneration committees also become exposed to the conflict of being involved directly or indirectly with their own nomination and remuneration. Describing some directors as "independent" does not remove the conflict of influence and loyalty to each other sitting around the same board table. It explains the unconscious bias reported by Page (2009). Dallas (1988) explained how boards form "power coalitions" and the systemic conflicts of directors (Dallas 1997).

So-called "independent" NEDs have also been shown to be impotent from preventing expropriation of value from the company in a number of corporate failures (Coffee 2005). Bhagat and Black (2002) found no correlation between board independence and long-term firm performance with Swan and Forsberg (2014) reporting that independent directors "destroy corporate value".

The findings of Swan and Forsberg are consistent with Bhagat and Black (2002) who reported: "We find evidence that low-profitability firms increase the independence of their boards of directors". One reason is that CEOs promote board renewals so there is a loss of board memory of CEO shortcomings. Clarke (2006) pointed out the lack of both theory and empirical evidence supporting the appointment of non-management directors to boards and audit committees, while Rodrigues (2007) noted: "The fetishization of independence".

It would seem that governments and their regulators have been captured by the corporate governance industry. Governments have exacerbated this problem by appointing industry experts to advise them. In addition governments are subjected to the lobbying of professional bodies that represent the interest of practitioners. Directors and rating agencies find the research and analysis of scholars inconvenient in promoting their power, status, influence and income.

The conduct of Annual General Meetings (AGMs) is another example of the ubiquitous mindless blindness of regulators and directors to unethical behavior. Unethical conflicts arise when a director chairs an AGM. This is because the purpose of holding an AGM is for directors to present their accounts to shareholders and become accountable to them. However, shareholders may find it difficult if not impossible to hold directors to account if a director controls the meeting. The chair has the power to control which shareholder can speak and for how long. Corporate constitutions may specify that the chair of directors chair shareholder meetings. This demonstrates how stock exchanges and regulators who seek to promote ethical standards have accepted unethical practices.

If regulators or directors wanted to be seen to act ethically and remove the above-mentioned systemic conflicts of interests they would require PTC to amend corporate constitutions. One approach would be for shareholders to elect two boards as suggested by Tricker (1980) and Dallas (1988, 1997) or as practiced in a number of non-English speaking firms around the world surveyed by Turnbull (2000c, pp. 141–173).

A basic approach for shareholders to consider in introducing two boards to create a constructive division of powers is illustrated in Figure 13.1. One board is to manage the business and the other to govern the corporation. This separation of powers is commonly introduced as a condition for providing finance by venture capitalists and bankers. It eliminates directors having absolute power to identify and manage their own conflicts of interest. It removes the power of directors to corrupt themselves and the business absolutely. It also provides a creditable basis for managing any residual conflicts that may arise from non-systemic operational conflicts arising from related party transactions.

While a European supervisory board separates some governance powers from those of management the conflicts remain because the management board is accountable to the governing supervisory board rather than being separately elected and accountable to shareholders. When shareholders appoint both boards different voting methods can be introduced to protect minority interests as well as provide additional checks and balances on power coalitions.

To protect minority shareholders in an Australian start up company I founded, I introduced cumulative voting to elect directors and one vote per investor to elect governors (Turnbull 2000a). Cumulative voting allowed our US investors to appoint up to 20% of the directors. Instead of being an impotent minority they could privately inform the governance board to exercise its veto power for any unauthorized board

Separation of governance powers from management allows independent bottom-up
and outside-in stakeholder intelligence to integrate governance into CSR management

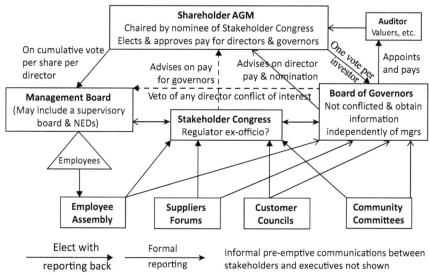

*Figure 13.1*  Generic Illustration of Network Governance

conflicts or other irregularities. This provided sufficient comfort for US investors to
contribute funds to a company controlled by Australians!

If minority shareholders had controlled the statutory audit board of Parmalat, its
accounting fraud might well have been discovered before the company became bank-
rupt in 2003. The fraud was not prevented because the CEO was a major shareholder
who controlled both the audit board and the supervisory board (Melis 2004).

Corporate Governance is fundamentally about power. Corporate constitutions create a contract between shareholders and directors to specify how corporate power is
organized. Regulators are irresponsible in allowing directors to obtain absolute power
to corrupt themselves, their business and so the well being of stakeholders. Regulator
irresponsibility is especially egregious with banks that can put the financial system and
the real economy at risk.

Most crucially, regulators, governance experts, practitioners and many academics
are in denial that Anglo governance practices are unethical and counter productive.
Yet as noted earlier a "key cause" of the 2008 financial crisis was a "dramatic failure
of corporate governance". Such "dramatic failures" did not arise because financial
institutions did not comply with what is thought to be best practice but because they
did. There are many other examples like Enron, Lehman and UK Banks failing with
so-called "good" governance.

Rather than admit that current governance codes and practices are unethically conflicted, regulators, practitioners and some academics are blaming the culture of individuals. Regulators have now obtained powers to regulate the illusive concept of culture
by requiring directors to be "fit and proper persons". However, it is the culture of

regulators that is the principle problem. It has created collective mindless blindness to recognising the unethical conflicted self-serving relationships in the firms they regulate.

Culture of firms being regulated is only a second order problem. The first order problem is to change corporate constitutions to remove systemic toxic conflicts of interest. This would lead the way for establishing more efficient, productive, self-governing and sustainable firms. It would also reduce the cost of regulation and enrich democracy (Turnbull 2013a). A basis would be established for introducing "Good Governance" as is next considered.

## 4 Defining good governance and its competitive advantages

A simply way to define good governance for any type of private, public or non-profit organization is: "Do no harm and act ethically". In the eighteenth century US charters of firms that did harm were cancelled (Grossman and Adams 1993). This was at a time when charters were only given for 20 years or less. The benefit of recapitalizing firms on a regular basis with "Time Limited Corporations" (Turnbull 1973) is to systematise "creative destruction" (Schumpeter 1976). An important result is that it makes executives continuously accountable to their investors.[4] Among other advantages it makes capital markets more efficient (Turnbull 2000b).

The above simple definition of good governance can be expanded to provide guidelines on how to design the governance architecture of organizations. The requirement "to do no harm" requires the organization not to incur costs for taxpayers in their regulation. These costs arise from the need for governments to establish laws, regulations, regulators and a legal system to protect citizens from harms and risks that organizations may introduce.

Good governance then depends upon organizations maximizing their ability to become self-governing (Turnbull 2014a) while imposing no costs, harms of risks on society while acting ethically and equitably in furthering the reason for their existence. To achieve this objective the governance architecture of organizations needs be designed to engage with any citizen who could be harmed or put at risk by its activities. As more organizations adopted good governance the cost and size of government would be reduced. More and more citizens would be able to become engaged in the governance of organizations that may affect them. Good governance would enrich democracy while protecting and furthering the interests of citizens.

The proliferation and continual failure of corporate governance laws, regulations, regulators and codes of practice, as discussed above, provides evidence that current practices are not achieving good governance. Good governance requires citizens who may be exposed to harms and risks to be included in the governance of the organization. Citizens then obtain the incentive to provide feedback to inform directors and their managers of not only their concerns but also to provide business intelligence for obtaining operating advantages. For example researchers have discovered that in some industries around 90% of innovations are obtained from customers rather than the Research & Development unit of a firm (Hipple 1994).

In addition, the involvement of stakeholders in the governance of firms can provide directors and other monitors such as governors included in Figure 13.1 with feedback information, independent of management, to cross check information provided by management. Without such independent feedback directors cannot possess a creditable way to carry out their fundamental fiduciary duty to monitor executives on a systematic basis. Without stakeholder feedback firms may not become aware if they are doing "harm".

However, it may not be in the interest of employees alone to report negative community impacts of the business, especially if they could be held responsible and/or it could diminish their ability to further their careers. Wider stakeholder engagement in corporate governance becomes essential for firms to achieve good governance. Importantly it also provides a way to integrate Corporate Social Responsibility (CSR) into corporate governance (Turnbull 2014b).

However, it makes no sense to include stakeholders on a management board of a firm. A board accountable to everyone becomes accountable to no one. It was for this reason that the advice of Porter (1992, p. 17) was ignored when he recommended that US corporations should: "Nominate significant owners, customers, suppliers, employees, and community representatives to the board of directors". However, the Porter analysis provides compelling evidence for corporate charters to formally include operational stakeholders in the governance architecture of firms to obtain competitive advantages. How this might be constructively achieved is illustrated in Figure 13.1. The firms cited in the introduction that possessed hundreds of boards indicates the legal possibility of introducing a division of powers with multiple boards that can also facilitate diverse types of stakeholder participation. Their existence also provides evidence of the competitive advantages of network governance over generations of managers. Instead of complicating the role of executives and requiring more executive time coordinating the various decision-making centers, the opposite occurs. While the governance architecture is more complicated the counter-intuitive outcome is that it can allow the role of each executive to be greatly simplified. This is illustrated by comparing the data processing load of directors of a firm governed by a single board with one governed by a network of boards as summarized in Table 13.1 reproduced from Turnbull (2000c: Figure 3). Another example is Visa International Inc. created with hundreds of boards within the one business entity. The founding CEO Dee Hock (1999, p. 181) explained: "No part knew the whole, the whole did not know all the parts, and none had any need to know".

The degree of simplification introduced by a Mondragón compound board is indicated by the how "Xs" are processed in each component. Components of a Mondragón board only have two or three Xs while a unitary board eleven. The simplification in increased by different individuals being involved in each component of a Mondragón board with all workers being included.

Distributed or "Network Governance" not only reduces information overload on directors and executives but introduces sources of intelligence independently of management to monitor management. Stakeholders can provide feedback on the Strengths, Weaknesses, Opportunities and Strengths (SWOT) of both management and the business. Stakeholders can be expected to have views that are contrary to those of management. In this way directors can not only cross check management reports on the known knowns but also obtain different views on the known unknowns and expose themselves to becoming aware of the unknown unknowns. This is not possible in command and control hierarchies where contrary behavior or views may not be tolerated.

In network governed firms like the UK employee controlled John Lewis Partnership (JLP), contrary views are encouraged. The JLP constitution and rules enshrine

*Table 13.1* Mondragón Compound Board Compared with Unitary Board (degrees of decomposition of information processing labour indicated by allocations of "X")

| Board Type | Mondragón Compound Board | | | | | Anglo |
|---|---|---|---|---|---|---|
| **Control centers**[a] | **Watchdog council** | **Supervisory board** | **Mgr. board** | **Social council** | **Work unit** | **Unitary board** |
| Members | 3 | 5–8 | 4–6 | ~5–25 | ~10–20 | ~4–12 |
| function[b] | Governance processes | Appoint mgt. board | Organize operations | Worker welfare | Production, elec.soc.c. | Manage |
| Activities | Efficacy & integrity of processes | Integrate strategic stakeholders | Efficient resource allocation | Establish working conditions | job organization & evaluation | Direct & control |
| Internal[b] | X | | X | X | X | XXXX |
| External[b] | X | X | | | | XX |
| Short term[b] | X | | X | | X | XXX |
| Long term[b] | | X | | X | | XX |

[a]Omits the General Assembly, which elects Watchdog Council and Supervisory board.
[b]Descriptions follow typology of Tricker (1994, p. 244 and 287).

complex bottom up feedback with checks and balances. For example, they include the right of any employee to publish criticism of managers anonymously in a weekly *Chronicles* published at branch levels by head office. The JLP constitution states: "the happiness of its members' is the Partnership's ultimate purpose".[5] JLP goes on to state our "Principles and Rules enables us over the long term to outperform companies with conventional ownership structures". Independent analysts have confirmed this statement for both JLP and the network-governed worker owned MCC in Spain (Turnbull 2000c, pp. 199–225).

There are wide variations in the control and communication architecture of network-governed firms. The architecture of each firm needs to be designed to not only recognise the limited ability of humans to receive, process, store and share data, information, knowledge and wisdom but to provide operating advantages. Without a division of powers and checks and balances introduced by network governance as suggested in Figure 13.1 it is not possible to achieve good governance.

It is not corporate law that denies good governance but corporate governance codes, principles and regulators. The UK Financial Conduct Authority web page states that it requires firms to act ethically but it accepts the systemic toxic unethical conflicts as described above. Australian Prudential Regulatory Authority (APRA), like The UK Prudential Regulatory Authority and the Sarbanes Oxley Act prescribes the adoption of toxic conflicted relationships that ethical directors and auditors would want to avoid. The time is long overdue for Parliaments to hold their regulators to account for accepting and promoting counter productive unethical governance practices.

The mind-set and remit of regulators need to be radically changed. Instead of regulators making rules and enforcing compliance, they should require firms and their shareholders to make the rules and enforce compliance to "do no harm and act ethically" in furthering their business interests. This would require sharehold-ers to adopt corporate constitutions that promoted self-regulation, self-governance and so good governance. The impossibility of any regulator or CEO to directly control complexity is revealed by the science of governance grounded in the laws of nature.

## 5 The natural laws of governance

The natural science of governance reveals that it is impossible to regulate complexity *directly*. The science of governance is grounded in "the science of control and com-munications in the animal and machine" identified less than 80 years ago by Weiner (1948). Transaction Byte Analysis (TBA) has extended the science of cybernetics to social organizations by adopting bytes as the unit of analysis (Turnbull 2000c). In this way the ability of social animals to understand, communicate and survive in dynamic, complex unknowable environments can be analyzed using the same unit of analysis for evaluating computers and the Internet.

Governance science explains why the human brain has "no Chief Executive Officer neuron" (Kurzweil 1999, p. 84). Instead different parts of the brain become respon-sible for making different types of decisions. This is what occurs in the network-governed organizations such as VISA, JLP and the MCC. The science of governance also explains how small creatures with simple brains obtain reliable ability to survive and reproduce in dynamic complex unknowable environments when organizations managed by highly educated humans with far superior brains may not.

The limited ability of human physiology and neurology to transact bytes can now be measured as reported in Turnbull (2000c: Table 3.5). This provides criteria for design-ing organizations so as to avoid humans being subjected to data overload in their com-munications, data processing and storage. Organizations can now be designed like computers so that the data processing capacity of human communication and control channels are not exceeded.

To avoid data overload organizations involved with complexity need to decompose communications, decision-making labor and control into simpler elements by intro-ducing distributed communication, decision-making and control networks. The most common strategy for decomposing decision-making is to form centrally controlled command and control hierarchies. But power hierarchies posses fundamental flaws as identified by Leibenstein (1987), Downs (1967, pp. 116–118). A crucial advantage of network governance is not that it just introduces distributed intelligence but that it also creates the capacity to introduce requisite variety of feedback signals and control channels to manage complexity as reliably as required. The importance of obtaining a "requisite variety" of channels to control (Ashby 1968, p. 202) and communicate (Shannon 1948) accurately has been established mathematically.

Ashby's law of requisite variety states that complexity can only be regulated *indi-rectly* through supplementary co-regulators (Ashby 1968, p. 265). It is the stake-holders and citizens who governments make laws to protect that are required to be involved as co-regulators to provide a requisite variety of both control and communi-cation channels. Network governance creates the ability to constructively engage with stakeholders to provide mutual benefits.

The inclusion of stakeholders in the governance architecture of firms and their regulators can provide many benefits for shareholders, directors, auditors, managers, stakeholders, regulators and civil society, as set out in Turnbull (2014b). Some of the general advantages are:

1  It is a condition precedent for directors to be able to creditably monitor management independently of management on a systemic basis.
2  It is a condition precedent for firms to reliably and comprehensively obtain access to intelligence about the complexity of their operating environments.
3  It is a condition precedent for reliably controlling complexity.
4  It is a condition precedent for improving self-regulation, self-governance and so good governance.
5  It creates a basis for cross checking management information of the known knowns.
6  It provides a check if management are aware of all the known unknowns.
7  It improves risk management and identification of new opportunities arising from what would otherwise be unknown unknowns.
8  It simplifies public corporate social and environmental reporting by either the firm or its stakeholders as these issues can be privately reported and resolved directly with the citizens concerned.
9  It removes the need to comply with CSR reporting standards as the citizens requiring the information either generate it and/or obtain it privately on a continuous basis to expedite amelioration and correction.
10  It reduces the size and cost of government to enrich the quality of democracy.

Table 13.2 assumes that NEDs have vacated the management board to take up the role of Governors. Advantages of network governance for auditors, management, stakeholders (other than shareholders), regulators and shareholders are detailed in Turnbull (2013a, 2014b).

## 6  Concluding remarks

The discussion above indicates some of the win-win advantages of network governance for corporations, their stakeholders, regulators, government and society. The existing system of Anglophone governance is conflicted, unethical, and counter-productive for all types of organizations. The imposition of this defective form of governance on financial institutions by so-called prudential regulators is not just unacceptable but dangerous for the health of national economies.

Many commentators are concerned about the stability of the financial system. Some expect that the next crisis could be more severe. Governments have not learnt the lessons of history such as documented by the US Financial Inquiry Report and the concerns of many other commentators. Since the 2008 financial crisis significant improvements have been made in improving the equity and liquidity buffers of the banking system. This is has been initiated by economists and bankers who apparently do apply their common sense to understand how unreliable and toxic is current system of governance. The current situation again demonstrates how good people can do bad things by peer group pressure (Milgram 1974).

*Table 13.2* Summarising Advantages of Network Governance for NEDs

| Systemic Problems for Non-Executive Directors (NEDs) on a Unitary Board | Systemic Solutions from Introducing Network Governance Used by Nature. Also Described as "Ecological Governance" |
|---|---|
| 1 Suspicion by outsiders that the absolute power of directors to identify and manage their own conflicts of interest might corrupt the directors and/or the business | Corporate charter establishes a governance board and a management board of directors elected by cumulative voting with one vote per share and Governors with one vote per shareholder. Governors control internal and external auditors, director nomination and pay with veto powers when conflicts exist for directors (Dallas 1997). |
| 2 No creditable systematic process for NEDs to determine when their trust in management might be misplaced | Corporate charters makes provision for any class of stakeholders to elect a representative board to meet with governors independently of management or directors to provide feedback and/or feed forward competitive intelligence to them and/or managers. |
| 3 Exposure of NEDs to personal liabilities and loss of reputation from management misdeeds | Misdeeds of executives are the responsibility of the directors' as Governors do not have power to manage business operations. As indicated in Figure 1 directors could include non-executives. |
| 4 No systemic access for NEDs to information opposing management views and so for evaluating management independently of managers | Feedback from establishment of one or more "Employee Assemblies", "Creditors Councils" and "Debtors Forums" who may appoint a "Stakeholder Congress" to advise on KPIs used to determine executive appointments and their remuneration. |
| 5 No diversity of information sources to cross check integrity of management information or obtain second or more opinions | Diversified feedback provided from specialized stakeholders groups and their Boards with informal access to Government regulator who chairs their Stakeholder Congress. Congress manages AGM that determines the pay and election of Directors and Governors. |
| 6 Coping with data and information overload | Compliance information and liabilities transferred to directors with option of strategic analysis transferred to a supervisory board as found in Europe. |
| 7 Difficulties in detecting biases, errors and omissions in reports from managers. | Access to a requisite variety of independent crosschecking sources of stakeholder feedback to obtain accuracy as much as desired as demonstrated by Shannon (1948). |
| 8 Inadequate knowledge for complex decision-making. | Simplification of decision-making (Von Neumann 1947). |
| 9 Board decision-making subject biases in its membership – Gender biases, etc. | Exposed to multiple diverse and contrary viewpoints raised by stakeholders to force consideration of taboo topics and avoid culture of don't ask don't tell. |
| 10 Lack of will to act against management. | Governors not captive to management information and/or executive powers and influence with independent power and/or influence on director nomination, pay and tenure. |
| 11 Lack of a systemic way to safely blow the whistle on errors, misdeeds, etc. | Provided privately by network of boards connected to the government regulator and/or firm specific employee ombudsperson. |
| 12 Impossibility of *directly* controlling/countering complex variables/risks. | Control amplified *indirectly* through requisite variety of stakeholders acting as co-regulators (Ashby 1968, p. 265). |

No less than parliamentary inquiry is required to provide intellectual leadership and confidence for regulators to change their approach. This could also force the vested interest of practitioners and their professional bodies to open their eyes to their mindless blindness to unethical practices. As noted above there is considerable power and influential vested interests in promoting or defending the current unconscionable unethical counter productive system of governance. Urgency is required because many commentators are anticipating another financial crisis.

## Notes

1  "We were shocked and surprised that, even after the ship had run aground, so many of those that were on the bridge were still so keen to congratulate themselves on their collective navigational skills", (PCBS 2013).
2  In referring to the role the auditor Lord Bridge stated: "No doubt he is acting antagonistically to the directors in the sense that he is appointed by the shareholders to be a check upon them" (Caparo 1990, p. 11).
3  An arrangement proposed for Australia by Senator Murray (1998) and for the UK by Hatherly (1995).
4  Limited life enterprises compel firms to continuously distribute all profits and grow through dividend reinvestment in successor "offspring" firms. This transfers the re-investment decision from executives to shareholders and the wider economy.
5  Refer to: http://www.johnlewispartnership.co.uk/about/our-constitution.html, viewed 10 February 2015.

## Bibliography

Adams, R.B. (2012), 'Governance and the Financial Crisis', *International Review of Finance*, vol. 12, no.1, pp. 7–28.
Analysitica (1992), *Board of Directors and Corporate Governance: Trends in the G7 Countries Over the Next Ten Years*, Oxford Analytica Ltd, England.
Ashby, W.R. (1968), *An Introduction to Cybernetics*, University Paper-back, London.
Bazerman, M.H., Morgan, K.P. and Loewenstein, G.F. (1997), 'The Impossibility of Auditor Independence', *Sloan, Management Review*, vol. 38, no. 4, pp. 89–94.
Bernstein, P. (1978), *Guidelines for the Design of Economic Feedback Systems*, Office of Technical Assistance, Economic Development Administration, US Department of Commerce, Washington, DC.
Bernstein, P. (1980), *Workplace Democratization: Its Internal Dynamics*, Transaction Books, New Brunswick, NJ.
Bhagat, S. and Black, B.S. (2002), 'The Non-correlation between Board Independence and Long-Term Firm Performance', *Journal of Corporation Law*, vol. 27, pp. 231–273. Available from http://ssrn.com/abstract=133808 (accessed February 10, 2015).
Caparo (1990), House of Lords judgment of Caparo vs Dickman, London, Available from http://oxcheps.new.ox.ac.uk/casebook/Resources/CAPARO_1.pdf (accessed February 10, 2015).
Clarke, D.C. (2006), 'Setting the Record Straight: Three Concepts of the Independent Director', *GWU Legal Studies Research Paper 199*, George Washington University Law School, Washington, DC.
Clarke, T. (2010), 'Recurring Crises in Anglo-American Corporate Governance', *Contributions to Political Economy*, vol. 29, no.1, pp. 9–32.
Coffee, J.C. (2005), 'A Theory of Corporate Scandals: Why the U.S. and Europe Differ', *Working Paper No. 274*, The Center for Law and Economic Studies, Columbia University Law School, New York.

Dallas, L.L. (1988), 'Two Models of Corporate Governance: Beyond Berle & Means', *Journal of Law Reform*, vol. 22, no.1, pp. 19–116.

Dallas, L.L. (1997), 'Proposals for Reform of Corporate Boards of Directors: The Dual Board and Board Ombudsperson', *Washington and Lee Law Review*, vol. 5, no. 1, pp. 92–146.

Downs, A. (1967), *Inside Bureaucracy*, Little Brown & Co, Boston.

The Economist (2015), *'Shareholder Activism: Capitalism's Unlikely Heroes'*, February 7th. Available from http://www.economist.com/news/leaders/21642169-why-activist-investors-are-good-public-company-capitalisms-unlikely-heroes (accessed February 10, 2015).

*Financial Crisis Inquiry Report* (2011), *The Financial Crisis Inquiry Commission*, Washington, DC. Available from http://cybercemetery.unt.edu/archive/fcic/20110310173545/http://c0182732.cdn1.cloudfiles.rackspacecloud.com/fcic_final_report_full.pdf (accessed February 10, 2015).

Grossman, R.L. and Adams, F.T. (1993), *Taking Care of Business: Citizenship and the Charter of Incorporation*, Charter Ink. Available from http://www.ratical.org/corporations/TCoB.html (accessed February 10, 2015).

Guthrie, J. and Turnbull, S. (1995), 'Audit Committees: Is There a Role for Corporate Senates and and/or Stakeholder Councils?' *Corporate Governance: An International Review*, vol. 3, no. 2, pp. 72–89.

Hatherly, D.J. (1995), 'The Case for the Shareholder Panel in the UK', *The European Accounting Review*, vol. 4, no. 3, pp. 535–553.

Hayward, J. (2003), *Thinking Not Ticking: Bringing Competition to the Public Interest Audit*, Centre for the Study of Financial Innovation, London.

Hipple, E.V. (1994), *Sources of Innovation*, Oxford University Press, New York.

Hock, D.W. (1999), *Birth of the Chaordic Age*, Berrett-Koehler Publishers, San Francisco, CA.

Jensen, M.C. (1993), 'The Modern Industrial Revolution: Exit and the Failure of Internal Control Systems', *The Journal of Finance*, vol. 48, no. 3, pp. 831–880.

Kurzweil, R. (1999), *The Age of Spiritual Machines*, Viking, New York.

La Porta, L., De Silanes, F.L. and Shleifer, A. (1999), 'Corporate Ownership Around the World', *The Journal of Finance*, vol. 54, no. 2, pp. 471–517.

Leibenstein, H. (1987), *Inside the Firm: The Inefficiencies of Hierarchy*, Harvard University Press, Cambridge.

Melis, A. (2004), 'On the Role of the Board of Statutory Auditors in Italian Listed Companies', *Corporate Governance: An International Review*, vol.12, no. 1, pp. 74–84.

Milgram, S. (1974), *Obedience to Authority: An Experimental View*, Tavistock, London.

Murray, A. (1998), *Minority Report on the Company Law Review Bill*, 1997 Parliamentary Joint Committee on Corporations and Securities, The Parliament of the Commonwealth of Australia. Available from http://www.aph.gov.au/Parliamentary_Business/Committees/Joint/Corporations_and_Financial_Services/Completed_inquiries/1996–99/companylaw/report/d01 (accessed February 10, 2015).

Neumann, J von. (1947), *Theory of Games and Economic Behaviour*, Yale University Press, New Haven, CT.

O'Connor, S.M. (2004), 'Be Careful What You Wish for: How Accountants and Congress Created the Problem of Auditor Independence', *Boston College Law Review*, vol. 45, no. 4, pp. 741–827.

Page, A. (2009), 'Unconscious Bias and the Limits of Director Independence', *University of Illinois Law Review*, no.1, pp. 237–294.

Parliamentary Commission into Banking Standards Report 2013, Joint Parliamentary Committee, House of Lords, House of Commons, 'Changing Banking for Good'. Available from http://www.parliament.uk/documents/banking-commission/Banking-final-report-vol-ii.pdf (accessed February 10, 2015).

Porter, M.E. (1992), *Capital Choices: Changing the Way America Invests in Business*, Harvard Business School, Boston, MA.

Pound, J. (1992), 'Beyond Takeovers: Politics Comes to Corporate Control', *Harvard Business Review*, March-April, pp. 83–93.

Pound, J. (1993a), 'Creating Relationship Institutional Investors and Corporations: An Introduction', *Journal of Corporate Finance*, vol. 6, no. 2, pp. 32–34.

Pound, J. (1993b), 'The Rise of the Political Model of Corporate Governance and Corporate Control', *New York University Law Review*, vol. 68, no. 5, pp. 1003–1007.

Rodrigues, U. (2007). 'The Fetishization of Independence', *The UGA Legal Studies Research Paper No. 07–007*, March, University of Georgia Law School. Available from http://papers.ssrn.com/sol3/papers.cfm?abstract_id=968513 (accessed February 10, 2015).

Romano, R. (2004), *The Sarbanes-Oxley Act and the Making of Quack Corporate Governance* Yale ICF Working Paper No. 04–37, ECGI – Finance. Available from http://papers.ssrn.com/paper.taf?abstract_id=596101 (accessed February 10, 2015).

Rose, P. (2006), 'The Corporate Governance Industry', *Ohio State Public Law Working Paper*. Available from http://papers.ssrn.com/sol3/Papers.cfm?abstract_id=902900 (accessed February 10, 2015).

Schumpeter, J.A. (1976), *Capitalism, Socialism and Democracy*, Allen and Unwin, London.

Shapiro, A. (2004), 'Who Pays the Auditor Calls the Tune? Auditing Regulation and Clients' Incentives', Legal Studies Research Paper Series, Paper No. 04–014, Cornell Law School, *Seton Hall Law Review*, 30. Available from http://papers.ssrn.com/sol3/papers.cfm?abstract_id=587972.

Shannon, C.E. (1948), 'The Mathematical Theory of Communications', *The Bell System Technical Journal*, vol. 27, pp. 379–423 and 623–656.

Shleifer, A. and Vishny, R.W. (1997), 'A Survey of Corporate Governance', *The Journal of Finance*, vol. 52, no. 2, pp. 737–783.

Swan, P.L. and Forsberg, D. (2014), 'Does Board "independence" Destroy Corporate Value?' Presented to 27th Australasian Finance and Banking Conference, Sydney. Available from http://ssrn.com/abstract=2312325 (accessed February 10, 2015).

Tricker, R.I. (1980), *Two Tiered Boards*, The corporate policy group, Nuffield College, Oxford.

Tricker, R.I. (1994), International Corporate Governance, Simon & Schuster, Singapore.

Turnbull, S. (1973), 'Time Limited Corporations' *ABACUS*, vol. 9, no. 1, pp. 28–43.

Turnbull, S. (1994), 'Stakeholder Democracy: Redesigning the Governance of Firms and Bureaucracies', *Journal of Socio-Economics*, vol. 23, no. 3, pp. 321–360.

Turnbull, S. (1995), 'Best Practice in the Governance of GBE's.' In Guthrie, J. (ed.), *The Australian Public Sector: Pathways to Change*, IIR Pty. Limited, Sydney, pp. 99–109.

Turnbull, S. (2000a), 'Corporate Charters with Competitive Advantages', *St. Johns Law Review*, vol. 74, no. 44, pp. 101–159.

Turnbull, S. (2000b), 'Stakeholder Governance: A Cybernetic and Property Rights Analysis.' In Tricker, R.I. (ed.), *Corporate Governance: The History of Management Thought*, Ashgate Publishing, Aldershot.

Turnbull, S. (2000c), *The Governance of Firms Controlled by More than One Board: Theory Development and Examples*. PhD thesis, Macquarie University, Sydney. Available from http://ssrn.com/abstract=858244 (accessed February 10, 2015).

Turnbull, S. (2002a), *A New Way to Govern: Organisations and Society after Enron*, New Economics Foundation, London. Available from http://www.i-r-e.org/docs/a002_organisations-and-society-after-enron.pdf (accessed February 10, 2015).

Turnbull, S. (2002b), 'The Science of Corporate Governance', *Corporate Governance: An International Review*, vol. 10, no. 4, pp. 256–272.

Turnbull, S. (2007), 'Borrowing From the Laws of Nature', *Company Director*, Australian Institute of Company Directors, vol. 23, no. 10, pp. 54, 56, 57.

Turnbull, S. (2008a), 'The Science of Governance: A Blind Spot of Risk Managers and Corporate Governance Reform', *Journal of Risk Management in Financial Institutions*, vol. 1, no. 4, pp. 360–368. Available from http://ssrn.com/abstract=1742584 (accessed February 10, 2015).

Turnbull, S. (2008b), 'Why Emerging Countries Should Not Follow US and UK Audit Practices', *The ICFAI Journal of Audit Practice*, vol. 5, no. 1, pp. 36–46. Available from http://ssrn.com/abstract=959332 (accessed February 10, 2015).

Turnbull, S. (2012), 'Discovering the "natural laws" of Governance', *The Corporate Board*, March/April, Vanguard Publications Inc., Okemos, MI. Available from http://ssrn.com/abstract=2062579 (accessed February 10, 2015).

Turnbull, S. (2013a), 'A Sustainable Future for Corporate Governance Theory and Practice.' In Boubaker, S., Nguyen, Bang D. and Nguyen, Duc K. (eds.) *Corporate Governance: Recent Developments and New Trends*, Springer-Vertag, Heidelberg, pp. 347–368, Working paper. Available from http://ssrn.com/abstract=1987305 (accessed February 10, 2015).

Turnbull, S. (2013b), 'How Can Non-profit Organizations Enhance Performance and Legitimize their Operations? Presented to 9th Workshop on Managing the Challenges of the Third Sector, European Institute for Advanced Studies in Management, University of Lund, Sweden. Available from http://ssrn.com/abstract=2223032 (accessed February 10, 2015).

Turnbull, S. (2013c), 'Re-inventing Governance using the Laws of Nature.' In Peters, J. (ed.), *Best Practice in Corporate Governance*, vol. 1, pp. 42–45. Available from http://www.iodonline.com/Articles/Re-inventingGovernance.pdf (accessed February 10, 2015).

Turnbull, S. (2014a), 'A Proposal for Self-governing Corporations.' In Blond, P. (ed.), *The Virtue of Enterprise: Responsible Business for a New Economy*, January, ResPublica, London, pp. 52–54. Available from http://www.respublica.org.uk/documents/jae_The%20Virtue%20of%20Enterprise.pdf (accessed February 10, 2015).

Turnbull, S. (2014b), *Designing Resilient Organisations: With Operating Advantages for Public, Private, Non-profit and Government Entities and their Stakeholders.* Lambert Academic Publishing: Saarbrucken, Germany, Available from https://www.morebooks.de/store/gb/book/designing-resilient-organisations/isbn/978–3–659–34586–9 (accessed February 10, 2015).

Turnbull, S. (2014c), 'How Might Corporate Charters be Amended to Enhance Investor Returns?' Presented to International Corporate Governance Network, Academic Conference, Nyenrode Business University, Amsterdam. Available from http://ssrn.com/abstract=2417843 (accessed February 10, 2015).

Turnbull, S. (2014d), 'How Might Network Governance Found in Nature Protect Nature?' *Journal of European Law*, vol. 11, no. 2, pp. 98–102. Available from https://www.kluwerlawonline.com/abstract.php?id=EUCL2014019 (accessed February 10, 2015).

Turnbull, S. (2014e), 'Integrating Social Responsibility into Corporate Governance', in Tchotourian, I. (ed.), *Company Law and CSR: New Legal and Economic Challenges (Analysed from a Comparative Perspective)*, Bruylant, Paris. Available from http://ssrn.com/abstract=2261518 (accessed February 10, 2015).

Williamson, O.E. (1985), *The Economic Institutions of Capitalism*, Free Press, New York.

Weiner, N. (1948), *Cybernetics: Or Control and Communication in the Animal and Machine*, MIT Press, Cambridge, MA.

# Conclusion

*Coral Ingley and Güler Aras*

Practical experience demonstrates that if an organisation is to be socially responsible then it needs the full commitment of the board of directors in conjunction with the senior managers of the organisation. In this sense, leadership does not reside with an individual (the CEO) within the organisation, but with all of those at the apex of corporate power and control. Unless there is recognition and acceptance of a distributed leadership responsibility at the head of an organisation it is likely that CSR and commitment to sustainability issues will be limited and remain non-strategic. Effective change management requires enlightened and capable leadership to instigate and drive the process of embedding a sustainable and socially responsible corporate philosophy and culture that supports good business decision-making. A profound understanding of the requirements of such a leadership process will help corporate managers become highly effective change agents.

This volume draws out a number of common themes which underscore the importance of good corporate behavior based on sound corporate governance practices which recognize the environmental challenges facing the globe now and into the future. The boards of responsible companies not only prioritize the issues they see and strategize their responses to them, they are also willing to be accountable to stakeholders by reporting publicly on their corporate sustainability performance.

Among the key themes that link the discussions in this book, corporations and their boards are urged to recognize the centrality of *values* in promoting and demonstrating good business behavior. Güler Aras and Paul Williams have highlighted the importance of moral values in addressing the agency problems implicated in the global financial crisis. Philippa Wells and Coral Ingley have drawn attention to prioritizing sustainability values, which include behaving ethically, as part of directors' fiduciary duty to act in good faith. Suzanne Benn promotes the need to understand the corporation as a moral entity based on principles of community, interconnectedness and cooperation in moving forward towards sustainability. Moral values and moral purpose are also emphasized by Bob Garratt in relation to developing the requisite organizational culture and effective leadership that are essential to the stability and development of society.

Integral to moral and ethical values – and also a noteworthy theme in the book – is the notion of *trust* as the basis for good corporate governance and sustainable business practices. Aras and Williams have argued that as well as moral values and ethical practices, responsible corporate behavior exists in an environment of trust if stakeholders' confidence in the corporate sector is to be restored and maintained. The significance of trusting in the leadership and in the ethical culture of corporations was highlighted by Jacob Dahl Rendtorff as being the foundation of good corporate citizenship.

Garratt's and Rendtorff's emphasis on responsible *leadership* – especially by the corporate board – is another key theme among the chapters of the book. Elke et al. have focused on "next generation" responsible leadership. They note the evolving definition of the concept and the collaborative forms this takes in addressing challenges to sustainable development through the transformation of corporations to "ecosystem" thinking instead of an "ego-system" orientation. Shann Turnbull highlights the involvement of lawmakers as a requirement for providing the leadership needed to achieve the objectives of good governance.

The growing attention given to the practice of integrated *reporting* as a more balanced approach to monitoring and measuring corporate performance forms another important dimension of the discussion in the book. Because stakeholders are more demanding in holding corporations accountable for their behavior, companies are realizing that their reputations may rest on how they are perceived as responsible corporate citizens. Stakeholders are also increasingly powerful in influencing policy makers as well as being more active in monitoring corporate performance. Miriam Green has highlighted the role of scholarship, especially in management studies, in influencing and effecting the discourse on sustainability among university students, business professionals, policy makers and the wider society. The influence of the media in framing CSR and encouraging responsible business behavior featured in Jamilah Ahmed and Suraati Saad's discussion. Suzanne Benn has also referred to the role of the media as a part of the information revolution driving the change agenda for corporations. Shallini Taneja et al. adopted a multi-stakeholder approach to measuring sustainability performance in Indian companies, while Alison Dempsey has emphasized the concept of materiality in measuring environmental and social impacts for integrated reporting on corporate performance. In his précis of corporate social accounting over the last 40 years, Douglas Branson has provided another perspective on CSR monitoring and reporting. In his discussion Branson has traced the progression of CSR reporting standards and noted the dominance of the large accounting firms in social auditing. While this evolution may signal steps toward standardizing social performance metrics and raising the quality of CSR monitoring and reporting, Branson has noted the resulting ever-denser corporate reports that risk generating expansiveness at the expense of relevance, so that the real purpose, intent and value in such reports may be missed.

In this book we have presented analyses and discussions of business behavior and sustainability issues which underpin the type of thinking and responses which are clearly vital for a sound global economy. Our authors have discussed what is needed to create working models that support resilient and sustainable business and markets. We believe our approach to this multidimensional topic, as developed by the authors in their respective chapters, will provide the reader with a fuller understanding of some of the many issues and controversies involved. We also aim to leave the reader with a useful reflection on matters relating to better corporate practices, in the hope that all constituents: governments, corporations and citizens, can move forward in working together responsibly to achieve long-term market and business, success and a sustainable environmental and social future.

# Index

abstract empiricism 46
Abt Associates 145, 146
Abt, Clark 146
academia: behavior 42; Burns/Stalker
  approach 48–9; ideological positions
  57–9; managerialism 57–8; neoliberalism
  58–9; political pressures 57; pressures
  56–7
accountability 103; social world complexity
  (reduction), trust process (usage) 104–8
accounting: corporate social accounting,
  benefits 139–45; social accounting 138
accounting-based measures 23
*Accounting, Organizations and Society*
  (AOS) 53
action, good faith duty 72–7
activist organizations, questions/criticisms
  (data provision) 142
activity-based management (ABM) 23
*Administrative Science Quarterly* 56
agency theory 9; argument 10; failure 13;
  implications 12; principles, usage 10–11;
  shift 11–13
agenda-setting theory 131
agent view 205
Ahmed, Jamilah 3, 121, 253
*Alice in Wonderland* 138
alliances, formation 183
alternative scholarship, examples 51–2
Amazon, policy change (scrutiny) 154
American Telephone and Telegraph (AT&T),
  takeover bid 140
amphibians, extinction threat 177
Annan, Kofi 181, 191
Annual General Meetings (AGMs),
  conduct 240
annual reports, usage 142
anti-sociological sentiments 57
Aras, Güler 1, 2, 9, 252
Arendt, Hannah 214
Arthur D. Little, Inc. 145

asbestos-related claims, total corporate
  liability costs 190
Atlantic Richfield, process audits 146
auditor independence, impossibility 239
Austerity Era 231
Australia, corporate responsibility regulation
  88–9
Australian Corporations and Markets
  Advisory Committee (CAMAC) 68, 88–9
Australian Prudential Regulatory Authority
  (APRA) 244
authoritarian corporate governance codes
  140
authority: procedural justice-based model,
  firm development 16; shift 214

bad faith, impact 108
Bank of America, process audits 146
Base of the Pyramid model 188
Bauer, Raymond 146
Beck, Ulrich 104
behaviour: academic environment 42;
  leadership focus, change 225; observation
  229
belief systems, developmental complexity
  analysis 202
Benn, Suzanne 4, 5, 175, 253
Bischoff, Win 228
BM&F BOVESPA 164
board of directors: fiduciary duty 77;
  leadership 93–5; responsibility 167
boardroom, ESG matters 152
Body Shop, The 212
Boltanski, Luc 112
bounded rationality, concept 106
Branson, Douglas 4, 85, 138
*Bribery Act* (2011) 165
bribery, decrease 187
British American Tobacco (BAT) document 148
British Petroleum (BP): settlement payment
  154; water/land pollution 67

Brundtland Report 186
*Brundtland Report* 70
Building and Wood Workers' International
   (BWI) 184
Burr, Donald 131
business: corporate social responsibility 87;
   corporations, trust (crisis) 105; Indian
   business, empirical tests 21; operations,
   CSR integration 123; requirements 17–18;
   scandals 154
Business Charter for Sustainable
   Development 181
business ethics 110–11, 113; trust/
   accountability, necessity 115–16
business models 187–92; risk management,
   incorporation 190

*Cadbury Report on The Financial Aspects of
   Corporate Governance* 226–7
Cadbury Report, The 13, 227
capitalism model 179
capital markets: corporate information
   sources 155; participants 166–7
carbon capture/storage technology, usage 188
carbon dioxide ($CO_2$) emissions, reduction
   188
Carbon Disclosure Project (CDP) 69, 161,
   187
Carbon Tracker 176
Center for Corporate Social Responsibility
   148
CERES, impact 185
Ceres report 158
change: business models 187–92; conduct,
   codes 186–7; co-regulation 186; cost
   avoidance, risk management (relationship)
   189–91; innovation, culture 192;
   innovation, technology (relationship)
   187–8; investors, pressure 191;
   knowledge-based organization 191–2;
   natural capitalism 187, business advantage;
   new business models 188–9; regulation,
   forms (evolution) 185–7; reporting
   requirements/concepts 187; supply chains,
   networks 184–5; technologies 187–92;
   user pays 185
change, drivers 175
Chapello, Eve 112
Chevron: shareholder resolutions, impact
   161; toxic waste 67
China, environmental impacts 178
chi-square/degrees of freedom (CMIN/DF) 32
civic cooperation, increase 106
civic engagement, importance 106
Clean Clothes Campaign (CCC) 184

climate change 175–6, 177
Coca-Cola, water extraction/pollution 67
Codes 226; creation 230
codes, examination 227
collaborative leadership: defining 209–15;
   first precondition 212; new kind,
   perspective 213–14; understanding 211
collaborative practice, communities 215
collaborative responsible leadership
   (collaborative RL): essence 220; practice
   212–13; theory/practice 209–19
collaborative RL 215–19
collaborative stakeholder engagement
   217–18
collaboratories 215–19; development
   217–18; holistic framing/facilitation 218;
   template 218
collective approaches 210
collective awareness (increase), facilitating
   (impact) 218–19
collective intelligence, second precondition
   212
collective purpose/starting, co-creation 217
Combined Code 13
communication, distortion 58
community: expectations, scales 28;
   principles 5
companies: best interests 75; good faith duty
   72–7; reputation, media (impact) 122, 127
Companies Act (1993) 70
Companies Act (2006) 70, 89–90, 157, 231
company-specific integrated strategic plan,
   development 96
compensation system 96
competitive opportunity 186
complex situations, assessment 220
compliance: function 75; increase 226–7
Compound Board 235
compound boards, impact 236
compound board, unitary board (contrast)
   *244*
condition precedents 246
conduct: codes 17, 186–7; examination 227
Confirmatory Factor Analysis (CFA) 27
Conley, John 143
consciousness development 204
consensual solutions, establishment 208–9
consensus values 139
consistency, footnotes (importance) 141
"consistently applied" notion 141
constructivist developmental theories 204
consultancy firms, raw data 139–40
consumer action, impact 183
content validity, testing 25
continuing success, development 228

*Continuous Disclosure Obligations* (National Instrument 53–104) 155, 157
contracts, nexus 16
*Cool Response: The SEC and Climate Change Reporting* (Ceres report) 158
cooperation, principles 5
COP21 176
coral reefs, value 177
co-regulation 186
corporate actions, social/environmental consequences 203
corporate activity: non-financial dimensions 152; voluntary nature 84
corporate behavior: ideas, popularization 129–30
corporate behavior, corporate culture (impact) 30
corporate citizenship 103; accountability 115; constitution 105; social world complexity (reduction), trust process (usage) 104–8; trust, dynamic movement 108–12
corporate concerns, focus 1–2
corporate constitutions, specifications 240
corporate economic, measurement (framework) 31
corporate economic social performance, measurement (proposed framework) 22
corporate environmental reporting, low level (Malaysia) 124
corporate governance: culture, relationship 227–8; effectiveness 5; failures 225; financial crisis, relationship 9; future corporate governance system, approach 226–7; laws, proliferation/failure 242; mechanisms 15; political sale 225–6; power, relationship 241; practice 226; usage 11–13; valuation 225
*Corporate Governance* (Tricker) 226–7
corporate information sources 155
corporate legitimacy, trust process (significance) 103
corporate management, theory (alternative) 11
corporate misconduct, reduction 4
corporate motives, skepticism 142
corporate news releases, purposes 128
corporate performance: enhancement 28; good governance ethics, relationship 15–17
*Corporate Practices and Conduct* 154
corporate profit, increase 166
corporate reports, focus 10
corporate responsibility 83; board leadership 93–5; challenges 84–5; change-management perspective 92; defining 83, 86–7; governance 83, 90–2;

implementation 95–7; improvement 84; PJC Report definition 86; pyramid, development 86; stakeholder engagement 92–3
corporate responsibility, regulation 87–90; Australia 88–9; United Kingdom 89–90; United States 90
corporate scandals, impact 13–14
corporate social accounting: benefits 139–45; goals/objectives, identification 139–40
corporate social behavior, presentation 130
corporate social performance (CSP) 22, 23
corporate social responsibility (CSR) 122–3; broadcasting, media role 121; compliance 201; concept-coverage, example 127; criticisms 142; development (Malaysia) 123–4; findings/discussion 124–7; global significance 84–3; integration 96, 234; mainstreaming/institutionalization 96; media interest 130–1; media, relationship 124; media, role 128; media, symbiotic relationship 128–31; methodology 124–7; monitoring 253; news categories *126*; news coverage *125*; notion 123; origin 124; pillars *125*; positioning, media reporting 121; reporting, quality scores 147–8; reporting standards, compliance (removal) 246; RL, compliance 201
Corporate Social Responsiveness 23
corporate sustainability 186; complexity 87; corporation DNA, social responsibility (embedding) 142–3; expenditures/results, measurement consistency 141; governmental intervention, protection 143–4; green washing 142; insincerity, allegations (deflection) 142; investors/institutional investors, bonds (establishment) 143–4; measurement, management 145; NGO/activist organization questions/criticisms, data provision 142; pathway 127; social goals, adjustment 140–1; stakeholder constituencies, dialogues (opening) 140
corporate value, destruction 239
corporation: CSR accounting/reporting 144; CSR activities 127; DNA, social responsibility (embedding) 142–3; public view/opinion 127; purpose 84
Corporations Act (2001) 70, 88
corruption: decrease 187; risk 43
Corrupt Noughties 231
cost avoidance, risk management (relationship) 189–91
costs, externalisation 166
*Coulter v. E.L. Huckerby and Associates Inc.* 73

country-level studies, number (increase) 15–16
"cover the waterfront" complete audits 146–7
creative destruction 242
credibility, basis 114
CRM practices, customer expectation 29
CSR Malaysia, network 124
cultural factors, impact 192
culture: corporate governance, relationship 227–8; description 229; hierarchy 228–30; learning system 228
customer expectations, scales 29, *30*
customer satisfaction 97
cybernetics 57

Davidson, Kirk 2, 21
Dayton Hudson, process audits 146
decision making processes, people (integration) 214
Deepwater Horizon oil spill 190
deforestation, impact 177
deliberately developmental organizations (DDOs) 213, 215
deliberative processes, sense 202
Deloitte Touche, experiences 145
Deloitte Touche Tohmatsu Limited, The 148
democracy, quality (enrichment) 246
Dempsey, Alison 4, 152, 253
determinist approach 46
developmental complexity 202
Development Research Center 178
*Developments in Corporate Governance and Stewardship* (UK Financial Reporting Council) 228
*Directive of the European Parliament and of the Council amending Directive 2013/34/EU* 164–5
distortion, risk 43
distributed governance 244
distributed leadership approaches 210
diversion, risk 43
Dodd-Frank Wall Street and Consumer Protection Act (2010) 14, 154, 165
dramatic failures 241
Drucker, Peter 213
DuPont, process audits 146
dynamic natural environment 175–7

eco-efficiency models 190
Eco-Index 185
ecological modernization 186
ecological value commitments 114
economic growth 179
economic irrationality 12
economic markets, globalization 103

economics, dependence 115–16
economic system, success 70
eco-system, well-being 70
ego-system orientation 253
Electric Utility Sustainable Supply Chain Alliance 185
Elkington, John 85
emancipatory knowledge 58
empirical actors, moral competencies/capacities 201
employees: commitment 49; expectations, scales 28–9, *29*; ignoring, impact 48; levels 24; training, prioritization 187
energy efficiency, improvement 188
Enlightened Shareholder Value Model 68
Enron scandal 9, 13
Entity Maximization and Sustainability Model 68
environmental agreements, tensions 180
environmental impacts 176–7
Environmental Management (EMS), implementation 192
environmental pollution, negative publicity 67
environmental reporting, simplification 246
environmental/social/governance issues, integration (UNPRI guidance) 167
epistemological standards 42
Equator Principles 162
*Equiticorp Industries Group Ltd v. BNZ* 73–4
equity, agency problems 12
"essential management tool" 148
ethical accountability, trust (dynamic movement) 108–12
ethical autonomy, Kantian concept 110
ethical consumer, myth 188–9
*Ethical Corporation Magazine*, respondent survey 96
ethical, environmental, social, and governance (ESG): agenda, regulatory change 164–6; considerations 163; factors, increase 158–9; information, market demand 158–62; integration 155; management, effectiveness 166; matters 152; metrics 167; performance/reward 166–9; reporting 162–5; targets 96
ethical management systems 17
ethical values, factors 252–3
ethics 103, 201; business ethics 110–11
ethics pays, argument 113
ethos (rhetorical figure) 108
evil orders 112
*Exchange Act* (Rule 12b-2) 157
expert opinions, analysis 25
exploratory factor analysis (EFA) 27

*ex post facto* interpretations 54
externalities, prevention 200
externality machines 11
external stakeholders, goals contributions 214
*Extractive Sector Transparency Measures Act* 165
extra-organizational stakeholders 209
Exxon Mobil: CSR reports 148; shareholder resolutions, impact 161

face validity, testing 25
facilitation, impact 218
feedback mechanisms 229
Fenn, Dan 146
fiduciary duty 73
financial Big Bang 231
financial crisis: aftermath 167; corporate governance, relationship 9
*Financial Crisis Inquiry Report* (US Government) 236
financial KPIs, manager performance assessment 97
financial leadership crisis 225
financials 162–4
firm: ecological value commitments 114; operation, social license 23
Fishermen's Association, Mangrove plantation project 128–9
fit and proper persons 241–2
flexible fuels, development 188
Ford Foundation, survey 143
forest loss, cessation 188
Forest Program, focus 161
Form 10-K, usage 155
formal networks 112
fossil fuel plants, carbon capture/storage technology (usage) 188
Frankfurt School 58
Freshfield Report 161
Fukushima nuclear disaster, costs 190
functionalism, approaches 47
functionalist approaches 46–8
functionalist scholarship, weaknesses 52–5
future corporate governance system 226–7
"Future We Want, The" 181

G4 intention 163–4
G20/OECD Principles of Corporate Governance 166
Garratt, Bob 5–6, 253
Geertz, Clifford 230
General Agreement on Tariffs and Trade (GATT) 179
General Motors, process audits 146
"get big fast" phenomenon 139

global averages, usage 176
global capitalism, social/environmental impacts 188
global climate, damage (absence) 188
Global Compact 165, 201; support 181
Global Crossing, scandal 13
Global Financial Crisis (2008) 237
globalization 178–85; planetary impacts 177
globalization from above 179–81; countervailing pressures 179–81
globalization from below 182
"Globalization with a Human Face" (Annan) 181
Global Reporting Initiative (GRI) 162–3, 181; annual reports publication 69; frameworks 165; guidelines 92; international standards/frameworks 84; recommendations 92–3; sustainability governance guidelines 91
Global Sustainable Investment Alliance (GSIA) 159, 191
*Global Sustainable Investment Review 2014* (Global Sustainable Investment Alliance) 159
goals, contributions 214
going green, benefits 76
good business, requirements 17–18
good corporate citizenship: concept, sense-making/organizing 103; foundation 105
good faith action 72–7
good governance 241; achievement 234; competitive advantages, defining 242–5; defining 234, 242–5; ethics, corporate performance (relationship) 15–17; practices, toxicity 237–9; principles, development 15–17; systemic director conflicts 239–42
governance: codes, formulation 234; corporate governance, usage 11–13; corporate responsibility, relationship 83; functions 238; good governance, principles (development) 15–17; mantra 226; natural laws 245–6; reform, efforts 16; sustainability, relationship 67; usage 9
governmental intervention, protection 144–5
government, size/cost (reduction) 246
Granovetter, Marc 116
Grantham Research Institute on Climate Change (London School of Economics) 176
Great Barrier Reef, World Heritage sites 180
Greenbury Report, The 13
green economy, concepts 181
greenhouse gases (GHG): emissions 162, 189; mitigation targets 187–8

Green, Mirian 2, 42
Greenspan, Alan (Tett, commonality) 231–2
greenspeaking 69
greenwashing 69, 85
green washing 142
Griffin, Jennifer 2, 21

habitats, loss/alteration/fragmentation 177
hard concrete reality 47
Henderson, Hazel 182
Hewlett-Packard (HP), Environmental
    Strategies and Solutions programme 189
hierarchical mechanistic structures 47
high-carbon coal, replacement 187
Hock, Dee 243
holding environment, creation 220
holistic framing/facilitation 218
homo reciprocans 16
horizontal comparison 139–40
human behaviours, usage 226–7
human constituent groups, identification 75
Human Development Index (HDI) 178
human expectations, subjectivity 107
human physiology/neurology, ability
    (limitation) 245
hybrid frameworks 68

ideological positions 58–9
in-date budgeting information, problems 48
independent NEDs, impotency 239
Indian business, empirical tests 21
individuals, empowerment 216
industrialization, planetary impacts 177
informal groupings, exclusion 44
informal networks 112
information-based economy 191
information subsidies 128
Ingley, Coral 1, 3, 67, 252
innovation: culture 192; relational innovation
    220; technology, relationship 187–8
insincerity, allegations (deflection) 142
Institute of Accountants of England and
    Wales 227
Institute of Chartered Accountants in
    Australia (ICAA) 183
institutional advertising 142
institutional investors: bonds, establishment
    143–4; Ernst and Young survey 155
intangibles, management 190
integrated reporting, concepts 181
integrative leadership behavior,
    developmental basis 202
intelligence (increase), facilitating (impact)
    218–19
interconnectedness, principles 5

interested investors, bonds (establishment)
    143–4
International Accounting Standards Board
    (IASB) 165
*International Corporate Sustainability Survey*
    (KPMG) 147
International Integrated Reporting
    Committee (IIRC): establishment 92;
    integrated reporting framework 165
International Labour Organization (ILO) 185
international political leadership crisis 225
International Stock Exchange of London 227
International Textile, Garment and Leather
    Workers' Federation (ITGLWF) 184
International Trades Union Federation
    (ITUC) 184
interpenetration, necessity 51
interpersonal trust 114; importance 107
introspection, practice 220
invasive species 177
investors: briefings 93; pressure 191;
    protection 14–15
ISO 26000 162
I-We-All-of-Us model 205, *205*

*Jantzi Sustainalytics* 76
Jaques, Elliot 206
Jiping, Chen 182
Johannesburg Stock Exchange 164; company
    listing 157
John Lewis Partnership (JLP) 235, 243–4

Kegan, Robert 205
Ki-moon, Ban 175
Klettner, Alice 3, 83
knowledge-based organization 191–2
knowledge management 191–2
known unknowns, awareness 246
Kohlberg, Lawrence 209
KPMG: *International Corporate
    Sustainability Survey* 147; monitoring
    83; survey 92; Survey of Corporate
    Responsibility Reporting 163

Laloux, Frederic 212, 215
landing strips, construction 211
language barriers 142
La Porta, Lopez-de-Silanes, Shleifer and
    Vishny (LLSV) study 15
large-scale eco-system transitions 216
law, usage 190
leadership 202; collaborative endeavor 199;
    control, loss 214; discussion/implications
    219–21; effectiveness 6; focus, change 225;
    levels *207*; post-heroic leadership concepts

216; purpose, defining 219–20; responsible leadership 199–209; strategy, 113–14; trust, degree 215
Leadership for Transition (LiFT) 216–19
leadership in the plural 209–10
learning: slowness 229; systems, usage 226–7
legitimate scholarship 44
Leverage Buyout Organisations (LBOs) 236
Likert-type questionnaires, usage 52
Listing Agreement, Clause 51A 25
*Living Planet Report* (WWF) 177
local community expectations, scales 27–8
logical positivism 53–4
logos (rhetorical figure) 108
Logstrup, K.E. 110
London School of Economics (Grantham Research Institute on Climate Change) 176
London Stock Exchange 164; company listing 157, 227
long-term goals, organization work (alignment) 214
lost-time injury rates 97
low-carbon gas, usage 188
low-emissions technologies, acceleration/ development 188
Luhmann, Niklas 106, 109

mainstream management scholarship 45–6; criticisms 52–3; principles, summary 49–50
mainstream scholarship, sustainability (investigation) 42
Malaysia, CSR development 123–4
mammals, extinction threat 177
management: Drucker perspective 213; information, cross checking (basis) 246; values-driven management 103
management control systems (MCS) 52
*Management of Innovation, The* (Burns/ Stalker) 42, 50; sociological emphasis 51
management scholarship: alternative 50–2; functionalist approaches 46–8; objectivist approaches, persistence (explanations) 55–9
Management's Discussion and Analysis (MD&A) 158
management studies: cross-fertilisation 57; mainstream scholarship, sustainability investigation 42
managerialism 57–8
managers: management, agency theory principles (usage) 10–11; performance, assessment 97; policies, failure 50; supervision, efficiency (increase) 187
manufacturing sectors, selection 176
*Map and the Territory, The* (Greenspan) 232
Marine Stewardship Council 184

market uncertainty 161
mass boycotts, impact 183
material information, defining 156
materiality, term (usage) 155–6
material matters, disclosure 157
Maximum Likelihood (ML) 27
mechanistic/organic dichotomy 48–9
media: corporate social responsibility, relationship 124; corporate social responsibility, symbiotic relationship 128–31; reporting, impact 121; role 128; usage 121
media setting, role 121
mental language 204–5
minority shareholders, protection 240–1
mismanagement, impact 13–14
mis-motivation, breach 73
*Model Guidance on ESG Reporting to Investors* (SSEI) 164
models fit indices 32
modernization, impacts 5
Mondragón, compound board/unitary board (contrast) *244*
Mondragón Corporation Cooperativa (MCC) 235
moral autonomy, Kantian concept 110
morality, societal characteristic 215
moral reasoning, 6th order 209
moral rights 86–7
morals/morality 201
moral values, factors 252–3
mutual economic rationality 12
mutuality, impact 110

National Association of Pension Funds (NAPF) pension fund survey 159
National Cash Register Company (NCR) 140
national cultures, impact 227
national stock exchanges 25
nation-states, self-seeking manipulations 182
*Natural Capital at Risk* 176
natural capitalism, business advantage 189, 190
negative publicity 67
neoliberalism 58–9
neo-liberalism, principles 44
networked society, impact 182
Network for Business Sustainability 184
network governance 243; flowchart *241*
networks: formation 183; supply chains, relationship 184–5
new business models 188–9
new corporate social responsibility movement, emergence 85
New Right, influence 57
news: CSR coverage *125*; defining 122; media, stakeholder role 130

New York Stock Exchange (NYSE) 164
next generation 213; RL 200, 253; theoretical challenges/practical implications 199
NGO Global Forest Watch, information 184
NGO Worldwatch Institute 188
Nike, footwear manufacture 141
non-compliance, business risk 189
non-executive directors (NEDs): independent NEDs, impotency 239; management board vacancy 246; network governance advantages, summarization 247
non-financial factors 158
non-financial information 163
non-financial measures 97
non-financial performance 156
non-governmental organizations (NGOs): CSR perspective 144–5; good governance 129; language barriers 142; questions/ criticisms, data provision 142
non-government organisations (NGOs), initiatives 93
non-shareholder constituency statutes, adoption 140
non-shareholder interests 89
non-systemic operational conflicts 240
normative discourses 210–11

objectivism, contrast 58
objectivist approach 46
objectivist scholarship: dominance 58; subjectivist aspects 55; weaknesses 52–5
object of inquiry 55
occupational ideologies, contrast 51
occupational pension schemes 160
OECD: Environmental Outlook 175; Principles of Corporate Governance 14, 17, 77, 156
Oliver, Justice 238
ongoing collaborative inquiry 209
operational performance 21
opportunities, identification (improvement) 246
opportunity seeker 202
organisational failures 225–6
organizational culture 114–15; trust, social capital 112–16
organizational governance, implications 45
organizational members, impact 52
organizations: ethical concepts 112; governance architecture 242; governance, responsibility 68; greening 175; information 49; integrity, concept 111–12; self-representation 107–8; social/economic goals, integration 23; study 46
organization work, long-term goals (alignment) 214
organizing, evolutionary ways 213

Paedophile Exchange 231
palm oil, usage (concerns) 182–3
Parliamentary Commission into Banking Standards Report (PCBSR) 237
Parliamentary Joint Committee on Corporations and Financial Services Report (PJC Report) 86, 88
Parmalat, scandal 13
Parsons, Talcott 108
partnership approach, necessity 190
pathos (rhetorical figures) 108
pedagogy, defining 42
People Express 131
performance 166–8; appraisal 96; board function 76; corporate culture, impact 30; measurement 190
performance-based rewards 21
personal leadership, role 190
philanthropy, classification 87
Piketty, Thomas 10
planet, direct pressures 177–8
Play Fair Alliance 184
Polanyi, Karl 116
political pressures 57
political stability, importance 106
political structures, relationship (analysis) 51
pollution 177; discharge 185
population growth/consumption increase, combination 178
positivism 53–4; non-subjective elements 44
positivist scholarship, scientific credentials 53–5
post-heroic leadership concepts 216
power: concept 214; corporate governance, relationship 241; differentials, shift 178–9; separation 234; shift 214
power-over 214
press coverage, quality 129
PricewaterhouseCoopers (PWC), process audit usage 146
primary sectors, selection 176
principal-agent relationship 14
Principal Components Analysis (PCA) 27
Principles-based Code 227
Principles for Responsible Investment (PRI) 162, 181
Principles of Corporate Governance (ALI) 77
Principles of Corporate Governance (OECD) 14, 17, 77, 156
problems, explanation/creation 9
process audits 145–6
production factor 48
profit after tax (PAT) 23
profit maximization 138
progress, monitoring 180
protests, impact 183

public corporate social/environmental reporting, simplification 246
public limited companies (PLCs) 235; CSR framework 124
Publicly Traded Corporations (PTCs), constitutional architecture 235
public space, organizations (self-representation) 107–8
public trust: creation 111; necessity 190
Putnam, Robert 105

Quaker Oats 146
quality control efforts 142
quality scores 147–8

rainforest destruction, result 183
Rana Plaza collapse 185
rational choice theory 109
rational self-interest, maximization 115
Ray, Rupamanjari Sinha 2, 21
reasonable investor, perspective 156
reciprocity: impact 110; norms 113
*Regentcrest Ltd v. Cohen* 73
regulation: co-regulation 186; corporate responsibility, regulation 87–90; forms, evolution 185–7; soft law regulation 84–5
Regulation S-K 155; Items 101/103 157–8
regulatory phenomenon 186–7
*Reinventing Organizations* (Laloux) 212
relational innovation 220
relationships, system 16
Rendtorff, Jacob Dahl 3, 103, 253
reporting requirements/concepts 187
requisite organization 206
researcher, situatedness 54
resource consumption/constraint 153
*Resource Extraction Payments Disclosure Law* 165
respectability, norms 113
responsibilities, defining 217
responsibility: defining, correctness 201; developmentally based criteria 201–2; notions 206, *208*; trust, dynamic movement 108–12
responsible business practices 146
responsible leadership (RL): collaborative effort 199–200; CSR compliance 201; definitions, comprehensiveness 204; developmental perspective 203–9; emphasis 253; good character, importance 219; literature, developments/shortcomings 201–3; moral person, importance 219; moral/relational qualities, importance 219–20; next generation RL 200; notions *208*; questions/challenges 199–200; redefining 201–9; service 200

return on equity (ROE) 23
return on investment (ROI) 23
Rio Conference (1992) 186
Risk Assessment areas 228
risk aversion 225
risk-free world, public demand 190
risk management: cost avoidance, relationship 189–91; improvement 246; trends 190
*Risk Society* (Beck) 104
risk, uncertainty/trust (relations) 104
Roddick, Anita 201
roles, defining 217
Root Mean Square Error of Approximation (RMRSEA) 32
Royal Dutch Shell: activist pressure 161; water/land pollution 67
*Rules-Based* compliance 227

Saad, Suraati 3, 121, 253
safety codes 142
safety management (lever), law (usage) 190
*Saloman v. Salomon and Co* 73
Salzberg, Barry 148
Sarbanes-Oxley Act (SOX) 14, 154, 201, 239, 244
Sartre, Jean-Paul 108
scale development process 24–7
scales for community expectations 28
scales for customer expectations 29, *30*
scales for employees expectations 28–9, *29*
scales for shareholders expectations 30, *31*, *32*
scale validity assessment 32–3
Scharmer, Otto 5, 206, 218
scholarship: legitimacy 44–6; validity, confidence 2–3
SEC Act of 1934 238
Second United Nations Conference on the Environment and Development (UNCED), occurrence 180
*Securities Act* (Rule 408) 157
self-aggrandizement 142
self-development, complexity levels 206
self development, levels 206, *207*; responsibility/responsible leadership, impact *208*
self-expression, freedom 182
self-governance 234
self-interest 109; rational self-interest, maximization 115
self-management 214
self, perception 211
self-regulation, theory/practices 235
self-respect, basis 110
Senge, Peter 211

sense-making processes 109
Seven Deadly Sins 230
Seven Virtues 230
shadows, impact 211–12
shareholders: agreements 235–6;
 audit committee, establishment
 238; expectations, scales 30, *31*, 32;
 inadequacies 22; interests, attention
 155–8; legal protection 71; minority
 shareholders, protection 240–1; models
 72; perspectives, stakeholder perspectives
 (contrast) 71–2; wealth, maximization 21
shareholder value maximization model
 (SVMM) 67–8, 73–4
Sharma, Radha 2, 21
short-term business strategies 199
6th order (moral reasoning) 209
small to medium-size enterprises (SMEs)
 184–5
Smith, Adam 11, 14
social accounting 138; corporate social
 accounting, benefits 139–42; definitions
 138–9; progress 145–7; services/reports,
 provision 147–9
social auditing 140
social audits 142
social capital 104, 112–16; improvement 111
social goals, adjustment 140–1
social issues 130–1
socially responsible investment (SRI): funds
 155; specialisation 159
socially responsible leadership 94
social networks, trustworthiness 105
social performance, measurement
 (framework) *31*
social phenomenon 210
social responsibility: definition 122;
 embedding 142–3
social screens, usage 144
social systems, stabilization 112
social world complexity (reduction), trust
 process (usage)104–8
society: development 106; empowerment 216
soft law: regulation 84–5; role 97–9
soft regulation: role 83; soft law, usage 84–5
stakeholder approach 22; expert opinions,
 analysis 25; literature review 22–4;
 profile, sample 26; research methodology
 24–7; results/discussion 27–33; scale
 development process 24–7; theoretical
 underpinnings 22–4; usage 21
stakeholder dialogue 140; processes,
 preconditions 220
stakeholders: collaborative stakeholder
 engagement 217–18; constituencies,
 dialogues (opening)140; dialogs,

importance 202; dynamic partnerships
 184; engagement 92–3, 218; expectations,
 transformation 95; external stakeholders,
 goals contributions 214; feedback 243;
 groupings, power (change) 1; inclusion,
 advantages 246; interests 90; involvement
 242–3; model 72; moral rights, respect/
 protection 86–7; movement 140;
 participation, types (diversity) 243;
 salience, model 93; statutes 90; viewpoints
 204–5, 220
stakeholder theory 14–15; emphasis 24
state-based law makers/regulators 152
Statements of Investment Policies and
 Procedures (SIPPs) 160
State Pension Fund, stakes (Norway sale) 160
status structures, relationship (analysis) 51
statutory auditor arrangements 238
stories, news content 122
Strengths, Weaknesses, Opportunities and
 Threats (SWOT) 243
structural complexity 204
subjectivities, claims 55
subject-object-balance 205–6
success, understanding: expert opinions,
 analysis 25; literature review 22–4;
 profile, sample 26; research methodology
 24–7; results/discussion 27–33; scale
 development process 24–7; stakeholder
 approach, usage 21; theoretical
 underpinnings 22–4
supply chains: networks 184–5; risk 156
Survey of Corporate Responsibility
 Reporting (KPMG) 163
sustainability: adoption 71; company
 pursuit 76; corporate culture, impact
 30; exemplary citizenship 138; framing
 69; meaning 70–2; networks/alliances
 182–4; next generation, implications 199;
 non-executive director responsibility 95;
 notion 199; reporting, impact 187; risks/
 opportunities, shift 178–9; shareholder
 perspectives, stakeholder perspectives
 (contrast) 71–2; strategy, development
 93; support/facilitation 17
Sustainability Accounting Standards Board
 (SASB) 165
sustainability governance 67; GRI
 guidance *91*
sustainable business 1; ethical behaviour,
 usage 9; governance, usage 9
sustainable markets, business contribution 1
systemic deficiency, evidence 236
systemic director conflicts 239–42
system trust, concept (emphasis) 108
system wide shocks 153

Taneja, Pawan 2, 21
Taneja, Shallini 2, 21
tasks, defining 217
team effectiveness, perspective 210
technological innovation 179
technologies 187–92; innovation,
    relationship 187–8
tertiary sectors, selection 176
Tett, Gillian (Greenspan, commonality)
    231–2
texts, meanings (decisions) 43
Thatcher, Margaret 57
The Economics of Ecosystems and
    Biodiversity (TEEB) Coalition 176–7, 181
them-and-us culture 226
Theory U 218
Time Limited Corporations 242
tipping points, impact 175
Tokyo Electric Power Co., costs 190
Toronto Dominion Bank 148
total direct environmental damage, revenue
    percentage 176
Transaction Byte Analysis (TBA) 236, 245
Transaction Cost Economics (TCE) 236
transnational corporations (TNCs): global
    economy context 72; operations,
    ecological soundness 74–5; public
    attention 67
transnational NGOs, impact 182
transparency, impact 187
Tricker, Bob 226, 240
tripod ontology 220
Trucost report 74
trust: atmosphere 218; basis 114; concept,
    analysis 109; crisis 105; culture,
    basis 111–12; degree 215; dynamic
    movement 108–12; dynamic process
    view 103; ethical definition 114;
    importance 115; indeterminacy 106–7;
    institutional foundation, necessity 115;
    interpersonal trust, importance 107, 114;
    phenomenological perspective 110–11;
    public trust, necessity 190; reducibility
    109; social capital 112–16; symbolic
    generalization/images 107; system trust,
    concept (emphasis) 108; uncertainty/risk,
    relations 104
trustful character/identity, expression 113
trust process: role, analysis 112; significance
    103
trustworthiness, norms 113
trustworthy business practices, basis 104
Turnbull, Shann 6, 253
Tyco, scandal 13
Type B Corporation charter 17

UK 1862 Company Act 238
UK Companies Act of 2006 77
UK Financial Conduct Authority 244
UK Prudential Regulatory Authority 244
"Unburnable Carbon 2013" 191
uncertainty, risk/trust (relations) 104
UNEP FI 159
UNEP report 94–6
uniform standards/rules, necessity 17–18
Unilever, WWF (partnership) 184
Union Carbide, gas/toxic chemical leak 67
unitary board, compound board
    (contrast) 244
United Kingdom, corporate responsibility
    regulation 89–90
United Nations Development Programme
    Human Development Report (UNDP HD
    Report) 178
United Nations Framework Convention on
    Climate Change (UNFCCC) 180
United Nations Global Compact (UNGC) 84
United Nations Sustainable Stock Exchange
    Initiative (SSEI) 153, 164; Model Guidance
    on ESG Reporting to Investors 164
United States: asbestos-related claims,
    total corporate liability costs
    190; corporate responsibility regulation 90
UNPRI, investor/company guidance 167
US Business Principles for Human Rights of
    Workers in China 181
user pays 185

Valdez Principles 181
values: financial meaning 229; leadership
    focus, change 225; usage 226–7; value
    230–1
values-driven management 103
value systems, developmental complexity
    analysis 202
Varimax with Kaiser Normalization 27
venture capitalists (VCs), shareholder
    agreement 235–6
virtual economy 104
"Vita Activa" 214
Volkswagen scandal 190
voluntary corporate commitment 122

Walmart, investigations 154
Water Program, focus 161
Watson, Tower 213
Wells, Philippa 3, 67, 252
Western Economic Failure (2008) 227
Western Financial Crisis (2008) 231
wild species' populations, overexploitation 177
Williams, Cynthia 143–4

Williams, Paul 2, 9, 252
workers, goals contributions 214
workforce involvement, role 190
work-organization, relationship
    (analysis) 51
world at risk society 4–5
World Bank 154, 165
World Commission of Environment and
    Development (WCED) report 180
WorldCom scandal 9, 13

World Economic Forum 179; business
    challenge 181
World Heritage sites 180
World Trade Organization (WTO) 179
World Wide Fund for Nature (WWF):
    *Living Planet Report* 177; Unilever,
    partnership 184

Zadek, Simon 114
Zedlmayer, Bagi 189

For Product Safety Concerns and Information please contact our EU
representative  GPSR@taylorandfrancis.com
Taylor & Francis Verlag GmbH, Kaufingerstraße 24, 80331 München, Germany

www.ingramcontent.com/pod-product-compliance
Ingram Content Group UK Ltd.
Pitfield, Milton Keynes, MK11 3LW, UK
UKHW051832180425
457613UK00022B/1220